INTERNATIONAL BUSINESS

International Business

Strategy and Operations

Edgar P. Hibbert

MACMILLAN
Business

© Edgar P. Hibbert 1997

First published 1997 by
MACMILLAN PRESS LTD
Houndmills, Basingstoke, Hampshire RG21 6XS
and London
Companies and representatives
throughout the world

ISBN 0–333–62825–X hardcover
ISBN 0–333–62826–8 paperback

A catalogue record for this book is available
from the British Library.

This book is printed on paper suitable for recycling and
made from fully managed and sustained forest sources.

10   9   8   7   6   5   4   3   2   1
06   05   04   03   02   01   00   99   98   97

Typeset by Footnote Graphics, Warminster, Wilts

Printed in Great Britain by
Creative Print & Design (Wales), Ebbw Vale, Gwent

A Merchant has no Nation

Mediaeval Proverb

Contents

List of figures

List of tables

Introduction

This text provides an integrated approach in understanding international trade as a basis for developing the overall business strategy of the firm; and this is the context within which effective international operations can be planned and implemented. The text is aimed at undergraduate and postgraduate degree level students taking courses in international economics, international trade, export management and international business/marketing. The data used, especially for the Case Examples, includes information from experiential data and secondary sources across many countries.

In the synopsis of chapters, the coverage of topics follows a progression from concepts, through strategy and planning, to operations. Chapter 1 explains key developments in trade theory and policy as they affect trading prospects and foreign market access. Chapter 2 explains the general principles of international business, including the concept of internationalisation, the role of the multinational corporation and the government/industry interface (with emphasis on trade policy and trade promotion). Chapter 3 deals with environment analysis, demand analysis across countries and multi-country market research. Chapter 4 examines the roles of innovation, design and manufacturing in international competition, following the section on strategic factors and options. Chapter 5 discusses some critical decision-making areas for management in planning international operations, from acquisitions to strategic business alliances. Chapter 6 deals with key financial aspects, including foreign direct investment, raising finance for international operations and profit improvement. Chapter 7 covers effective management of operations such as risk and crisis management, agencies and subsidiaries, international contracting and countertrading. Chapter 8 consolidates the planning and operations aspects with a sharp focus on marketing: this Chapter will also show the link with demand analysis and research (Chapter 3) and marketing planning (Chapter 5), explaining the outcome in terms of effective marketing and promotion programmes.

The text contains new material, particularly topical case examples from industries and countries to illustrate applications and so forth. The coverage is broadly-based: there is a selective treatment of market regions (for example the European Union is already extensively documented elsewhere); this approach also ensures a wide international appeal.

This is a text on international management, but it is more than that: it provides the global context within which the manager can operate effectively (Chapters 5, 6, 7 and 8); as such there is the constituency of senior managers in trade and industry responsible for, or in a position to influence, their companies' international trading who would also benefit from this text (these include directors of operations, marketing and export directors, managing directors of subsidiaries, directors of corporate affairs, and so on).

Other topical highlights which differentiate this text include: an analysis of the significance of technology transfer; a critique of international competitiveness, both inter-firm and inter-country; an analysis of the government/industry interface; an assessment of the growth of business alliances; the emerging role of the global manager; risk and crisis management, profit and performance improvement and implementing effectively international promotion. The text is analytical throughout with some detailed trade statistics for reference.

The text is designed for taught undergraduate and postgraduate courses in international business. The Case Examples are intended to go some way towards meeting the demand for case material and thereby provide managerial applications in specific contexts of the concepts and principles.

EDGAR P. HIBBERT

Acknowledgements

The author and publishers are grateful to the International Trade Centre UNCTAD/WTO Geneva for the use of excerpts from the 1992 ITC publication *Financial Appraisal of Export Projects* in Chapter 6.

'Profit and Performance Improvement' in Chapter 6 is adapted from E.P. Hibbert and J. Liu (1995) *International Market Research: A Financial Perspective* (Blackwell: Oxford) pp. 160–7, authors' copyright material.

The Case Examples, of which there are 108, are adapted from wide reading of the trade, management and business press, and other sources. Every effort has been made to trace all copyright-holders, but if any have been inadvertently overlooked the publishers will be pleased to make the necessary arrangement at the first opportunity.

CHAPTER 1

International trade: concepts and strategy

INTRODUCTION

This chapter explains how developments in international trade theory influence our understanding of the changing pattern of competitiveness at the levels of the country, the industry and the firm. There is emphasis on the structure of demand and optimising the use of resources in trade. Porter's Diamond Theory is re-visited, where the importance of a strong domestic market for firms trading internationally is highlighted. The spectrum of government trade policies from 'non-interference' to economic planning is discussed, together with the roles of international agencies. There is an analysis of the impact of tariffs and non-tariff measures (NTMs) on foreign market access, and on the levels of and prospects for inter-country trade. Finally there is a detailed analysis of trends in world trade by country, region and industrial sector.

■ Strategic trade theory

■ Competitive advantage

The traditional approach to international trade is based on the concepts of 'absolute' and 'relative' comparative advantage. In international trade each country possesses resources which have a higher value externally than in the domestic economy. This can be due to surplus of production, high demand for finite resources, superior technology, higher labour productivity and other factors enabling one country to 'trade off' these with other countries endowed with other complementary resource factors. Such economic exchanges, according to this approach, form market forces which determine the pattern of international trade.

Indeed, the principles of 'absolute' and 'relative' comparative advantage first propounded by Adam Smith in *The Wealth of Nations* remain the principal justification for international trade. A country should export a commodity that can be produced at lower cost than that of other nations, and, conversely, should import a commodity that can be produced only at a lower cost by other nations. Note, however, that the advantage principle does not refer only to cost; it can be applied through gains in factor resources such as labour sophistication and specialisation, technology and other expertise. Indeed each country has a unique set of resources enabling it to benefit from the 'experience curve', where specialisation enables the country to improve its prosperity by increasing productivity as trade volume increases. Moreover, because countries trade in those commodities where each has an advantage, trade generates wealth in a situation where gain is anticipated without a high risk of loss; trade is therefore a 'positive sum' game (whereas in a zero sum game, one participant can gain only to the detriment of another).

This traditional approach is based on the premise that free trade operates to the general advantage of trading countries. This came to be questioned more after the First World War when, partly in response to the Depression of the 1930s, it was argued that some macro-economic developments had taken effect; these were:

1. Enormous scale economies in some industries such as steel, chemicals and so on, giving rise to monopolies and monopsonies.
2. Multi-national corporations (MNCs) with operations large enough to influence global markets.
3. Growth of protectionism and the increasing intervention of governments to influence trade.
4. The emergence in the 1970s and after of regional trading blocs, especially in Europe and North America.

The impact of these factors on trade theory has been profound: in particular a recognition that in place of the 'perfect' competition postulated by the classical theorists, competition in global markets is seen to be imperfect, and that firms and governments can act strategically to affect trade flows and the position of national economies. Moreover, mature industries in Europe and America have put increasing pressures on government for protection against low cost competitors particularly in the Pacific region (these include vehicle manufacturing, semi-conductors, electrical appliances and textiles). So large-scale operations involving concentration of power in both markets and supply have effectively eroded the base on which classical theory was founded, where multitudinous firms were competing in conditions of perfect competition; this concentration has enabled firms and governments to make strategic choices to build competitive advantage in global trade at these levels:

1. the firm;
2. the industry;
3. the country.

The Single European Act 1987, the Maastricht Treaty 1990 and the North American Free Trade Agreement (NAFTA) 1992 provide for the elimination of all internal restrictions on trade, harmonisation of trade practices, and, of course, the operation of a common external tariff (CET). Maastricht indeed goes much further with provisions for political and social integration in Europe. So trade theory from the 1980s has had to come to terms with a new set of macro-economic parameters, and this has led economists to explain how companies in oligopolistic industries compete while at the same time recognising their interdependence and the fact that differences in cost-bases and market-shares also lead to conflict and sub-optimisation of profits. So what has developed is 'strategic trade theory' in the 1980s and 1990s which recognises that Governments and MNCs can intervene strategically in trade, in defined ways:

1. Creating barriers to entry by heavy promotional or investment expenditure.
2. Using 'economies of scale' to force down prices so deterring new competitors.
3. 'Dumping' to capture volume market share by pricing below cost.
4. 'Preemptive strategies' in innovation, design, R&D and market penetration to deny competitive advantage to rival companies/industries.
5. Government 'supply side' subsidies for R&D or new technology, altering the 'pay offs' to domestic companies thereby discouraging entry into the market by foreign competitors, and precluding the latter from preempting the entry of domestic firms.

CASE 1.1

The position of Japan in international trade is a highly topical illustration of 'competitive advantage'; Japan is very poorly endowed with natural resources, and has therefore concentrated on developing to a high degree other 'factor resources' such as innovation, technology, labour productivity, design – in short 'adding value'. Japan is in fact the world's largest importer of natural resources. Having only 3 per cent of the world's population, Japan accounts for a quarter of the world's total exports of raw materials. It imports virtually all of its crude oil, iron ore, uranium, bauxite, nickel, cotton and natural rubber. Furthermore it has to import 92 per cent of its copper, 85 per cent of its coking coal, 40 per cent of its fish and 30 per cent of its farm products. Yet Japan is also the world's largest exporter of machinery and capital. Because the country has little in the way of natural resources, it has been necessary for Japan to become a processor of raw materials which are then transformed into value-added merchandise for export. By investing in technology, innovation and design, Japan has become the world's leading exporter of cars, electrical appliances, electronics, and other industrial products. However, the advantage of labour costs formerly enjoyed by Japan has been increasingly eroded by cheaper manufacturing costs in the Pacific countries such as Taiwan and South Korea, where Japanese companies are now sourcing much of their volume production, particularly in labour-intensive industries.

■ Developments in trade theory

We have seen that Adam Smith (*Wealth of Nations*, 1776) established that trade between countries is mutually beneficial if each has absolute advantage over the other in the production of a commodity. Ricardo took this argument a step further (*Principles of Political Economy*, 1817); he concluded that trade was mutually profitable even in the case where one country had an absolute advantage over the other in the production of both commodities (but where its advantage was greater in one commodity than in the other). But both the Adam Smith and Ricardo models are based on only one factor of production. Heckscher (1935) and Ohlin (1933) addressed the situation where more than one factor of production was available: the basic tenet of the Heckscher–Ohlin model is that trade is profitable only when countries take advantage of their different factor endowments. Even if two countries are equally endowed, opportunities for mutually profitable trade still exist due to differences in factor prices and differences in demand patterns between the two countries. The different demand patterns may be a result of different income distributions or differences in taste between the two countries (see Chapter 3).

Indeed, Keesing (1981) provided the evidence that skill availability was a major determinant of international trade patterns. He measured the skill content of exports and imports from the USA, Japan and seven European countries; he found that those countries with the most skill-intensive exports had the least skill-intensive imports. The training and competence of the labour force is the one key factor which distinguishes one country from another. Countries which are relatively well-endowed with highly-trained professional personnel (managers, technicians, engineers or scientists) will specialise in and export skill-intensive products, while countries with a relative abundance of unskilled labour will specialise in and export non-skill-intensive products.

Helpman and Krugman (1989) have drawn attention to the fact that there has occurred a major change in our understanding of international trade. They note that the theory of trade based on comparative advantage has been complemented, and to some extent supplemented, by a new theoretical view in which 'increasing returns are a major source of trade'. These have played a co-equal role with comparative advantage in explaining the pattern of trade, where global industrialisation has contributed to rising trade values. Increasing returns are inconsistent with perfect competition, as in this model markets are imperfectly competitive. This theory incorporates industrial organisation; in other words, there is a link between business organisation and national trade performance.

■ Porter's 'diamond' theory

In *The Competitive Advantage of Nations*, Porter (1990) investigated, on an empirical rather than a theoretical basis, why some nations' firms succeed in international competition. More specifically:

- Why does a nation succeed internationally in a particular industry?
- What is the influence of the nation on competition in specific industries or industry sectors?
- Why do a nation's firms select particular strategies?

In resolving these questions Porter has postulated four particular premises:

1. The nature of competition and the sources of competitive advantage differ widely among industries (and even among industry segments);
2. Successful global competitors perform some activities in the 'value chain' outside their home country and draw competitive advantages from their entire worldwide network rather than from just their home base;
3. Firms gain and sustain competitive advantage in modern international competition through innovation;
4. Firms that successfully gain competitive advantage in an industry are those that move early and aggressively to exploit a new market or technology.

Porter's argument is that there are four national attributes which shape the economic environment faced by domestic firms, and that they have a direct impact on the firm's ability to compete globally. These four attributes are illustrated in Figure 1.1.

☐ *Factor conditions*

The success of nations in particular industries is created, not inherited. Thus, success is not based on natural endowments such as land, labour, capital and

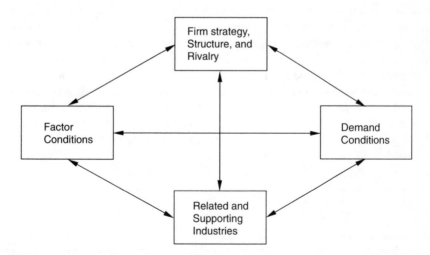

Figure 1.1   Porter's 'diamond' theory

Source: Adapted from Porter (1990).

natural resources. Competitive advantage (a nation's ability to compete in a given industry) is therefore created. This ability to compete requires skilled labour (an educated workforce) and good infrastructure as a back up. A nation possessing skilled labour can turn natural resources into a specialised advantage or competitive advantage; whereas a nation with abundant natural resources, but without skilled labour, is unable to turn the natural resources into a competitive advantage. Also, a nation with skilled labour is innovative (broadly defined to include improvements in technology and production processes, new product design, and better methods or ways of doing things, such as a new approach to marketing). Porter argues that the key to sustaining competitive advantage is to continue upgrading skills in a nation. The value-added concept constitutes an integral part of the explanation of why a particular industry is internationally competitive, since value added is related to productivity, which depends on skills.

☐ *Demand conditions*

The nature of home-market demand influences the success of a nation's industry in international markets. This is dependent on the size of the home-market, the number and level of sophistication of the consumers, and media exposure of products on the home-market. The behaviour of the consumers and local retailers is of crucial importance. If consumers are strict and discriminate among producers, this would stimulate producers to make products which satisfy the strict demands of the consumers. Similarly, if the local retailers are strict and discriminate among the producers, this would also stimulate the producers to make products which satisfy the strict demands of the retailers. For instance, if domestic consumers demand high-quality products, this would force producers to pay particular attention to quality; on the other hand, if consumers are not strict on quality, producers are less likely to pay particular attention to quality. The same applies for local retailers.

Porter's contention is that if an industry is used to satisfying strict and discriminating consumers on the home-market, it will not have difficulties satisfying the same demands on the international market, and will have a competitive advantage over industries from other nations where consumers are not strict and discriminating.

☐ *Related and supporting industries*

These play a major role in an industry's ability to compete internationally. An industry vying for export competitiveness needs suppliers at home with internationally – competitive inputs. Their absence will negatively impact on the industry's ability to compete. Related industries must also be internationally competitive.

□ *Company strategy, structure and rivalry*

Porter's central argument is that the creation and sustaining of competitive advantage is a highly localised process. It is the differences in national economic structures, values, cultures, institutions and histories which have significant contributions to competitive success. It is these national circumstances and the local environment which determine how companies are created, organised and managed, as well as the nature of domestic rivalry. Thus, the home nation is pivotal to competitive advantage, and hence competitive success. The home nation is also the source of the skills and technology that underpin competitive advantage. Porter concludes that 'among all the points on the diamond, domestic rivalry is arguably the most important because of the powerfully stimulating effect it has on all the other points'.

Therefore, the central thesis of Porter's model is that competitiveness is born of intense (or fierce) domestic rivalry. Accordingly, he advocates an active anti-trust policy and avoidance of protection as policy prescriptions. Regarding the role of government in the economy, Porter challenges the argument that government should be a helper or supporter of industry, using various policies that contribute directly to the competitive performance of strategic or targeted industries. He challenges also the argument that the operation of the economy should be left entirely to the workings of the invisible hand (free market forces). Porter's contention is that government cannot create competitive industries, but only companies can create competitive industries. Porter concludes by saying that government's proper role should be creating an environment in which companies can gain competitive advantage (rather than involve itself directly in the process) by influencing the four points (attributes) on the diamond – the determinants of national competitive advantage (this important aspect is discussed further in depth in Chapter 2 in the discussion of the government/industry interface).

■ International trade policies and organisation

■ Trade promotion

Government and industry need to work effectively to improve all aspects of trade promotion in order to open up and maintain international market access. In national trade promotion policy, dilemmas face many governments attempting to improve their trade balance in terms of import substitution or export promotion. The topical importance of such dilemmas to all organisations involved in overseas trade is illustrated by the stresses currently afflicting the world system. Domestic unemployment and inflation have caused some countries to become protectionist in their overseas trade policies. Other governments, many with substantial payment surpluses, have been reluctant to reflate or pursue economic growth for fear of accelerating their own inflation rate. Yet

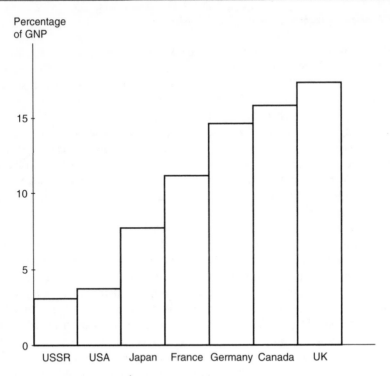

Figure 1.2   Foreign trade by value as a percentage of GNP

Source: Adapted from World Bank, *World Development Report 1990*, New York.

only if there is growth in world trade will prosperous industrialised nations be in a position to absorb more imports from countries with balance-of-payments problems. Also, there needs to be continuing cooperation between government and business in sponsoring research into new product uses in new markets for traditional exports, and in diversifying industrial goods for export. Particularly vital is the provision of venture capital for investment in new industrial plant and processes.

The role of national trade promotion organisations, both in function and in organisation, is to promote their countries' exports cost-effectively. Particular reference is made here to the UK, since that country is singularly dependent for economic solvency on foreign trade (see Figure 1.2).

Industrialists must not, however, rely entirely on governments to open up markets; much can be achieved, both at home and abroad, by the activities of national trade or industry exporters' associations. Indeed, the discipline of a pricing policy for all government trade services in many countries is now widely recognised: it ensures more cost-effective use of these services, particularly those involving commercial risks.

■ **Expansion in world trade**

Multilateral trade and regional trading blocs are increasingly the focus for collective action by both developing and industrialised countries producing and exporting raw materials and manufactures. An important aspect of this two-way trade is what is termed the 'North–South dialogue', and its significance lies in the balance of power in world trade between the producer countries of the Third World and the industrialised, consuming countries in terms of preferential tariffs, debt relief and investment. The need of Third World countries to derive higher levels of export earnings from new industrial development projects is urgent, because only in this way can they increase earnings of hard currencies with which to purchase industrial goods and services and technology from the industrialised countries. The capacity of Third World countries to continue to finance imports of technology from the Western industrialised world will also rest on their improved promotion of the whole range of commodities and produce, and on the increased purchasing capacity of the industrialised countries themselves.

The Tokyo and Uruguay Rounds held in the 1970s and 1980s under the auspices of the General Agreement on Tariffs and Trade (GATT), have sought, through multi-lateral negotiations and notification of agreements to ensure some continuing and measurable growth in world trade, and above all increased domestic industrial output levels which will have some impact on reducing both inflation and unemployment. The significance of movements in world trade in this context is illustrated in Figure 1.3.

The strategic importance of expanding trade can be spelt out as a result of these conferences in terms of (1) monetary stability and (2) economic growth. Germany pledged to stimulate demand by the equivalent of 1 per cent of its GNP, and Japan undertook to stabilise the volume of its exports while achieving a real growth rate of 7 per cent; the OECD reckons that the growth rate of OECD member countries will reach barely 2 per cent even if these pledges are fulfilled. The Tokyo Rounds and Uruguay are concerned with the further liberalisation of international trade within the framework of the General Agreement on Tariffs and Trade (GATT); the World Trade Organisation (WTO) took over from GATT in January 1995 with increased powers of investigation, arbitration and compliance.

■ **Trade policies**

Furthermore, developments in world trade in recent years have brought both opportunities and problems in formulating national trade policies (the value of world trade has risen from US $200 billion to more than $2 trillion in the last 20 years). Opportunities have occurred by increased demand for traded goods as exports, but problems have arisen through increased competition, particularly price competition, from newly-industrialising countries. Such trade

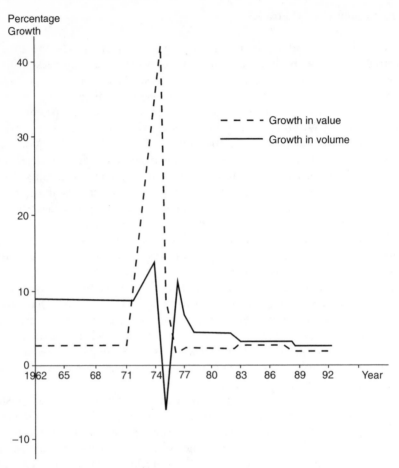

Figure 1.3   Growth in world trade 1962–92

Source: Adapted from *World Bank Atlas*, Washington, DC, 1992.

expansion has also brought about increased interdependences among trading nations, and this, in turn, has important implications for trade promotion. Such interdependence first emerged as a critical factor in world trade during the oil crisis of the 1970s, when it was seen that concerted action by a number of relatively unknown countries could have major repercussions on the international as well as the domestic economic levels. Difficulties in meeting demand from domestic output, currency shortages and increasing trade deficits have, since that time, come increasingly to influence the shaping of both trade policy and trade promotion by national governments. The reality is that, increasingly, national and industrial needs on the domestic front (increasing employment, supporting new industries, reducing trade deficits) can conflict with developments in international trade.

The globalisation of the world economy has made protectionism more difficult to implement. Take for example the global reorientation of production. A few decades ago it would have been impossible for an automobile to be partially produced in a variety of countries, assembled in others, and then sold elsewhere as Ford has done in Europe. Such operations are further evidence of comparative advantages increasingly dominating manufacturing as well as trading across national boundaries (see for example Ludlow, 1990).

Three possible trading options can be postulated to resolve such conflicts of interest, they are:

1. To diminish economic interdependence by reducing trade through trade restriction. As a result, domestic economic policy-making would be restored, but each individual country and the world community would be deprived of the benefits gained through trade.
2. To aim for 'damage control'. Nations would not only offset trade liberalisation measures against each other, but trade liberalisation against trade restrictions. For such an approach to work, however, it would also require those industries gaining from liberalisation measures (a gain which concurrently is obtained without a *quid pro quo*), to share these benefits with those less-fortunate industries suffering from restrictive trade measures.
3. Alternatively, to bring about 'reasonably free' trade. Market forces would be accepted as the primary engine of trade activities with the minimum of distortion through policy measures. Such an approach requires close cooperation in terms such as harmonisation of monetary policies, increase in the transparency of domestic economic policies, and opening up of trade flows for firms rather than products.

These and other trade policy options for governments are illustrated in Tables 1.1 and 1.2.

A policy of non-interference is based on the view that market forces, left to take their course, produce beneficial results for the economy if not subject to controls. The contrary argument is that complete non-intervention is never practised in commercial affairs, that indeed it has become impracticable and irrelevant in a world in which every type of competition, fair and unfair, is being practised. There are strong pressures on any government to support its country's business in the world marketplace. It is not unknown for businessmen who are noted as spokesmen against government controls to be equally, though less publicly, advocating intervention on behalf of their companies or industry sectors, especially when they are threatened by competition; this is particularly true where problems of market access arise. However, establishing precisely what constitutes non-interference is by no means straightforward and reflects the subtleties of official policies.

The USA, for instance, is generally regarded as the arch-supporter of freedom for market forces, but executives of companies which have to compete with the Americans are quick to point out that government purchasing in that country is

Table 1.1 Trade categories, the source of trade, and the gains from trade to a domestic economy

	Category 1	Category 2	Category 3	Category 4
Imports	Specific factor non-existent	Specific factor scarce	Standardised goods	Differentiated products
Basis of trade	Absolute disadvantage	Comparative disadvantage	Comparative disadvantage	Non-price features
Gains from trade	Consumption of non-indigenous goods	Overcomes domestic shortages	Higher consumption: increased competition	More consumer choice; increased competiton; higher domestic efficiency
Exports	Sole possession of specific factor	Abundant possession of specific factor	Standardised goods	Differentiated products
Basis of trade	Absolute advantage	Comparative advantage	Comparative advantage	Consumer choice; imperfect markets
Gains from trade	Increased specialisation	Increased specialisation	Bigger markets; economies of scale	Bigger markets

Source: Burton (1984) *Contemporary Trade*, Philip Allen Industrial Studies, Chapter 1, p. 18.

Table 1.2 Spectrum of trade policies

Policy	Advantages (claimed by supporters)	Disadvantages (indicated by opponents)
Non-interference type	Allows optimal solutions to emerge	Impractical in or irrelevant to a world in which competition, fair and unfair, is being practised
Minor intervention necessary	Allows optimal solutions but with discriminatory assistance especially with those aspects (like market research and special promotions) where government is able to help most economically	Any intervention produces inefficiency, hampers innovation and change and brings reprisals from other countries
	Provides a breathing space for hard-pressed domestic producers	Firms may be hampered without any compensating advantage
	Ensures that foreign investors, both home and foreign based, bring minimum damage and maximum assistance to the national economy	Needed investment may be turned away
	Is what most western industrial nations, and many others, claim to be doing	
Oversight of foreign trading policies	Makes possible the determination of priorities and enables the country's businessmen to make the greatest possible impact on foreign markets	Increases still further all the disadvantages of minor intervention
National trading policies	Operated by many developing countries to produce rapid industrialisation along predetermined lines	Considered unacceptable in democratic countries – restricts the liberty of individual entrepreneurs

Source: Brooke and Remmers (1978) *The Strategy of Multinational Enterprise.*

still a form of intervention. There are also laws, like the anti-trust Acts, which influence corporate policies. Switzerland, the country with the world's highest income per head, is officially non-interventionist, while Sweden lies second and pursues different policies. Even in Switzerland, lack of interference on the part of the federal government is sometimes matched by a different approach in a particular canton. Japan is even more enigmatic – the country in which government spending is the lowest proportion of national income of any industrial nation, yet with a reputation for extensive government coordination of corporate trading policies.

Minor intervention is usually considered to be the policy adopted by the UK. If this is the case, a wide range of activity is included, for example:

1. Support for exporters both directly, by subsidised market research and promotion, and indirectly, by support for ailing companies, by the use of government purchasing and by the tax system.
2. Restraints on importers, by tariffs and by restrictions including participation in international measures like the multi-fibre agreement.
3. Controls and incentives for inward foreign investment – nowadays most of the constraints operate as conditions on the incentives, some of which are provided by local authorities (see Chapter 6).
4. Controls on outward foreign investment: at present there are no exchange controls in the UK, but taxation influences company policies.
5. International agreements on exports, imports, investment and all other means of conducting foreign investment are influenced by government participation in international treaties and trading agreements.

Selective interference is justified on the grounds that temporary problems (like the adjustment of domestic manufacturers to fresh sources of competition) can be met without causing disruption to trade and reprisals on the part of other countries. This latter hope, at least, is sometimes proved incorrect as critics have no difficulty in demonstrating.

Oversight of foreign trading policies is yet another option; the development of national trade policies facilitates the fixing of priorities and enables the nation's businessmen to make the greatest possible impact on foreign markets. Many executives who dislike government intervention on principle would support some such policy as they find themselves face to face with competitors who appear to have considerable official support. The opponents of this view consider that any form of assistance leads to inefficiency and a failure to make the best use of resources.

A further factor affecting inter-country trade and market access of strategic importance is the supply situation of commodities, fibres, minerals, metals, ores and other raw materials essential to the functioning of the manufacturing industries and technologies of the Western industrialised world. The commercial and, indeed, strategic implications of this supply situation world-wide are illustrated in Figure 1.5.

Table 1.3 Balance of payments audit (indicative figures only)

Possible action to reduce outflows	Outflows ($ million)	Inflows ($ million)	Possible action to increase inflows
Reduce expenditure on shipping owned by other but we need to use shipping for our exports	Shipping and insurance 13	**Services** Use of shipping/insurance 3	Increase the hiring out of our shipping space to other countries but do we have enough shipping to do that?
Reduce expenditure on tourism/visits abroad but restrictions on travel could hit exports	Tourism/visits abroad 2	Tourists to our country 32	Promote tourism to our country but this requires tourist facilities at home and publicity abroad, and may be socially harmful
Reduce expenditure on foreign experts but can be afford to do without their expertise?	Payments for foreign know-how 5 / 20	Receipts from our know-how 1 / 36	Increase income from know-how sold abroad but do we have enough expertise to do this, and can we spare it?
Limit our investment and loans abroad but are these significant?	Our investments abroad 1	**Capital flows** Foreign investment here 7	Encourage more foreign investment here but interest will be needed (an outflow)
	Our loans abroad 1	Loans made to user 10	
Make repatriation of capital more difficult but will this discourage investment and encourage illegal methods?	Repatriation of capital 12 / 14	Repatriation of capital 1 / 18	Seek more loans but we shall have to pay interest (an outflow) and to repay the loan eventually
Limit amount of pay that foreign experts in our country can send home but will this make it more difficult to get foreign expertise?	Remittances sent home by foreigners working here 1	**Other flows** Remittances from our people working abroad 3	Encourage more repatriation of our capital from abroad for investment at home but remember this might provoke retaliation
	Interest on loans made to us 2	Interest on our loans abroad 1	
Only get loans we really need, at lowest interest rates but we need loans for our own development	Dividends on investments here by foreigners 1 / 4	Dividends on our investments abroad 1 / 5	Encourage our people abroad to remit more of their earnings to our country but how? And with what effect?
Reduce payment of dividends on foreign investments in our country but can we do this without reducing essential foreign investment	VISIBLE IMPORTS 150	VISIBLE EXPORTS 99	Invest more abroad but this is an outflow
Reduce our imports of goods but what about goods vital for our economic development, our health and education, and even our export trade?	TOTALS 188	Deficit = $30 million	Encourage our exports of goods. How?

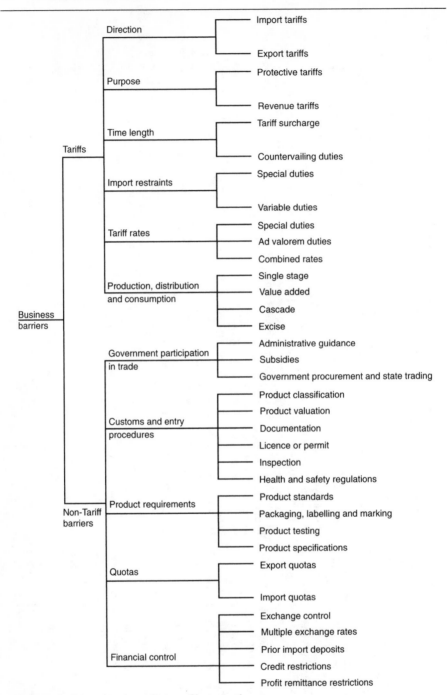

Figure 1.4   How trade policies affect market access

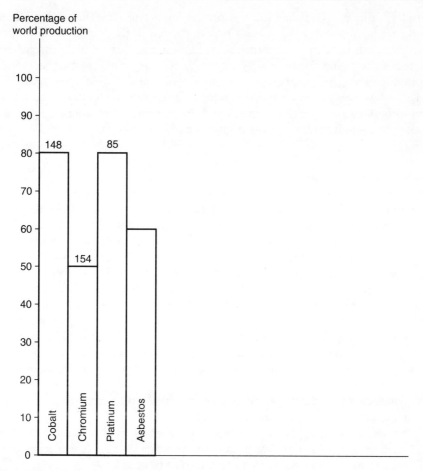

Figure 1.5 Reserves of strategic minerals

Note: Figure at top of each bar indicates the number of years remaining with 5 times the present known reserves.
Source: Adapted from the *Commodity Yearbook*, 1992.

Thus, it is essential that the trading system should contribute to economic development by encompassing an orderly approach to world trade in raw materials, commodities and semi-manufactures, and should not be used so often as in the past to gain advantages of price manipulation. There must be recognition that developing countries need to industralise on the basis of their comparative advantage, if only to accommodate productively the large increases in their population. GATT therefore proposed that an important component of multilateral trade rounds must be a negotiated 'trade-off' in terms of assurance of unimpeded access to markets by a *quid pro quo* for assurances of unimpeded access to supplies.

Indeed, this proposal has focused on the impact of changing technology on world trade, and on the need for a new approach to the 'inputs' and 'outputs' of trade, both in terms of internal consumption and distribution, and in terms of resources being more widely shared and controlled worldwide. Socio-economic needs, for instance, have themselves generated much new technology in the last 30 years: agricultural techniques which improve per-acre productivity, new processes for recycling waste, and improvements in energy technology leading to cost-effective energy consumption.

■ Trade liberalisation

The trade policies so far discussed at the macro level have been developed under the general auspices of the General Agreement of Tariffs and Trade (GATT), set up in 1948. This has provided a forum for substantial trade liberalisation measures through a series of multilateral trade 'Rounds' (already referred to). It is important to grasp that GATT (now replaced by the World Trade Organisation) has provided a set of rules for these multilateral tariff and non-tariff conferences and, more importantly, some mechanisms for monitoring the implementation of these rules. Signatories to GATT must, for example, conform to the principle of most-favoured nation (MFN), which requires a country to extend any concession on tariffs, licences or quotas granted to one trading partner, to all others; there are some exceptions to MFN which require mention:

1. Manufactured products from developing countries can be given preferential treatment compared to those from other countries.
2. It does not apply to those commodities covered by the Generalised System of Preferences (GSP) under which industrialised countries offer special tariff concessions to imports from developing countries on a bilateral basis.
3. Concessions granted to other members of a trading bloc do not have to be extended to other countries.
4. Countries whose products are arbitrarily discriminated against by another country are not obliged to give MFN treatment to that country's products.

The importance of MFN clearly is that all signatories have undertaken to apply the same trade regulations to nearly all the world's trading countries, thus further increasing the process of liberalisation. It also has the effect of simplifying the process of negotiations by allowing exporters from most nations to have the same access, in terms of regulations, to the market of any participating country.

The United Nations Conference on Trade and Development (UNCTAD) has also been convened (six times since 1964) to improve access of developing countries' exports into industrial countries and to raise these countries' shares of trade in manufactures. Special agreements have also been made by commodity producers in attempts to allocate markets and production to raise export earnings. Note should also be made of international agencies such as the Asian Development Bank and the World Bank which make finance available for capital projects, particularly in communications, port installation, dams and irrigational schemes, welfare and housing projects, and so on. This is particularly so where such loans would not be forthcoming from the private banking sector and where equipment, plant and technology, and so forth, have to be imported because they are not available locally.

UNCTAD has also been concerned to promote intra-regional trade, and the priority tasks of government can be defined as follows:

1. To examine the present restraints on intra-regional trade covering such fields as availability of goods, their competitive price, the delivery schedule, availability of finance for export trade, the administrative formalities for export, the infrastructure facilities available, shipping and freight, port handling operations, availability of managerial personnel and, most important, the trade policy with particular reference to tariff structure, quotas and exchange regulations.
2. To consider what liberalisation measures are necessary so as to facilitate intra-regional trade. The liberalisation measures that could be adopted are several and varied, some of which could be:

    *   preferential cuts in tariffs on imports of specific commodities;
    *   preferential relaxation of quantitative restrictions or restrictions on allocation of foreign exchange in respect of quantity or value of trade;
    *   bulk purchase by importing countries from intra-regional sources;
    *   preferential purchases by public authorities from intra-regional sources;
    *   preferential dismantling of other non-tariff barriers;
    *   negotiations for discounts on freight of commodities moving under an intra-regional programme, customs facilitation for import and export of commodities included in the trade programme.

It is interesting to note the original objectives of national and international action when GATT itself was first established. The Geneva draft charter contains these objectives:

1. To assure a large and steadily growing volume of real income and effective demand; to increase the production, consumption and exchange of goods; and thus to contribute to a balanced and expanding world economy.
2. To foster and assist industrial and general economic development particularly of those countries which are still in the early stages of industrial development, and to encourage the international flow of capital for productive investment.
3. To further the enjoyment by all countries, on equal terms, of access to the markets, products, and productive facilities which are needed for their economic prosperity and development.
4. To reduce tariffs and other barriers to trade and to eliminate discriminatory treatment in international commerce.
5. To enable countries, by increasing the opportunities for their trade and economic

development on a mutually advantageous basis, to abstain from measures which would disrupt world commerce, reduce productive employment, economic development, commercial policy, business practices and commodity policy.

There is a second draft on commercial policy laying down several important principles. It stipulates unconditional most-favoured nation (MFN) treatment among members, ruling out any new preferential arrangements or any increase in existing preferential margins. It demands the general elimination of quantitative import restrictions such as quotas and licences, and in the special cases where such restrictions are continued they are to be applied indiscriminately to all countries. Tariffs and preferential margins are to be reduced. Direct export subsidies are to be phased out.

The United Nations Conference on Trade and Development (UNCTAD) has also been concerned with policy aspects of trade liberalisation, and has concerned multilateral Trade Rounds administering in UNCTAD VI. Manufacturing production in developing countries has been growing and the composition of this trade (and production) has altered considerably in recent years. Production and trade in other industries have not declined but growth in industries such as engineering products, clothing and light manufactures (especially electronic goods) has been particularly rapid. This transfer of specific manufacturing industries to developing countries involves both these and industrialised countries specialising in specific manufactures or semi-manufactures (and trading in these). Essentially, industrialised countries are cutting back on less-profitable (normally older technology) industries, and these are being relocated in developing countries which possess cheaper inputs (labour, raw materials) or other inducements (for example incentives offered by governments or the Generalised System of Preferences) or treatment of exports into industrialised countries.

One of the factors restricting the growth of world trade is protectionist trade policies in some industrialised countries. Although tariff barriers are being reduced, non-tariff measures (NTM) are still used by governments to protect their economies; NTMs include variable levies, anti-dumping and countervailing duties, minimum prices (price controls), prohibitions, quotas, seasonal restrictions, discretionary licensing, volume controls and a variety of restrictive practices. The last measure is normally imposed by national or international firms, whilst most of the other NTMs are imposed by governments. Certainly, from the viewpoint of UNCTAD VI, protectionism affects export sales and balance of payments, and delays international transfer of technologies in a period of rapid change. So any reduction in protectionism will benefit the entire world economy. Policies under the auspices of GATT to reduce or resolve NTMs are dealt with shortly.

■ **Impact of tariffs**

Balance-of-payments deficits are allied with high interest payments, and many developing countries are facing ever increasing 'debt service' ratios (the proportion of a country's export revenues spent on payment of interest on external debts). Again, trade policies to increase the flow of resources to developing countries and a softening of the conditions imposed by the International Monetary Fund (IMF) were agreed at UNCTAD VI.

Commodity policies concern the perennial issue of commodity market stabilisation, access to processing distribution and marketing, and compensatory financing for export-earning shortfalls. Indeed, the number of countries signing the Common Fund for Commodities at UNCTAD VI has increased to 108 (54 ratifications), thus bringing the date for its operation (and hence price/demand stabilisation) closer. Commitments were also made to continuing support for the Generalised System of Preferences (GSP) and International Commodity Agreements (ICAs).

The Tokyo Round (under the auspices of GATT) nevertheless achieved a substantial cut in tariffs, overall by about 33 per cent, starting in 1980 for an eight-year period; for example, tariffs between the EEC and the USA were reduced by 35 per cent each way, and US imports into Japan by 45 per cent. The comparable overall cut in the Kennedy Round in 1962 was 35 per cent; all tariff reductions are on a most-favoured nation basis. To take two products as an example, the EEC tariff of 13 per cent on photographic equipment and cameras and 6 per cent on office machinery was cut to 7.2 per cent and 4.4 per cent respectively by 1987 (the reductions occurred slowly and were hardly noticeable to consumers); but they have some beneficial effect on company pricing policies.

Although tariff cuts may be beneficial, currency fluctuations are likely to be much more important. The major currencies' exchange movements over the past few years have greatly offset or compounded the effect of differential tariff rates. And although tariffs will no longer be significant for most industries, a few products such as textiles, clothing, footwear and some chemicals will continue to have substantial protection. Even after the cuts, US tariffs on clothing are as high as 35 per cent, and outer garments in the EU still carry tariffs of up to 14 per cent. While some tariffs will remain high, other industries will experience a significant drop; those products benefiting most will include, for instance, forest product imports into the USA, office computing equipment into the EEC and Japan, and certain types of machinery imports into Canada. Some tariffs on industrial goods have been cut by as much as 60 per cent, and the number of industrial products subject to tariffs of under 5 per cent increased substantially. It has to be recognised, however, that average tariff reduction figures are practically meaningless for most companies, which face a specific rate for each product that can vary considerably from the average tariff rate in that industry. Companies should obtain comparable tariff reductions for their products in key markets. The implications for management are that tariffs should be identified with precision as they will affect the prices at which the company can place the product on the market; also it is essential to secure the most favourable tariff rate levied on entry, and this can involve modifying the product (for example exporting for assembly or in bulk form).

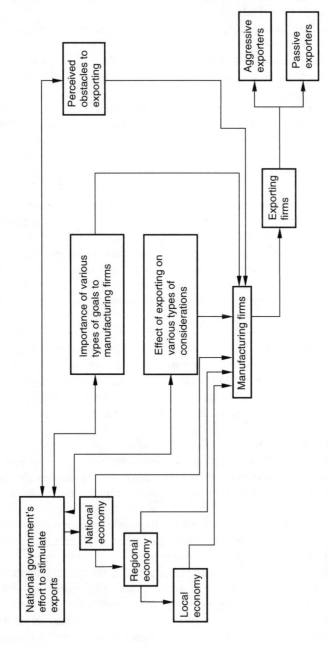

Figure 1.6 Government policies to stimulate exports

Source: G. Tesar and J. S. Tarleton (1983) 'Stimulation of Manufacturing Firms as Part of National Export Policy', in *Export Promotion: The Public and Private Sector Interaction*, ed. M. R. Czinkota, Prague, p.26.

■ Inter-country trading and market access

■ Recent developments

Developments in inter-country trade in recent years have brought about both opportunities and problems for the international trading company. Opportunities have occurred in terms of increased demand for traded goods as exports, but problems have arisen in terms of increased competition (particularly price competition) from newly-industrialising countries (NICs) such as South Korea, Taiwan, Hong Kong and Singapore.

Increases in all forms of international trade in this period have been large, not only in real terms – well ahead of inflation – but also well ahead of other relevant factors such as the amount of goods manufactured. This relative advance of trade is remarkable by any standard, but it also masks a number of differences between countries and industry sectors. The industrialised nations have come out better in percentage terms, even though they start from a higher base, while a steep fall in the demand for oil in the 1970s and early 1980s led to the first decline for a quarter of a century; but inter-country trade in agricultural and manufactured products has continued to increase. Later in this section, we shall study some specific trade trends in these products.

The most important recent development in the African, Caribbean and Pacific (ACP) countries has been the enormous growth in international tourism, and the potential for increasing foreign currency earnings from services supplying the tourist sector, and the growing financial services sector in the Pacific Rim.

Since 1970, the 24 major industrialised countries, led by member countries of the Organisation for European Cooperation and Development (OECD) have expanded both their exports and imports tenfold, some by much more. One reason is the expansion in the number of companies entering international trade in one way or another; existing enterprises are also anxious to reduce their dependence on any one particular national economy. Whereas export used to be confined to certain industry sectors, and investment to large companies, now numerous pressures are compelling companies into international trade. These include six key areas:

1. Searching for overseas sales in countries with high growth economies.
2. Adapting pricing policies to increase profits in overseas markets.
3. Spreading commercial risks across national frontiers.
4. Intensive marketing in countries undergoing economic 'upturns' in demand when the domestic economy may be stagnant.
5. Developing international competitive strengths in product design and quality, and supply.
6. Securing overseas market access for future investment.

■ The trade cycle

It should be noted that even at a time of world boom or recession, economic activity does not rise and fall simultaneously everywhere: under more stable economic conditions the cycle of business activity can vary considerably between countries, and rates of industrial production and currency values can fluctuate substantially.

The role of the trade cycle is particularly important in this context. Clearly any enterprise affected by the trade cycle can protect itself by operating in more than one economy, though investing in a very large number of countries is more appropriate to the multinational corporation (MNC) than to the small firm. Table 1.4 illustrates how world trade is structured, and the mechanisms used by companies to enter and engage in international operations.

■ Selected markets of the world

This section profiles some key regions and explains how differences of culture, demography and economic organisation represent opportunities for business development; it is not a comprehensive geographical coverage which is widely available in other relevant texts.

The North American market, comprising Canada and the USA, is a large and varied continent; more than 200 million people live in the USA, but although they are all 'American' there are many different cultural groups. There are concentrations of people of Polish descent in Chicago, of Irish descent elsewhere, and European languages are still spoken by such communities; also due to recent immigration from Central and Latin America, Spanish is widely spoken in parts of Texas and New Mexico where even some advertising is in Spanish.

Table 1.4   Components of world trade

Trade components			
Sale of goods in international markets	Sales of services in international markets	Sale of technology in international markets	Investment in international operations

International trading system Modes of operation			
Direct export	Banking	Licensing	Direct investment
Indirect export agents	Insurance	Franchising	Acquisitions of
Direct selling	Commodity brokerage	Management contracts	brands
Export management	Tourism	Technical agreements	Distributors' 'Buy
	Retailing	Contract	outs'
	Transportation	manufacturing	Portfolio investment

And while the main language spoken in both Canada and the USA is English, in the Canadian province of Quebec the dominant language is French.

Economically, North America is the world's richest and largest market at the present time. The standard of living is the highest in the world. It has great resources of raw materials of every kind and the biggest industries in the world. There is a vast labour force and the USA has more concentrated technical knowledge and skill than anywhere else. The North American Free Trade Area (NAFTA) will further consolidate the region as an integrated market.

The consumption of North America is so great that it is ready to buy from everywhere, even those products that it can make for itself, thus making it the world's foremost region for access. Among world markets, North America is surpassed only by Western Europe in terms of total imports, and by Western Europe and Australasia in terms of imports per head. Americans and Canadians are good businessmen and prices are keen. But because of high wages, hand-made goods and labour-intensive products are very expensive indeed so it is a good market for an exporter of these items. It is a buoyant market that is always looking for goods that are new, different and unusual. What sells well one day may be quite out of fashion and impossible to sell during the following week. And because the market is so large, an exporter must be willing to accept very large orders and to fulfil them quickly. The USA is not a place for the small producer to sell to direct, unless he concentrates on one small region or state. Because of its good communications and nationwide radio and television networks, North America is a remarkably homogenous market in spite of the many racial and cultural differences.

Government interference is very small and there are few restrictions. Exporters deal with individuals or private companies who are relatively free to buy what they like. Government is stable, with each state of the USA, for example, administering the details of everyday affairs, very much like local government on a larger scale. Each state is proud of its autonomy, but this is not important to an exporter.

Eastern and Central Europe comprise the former Communist countries such as Roumania, Poland, Bulgaria and the Newly Independent States (NIS) of the former Soviet Union, a vast land area larger of course, than the whole of Western Europe. In economic terms these countries are sometimes referred to as "Economies in Transition". In such a large region there are many great natural barriers of all kinds. There are high mountain ranges in the Urals, and elsewhere there are dense forest, wide rivers and great plains. The tremendous distances between towns can make transport and distribution difficult and costly, and communications are not nearly so well developed in this region as they are in the rest of Europe. Land communications are especially bad over long distances. The weather is much more extreme than the rest of Europe. The summers are much hotter and the winters are very cold indeed – often so cold that land transport is delayed, and sometimes impossible by road. Socially, this region of the CIS is a huge market. The population is more than 250 million. Rumania has 20 million people; Bulgaria and Hungary 10 million each. But these figures are not so important for inter-country trade in produce as there is a high degree of rural self-sufficiency.

This entire region has been undergoing a process of transition from centrally-planned to market-based economies with highly significant implications for inter-country trade, particularly the European Union, the Middle East and Scandinavia, and for opening up market access. There has already been substantial economic growth in the most vigorous reforming countries (EBRD, 1995). Output in Eastern and Central Europe grew at an average 3 per cent in 1994; and in Poland, Slovakia, Slovenia and Estonia output grew by 4–5 per cent (for Poland this was the third successive year of growth). And Hungary, Latvia, Rumania, Bulgaria and Croatia have experienced a return to growth. Indeed inflation fell throughout Eastern and Central Europe in 1994, taking in the Czech and Slovak Republics, falling substantially in Rumania, Croatia and Macedonia. Although further sharp falls in output were recorded in the CIS, there was progress in controlling inflation, with a decline in Russia, Ukraine, Kyrgyzstan, Uzbekistan and Moldova.

Liberalisation and reform are moving forward in many areas. Inflation and foreign trade flows, which were previously fixed by bureaucrats in annual plans, are now heavily influenced by fiscal, monetary and exchange in most East European and CIS countries. This is a consequence of comprehensive deregulation of prices and trade which was implemented in many of these countries as early as 1989/91. In inter-country trade, the Czech and Slovak Republics, Poland and Hungary, South Eastern Europe and the Baltic States have seen their trade with Western market economies more than double in dollar terms since 1989, facilitated in most cases by competitive exchange rates and Association agreements with the European Union. Internally, privatisation of commerce and industry has advanced more unevenly, but in the last three years there have been big privatisations notably in the Czech Republic and Russia. Indeed, most of the output growth in East and Central Europe derives from the private sector which, from very small beginnings, now accounts for more than 5 per cent of GDP.

The People's Republic of China is, in population, the largest country in the world; its vast natural wealth and enormous population means that it is largely self-sufficient in its need for everyday products, both consumer and industrial. The main constraint on the expansion of China's foreign trade is its limited supply of foreign currency; nevertheless, there has been more emphasis in recent years on importing technology products from the West to modernise Chinese industry, and to build up the underlying industrial strength of the country.

Since 1979 China has been undergoing a fundamental transformation from a central command to a market-led economy, culminating in the official adoption by the Chinese Communist Party of the 'Socialist Market Economy' in 1992. With the development of this new market system, 400 000 state-owned enterprises will be transformed from government production units to independent economic entities managed according to conventional open-market principles. This new policy envisages the development of new markets, including those dealing in commodities, finance and capital, labour, technology and so on. An important milestone was passed in 1992 when output from non-state sectors accounted for more than half (52 per cent) of GDP. This market development also has important implications both for China's inter-country trade and for access to the vast domestic market of China. The modernisation of Chinese industry and other 'structural adjustments' in distribution and so forth are already creating a huge potential market for industrial and technical products from Western Europe. At the same time, Chinese industry is expanding its production of consumer goods (where it holds a substantial labour-cost advantage) which are already being traded internationally in volume. The main constraints facing China are shortages of foreign currency and foreign direct investment (FDI).

The Middle East region is not a market in the same sense as the European Union. There is little formal association of countries (apart from the Gulf Cooperation Council), nor do they always have the same policies. They do share the same religion and have similar economies, though even here the Moslem fundamentalist movement in Iran, the Iran/Iraq war and the civil war in Lebanon have caused bitter divisions; it is also true historically that different Arab factions have always found it difficult to work together politically and economically. Geographically, the Middle East includes the countries in the North of Africa (such as Egypt), those to the East of the Mediterranean (such as Syria and Jordan) and the countries and states round the Gulf (such as Saudi Arabia and Oman). They are all hot, dry countries, and much of the land is sandy desert; the *lingua franca* is Arabic. Israel is a part of the Middle East, but for political and religious reasons is best thought of as a quite separate market, though the recent peace agreement with the PLO has at least lifted the burden of trade boycotts. Land communications are generally poor.

Socially, each country of the Middle East has its own way of life and its own language. The languages are all very similar (they are varieties of Arabic) except in Iran which has a quite different language, Farsi. The Iranians are not Arabs, although they have much in common with the Arab nations. All the States of the Middle East except Israel share in the Moslem religion, and this is perhaps the most important tie that holds them together. The States are sometimes known collectively as 'The Green Crescent'. All the countries and states have great extremes of poverty and wealth although in the oil-rich countries this is changing fast. Economically, the Middle East states are dependent on their oil industries, and about half of the world's oil supplies come from these countries. Because this is an essential requirement of modern civilisation, the Middle East states find a ready world market for their oil, and all the oil states are very wealthy indeed. Because they are interested in developing their other industries quickly, they are a good market for industrial goods. The Middle East is also a growing market for consumer goods as greater wealth becomes more available to the mass of the population.

Each country in the Middle East has its own government and its own laws, and it is not possible to make a general statement that applies to them all. Some of the countries have a very firm autocracy with power held by a very few people. Other countries are moving towards the beginnings of democracy. There are other political systems between these extremes, and each one has its own trading policy. In Algeria, Libya and Saudi Arabia most of the trading is done through the public sector, very much like a planned economy. In the Lebanon it is mostly a free market economy with the government taking less part. In other Middle East countries, trading is a mixture of both planned and free. An exporter who wishes to trade in the Middle East must study each country separately; he must also be prepared for changes in policy from time to time.

Developing countries comprise a wide diversity of countries which are in receipt, in one form or another, of development aid. The term also encompasses a division between developing countries and least-developed countries (LDCs) which, largely because of geographical and economic factors such as being islands or landlocked, are classified as the poorest countries in the world. The developing countries have in the last few years formed a trading bloc in negotiating improvements in trade terms with industrialised countries; this is the African, Caribbean, and Pacific bloc (ACP).

Table 1.5 summarises some key world trade statistics.

The developing countries occupy most of Africa, all of Latin America, the Indian sub-continent and South-east Asia. It is clearly difficult to generalise but climate is generally tropical with extremes of drought or excessive rains. Communications are usually poor and links with other countries owe more to colonial history than to current conditions.

The mass of the population do not have the money for consumer goods like

Table 1.5   World market data

Market region	Area (million square miles)	Population (million)	Total imports (US$ million)**	Imports per head (US$ million)
Western Europe	4.00	400	360 000	900.0
North America	9.40	232	148 000	638.0
Middle East	3.70	100	30 000	300.0
Eastern Central Europe & CIS countries	9.00	320	80 000	250.0
China*	3.70	900	5 000	5.5
Japan	0.14	110	50 000	454.5
Australasia	3.10	16	12 000	750.0
Developing countries	19.00	1 900	100 000	52.5

Notes:
*   No recent trade data available.
** These are approximations based on IMF statistics and UN sources to 1990.

televisions and refrigerators. But they have a great need for basic necessities such as clothes, food, simple machines, agricultural products and educational supplies which find a ready market.

Following this analysis of the main market regions of the world, it is now appropriate to consider the major trends in inter-country trade by economic sector.

■ Trade in manufactures

One of the most significant trends in the last decade has been the expansion of the industrial base of newly-industrialising countries (NICs), evidenced by the increase in their machinery and equipment exports and their increased sales to Europe and North America of a range of durable and other consumer goods. At the same time, the member countries of the OECD have expanded their intra-regional trade at a greater rate than their trade in those sectors with developing countries.

During the decade up to 1990, the world's ten leading industrial countries at least doubled – and in some cases trebled – their total trade: Canada and the UK doubled their trade (by value), West Germany and USA increased their trade two and a half times, and Japan and the USSR increased their trade approximately threefold.

In developing countries, governments have endeavoured to force the pace of industrialisation, thereby taking resources away from traditional export products, the prices of which in some cases have been forced up, so encouraging the development of synthetic substitutes by industrialised countries.

Table 1.6 and Figure 1.7 quantify the main statistical trends in world trade in manufactures.

1. The effects of the change in the size of the world market for manufactured goods as a whole.
2. The effects of changes in the location of production and trade patterns by type of product.
3. The effects of the changes in shares of production and exports by countries, reflecting changes in their competitive positions.

Figure 1.7 shows the composition of the industrial sectors in world trade since 1937, and two outstanding changes can be discerned:

1. The rise in trade in machinery and transport equipment.
2. The fall in trade in textiles and clothing.

From Figure 1.7 it is clear how the pattern of manufacturing output has changed. Industry has to respond to changes in demand as income levels rise; typical of this process is the relatively rapid growth in demand for capital

Table 1.6   Shares of world production and exports of
manufactures

		1937 (%)	1959 (%)	1990 (%)
France	P	8.2	7.1	8.5
	E	5.8	9.7	9.4
Germany	P	15.3	10.6	13.5
	E	16.3	19.2	20.1
UK	P	14.7	11.2	4.8
	E	20.3	16.8	9.3
Other W	P	9.1	9.1	10.9
Europe	E	19.4	21.6	32.0
Canada	P	2.7	3.1	2.8
USA	P	47.0	55.4	47.0
	E	20.5	19.3	14.8
Japan	P	3.0	3.5	16.2
	E	9.5	6.8	14.3

Note:
P = net value of manufactured production.
E = value of manufactured exports in US$ at current prices.
Source: Adapted from UN *Statistical Yearbook* and OECD,
Department of Economics and Statistics, *Foreign Trade by Manu-
facturers and Commodities*, Vol 5. 1995, Paris.

goods, chemicals and consumer durable goods, and a slowing down in demand
for food, textiles and clothing.

Much also depends on the resources of each manufacturing country – for
example, capital, supply sources and technical expertise. The extent of these
will determine both the economies of scale that are possible and the volume of
imports needed to sustain industrialisation. Much depends on the value-added
content which the manufacturing sector can earn by improved technology.
changes in the volume of manufacturers, therefore, are affected by two major
influences:

1.   Changes in the level of consumption of manufactures.
2.   Changes in the proportion of consumption which is met by imports.

■ Trade in primary products

Primary products are those products and commodities which include deposits
of essential but exhaustible – as distinct from renewable – resources. Renewable
resources include commodities (such as fibres, beverages, seed and oil products)
sold by developing countries to industrialised countries, and processed mostly in
industrialised countries. There are also deposits of exhaustible resources (again
mostly sold in their primary state by developing to industrialised countries)

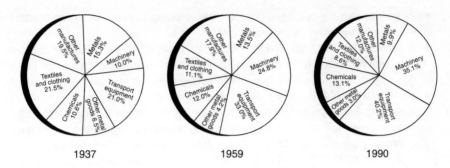

1937   1959   1990

Figure 1.7   Sectoral composition of world trade in manufactures

Source: Adapted from United Nations *Statistical Yearbook* and *Bulletin of Statistics*.

including iron and other ores, and steel-strengthening minerals like bauxite and titanium which are used in almost every type of finished manufactured product; precious metals too (for example, photographic manufacturers such as Kodak buy up every year one-third of the world's output of silver).

International trade in such commodities has been influenced by various international agreements, for example in sugar, wheat, coffee, tin and copper, and the Multi-Fibre Arrangement which applies to textiles. Such agreements, negotiated on a multilateral basis between the main producing and consuming countries, are intended to ensure price stability for a fixed term, and typically contain four clauses.

1. Purchasers (mostly industrialised countries) undertake to buy minimum quantities over a fixed term.
2. Brokers or other authorised intermediaries act on behalf of commodity producers.
3. Producing (most developing) countries agree to supply forward at a contracted price and to deliver at minimum specified quality.
4. Quotas among producers are often implemented to prevent over-production forcing down prices, causing loss and precipitating future shortages of supply.

The other important aspect is the balance of market power between producing and consuming countries. A study by the Economist Intelligence Unit examined this aspect with reference to 13 commodities: bananas, bauxite, cocoa, coffee, copper, iron ore, pepper and other spices, phosphates, natural rubber, sugar, tea, tin and wool. The study found that there were five significant limitations on the market power of the producers:

1. *Monopoly of supply:* where a major producer remains outside an agreement, clearly market power is reduced (for example, neither USA, the world's largest copper producer, nor Canada, are members of the International Council of Copper Exporting Countries (ICEC)).
2. *A 'slow down' in the trade of industrialised countries* directly affects the export

earnings of producer countries (for example, a slump in construction contracts in the USA reduces timber imports).

3. *Fluctuations in prices and shortages of foreign exchange* have the result that producers' groups do not have the financial stability to restrict exports over a period to push up consumer prices (the exception was the Organisation of Petroleum Export Countries (OPEC) which did just this during the 1970s).

4. *Competition from synthetics and substitutes*: where manufacturing and output costs are forced to rise by actions of producer countries, the industrialised countries intensify development of substitutes (for example, when member countries of the International Bauxite Association (IBA) forced up taxes on foreign companies mining their land, consumer countries found an alternative primary resource for aluminium in non-bauxite clays).

5. *Elasticity of demand*: for many commodities sold internationally, rising prices can cause consumers to switch to other available products (for example, the Union of Banana Exporting Countries (UBEC) faces the possibility of consumers buying more of other fruit if banana prices are pushed higher).

■ Conclusions

Both conceptual and empirical aspects of international trade have been explained in this chapter as a foundation to build an understanding of how trade policies of governments influence business opportunities. Key economic regions of the world have been profiled to show opportunities for trade, and the chapter has included a statistical analysis of trade patterns by region, industry sector and commodity. It is clear that market access and stimulation of demand are the keys to sustained international expansion for the company. It is also clear that the pattern of trade is changing, both in terms of regional markets and industry sectors, and these changes represent significant business opportunities for alert managements, particularly the growth of regional trading blocs, and in the global provision of services where growth is outpacing that of manufacturing in many countries' markets.

QUESTIONS

1. What recent developments in trade theory have, in your view, undermined the classical concept of 'comparative advantage'?
2. Which international trade organisations have been most influential in reducing, if not eliminating, tariffs and why?
3. What have been the most significant recent trends in inter-country trade in manufactures and semi-manufactures?
4. To what extent has the emergence of regional trading blocs improved market access in international trade? Discuss one example.
5. How has political change impacted on market access in any region of your choice?
6. Is it arguable that, for those countries dependent on primary products for export, their terms of trade can only deteriorate further in comparison to countries exporting manufactures to them?
7. How has the changing composition of 'factors of production' influenced the location and organisation of manufacturing among the principal trading countries?

CHAPTER 2

International business: concepts and organisation

INTRODUCTION

This chapter explains how companies develop international operations through direct exporting and then investing overseas, and the implications for management. The key point here is that internationalisation is a developmental process where, though the firm may not have initially planned to expand abroad, forces in competition and in its domestic market have impelled it to do so, and thereby foreign experience is accumulated. The critical factor seems to be the quality and the philosophy of management, but the operational aspects are also covered in detail.

The changing role of the multinational corporation is another focus in this chapter, which explains how MNCs have developed their business with particular reference to cross-border expansion. Finally, the significance of the interface between government and industry in trade promotion and industrial policy is examined and different policy aspects evaluated.

The internationalisation process

Determining factors

The factors which impel firms to operate internationally have been extensively researched over many years and cover a wide spectrum; indeed firms are having to internationalise their operations to remain competitive. For example, an increasing number of firms undertake local manufacturing through licensing arrangements or direct investments. This has created new market opportunities for management and, at the same time, has brought about the development of a cadre of international managers able to operate effectively across national and cultural boundaries. International business accounts for an important share of large companies' operations, and increasingly small and medium enterprises (SMEs) are developing their own overseas markets.

The internationalisation process describes the sequence in which a firm evolves from a domestic organisation, serving a relatively homogeneous home market, to becoming an active exporter, and subsequently an international corporation serving a large number of diverse multinational and cultural markets.

The internationalisation theory is based on certain assumptions. The firm that invests abroad is assumed to have developed a company-specific advantage in its home market, usually cited as superior knowledge/expertise in production or marketing of a product or service. Furthermore, it is assumed that this expertise, as an intangible asset, is developed within the firm, which then tries to exploit it profitably in international markets by acquiring local companies as a base for exploiting market potential overseas. There is also an assumption that the costs of market transactions between independent firms are higher than the administrative costs associated with exploitation within a wholly-owned corporate structure. The theory also predicts that this tends to be the case: the more knowledge- or technology-intensive the company-specific asset is, this is reflected in a propensity to invest abroad rather than market through intermediaries. Of course, the greater the uncertainty about the foreign market, the higher will be the coordination costs of the investing company, and this in itself tends to reinforce the policy of acquisitions, with more market control, intelligence and contacts and trading expertise provided by the acquired enterprise.

Thus, in the internationalisation process, the firm tends to choose acquisitions rather than direct investment in new plant and so forth, to get a lower but less uncertain expected rate of return. So the theory predicts a correlation between a firm's degree of internationalisation and its propensity to use foreign acquisition as its primary mode of expansion; indeed, the theory is based on the view of direct foreign investment as a mode of entry into a foreign market to exploit company-specific assets and expertise (see Chapter 5, on acquisitions and divestment).

Figure 2.1 illustrates four key phases in the development of international business. As the scope of operations widens, so the elements of risk and investment in countries' markets increases; moreover, with the growth of regional trading blocs (EU, ASEAN, NAFTA) international companies are increasingly pursuing multi-country or regional strategies through 'complementation' agreements such as that between IBM and the Latin American Integration Association (LAIA).

An important issue throughout this process, however, is to what extent do firms typically plan to internationalise and how far are they drawn into international operations by external factors? Notwithstanding the high level of interest in the study of international business, much involvement by firms seems developmental, rather than planned, in the long term; indeed the failure to develop long-range international objectives prior to moving overseas has resulted in many unsuccessful foreign ventures. Further, decisions relating to entry into foreign markets are complicated by many variables not found in domestic market decisions. Some of these variables are external to the com-pany such as pressure from international competitors, or the effects of foreign governments' trade policies: the point is that few of these external variables are predictable with the precision required for forward planning.

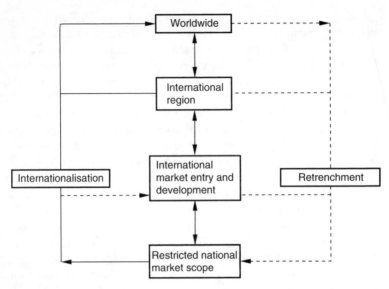

Figure 2.1   The development of international business

Source: Ellis and Williams (1995), p. 54.

The model that is frequently quoted to explain the internationalisation theory is the Swedish internationalisation model (Johanson and Vahlne, 1977). According to this, a firm's internationalisation starts when the domestic market is close to saturation and it seeks new alternatives abroad; hence, the process proceeds as a consequence of a growth and profit motive. Abroad, the firm faces uncertainty and risk to a degree not encountered in the domestic market, and these can be reduced only through the steady accumulation of experience of foreign operations.

The general question, therefore, arises: what are the key 'movers' in internationalising the firm; this is illustrated in Figure 2.2 showing the interaction of different forces such as latent and direct influences on the behaviour of the firm; some of these are internal to the firm and some are external. But perhaps the more significant distinction is between what have come to be termed reactive and proactive motivations to internationalise.

Firms react to changes in the business environment by exploring overseas markets; these reactive factors apply especially to,

- the competitive position of the firm;
- the state of the domestic economy.

As far as reactive factors are concerned, firms typically react to overproduction or excess capacity in manufacturing by seeking overseas outlets for sales; allied to this situation may well be stagnant or saturated domestic markets which force the firm to go overseas; similarly, declining domestic sales or increasingly

---

CASE 2.1

This concerns the only British-owned soup firm to have survived shortages of tins, jars and 172 takeover bids. Gordon Baxter, chairman and managing director of W. A. Baxter & Sons, and Audrey Baxter, managing director of the Baxters of Speyside subsidiary, gave a presentation to the 1994 Institute of Directors Convention in London to explain how the company had developed from a grocery shop, founded 126 years ago, into an international business with a turnover of £40 million, pre-tax profits of £3.8 million, 600 staff and a determination to resist takeovers. According to Mr Baxter, the third generation of the family to run the firm, it has been carefully planned to keep full family control of the company; as this is the only way to guarantee that standards will be maintained. His inventive mother provided the basis for the firm's success in 1929 with Royal Game Soup, now claimed to be the biggest selling quality soup in the world, pioneered soft-fruit canning and added to the jams made by her mother-in-law. Exports started when a buyer from Macy's, the American store, saw Baxter's jams in Harrods and placed orders. The company now exports to 12 countries. In 1945 it had 11 employees and had to 'beg' for a can allocation while scouring the country for used jars for jams. New products were developed by Mr Baxter and his wife, Ena, with the aid of a soup pan, a wooden spoon and a Bunsen burner. Then, there were 20 jam-making firms in Scotland. Baxter's is one of the two survivors.

The 40 soup-makers of 1946 are now three, of which Heinz and Campbell are American. According to Mr Baxter, rivals had died 'or were on somebody else's menu'. His rejected suitors included General Foods, General Mills, Distillers, Campbells, United Biscuits, Quaker Oats, Rowntree and Heinz. These approaches just reinforced the policy to remain independent, to remain profitable and for Baxter's to remain in Scotland.

---

severe competition in the home-market can alert management both to their vulnerable reliance on home sales and to missed sales opportunities abroad. Logistics-management enables firms to serve overseas customers cost-effectively, and to offset over-reliance on one or two markets. The point is that in this context, management tends to await events and react to change rather than plan ahead and control events. It is essentially the difference between a sales-oriented approach – reacting to enquiries, fulfilling orders and 'selling what the company makes' – and a marketing-oriented or proactive approach, where a marketing plan, based on a thorough analysis of target-country markets, means that the firm is manufacturing what customers want to buy.

■ **The role of management**

So what are these proactive factors which distinguish the marketing-led firm from the reactive firm. First and foremost is the drive and philosophy of the

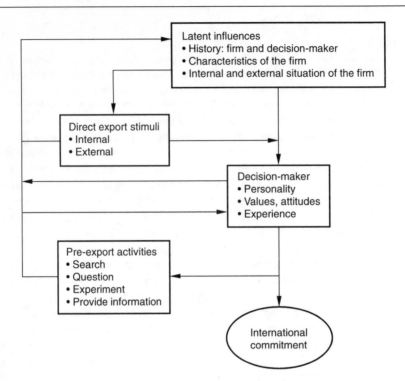

Figure 2.2   Key influences on initial international involvement

Source: Czinkota (1982).

management: studies of international performance over many years have shown that it is the quality of management, not just marketing expertise, which is the key proactive factor, though certainly most proactive factors are marketing-based. Other proactive factors include:

1. *Economies of scale* – achieved by driving up volume across country markets and reducing unit costs and prices, without lowering quality; this then improves the competitive position of the firm in a situation where the domestic market is not big enough to achieve scale economies.
2. *Tax benefit* –this is a complex issue for the firm operating across frontiers including currency management, transfer pricing and remission of profits. Basically, only a firm with a strong international presence can capitalise in this way by optimal use of assets and by minimising corporate tax liabilities.
3. *Exclusive information* – management must have an intelligence system, or network, through which new information about markets is filtered and acted on; this can be through the use of agents, the government's Export Intelligence Service in the UK, or other information services offered to subscribing companies by media owners

such as Croners or Dun and Bradstreet. The information will not be exclusive for long, and acting on it promptly signifies a proactive approach.

4. *Technological advantage* – companies which invest in technology, new designs, formulations and products are characterised by proactive management, which sees competitive advantage as the key outcome of such investment; but again this requires forward planning and the drive to stay ahead. Black and Decker's international strength is partly due to the management's decision in the 1990s to invest a higher percentage of turnover (about 6 per cent) in design than its competitors.

5. *Unique products* – this is the best case of proactive marketing as the basis of the firm's internationalisation. Products which offer a unique benefit and which enjoy consumer acceptance in overseas markets provide the firm with a strong foundation for international expansion.

6. *Profit advantage* – market-based pricing requires proactive management: that is market research as a basis for profitable pricing taking account of demand trends in different countries' markets; otherwise, a firm's ignorance of consumer prices in foreign markets may be exploited by its agents, thus depriving the firm of a higher profit margin. Studies over some years have shown that in some industry sectors such as high quality reproduction furniture, fashion-wear, security and emergency lighting, some UK firms have actually lost business overseas by underpricing, damaging the product's reputation.

CASE 2.2

The Texas Instruments Group, the engineering conglomerate, seeks to expand its international operations through its three main businesses: John Crane, Bundy and Dowty aerospace, without resorting to acquisitions: these represent TI's core business for sustained growth, and are market leaders. In 1994 all of them reported double-digit increases in profit: Bundy makes fuel and brake systems for cars, John Crane makes industrial seals, and Dowty makes aircraft landing gear.

TI management now intends to develop its international presence by globalising some products that have achieved regional success; this is because management considers that the company's main weakness is that many of its best products are not reaching enough international customers, particularly in the light of a buoyant automotive market in the USA and an upturn in the European market. For example, TI's leakless or zero-emission seal, a world first, sells well in the USA but has international potential.

The key point is that the policy to make TI a global player will involve a cultural change within the company, which traditionally has devoted more time to engineering than to marketing; this will involve training product managers in sales and marketing, and generating a more positive international orientation (including language training) among middle and senior management. The immediate task is to develop a cadre of managers able to operate effectively in a multi-cultural environment.

■ Operational aspects

Many companies recognise that, as their overseas business develops, decisions have to be faced about the extent of investment in and commitment to major markets, in order to secure the company's long-term market position. Such decisions concern investing in and setting up overseas production operations and, sometimes, buying sales and distribution companies locally in order to ensure sales outlets for the required investment in output. Direct investment of this sort is increasingly required to secure a long-term market position, whether or not this has been established by another route, such as exports. In many overseas markets the establishment of such a presence by a manufacturer (production operations, assembly and distribution facilities) can increase local demand. Government incentives in the form of tax concessions and grants will often be available to reduce the costs of capital outlay. Worldwide operating costs associated with exporting finished goods can be reduced, and closer links with the market will often enable marketing effectiveness to be improved.

Of course, direct manufacture overseas means financial investment in overseas operations, or perhaps the acquisition of a local manufacturing firm; in either case there is the element of risk of loss. So the decision to set up local manufacture in a country previously supplied by imports of finished goods must be a major step in the international growth of any company. The extent of the commitment will vary according to whether it is full or partial manufacture/ assembly or a joint venture. Whereas a decade ago the standard advice to the management might have been to set up a foreign plant with 100 per cent ownership (and control), if this was legally permitted, now conditions of both ownership and control are much more complex and often involve some sort of participation by host-government agencies. Also, more use is being made of options such as management contracts (See Chapter 7, section on international contracting). In reality, many companies operating internationally face little option but to consider some form of investment outlay; this is because many

---

CASE 2.3

A manufacturer of industrial equipment had for a long time followed implicitly a policy of undertaking local production only when it was forced into it by competitive pressure or actions of the host government. When management became aware that the company was being squeezed out of some promising markets because of this policy, it reversed its position and began actively to seek opportunities for direct investment overseas. A senior executive of the firm noted that the company was experiencing considerable difficulties in regaining the lost ground, as it was practically locked out of some markets owing to governments' concessions granted to earlier entrants, while in others competition was too entrenched for the firm to develop a viable market position to justify any direct investment.

host governments, concerned to expand the local manufacturing base and to increase export earnings from output, now operate various forms of tariffs, non-tariff measures and other restrictions and regulations that make direct exporting of finished goods into their countries increasingly costly and difficult. All this requires a positive policy on the part of the company's management towards direct investment in overseas operations.

■ **Decision criteria**

Clearly, a major set of decisions about internationalisation confronts management. Analysis and decision-making are required in the following areas:

1. *Where to locate* – which country and which region in which to locate or build the plant.
2. *Demand analysis* – is the expected, quantifiable demand likely to make the plant commercially viable when the output can,

   - be sold locally?
   - be sold to neighbouring countries/regionally?

3. *Market access and proximity* (as distinct from demand analysis) – regional economic communities such as the EU, CARICOM, ECOWAS, LAIA and ASEAN can provide tariff-free and unrestricted access for output among member countries; also the type and number bilateral trade treaties.
4. *Access to sources of supply* which can bring economies of manufacture together with improved procurement arrangements for sub-components, materials, and so forth.
5. *Financial aspects* – this would include an assessment of the availability and sources of capital (and the terms on which it is available), the expected return on the investment over what period and the position regarding repatriation of profits and dividends.
6. *Analysis of costs* – this of course, covers a spectrum including labour costs, expected operating costs, improvements in raw materials and other supply costs (related to point 4 above).
7. *Manpower* – this refers to the availability, quality and technical levels of local labour and of course labour costs; all these must be related to estimated levels of productivity.
8. *Competitor analysis* – strengths, weaknesses and assessed marketing policies of both locally-based and international competitors, particularly pricing policies and the quality/level of service offered.
9. *Technical and logistical factors* – these refer to such items as the availability and costs of distribution channels for the output, quality control standards, energy sources/costs, local availability of chemicals and any other supplies required for manufacturing.

10. *Fiscal aspects* – assessment of the types of customs 'drawbacks', and so on, offered by the host government of the proposed country of supply.
11. *Political factors* – many overseas Governments favour policies related to import substitution and export development; this means that once agreement has been reached with the appropriate government agency, continuing support with trade promotion, planning consents, mobilisation of labour, direct equity participation and special exemptions from foreign exchange restrictions for the importation of essential supply components and so on, can be forthcoming.
12. *Risk assessment* (see Chapter 7, section on risk and crisis management) –

- political risks (practically impossible to foresee fully) – change of government, nationalisation/expropriation, security measures against terrorism, change of laws, embargoes, strikes, political stability, political relationships with neighbouring countries which are target markets;
- financial risks – insolvency laws, foreign exchange transfers and delays, level of indebtedness to international banks, currency, inflation and interest rate trends, availability of credit, capital repatriation, and so on;
- commercial risks – laws regarding contract repudiation of agencies, takeover of partner by competitor, market shrinkage, patent or trademark infringement or revocation, loss of control of technology, product liability risks, performance of technology or equipment, and so forth.

Many aspects of the international process in this checklist, such as risk management, relations with host governments, competitive strategies and market entry are explained in detail in Chapter 4 and the section in Chapter 8 on the matrix approach.

■ The role of the multinational corporation (MNC)

■ Background developments

To understand the origins and role of the MNC it is first necessary to examine the home-base from which many MNCs have developed. The national base of the US and Japanese economies has been sufficient for these countries to nurture many stable, global businesses. This has not been true of all of Europe, in which the critical mass of most countries is insufficient to easily support global corporations, which look for alliances with other companies in order to grow. Electrolux long ago outgrew its home market, Sweden, and through many years of diversification and acquisitions has become a truly global company. At the same time, American and Japanese companies have set up large and successful pan-European operations in vehicles – Ford and GM followed by Nissan and Toyota; in food – Coca Cola, Pepsi and McDonald's; and in services – such as consultancy, McKinsey and Arthur Anderson.

■ The European perspective

And the European corporate expansion has certainly not been an unqualified success: for example the failure of Dunlop–Pirelli (tyres), Hoesch–Hoogovens (steel) and Volvo–Renault (cars); undoubtedly cultural and national factors have played a part in frustrating cross-border expansion in Europe.

Perhaps one of the difficulties is that there is no pan-European corporate tradition comparable with the clear and comprehensible corporate traditions of Japan and the USA. But because there is no consistent European culture with which every European company will be familiar, the company expanding beyond national frontiers either has to create a new culture of its own, impose its existing culture on its partner, or come to some uneasy compromise. In some industries, paper-making, defence and heavy vehicles for instance, companies go first for national convergence in which the strong country champion emerges, then for pan-national convergence in which the global competitor emerges from a number of national champions.

CASE 2.4

In vehicles, the main pan-European company to emerge is IVECO, a Dutch-registered but Italian-dominated company embracing Fiat, Lancia and OM of Italy, Magirus Deutz of Germany, Unic of France, Pegaso of Spain and Seddon–Atkinson and Ford of Britain. IVECO is attempting to build itself up as a global force in the heavy vehicle industry on this multi-national foundation; it is, however, essentially an Italian-run business with aspirations to worldwide dominance. And IVECO management is not finding the blending together of different corporate cultures easy; the conglomerate was formed largely through takeovers, and the bulk of the shareholding and the composition of the board and very senior management are predominantly Italian.

Some European companies have sought to avoid the cultural and political pitfalls of outright acquisitions by forming alliances. GEC operates through a series of affiliations, alliances and joint ventures with different companies in different places. Some of these alliances are European. GEC Alsthom, a Franco-British venture is, it happens, a direct competitor of ABB. Guinness and Moët–Hennessy, the drinks division of the French company LVMH, have shares in each other's businesses and find it convenient to work together in many parts of the world. They do not operate as a single business entity, although no doubt they rationalise where they can. However it seems to be a hands-off approach rather than a hands-on relationship, a policy which does not unduly disturb national corporate behaviour patterns. Interestingly, both Guinness and Moët–Hennessy sell national brands. All those Scotch whisky brands, perfumes, cognacs and champagnes derive their names and images

CASE 2.5

In 1988 Swiss Brown–Boveri and Swedish ASEA, two of the giants in the European power engineering business merged to create ABB. The conglomerate is headed by an inspirational and dynamic Swedish Chief Executive, Percy Barnevik. He is driving hard to create a truly European global company as opposed to one where a single national company dominates. He has some advantages: first he heads what was at least in theory a merger; and, second, Sweden and Switzerland have small domestic markets for corporate products, and firms can take a more realistic and objective view of their world significance.

Nevertheless, in order to be competitive internationally, the management of ABB has had to undertake some ruthless pruning which has meant plant closures and other cost-cutting measures; this has not made the company popular amongst its own people in a number of countries in which it operates, but in spite of these strains, the prospects for ABB globally look positive.

directly from English, Scottish, Irish and French caricatures. In so far as one can judge from the outside, the arrangement seems to suit both parties, who have recently moved further together.

Undoubtedly, MNCs operating either within or out of Europe do have world-class products in certain key industry sectors, but across all industries the pan-European scenario is still somewhat fragmented. As one analyst has put it:

Europe has a few pockets of excellence in manufacturing, particularly in the upper-middle technology range, which neither North America nor Japan can match. But there are not many where it is objectively the best. It has some excellent pharmaceutical and oil companies and the greatest export centre for financial services. But Europe's comparative advantage in conventional industry is quite thin. If, however, one looks at the individual European countries in detail the picture is more encouraging. All, for example, have a high quality craft manufacturing centre, but each produces very different items. England has racing car manufacturing (which includes research on advanced engine technology for European companies); Scotland, whisky; France, perfume and toiletries; Italy quality clothing; Germany, medical and dental equipment. It is very hard to see Taiwan – or looking ahead, mainland China – competing effectively in any of those areas.

(Macrae, 1993)

Nevertheless, the 'lead' companies in Europe such as ABB and Akzo–Nobel are determined to make a success of an organisation which goes above and beyond national boundaries. They will focus their efforts on creating a unified culture and a corporate personality which complements the national loyalties of the employee. The effort involved in creating such structures is immense, extremely costly and takes a long time.

■ Organisational aspects

The organisation of MNCs has to be highly decentralised but very well co-ordinated. The organisations that succeed, increasingly find that being bound into a nation-state or even two nation-states, with their idiosyncrasies of culture and personality and their fiscal and financial regulations, is increasingly irksome.

They will move ever closer to a world in which they and their people have no national provenance, no national bias, no national prejudices – although it is perfectly possible, indeed likely, that some of these companies will market products with powerful national or regional characteristics. They become global companies, owing allegiance only to their stakeholders – their employees, their customers, their suppliers, their investors and to their host countries.

So the phenomenon of the MNC can be said increasingly to dominate international trade. The MNC operates across national boundaries, and becomes a corporate citizen of those nation-states in it which have production, marketing and other management responsibilities. To remain effective as an entity, the company has to coordinate and control its activities in multiple environments, making decisions that may not be optimal for one or more of the country markets in which it operates. As a result, the company may come under scrutiny by private and public organisations such as government Departments of Trade and Commerce, the European Commission, the World Trade Organisation (WTO) and Agencies of the United Nations (see for example OECD, 1992).

The UN defines MNCs as 'enterprises which own or control production or facilities outside the country in which they are based'; the key criteria are that the firm controls its production facilities abroad, and manages them (and its domestic operations) in an integrated fashion in pursuit of global opportunities.

There are some definitional points which must be addressed in any analysis of the role of the MNC; first their number has been estimated by the International Labour Office (ILO), Geneva, at about 10 000, with 90 000 affiliates around the world.

Traditionally, companies expanding internationally have organised themselves in a decentralised way, meeting the requirements of host governments to 'fly the local flag' and the desire of country managers for local autonomy from head office. It is generally accepted that, in addition to multi-country operations, the proportion of revenue generated from foreign operations should be of the order of 25–30 per cent. And the degree of foreign market involvement must be substantial enough to make a difference in decision-making. In a few cases, several nations own the MNC, as is the case with Royal Dutch Shell and Unilever. However, production abroad is insufficient alone as a criterion: the behaviour of the firm and its degree of, and commitment to, internationalisation (explained earlier in this chapter) are the determining factors.

There are a growing number of global industries, for example pharmaceuticals, defence and telecommunications, computers, television and electrical appliances. Indeed many of the world's largest corporate entities are larger than their host nations. Some operate in well over 100 countries; for example IBM has operations in 131 countries. Of the top 100 firms listed in the 500 largest industrial corporations of *Fortune* magazine, the USA holds a commanding lead with 39, followed by Japan with 15 and Germany with 12. But this group is more diversified than the numbers suggest; for example General Motors, while classified as American, includes large subsidiaries that employ thousands locally in Canada, Germany, the UK, Spain, Belgium, Brazil and Mexico. So the role of country management is still crucial: the economics of identifying a global market niche and organising the company to exploit it.

But the organisational difficulties involved in operating across multi-markets are considerable and must be borne in mind when considering the role of the MNC. Historically, they have been organised on the basis of regional or functional divisionalisation. For example, Sony has organised itself into world product divisions based in Tokyo; but it also has the Sony Corporation of America, a legacy of Sony's policy to go international. Country managers and product managers have to share responsibilities for decision-making and profit.

■   **Organisational modalities**

This raises a more general question: how far is there an optimal organisational mode for effective global operations? Porter has proposed a critical review of a company's main activities (manufacturing, marketing, R&D, personnel and so forth) along two axes which are illustrated in Figure 2.3.

On the two axes are shown:

(a) *Configuration.* Where should each activity be performed to maximise economies of scale? At one limit, each activity could be performed in every country (low configuration); at the other each activity in only one country (high configuration).

Figure 2.3   Global operational strategies

Source: Adapted from Porter (1990) *Competitive Strategy.*

(b) *Coordination.* What is the relationship between like activities in different countries? Are decisions all taken locally (low coordination) or centrally (high coordination)?

If the business is local and best served by local production, the company may not need a global strategy, even though it has multi-country operations (for example Unilever). If the country manufactures centrally, but markets in each

---

CASE 2.6

In 1995, Royal Dutch Shell initiated a massive corporate restructuring exercise which should sharpen competition in the international oil business. Following the sale of Shell's mining interest, a review of operations found that the rate of return on assets employed was not high enough to sustain the company in the long term. The main outcome of this restructuring is the dismantling of the 35-year-old matrix organisation based on regions, functions and operations, and its replacement by a grouping of Shell's five main business sectors: exploration and production, oil products, chemicals, gas and coal.

For historical reasons, Royal Dutch Shell has been organised mainly on geographical lines, each country or region having its own companies and managers which report back through layers of command to the corporate centre which is split between London and the Hague. At the top is the four-strong committee of managing directors, each responsible for one of Shell's four regions and a number of businesses. Regional coordinators ensure there is no overlap between different companies. This organisation evolved into a traditional matrix structure but it has become increasingly complex: a given operating company could be defined by its geography, its sector within the company and its line of business.

The restructuring around Shell's five core business organisations means that each operating company will report to whichever of these organisations (headed by new business committees) are relevant to its activities. Executive authority will remain with the operating companies so that they retain the 'localness' which is a key part of Shell's policy.

A central aim of this new structure is to reflect the different types of decision that are taken at various levels within the group. The executives who run the operating companies need a lot of local authority – and to be personally responsible for their companies' performance. The business committee will look at wider strategic issues that require a more collective approach. Their decisions will affect many companies and their focus will back up the chain of command to the committee of managing directors and ultimately to the shareholders. In this way, Shell hopes to encourage maximum local initiative within a structure that keeps the group as a whole heading in the right direction and provides the right checks and balances.

The restructuring is shown in Figure 2.4.

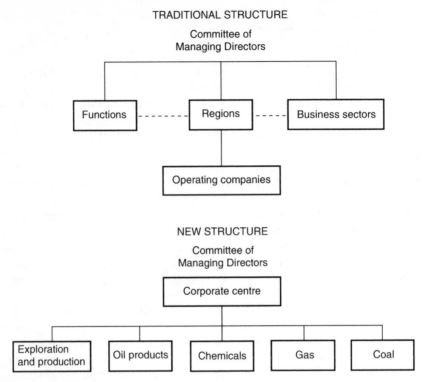

TRADITIONAL STRUCTURE

Committee of
Managing Directors

Functions ------- Regions ----- Business sectors

Operating companies

NEW STRUCTURE

Committee of
Managing Directors

Corporate centre

Exploration and production | Oil products | Chemicals | Gas | Coal

Figure 2.4   The re-organisation of Shell

Source: Adapted from Royal Dutch Shell and the *Financial Times*, March 1995.

country, the organisation should be built around exporting (for example Mercedes Benz). If its operations depend on much local investment, but need to be tightly coordinated, then the company is positioned in the upper left of Figure 2.3; this company would be vulnerable to a competitor who can undercut by moving right and getting economies of scale by making each component in the cheapest country and shipping around to markets.

Other big oil companies have already gone through corporate upheavals to adjust to 'flat' oil prices, including Exxon, British Petroleum and Amoco.

■ MNCs and world trade

The above discussion raises an important question, the need of the MNC to adjust to changing international trading conditions, particularly in view of the way they influence entire sectors and, in some cases, the economies of their host countries. MNCs operate in over 100 countries and the economic power that they command is immense: according to one estimate, the 500 largest industrial corporations account for 80 per cent of the world's affiliates. Corporate head-quarters for the 500 corporation are in 20 different countries; and direct invest-ment activity by firms from Africa, Asia and Latin America has increased dramatically.

Of course the impact of MNCs varies worldwide by industry sector and by country. To take oil again as an example, they command 30 per cent of global production and their share in refining and marketing ('downstream' activities) is still 45 per cent. In several agribusiness sectors, such as pineapples, MNCs account for approximately 60 per cent of world output. Similarly, the contribu-tion of multi-national corporations' affiliates may account for more than one-third of the output of the manufacturing sector in certain countries. For example, US companies owned 32 per cent of the paper and pulp industry, 36 per cent of the mining and smelting industry, and 30 per cent of manufacturing overall in Canada before the foreign direct investment climate changed in the early 1980s. The importance of the world marketplace to multinational corpo-rations also varies. The foreign sales share of total sales for the world's largest industrial corporations is approximately one-fourth. This will naturally vary by industry (for example oil company ratios are well over half) and by country of origin. For many European-based companies, domestic sales may be less than 10 per cent of overall sales.

But the traditional multinational structure has been a complex one, and increasingly management has had to adopt a policy of streamlining both head-office functions and its relationships with operating divisions. British Petroleum and ICI have abandoned matrices, while others, for example IBM and DOW, have opted for streamlining. Others, for example ABB, Deutsche Bank, Cater-pillar and Ford have installed new 'slimmer' matrices, in some cases for the first time. In almost every case, most of the power has been put into the hands of international business or product division managers, relegating geographic and especially functional management to subordinate roles. Of course there are certain inherent conflicts in the diverse activities which multinationals carry out: they must deploy their resources across the globe more effectively, rapidly and flexibly; they must reduce drastically the cost-base of head-office coordina-tion required to do that; and they must enhance their ability to respond to different market and competitive challenges in countries and regions of opera-tions, to say nothing of formal planning, risk analysis and management, and financial performance. Indeed, the multinationals most at risk of losing national and regional market responsiveness are those which have gone over to one-dimensional organisations in which their business divisions are all powerful. Where geographical units are reduced to playing little more than supporting roles in sales and service, the company risks alienating customers and staff in countries other than those where the business divisions have headquarters.

And even when organisational problems have been resolved, and competi-tiveness sharpened, the multinational has to come to terms with another prob-lem: political autonomy versus corporate centralisation. The directors of Shell Oil of America (excluded for legal and technical reasons from the restructuring explained in Case 2.6), who are obliged by US law to serve the best interests of their American company, saw a conflict between that loyalty and their loyalty to their Anglo-Dutch parent when it wanted to buy full control. Strife within multinationals and between them and host governments is not new. Renewed centralisation of key strategic decisions may well exacerbate frictions with some host governments; the solution seems to lie in retaining a strong regional presence with operational autonomy.

It would be unreasonable to expect anything more than this of Siemens at

---

CASE 2.7

Whenever a multinational company upgrades its growing network of foreign factories by opening a new research or design and development centre abroad, it reinforces a fashionable view held by many academics, politicians, government officials, and even top executives that, in this world of supposedly stateless companies spinning webs of increasingly high value-added activities across national borders, nationality of ownership is becoming irrelevant. The most influential proponent of this view has been Robert Reich, a Harvard economics professor who is US Labour Secretary, and he has been echoed by other senior figures from the top management of Motorola and Sony.

This attitude was exemplified in the reaction of UK ministers and officials to the plans in 1995 by Siemens, the German electronics giant, not only to build a £1.1 billion semiconductor factory near Newcastle, in north-east England, but to extend its international chain of electronics design and development centres by opening a 50-person unit on the same site.

The Siemens investment is undoubtedly welcome from a British point of view. It will also certainly strengthen the German company's drive to internationalise not just its production, but also the more critical – and more highly skilled – processes by which it conceives and develops new products. With a few exceptions, German multinationals – like French ones – are far behind UK, Swedish, Swiss and Dutch companies in this process.

But the significance of the Newcastle design centre should not be exaggerated. At least to begin with, it will merely put Siemens' UK semiconductor activities on a par with those in Singapore, where it already has a design centre, and behind Austria, where it has a much larger one. Most importantly, it will now lessen Siemen's dependence on its home technology base – mainly in Munich, but also increasingly in Dresden – for most of its basic technological innovations, and for its most advanced new products and processes. Company executives say that, initially at least, the UK centre will have a similar orientation towards local and regional customers as the Singapore centre. It is unlikely to be given responsibility for global designs for some time. They say that, as in Singapore and Austria, much of its activity will involve theadaptations of basic designs from libraries of ones already done in Munich.

this stage, for several reasons. First, far fewer multinationals than suggested by all the hype have built real research or product development webs around the world, in electronics or any other industry. As a report by the Washington-based Economic Strategy Institute concluded in 1995, the reality is that most multinationals' cutting-edge research and development remains in the home country. The same applies to their design and development of really advanced new products, since in the majority of companies most foreign work still consists mainly of local or regional adaptation and testing. (Source: *Financial Times* 18 August 1995.)

Finally the overwhelming home bias of multinationals was thought to be a temporary phenomenon, which would lessen inexorably as a natural cycle of internationalisation occurred in the wake of the spread of production around the world. But a series of recent studies by three British academics, John Cantwell of Reading University and Pari Patel and Keith Pavitt of the Science Policy Research Unit, has shown just how overwhelming the home-country bias still is for most large companies, especially those based in large economies. Their research shows that in the late 1980s less than 10 per cent of American multinationals' technology activity was carried out abroad – a proportion barely higher than in the 1930s, before it plunged sharply because of the war.

For European companies as a whole, the foreign proportion of their technology activity in the late 1980s was 31 per cent; of the major countries Germany was at one extreme with only 18 per cent done abroad, with Britain at the other extreme with a foreign rate of almost 50 per cent. Only in German and Swedish companies did the rate surge sharply in the 1980s. A third revelation is the limited geographic spread of those foreign development networks which do exist. Except for local adaptation work, the majority of companies still operate in a couple of countries outside their home base.

Some statistics on the activities of the world's largest industrial corporations are shown in Table 2.1.

■ **The interface between government and industry**

■ **Competition**

The accelerating pace of technological, economic and structural changes in the world (for example the telecommunications industry) is requiring both governments and multinational corporations to reassess their policies regarding competition, investment and trade. Moreover, governments have a role in influencing, both directly and indirectly, the internationalisation process.

As regards competition, in many countries government and the service providers have in general used a variety of methods that have affected competition both in home and overseas markets. In recent times, some governments have introduced policies designed to reduce the monopolistic tendencies of the

Table 2.1 The world's biggest industrial corporations

Company 1989 millions	Headquarters	Industry	Sales $ millions	Profits $
General Motors	Detroit	Motor vehicles	121 085.4	4 856.3
Ford Motor	Dearborn, Mich.	Motor vehicles	92 455.6	5 300.2
Exxon	New York	Petroleum refining	79 557.0	5 260.0
Royal Dutch/Shell Group	London/The Hague	Petroleum refining	78 381.1	5 238.7
International Business Machines	Armonk, N.Y.	Computers	59 681.0	5 806.0
Toyota Motor	Toyota City (Japan)	Motor vehicles	50 789.9	2 314.6
General Electric	Fairfield, Conn.	Electronics	49 515.0	3 386.0
Mobil	New York	Petroleum refining	48 198.0	2 087.0
British Petroleum	London	Petroleum refining	46 174.0	2 155.3
IRI	Rome	Metals	45 521.5	921.9
Daimler-Benz	Stuttgart	Motor vehicles	41 817.9	953.1
Hitachi	Tokyo	Electronics	41 330.7	989.0
Chrysler	Highland Park, Michigan	Motor vehicles	35 472.7	1 050.2
Siemens	Munich	Electronics	34 129.4	757.0
Fiat	Turin	Motor vehicles	34 039.3	2 324.7
Matsushita Electric Industrial	Osaka	Electronics	33 922.5	1 177.2
Volkswagen	Wolfsburg (W. Germany)	Motor vehicles	33 696.2	420.1
Texaco	White Plains, N.Y.	Petroleum refining	33 544.0	1 304.0
E.I. du Pont de Nemours	Wilmington, Del.	Chemicals	32 514.0	2 190.0
Unilever	London/Rotterdam	Food	30 488.2	1 485.6
Nissan Motor	Tokyo	Motor vehicles	29 097.1	463.0
Philips' Gloeilampenfabrieken	Eindhoven (Netherlands)	Electronics	38 270.5	477.1
Nestlé	Vevey (Switzerland)	Food	27 803.0	1 392.7
Samsung	Seoul	Electronics	27 386.1	464.3
Renault	Paris	Motor vehicles	27 109.7	1 496.7

Company	City	Industry		
Philip Morris	New York	Tobacco	25 860.0	2 337.0
Toshiba	Tokyo	Electronics	25 440.8	438.9
ENI	Rome	Petroleum refining	25 226.8	917.3
Chevron	San Francisco	Petroleum refining	25 196.0	1 768.0
BASF	Ludwigshafen (W. Germany)	Chemicals	24 960.5	802.2
Hoechst	Frankfurt	Chemicals	23 308.1	1 037.8
Peugeot	Paris	Motor vehicles	23 249.7	1 485.8
Bayer	Leverkusen (W. Germany)	Chemicals	23 025.9	1 055.5
Honda Motor	Tokyo	Motor vehicles	22 236.5	819.5
CGE (Cie Générale d'Électricité)	Paris	Scien. & photo. equipment	21 487.5	362.4
Elf Aquitaine	Paris	Petroleum refining	21 175.0	1 209.9
Amoco	Chicago	Petroleum refining	21 150.0	2 063.0
Imperial Chemical Industries	London	Chemicals	20 839.0	1 490.9
NEC	Tokyo	Electronics	19 626.1	183.4
Occidental Petroleum	Los Angeles	Food	19 417.0	302.0
Procter & Gamble	Cincinnati	Soaps, cosmetics	19 336.0	1 020.0
Ferruzzi Finanziaria	Ravenna	Chemicals	18 311.1	425.6
United Technologies	Hartford	Aerospace	18 087.8	659.1
Atlantic Richfield	Los Angeles	Petroleum refining	17 626.0	1 583.0
Asea Brown Boveri	Zurich	Indus. and farm equipment	17 562.0	386.0
Daewoo	Seoul	Electronics	17 251.2	33.3
Nippon Steel	Tokyo	Metals	17 108.9	291.7
Eastman Kodak	Rochester, N.Y.	Scien. and photo. equipment	17 034.0	1 397.0
Boeing	Seattle	Aerospace	16 962.0	614.0
RJR Nabisco	Atlanta	Food	16 956.0	1 393.0

Source: *Fortune* 1990.

industry as well as to give aid to new entrants. This is highly important in the light of prevailing conditions so prohibitive as to make entry into the industry in some countries a non-viable proposition for foreign suppliers. Other efforts, such as policies directed towards encouraging innovation in industry will, for example, have long-term effects worldwide by opening up export market opportunities for supplying companies.

CASE 2.8

From 1986 until 1991, top executives from as many as 19 major European car-ton-board makers met several times a year for what they called 'social occasions', usually in Zurich. According to the European Commission, the purpose of these meetings was to orchestrate price increases in the huge, £3 billion market for the stiff, card-like material widely used for packaging everything from toothpaste to frozen food.

The European Commission found that, on a carefully scheduled basis, they boosted list prices in each EU member country about twice a year by 6 to 10 per cent – even though at times pulp prices were actually falling. Purchasers were literally boxed in: the 19 suppliers represented the majority of the European carton-board market. Buying from North America was not worth it because of the extra shipping expense.

Finally alerted by the British Printing Industries Federation and the French carton-printers' trade association, the European Commission launched a coordinated series of surprise raids on company offices, uncovering the price-rigging scheme. The companies were fined £159 million.

Last year the Commission also acted against other major price-fixing cartels, including 14 of Europe's biggest steel producers who set up arrangements for market-sharing that helped to keep prices higher than the world market price; and another involving 42 companies and trade association who were fined for 'carving up' the European cement market.

Cartels eventually fail if they are not protected from outside competition by import tariffs and quotas or by price supports for local goods. However some EU governments, concerned about unemployment, have kept these price-boosting measures in place for a vast range of goods to prop local companies. Perhaps it is time Governments made clear to consumers just how much they pay in the shops and as taxpayers for decisions to protect domestic industries from import competition.

European governments are especially quick to protect national-champion enterprises. One of the longest-running examples is the airline industry, where some governments have subsidised companies to the tune of billions of pounds of taxpayers' money and have kept competitors like British Airways – an unsubsidised model of privatisation – out of their protected markets.

In the European Commission efforts are being made to design policies that are aimed at encouraging international competition in a concerted manner. This, it is hoped, will have considerable long-term benefits for all the member states.

In recent years, the escalating cost of research and development has meant that satisfying just the home market is no longer enough to cover these expenses. As a result more companies have begun to compete in international markets, and the response to this by governments has been to seriously consider both national and overseas markets when drafting new policy legislation. Although in most cases the first priority is to ensure that domestic production and sales are encouraged, governments have realised that it is becoming important to design products that can be used and sold abroad as well as at home; this in itself is likely to have long-term implications for change. In the first place, it may be a step forward towards truly worldwide common technical and industrial standards. In the second place it may achieve some degree of price stabilisation within the industry sectors concerned.

However, with so many countries and companies entering the international markets, it is possible that the benefits that are being sought by going international may be eroded by the competition that is occurring as a result. As a consequence of this, some governments have subsidised exports and imposed political pressure on imports to protect the domestic market. This state of affairs means that some industry sectors are at present being forced from one distorted market system to another. It is important therefore to assess some of the background aspects that contribute to the situation.

◼ Trade and industrial policies

The key point arising out of this analysis is that government trade policy (the demand side) cannot be entirely separated from industrial policy (the supply side); indeed the former should be gaining market outlets and access for the latter, while industrial policy is concerned with government support for industry to ensure quality and investment. At the strategic level firms can be supported to capture control of markets and anticipate the reactions of competitors through innovation, aggressive pricing (to drive competition from the market), design and market penetration.

The central proposition of this strategic approach is that firms and governments can behave pro-actively in imperfect global markets and thereby affect a country's balance of trade and national welfare. This raises a fundamental point of policy as to whether a government should adopt a dirigiste role in supporting industrial investment, or whether a country's industrial performance should be left entirely to market forces.

As far as government intervention in trade is concerned, two key questions arise at this stage:

1. Should governments control access of foreign firms to domestic markets?
2. How should governments promote the activities of domestic firms in foreign markets?

Both questions are controversial because some economists believe that government intervention in free markets can disrupt the general equilibrium of the economy, as well as the efficient functioning of markets. The general equilibrium argument is that every industry competes with every other industry for resources. Therefore, if one industry were to receive privileged access to resources, other industries would be deprived of these resources. The efficient markets argument is that resources will flow to their best use in a free market: government interventions can only distort these markets and lead to inefficiencies.

Then, there is the question of distinguishing the strategic implications of tariffs versus quotas versus voluntary export restraints (VERs). Each technique, under varying imperfect market conditions, can have positive or negative effects on welfare and trade. Some 'new trade' theorists argue that quotas can promote exports in the presence of imperfect competition and economies of sale. The idea is that by shutting a market to foreign producers, domestic producers would have a larger market-share. As a consequence, firms would be able to

---

CASE 2.9

In research into the tariff for a particular product, both its structure and its effect must be discovered. The tariff will take one of three forms.

Ad valorem tariffs are levied as a percentage of the cost, insurance and freight (CIF) price of the goods imported. For example, if there is a 20 per cent *ad valorem* tariff on imported watches, then duty on a watch imported at $100 CIF will be $20.

Specific tariffs are flat rate charges per physical unit imported. If there is a $5 ton duty on imported rice, $5 will be payable on every ton entering the country, irrespective of the CIF price.

Mixed or combined tariffs are composed of both a specific and an *ad valorem* element. If the duty on rice is $5 per ton plus 10 per cent, then the duty on a ton of rice valued at $100 CIF will be $15: $5 plus 10 per cent of $100.

Markets protected by an *ad valorem* tariff are sometimes easier to penetrate by undercutting prices than those where a specific tariff prevails. Suppose, for example, that the prevailing CIF price of a product of a particular country is $100 per ton and an exporter undercuts this price by $10, offering the product at $90 per ton. If that country's duty on the product is assessed on a specific tariff basis, the price advantage for the buyer would simply by $10 per ton.

However, if the duty were levied on an *ad valorem* basis, the exporter's price advantage would be greater because the amount of duty payable would be reduced along with the price. If the *ad valorem* duty is 20 per cent, then the duty on a ton of a product with a CIF price of $100 would be $20; if the CIF price were cut to $90, then the duty would be reduced to $18. Therefore, the price advantage for the buyer would be $12 per ton – he or she saves not only $10 on the price but also $2 on the duty.

move down their average cost and learning curves and capitalise on their learning in the protected home market, which would become a competitive advantage for serving foreign markets. For this outcome to be efficient, however, there would also have to be a mechanism for preventing excessive entry into the domestic industry in the short run.

■ Government intervention in trade

Furthermore, it is sometimes argued that through such intervention governments can encourage activities that generate *positive externalities* and *shifted profits* from foreign economies to the domestic economy. The positive externalities argument is concerned with situations where society can benefit from an action that might be too costly for an individual rational firm to undertake; in other words, a market failure has occurred. Suppose a firm's research and development activities would generate benefits for themselves and others (suppliers, customers, workers) in excess of the cost of the R&D, but the innovating firm's share of the benefits was inadequate to cover its costs. In such a case, it would make sense for the government to encourage the firm to undertake those activities, even if a subsidy (or protection) was required. The social benefits of the government's action would outweigh the social costs.

The profit-shifting argument is built on the assumption that a domestic government seeks to maximise national welfare, and not the welfare of the world or foreign consumers and producers. According to strategic trade theory (see Chapter 1), some economists believe that governments can help domestic firms to capture profits that would otherwise accrue to foreign firms. Governments could use tax relief or subsidies, for example, to increase the profitability of private investments. If government policy facilitated a domestically-based firm to make a credible commitment to expand production facilities, foreign firms might be discouraged from expanding their own operations. The result would be increased market shares and profits for domestic firms.

The key issue here is that of strategic government intervention to support home industries by creating conditions under which profits could be shifted from foreign firms to domestic firms, production runs could be lengthened (reducing marginal costs), the entry of domestic producers could be promoted, and external economies could be captured.

Other economists, however, counter that controlling market access can be damaging in the long run because excessive numbers of domestic firms would be induced to enter into an industry by the prospect of earning above-average profits. Government policies could also inadvertently promote production inefficiencies, facilitate collusion among both foreign and domestic firms, and potentially redistribute income in undesirable ways (for example as surplus was shifted from consumers to producers through higher prices).

As far as government intervention in industry is concerned, the difficulty in policy analysis is the calculation of the net benefit: exactly what constitutes market failure and when and how do the benefits of intervention outweigh the costs? Economists have found that the gains from strategic intervention have often been small. In addition, if other governments intervened in retaliation, even these small gains might be wiped out.

A second policy question raised in this context is how governments should promote the activities of domestic firms in global markets. Governments have available a number of policy instruments including government procurement to stimulate domestic demand, production subsidies to lower the cost of goods and increase their competitiveness in international markets, and R&D subsidies to encourage domestic firms to improve performance in innovation and design. Governments could use these instruments in a strategic manner to alter the competitive environment in favour of the entry of domestic firms.

A simple example of a strategic trade policy would be the subsidisation of research and development of an industry. By altering the payoffs to domestic firms, a government could attempt to discourage entry into the market by foreign firms and to preclude foreign firms from preempting the entry of domestic firms.

At an empirical level it can be observed that an active role by government can enhance the competitiveness of key sectors of a nation's industry. The key ingredient to success seems to be collaboration between government and industry. The government played a central role in the industrial competitiveness of South Korea; and the collaboration between the United States Government and the defence industry led to the USA dominating the world in aero engines and aircraft manufacturing.

In addition to collaboration with industry, governments can, as explained, alter the balance of cost advantage (altering the relative balance between firms) thus influencing the competitiveness of a nation's economy (and the direction of international trade). Governments can influence the four determinants of competitive advantage, advanced by Porter (1990) in *The Competitive Advantage of Nations*.

But more than this, government policies in their own right shape the national environment; they include foreign investment policy, competition policy, trade policy and export promotion. For example, when foreign-owned companies scan other countries to locate international production, factor conditions are a key consideration in the decision-making process. The foreign investment climate can also be added to factor conditions; critical here is the observed return from foreign direct investment (FDI) on the competitiveness of a country's industry. For example, FDI by Japan in the UK car industry is expected by the year 2000 to produce a positive trade balance, and 70 per cent of the output of the Japanese-invested plants will be exported. And the *World Investment Report* by the United Nations (UN, 1993) calls on the governments of 'transition economies to play an active role in improving their economies as locations for foreign investment' (these are the Newly Independent States (NIS) of the former Soviet Union and Central Europe).

Table 2.2 illustrates those policy areas where the interface between government and industry is especially significant.

Table 2.2 Policies of international business and national governments

Policy area	Policies of international business	Policies of national government (host countries)
Overall policy		
National economic and political policies	May extend government policies of investing country to subsidiaries in host country, e.g. US restrictions on exporting to communist countries	Defence of national sovereignty. Makes own policies apply to all firms established in the country
Proportion of industry in foreign ownership	Seeks freedom to invest, manufacture and sell in any selected market	Limits foreign-owned proportion, particularly in key sectors from security or development point of view
Investment		
Use of local or imported capital	Makes choice on basis of availability-cost, and effect on control of business	Policy may differ, depending on availability of local capital, effect on balance of payments, and governments usually favour participation by local capital
Return of profits to investing country	Freedom to decide whether to return profits or reinvest	Governments frequently place restrictions on return of profits
Tax evasion	May evade by costing and pricing policies	Enforcement of tax regulations
New products, research and development		
Imported versus local R&D	Seeks optimum international location, there may be economies of scale and concentration	Seeks R&D located within host country
Introduction of new products	According to stage of development in market	In favour of development, manufacture and marketing of products in 'early' and 'growth' stages of product cycle
Manufacturing		
Proportion of products to be produced locally	Locates manufacture internationally according to suitability and costs of various locations	Often encourages local manufacture of a high proportion of products
Location of subsidiaries within host country	Seeks optimum location within country	May require or encourage location in declining or underdeveloped areas
Marketing		
Freedom to import and export	Freedom essential to operation of a worldwide business	Restrictions frequently placed on imports, e.g. to protect indigenous industry, assist balance of payments, exports generally encouraged

Table 2.2   Policies of international business and national governments

Policy area	Policies of international business	Policies of national government (host countries)
Pricing policy	Differential pricing according to nature of demand in each market	Prevents dumping and operation of price advantages of international business
Staffing Employment of local or imported staff Relative status of these two types of staff	Optimum staffing for effectiveness in job, maintenance of centralised control	Maximum employment of local staff and development of technical and managerial skills, appropriate promotion for these staff
Redundancy	Redundancy may be a consequence of international rationalisation	Usually full employment

Source: Adapted from Tookey (1985) *Export Marketing Decisions.*

■ Conclusions

In the internationalisation process, the aspect of quality of management cannot be emphasised too strongly. Management must be alert to business opportunities, but at the same time take a strategic view so that planning and investment can be implemented: this is a more enlightened approach than the reactive approach. Such enlightened managers are likely to have some linguistic skills and cultural sensitivity and have proven experience in operating effectively across national and cultural boundaries, and in identifying competitors' strengths as a basis for formulating counter strategies.

Of special importance too is the way MNCs are having to adapt their organisational structures both to remain globally competitive, and to take account of the interests of their host governments. Also the extent to which governments can beneficially intervene directly or indirectly in trade and industry has been fully explained.

QUESTIONS

1. What is the key role for management in the internationalisation process?
2. How far is it feasible to adduce an optimal organisational structure for the MNC?
3. What should be the government's role in bringing about investment in innovation, design and technology?
4. How far can governments sustain economic conditions favourable to domestic industry through fiscal, social and industrial policies?
5. Should governments have planned programmes of trade expansion by targeting key industries through sector supply studies?
6. How far should the supply side be left entirely to market forces so that only the strongest industries survive?
7. How can the interface between government and industry be improved for international competitiveness?

CHAPTER 3

The international business environment

INTRODUCTION

The operating environment for the business is the keynote in the first part of this chapter, with an explanation of how environmental analysis can be used to identify new business opportunities through approaches such as scanning. Cultural and socioeconomic concepts are explained, based on socioeconomic factors that impact on demand levels. The concept and applications of environmental management are also discussed to show how it is possible to influence the operating environment in the company's favour. This entire aspect can be summed up in the words *environmental sensitivity* and its awareness by management.

The last section of this chapter is concerned with the uses of research methods in international markets, initially to assess demand levels and trends, and then to be applied to more qualitative aspects such as buyer behaviour. Some approaches to resolve hazards in multi-country research are also explained.

■ **Environmental Appraisal**

■ **The company and the environment**

This is concerned with the interactions between the company and its environment, which is made up of many different forces – political, cultural and legal. The international environment is more complex and turbulent than the domestic environment, and management must shape the company's strategy accordingly. Central to this theme is some understanding of the term *market ecology*, and how it impacts on business strategy; then there are external factors in the environment which influence both access to markets and demand. Further, there is the question of how companies can influence or even manage their operating environment.

Assuming the necessary corporate resources exist, management must use those under their control – finance, personnel, marketing supply and technology – to capitalise on anticipated demand. These controllable activities can be assessed in the long run – and often in the short run – and adjusted to changed market conditions or corporate objectives.

Other factors in the environment can also have a direct effect on the success of overseas ventures; they are not directly controllable by the company, but they can be used to identify new market opportunities. For example, a political decision involving fiscal policy can have a direct effect on a company's international market access.

Also the economic climate is a home-based but uncontrollable variable which can have far-reaching effects on a company's competitive position in foreign markets. The capacity for investment in plant and new technology in domestic or foreign markets is to a large extent a function of domestic economic vitality. It is generally true that capital will tend to flow towards optimum use, but capital must be generated before it can possess mobility. If internal economic conditions deteriorate there will be less scope to generate capital, less investment, and even restrictions against foreign investment being able to strengthen the domestic economy.

Market ecology is therefore an important concept in understanding not just the environment, but the interactions between it and the company. Market ecology is not simply the study of the cultural, political, economic and social environment of foreign markets; it also enables management to analyse what impact these parts of the environment have on the operations of the company.

So far the term environment has been used in a general sense to encompass all the external factors confronting the company internationally. It is important to analyse these factors and to include some mention of the natural environment. This is particularly relevant at the present time as companies are increasingly having to adjust both policies and operations to take account of social and political concerns about protecting the environment; damage has already been caused by industrial pollution and by waste generated by mass consumption: air, earth and water have all been affected.

CASE 3.1

On Sunday 3 December 1984, the life of an American multinational corporation was suddenly disrupted. The Union Carbide plant at Bhopal, a city less than 400 miles from New Delhi, India, had leaked poisonous gas into the air. Within one week over 2000 people died and more remained critically ill. Over 100 000 people were treated for nausea, blindness and bronchial problems. It was one of history's worst industrial accidents.

Union Carbide is America's 37th largest industrial corporation, with more than 100 000 employees, and an annual sales volume of over $9 billion. The company is active in petrochemicals, industrial gases, metals and carbon products, consumer products and technology transfers.

Union Carbide operates 14 plants in India. Total Indian operations accounted for less than 2 per cent of corporate sales. In spite of a policy by the Indian government to restrict foreign majority ownership of plants, Union Carbide owned 50.9 per cent of the Bhopal plant. This special arrangement was granted by the government because the plant served as a major technology transfer project. In order to achieve the goal of technology transfer, management at the plant was mostly carried out by Indian nationals. General corporate safety guidelines applied to the plant, but local regulatory agencies were charged with enforcing Indian environmental laws. Only three weeks before the accident, the plant had received an 'environmental clearance certificate' from the Indian State Pollution Board.

The accident resulted in wide public awareness in the United States. A poll showed that 47 per cent of those questioned linked Union Carbide's name to the Bhopal disaster. Most American consumers, however, do not connect the Union Carbide name to its line of consumer products. Industrial users, on the other hand, are highly aware of the corporation's products. One area that could be particularly affected is that of technology transfer, which in 1983 accounted for 24 per cent of Union Carbide's revenues. The firm had concentrated increasingly on that sector, selling mainly its know-how in the fields of engineering, manufacturing and personnel training.

Internationally, the reaction was one of widespread consumer hostility. Environmentalists demonstrated at Union Carbide's plants in West Germany and Australia. Plans for plants in Scotland had to be frozen. The operation of a plant in France was called into question by the French government.

And, major changes occurred. Union Carbide stock dropped by $10 in one week, a loss in market value of nearly $900 million. A $1.2 billion line of credit was frozen. Five days after the incident the first damage suit had been filed in a Federal District Court, asking for $15 billion.

The lessons learned? 'Don't lose control', said the Union Carbide Chairman. 'Bhopal has made it painfully obvious how dangerous some chemical plants can be if things go awry', commented *Business Week*. The stakes in accidental environmental mishaps are 'bigger than any other insurance I can imagine, except the space programme' said a representative of the insurance industry.

This concern for our environment has many important implications for international business; it means that management has to react, in its marketing operations, to reflect this concern; here are some examples:

1. In product development, many cosmetics companies are no longer using animals for testing purposes or research.
2. In promotion, many multinational corporations (MNCs) are using advertising to show corporate concern for the environment.
3. In packaging, food companies are making use of healthier organic ingredients and using biodegradable packets, cartons, and so forth.

4. In industrial products, manufacturers are having to invest in new technology for waste disposal.
5. In many countries the 'green' party or lobby is increasingly influential and vociferous and companies operating there must ensure that their 'marketing mix' is acceptable to such opinion.

CASE 3.2

In Scandinavian markets there are very strict environmental protection standards, and both a power-tool maker and a detergent manufacturer have had to make technical adjustments to their standard products to gain market acceptance: these adjustments were not to do with the technical performance of the products but concerned their impact on the environment. The tool manufacturer was required to reduce the noise level of his tools and to change the sound frequency on which they operated; the detergent manufacturer had to introduce a new formula which substantially reduced lather and sudsing in the washing process to eliminate water pollution.

■ **Components of the environment**

Environmental factors can be analysed under four broad categories:

1. Legislation and procedures about conforming to standards of environmental protection.
2. Communications systems: state of infrastructure, extent of networks, location of ports, tax-free zones and air cargo facilities.
3. Climate and topography: effects of high temperatures and humidity on design of products such as car engines.
4. Logistics: proximity of sources of supply to ports, markets and freight routes.

Political and demographic factors are very closely linked: the power structure of societies usually reflects the social make-up of the population; and there are two key marketing implications of demographic factors. First, the age distribution of populations directly influences purchasing patterns: demographic trends in Western Europe are downward – this means an increasingly ageing population; indeed, in some Western countries the population is failing to renew itself because the death rate outstrips the birth rate. Demographic trends in South America and in the Pacific region are upward; here the fastest growing sector of the population are young people in their late-teens to early-wenties. Second, differences in the densities of populations have a direct impact on organisation and the cost of marketing communications; also the proportions of the population of a foreign country that are still rural as opposed to urbanised has a similar effect; indeed, the growing drift of urbanisation in many countries (such as those in Latin America) pose social and economic problems – in terms of poverty, unemployment and social deprivation – which can have severe adverse effects on demand.

Political factors can also impact directly on marketing policies; indeed the political environment offers the best example of what is sometimes referred to as 'alien' status. Even in the domestic market, management must consider any political ramifications of decisions, though the consequences are likely to be minor. But internationally the political environment can be critical, and changes in foreign governments can often mean sudden changes in attitude or policy, affecting:

- movement of capital;
- of profits;
- level of and return on investment;
- pricing;
- taxation;
- import/export restrictions;
- management personnel (home-based or local to the country invested in).

■ Environmental analysis

This is critical when the time comes for a company to invest abroad or to review its overseas assets (and the decision to market internationally is an investment decision). Some of the most important risks, such as the political ones, are unquantifiable. So in addition to commercial expertise management must possess political judgement to assess both market potential and the investment climate. Policy stability is the most important dimension of political stability; it may not matter too much to foreign investors, for example, which regime is in power in the foreign country, as long as the regime has the capability to sustain policies favourable to private sector business and foreign investment.

Five political and demographic factors are also central to environmental analysis, and must be used by management as a basis for planning strategy:

1. The Power structure of society.
2. The Density and distribution of population.
3. Government procurement policies.
4. The Legal system (particularly the laws relating to commercial contracts and payments, agency and licensing agreements, arbitration of disputes, and those governing sales, advertising and promotions).
5. The stability or other aspects of the military/regime.

■ Socioeconomic factors

Among these the following are particularly relevant to marketing:

1. The distribution of wealth;
2. Comparative costs of living;
3. Comparative standards of living;
4. Average annual disposable per capita incomes;
5. Comparative purchasing power of the average industrial wage;
6. The make-up of average monthly household budgets;
7. The centres of purchasing influence;
8. New industrial development and free trade zones;
9. The availability, mobility and quality of labour in sales and distribution;
10. The structure of the social classes;
11. The balance-of-payments position and terms of trade of the foreign country;
12. Government fiscal policies.

Measurement of these and other socioeconomic indicators is not an exact science: this is due to inter-country fluctuations of currencies, interest and inflation rates, taxation, and so forth.

The overall economic health as well as the political stability of a country are important, but other economic factors may be just as important, depending on the type of product sold in the market as well as the target country market itself. For example, an oil-rich state may have been identified as a potential market for consumer products, but it transpires that the wealth of the country is concentrated into a few hands and therefore the actual disposable income per head of population is very low, as are actual sales. Distribution of wealth is, therefore, of key importance.

Many international trading problems have to do with the inability of so many countries, particularly in Africa and Latin America, to be able to settle their accounts with creditor nations. This situation was brought about by the rise in national expectations due to the oil price rise; these precipitated much industrial and other development, to be paid for with future expected earnings. In other words, many countries in these regions mortgaged themselves to international banks to accelerate their industrialisation; their governments are now paying for these past decisions at high rates of interest with current earnings well below those expected when the credit was negotiated. This problem of indebtedness is now so vast that it is international in scope, and only some kind of concerted international action will resolve it. Indeed many economies have and still do depend on international agencies for support and financial aid: these include the International Bank for Reconstruction and Development (IBRD) and the International Monetary Fund (IMF).

■ Cultural factors

These relate to many aspects of a society (and thus the target market), as follows:

- Levels of education;
- Social systems and social behaviour (including status of women, status of family, and status of ancestors);
- Levels of technical and managerial expertise;
- Language and literature;
- Customs, beliefs and attitudes;
- Arts and aesthetics;
- Morality and religion;
- Historical background and traditions;
- Reference and membership groups;
- Social and consumption values;
- Concepts of time and manners.

By far the most important marketing aspect of *culture* is that it is concerned with social behaviour, and is especially relevant to international operations. Hoebel defines culture as:

the integrated sum total of learned behaviour traits that are manifest and shared by members of a society.

(Hoebel, cited in Lee, 1976)

A major consideration is the structure of the family unit, and the roles and importance of various members within it. The structure of the Arab family and the power of the extended family in the Far East are key examples; the former is of importance when considering marketing activities for consumer products and in deciding whom to target. In the latter case, strong family loyalties will have to be taken into account when setting up a distribution strategy in an Oriental country.

Consider also the question of time: a western manager may find that the time frame for an overseas itinerary in Australia or the USA may not be applicable to the business environment in other countries.

The relationship of time and business decision-making also various from culture to culture. In some, the time required to make a decision is directly proportional to the importance of the decision. To try to hurry the decision-making process is likely to be counter-productive, as, in the eyes of the other party, it can diminish the importance you attach to your own proposal.

Obviously, different languages are spoken in different countries, but the languages themselves differ in how precisely they differentiate experience and the way in which they convey meaning. The way meaning is conveyed varies in matters such as the way things are said, the tone of the voice, the pitch of the voice, what is left unsaid, gestures when speaking and the degree of loquacious-

---

CASE 3.3

In some Asian countries, for instance, time is viewed differently but no less mean-ingfully in terms of cultural values than in some industrialised countries where the time-is-money philosophy prevails. As a result of this different attitude towards time, a businessman visiting an Asian market may need to allow himself a longer period of time to transact business than he would, for instance, in the United States. He may find that, in the Asian market, although he has a firm appointment he is kept waiting. When he is finally ushered in to see the business executive or official, his annoyance because of the delay may be reflected in his face – if he is not familiar with the customs of that country – and the business discussion will begin in a strained atmosphere. The person he has been waiting to see, on the other hand, considers that to tell his previous business visitor that his time is up is far ruder than to keep his next visitor waiting an extra half hour.

---

ness or brevity. Languages convey differences between cultures as far as formality and informality are concerned. In some languages there are a number of different words for you which vary according to the status of the person speaking and the person spoken to, while in others – English, for example – there is only one.

Cultural differences are also reflected in ways of negotiating and conducting business. In some countries in Asia, for instance, the nominated price is often the starting point for negotiations, not a take-it-or-leave-it figure as it is in many western countries. What is important in such situations is to ascertain the normal relationship between the asking price and the expected price and, if you are the buyer, for instance, to offer a little below the expected price so that each party is seen to give a little in the negotiations. To do otherwise is to force the seller into a position of losing face or to allow yourself to be taken-for-a-ride and lose the seller's respect.

In some cultures, logic is respected when arguing a business deal, in others it is emotion which is called for. In some environments it is customary to talk around the subject, moving inch by inch towards it over time – to come straight to the point in such negotiations is regarded as offensive. In other cultures the practice is just the opposite.

The basis for business negotiations may be in the form of technical or legal rules, mutually agreed practices or informal customs. These may cover matters such as the point at which negotiations cease – is the signing of the contract the conclusion of negotiations or the starting point for a second round of discus-sions? The customary nature of an agreement is another variable between cul-tures – how binding is a verbal agreement and will insisting on a written contract be regarded as offensive? A few enquiries along these lines by the busi-nessman before proceeding to the overseas market will prevent much heartache and disenchantment.

In commercial negotiations of substance, a legal agreement provides many businessmen with a feeling of security. However, not only does the basis of the legal system vary between cultures (for example English Common Law compared with the Napoleonic Code compared with the Shari's Law of Islam), but the interpretation of the law will also differ. In some cultures the law is absolute and is modified in its interpretation after it has been broken. In other cultures, the law has some flexibility, but once broken its interpretation is rigid. Familiarity with the legal system and its operation is a prerequisite to doing business in a different culture.

In researching the approach to overseas markets it is wise to consider that culture can have an impact on the product and its promotion. The culture in which a person lives affects his consumption patterns and also the meaning that he attaches to specific products. When promoting the product in a new culture it is easier initially to appeal to existing culture requirements or expectations than to try to change them. Product promotion must be sensitive to the basic values of the country and the differences in patterns of consumption. For example, promoting a do-it-yourself time-saving device in a country having widespread unemployment may be not only pointless but also yield unfavourable criticism of the exporting company.

Any colours used in national flags of host countries are often better avoided in promotion and packaging. Women as symbols cannot be used at all for promotion in Moslem countries, nor can there be any mention of alcohol or tobacco. The position of ethnic minorities in many overseas markets has to be fully understood, and approached with sensitivity by the businessman: some ethnic groups comprise major sub-sectors of the mass market in the USA, with specialised tastes and consumption styles; other ethnic groups dominate particular trade or distributive sectors of the economy, and government trade policies often take into account the position of these ethnic minorities and the company should, therefore, be fully conversant with them.

CASE 3.4

In Switzerland, foreign dishwasher manufacturers expected the same rapid sales as they had first obtained in other West European markets; but sales in Switzerland were so slow that research had to be done to find out why (this research should, of course, have been done before not after market entry). The research showed that the Swiss housewife had a different set of values to, for example, her French and English counterparts; she was very conscious of her role as strict and hardworking, and her responsibility for the health of her family. To the Swiss housewife dishwashers simply made life easy, and this conflicted with her Calvinistic work ethic. As a result of this research, dishwasher manufacturers had to change their advertising – promoting, instead of ease-and-convenience, hygiene-and-health. They did this by emphasising that because dishwashers used temperatures higher than hand-hot, the process was more hygienic than washing up by hand. Thereafter, they had no problems selling automatic dishwashers in Switzerland.

CASE 3.5

To appreciate the Japanese company it is necessary to understand the culture in which it exists. With a strong sense of obligation, Japanese culture is highly organised, harmony-oriented, hierarchial, self-effacing, ego-denying and security-risking. Lifetime employment, Japanese style (though this is increasingly under threat due to changed economic conditions) cannot be indiscriminately trans-planted to a Western culture that is ego-oriented, individualistic and competitive; a culture where product quality and social welfare philosophies have become so intertwined that the price of the former often expresses the expense of the latter.

Japanese companies take certain obligations and responsibilities very seriously. The risk of losing highly trained personnel to another firm is not great because companies do not want to upset their own employees by employing outsiders in mid-career. The company may continue to provide workers with jobs and/or income, even at great cost to the company: its commitment is based on cultural values. For example, when Toyota's automotive markets and production were slowed down by the oil crises, the company had to find work for many of its employees, especially its engineers. To solve the problem, it entered the construc-tion business by seeking contracts to construct houses and commercial buildings.

Another important practice in Japanese business is that an employee's in-adequacy or incompetence is not grounds for dismissal. The employee is simply transferred to a unit where he or she is less likely to do serious damage. The worst that could happen is that a bonus is used to induce an unwanted employee to resign. The culture of Japanese organisations does, however, have limits. Life-time employment is usually restricted to large firms, or those in the upper echelon of industry. Among small and medium enterprises (SMEs), labour mobility is more prevalent. Moreover, only 'regular' and male employees are entitled to this benefit. Neither part-time workers nor women are part of the system. Recruitment into an organisation is based largely on personal qualities rather than on particu-lar work-skill or jobs requirements (that is, professional qualifications). The same basis is also used to select employees for positions within the organisation. Indeed, status acquired in an organisations is a continuation and extension of the worker's status in the society at the time of initial employment; and it is customary for a worker to be entitled to a particular status based on education. Just as important is the worker's family background, since the parents' status is a large determinant of position as well.

And the pay system in Japan is based primarily on broad social rather than on production criteria. Promotion is decided on seniority; as a result, in addition to allowance for educational background, the reward criteria include the worker's age, length of service and family size. Reward is thus a function of loyalty and fidelity to the organisation and to the needs of the worker as husband and father. Occupying secondary importance are such criteria as job rank, competence and productivity. And the high output achieved shows that employee loyalty and group identification can be important motivational factors.

And companies in Japan are not only substantially responsible for their workers' job-related activities, but are also greatly involved in their employees' non-business activities; the responsibility is so complete that intimate or personal matters are not exempt. Companies may advise workers (who do not view this as an intrusion) on how to manage their personal lives, their spending, their children's education, religious activities and so forth. The corporate culture requires the firm to ensure that its responsibility to its employees is complete.

In decision-making and leadership, the negotiating style of the Japanese is dictated by minimising risk and avoidance of confrontation; Japanese managers tend to act only when events pressure them into some kind of action. Moreover, because of the desire not to become individually responsible for the consequence of a decision, staff avoid making decisions on their own; the group, rather than the individual, exercises the decision-making function, and the entire process is designed to achieve consensus. Indeed Japanese management is characterised by a style of middle-up consensus management: top management is not dictatorial in making decisions, which are initially made at the lower positions in the organisation. Participation is encouraged, and management at all levels is moderated by the views of workers at lower levels. So the implementation of a strategy, once agreed upon, can move swiftly towards the chosen objective in a coordinated way because all parties have already been involved and are in agreement. One important outcome of the Japanese decision-making approach is that middle managers cannot be bypassed; it is critical to identify and consult with those who will make decisions, as well as to gain support for a plan before it reaches the top decision-makers.

In spite of some changes and economic pressure, therefore, the Japanese have been able to maintain many of the country's traditional values: the nation has experienced cultural blending rather than cultural borrowing. The embracing of Western ideas has not radically altered Japanese fundamental values.

■ Appraisal and scanning

The next issue is: how can environmental analysis be effectively implemented by management? Obviously, sensitivity to economic and cultural parameters of a country market can ensure a high and continuing level of acceptance for the company's products. But as a basis for strategy, a two-stage approach can be usefully adopted. First environmental scanning, and second environmental management.

Research has shown that scanning by companies is a developmental process, and has been refined through a process of learning. Some companies have a basic awareness of some of the key factors in the environment but have no active or systematic search methods. Other companies actively collect information on their environment for planning and decision-making purposes but largely on an informal and *ad hoc* basis. Again, some other companies do have a structural process for the collection of specific information for a specific purpose, and more companies are now developing formal scanning systems.

An important study by Jain (1987) has confirmed that companies do move through an evaluating process with regard to scanning systems, in four phases:

- *Primitive* – information asked for but no purpose or effort in scanning; little or no effort used to distinguish between strategic and non-strategic information.
- *Ad hoc* – no formally planned screening as such, but increased sensitivity to information on certain issues/events which may be explored further.
- *Reactive* – scanning still unstructured and random but often specific information collected with a view to making appropriate responses to markets and competition.
- *Proactive* – scanning structured and deliberate using pre-established methodologies with a view to predicting the environment for a desired future.

Many companies have not achieved the proactive level of scanning because environmental appraisal is difficult and has to be future-oriented, not simply a straight-line projection of past trends. Management must first establish what should be appraised: the key elements of the environment have been explained, but appraisal itself is only useful where it can be linked to marketing strategy; that is, the research should be useful and used in strategic decision-making. And both the extent and scope of environmental appraisal activity that a company will require is company-specific and will take time to establish and build.

The key steps in this scanning approach system are therefore as follows:

1. Seek to maintain an awareness of broad trends in each of the key environmental factors outlined earlier. At this stage, scanning need not be detailed so long as trends are monitored.
2. Delineate more trends which are deemed not relevant, that is to have no political significance to the company for further more detailed investigation.
3. Undertake an in-depth analysis of the possible impact of these selected trends on the company's current products/markets. In particular, this analysis should delineate the extent to which the trend is an opportunity or a threat, and the potential magnitude of its impact.

In addition, an analysis should be made of how far market and social trends can open up new opportunities. In forecasting the future direction of the trends isolated:

1. Further analyse the possible effects of the forecast trends on future product/market momentum on the assumption of 'no action', and on the assumption that trends are responded to.
2. The final step in the procedure is to assess the implication of the preceding analysis to overall strategic decision-making.

■ Environmental Management

Although this framework for appraising the environment represents a structured and logical approach to systematic appraisal as an input to strategic decisions, it needs to be backed up and followed by the second stage: environmental management. This has been defined as:

the application of economic, psychological, political and PR skills to gain cooperation of a number of parties in order to enter and/or operate successfully in a given overseas market.

(Zeithaml and Zeithaml, 1984)

The significance of environment management stems from an appreciation by managers that the environment is dynamic, particularly in a marketing context, and that the concept of uncontrollable, or fixed unchanging parameters is increasingly unrealistic.

It is an approach to the environment that recognises the need on the part of management to influence and bring about improvements in trading conditions and market access which will benefit both the company and its customers. Of course this is a long-term process, and one that often requires a consortium approach to improve market access overseas (for example by joint government/ industry missions, trade and industry associations acting on behalf of small and medium-sized firms). In short, the traditional concept of the *mix* postulates a largely re-active role by management, while environmental management demands a pro-active role in all phases of the marketing process, from market entry to direct investment operations overseas. This is the only way, now, to open up access for products in difficult markets where import restrictions, invisible tariffs and *gatekeepers* otherwise bar market entry for high-quality products, even when there is effective demand among consumers. Clearly, the company's management often cannot achieve all this on its own: embassy staff may have to be used to tackle or bypass gatekeepers and advise on negotiating positions; trade missions can be used to open up particular industry sectors of the market; ministerial pressure in the manufacturer's home country may have to be applied to ministerial counterparts on official overseas visits; and so on.

A recent analysis (Varadarajan, Clark and Pride, 1992) has proposed a process by which scanning and management can be integrated in strategic analysis and planning; the three steps are:

1. Identification of issue – the key trends and influences impacting on the company's strategy.
2. Prioritisation of issues – the nature and scope of the issues must be carefully considered. Some issues, such as incidents of product tampering, or source contamination (as happened to Perrier), need to be managed immediately. Other issues require a sustained effort over a long time period to bring about market access (perhaps even involving political changes). Not all environmental opportu-

nities should receive managerial attention. Issues should be prioritised by considering both the probability that they will affect the firm's interests (for better or worse) and the probable impact they will make on the firm given a desirable or undesirable outcome.

3. Manageability of issues – high-priority issues may or may not be subject to managerial influence and control; it may be necessary to influence attitudes in key areas; even if it is not possible to change behaviour, at least communications with the media must be effectively and professionally managed whether the issue concerns a success (a new factory opened) or a crisis (retaliatory action on trade by a foreign government).

These three aspects are explored in more depth in Chapter 7 in the discussion on risk and crisis management.

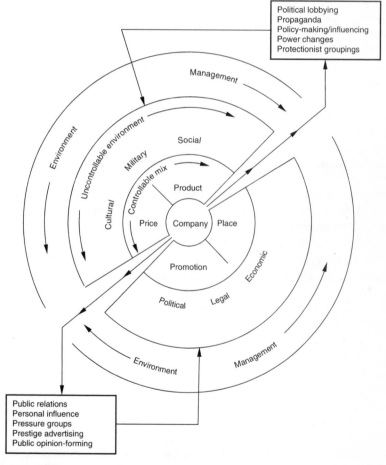

Figure 3.1 Environmental management

CASE 3.6

The health risks of tobacco are well-documented and propagated by governments. But the case of Philip Morris provides one of the clearest examples of a company's attempts to influence and shape its environment. It shows the multi-faceted efforts a company can make. Among the US tobacco product manufacturers, Philip Morris has most aggressively defended the industry's legitimacy. Amid increasing hostility the company has wielded every conceivable legal public-relations and marketing tool to defend cigarettes. Renowned among corporate donors for no-strings-attached philanthropy, Philip Morris has laboured hard to polish its public image through a strategic giving campaign. More than two decades of tax deductible beneficence has no doubt created plenty of goodwill. The company has reportedly gained access to presidents and prime ministers, Kings and Queens.

In 1988 the company launched a $5 million advertising campaign drawing attention to the economic clout of smokers. A full-page advertisement placed in several major newspapers argued that '$1 trillion is too much financial power to ignore'. When anti-smoking activists lobbied automobile makers to stop installing ashtrays as standard fixtures, Philip Morris quickly pointed out the size of the automobile market's smoking segment. One of its advertisements claimed that US smokers owned 35 million cars and had purchased more than 5 million new cars the previous year.

On another front the company ran advertisements in various trade magazines touting the number of smokers who stay in hotels, attend sporting events, and so on, to ward off restrictions on smoking at public gathering places.

In 1986 when Congress was considering a bill to ban all tobacco advertising, Philip Morris sponsored an $80 000 essay contest, which was judged by a panel of educatory writers and journalists. The company viewed the proposed bill as 'an unfortunate and dangerous trend toward control and censorship by an array of self-appointed social guardians'. The essay topic was freedom of expression.

Source: Varadarajan, Clark and Pride (1992).

■ Analysis of international markets

■ Market access

The important concept of market access has been discussed in Chapter 1, and it relates to the terms on which a company can obtain entry to a foreign market; there are both trade factors and competitive factors to consider. Access is critical to exploiting demand in a market; sometimes access is denied to companies for political or economic reasons. For example, when Searle Pharmaceuticals (UK) was taken over by the US Monsanto Chemical Co. it found that access to some Middle Eastern markets was cut off because of a political embargo on the products of its new parent company.

Then there are trade policy aspects (see Chapter 2); these refer to all the conditions that apply to the importation of manufactured goods into a foreign country. The major instruments include import duties, import restrictions or quotas, foreign exchange regulations, and preference arrangements:

1. A government may limit some kinds of imports because the country is short of foreign currency to pay for them.
2. A government may put a high tax on imported goods so as to price them out of reach of all but a small rich minority, foreigners and tourists (from whom foreign exchange is also earned); in this way, money stays in the country and helps to support home production.
3. A government may impose restrictions on imports of certain goods so that their own industries are protected from competition.
4. A government may impose restrictions for sound social or legal reasons, as in the case of arms, drugs and alcohol in Moslem countries.
5. A government may sometimes insist that some goods should be imported only by state buying agencies.
6. A government may sometimes insist that the goods made in their country shall not be sold to certain countries, usually for strategic or political reasons.
7. A government may prohibit competitive entry into designated national industries: examples are power generation and telecommunications supply contracts; or railway and defence procurement.

While companies may have physical entry for their products into foreign markets, the terms on which access must be sustained may be totally uneconomic, particularly in terms of barriers to entry: these can make it too costly for a company to enter a market in the light of,

- effective demand;
- strength of competitors; or the
- likely return to the company.

Four barriers to entry for companies seeking out new markets are:

1. Economies of scale in both production and distribution, which means the decline in unit costs of a product as absolute volume per period increases, for the established firms.
2. High initial cost of heavy media advertising, promotion, publicity work and so on needed to take market share from established brands.
3. Access to distribution channels; to the extent that channels are full, or unavailable, the cost of entry is substantially increased because a new entrant must create (and establish) new channels, which is always costly.
4. Cost of sourcing new markets, if existing suppliers' capacity to the manufacturer seeking entry is already fully taken up.

It can be just as important for some companies to try to maintain their access to existing markets as it is for others to secure access to new markets. Indeed, the extent of access can be damagingly reduced – sometimes completely taken away – by the actions of overseas governments or competitors.

Then there is the important question of government policies on access. Of course, companies expect their home government to use trade policies which keep access to markets open, or to improve access further, through:

- Multilateral trade negotiations to reduce obstacles to international trade under GATT, or EC reciprocal arrangements.
- Bilateral trade negotiations to open up access to mutual advantage, often accompanied by lines of credit.
- Remission of taxes and other national fiscal measures to facilitate exports by home manufacturers.

These measures can remove or mitigate trade obstacles to access; indeed such trade policies are an essential basis for effective incentives to exporters. But some restraints on international trade, such as embargoes, are political in nature and only political action at a high level can restore market access.

What options, then, are available to the management of companies to cope with the obstacles to access posed by competitors?

1. Use indirect methods of exporting, such as agents who are nationals of the target countries, where direct exporting is too costly or actually barred.
2. Both market access and development increasingly require some form of direct investment by companies in international markets: acquisitions policies are used to secure access to, often to gain control of:

CASE 3.7

A UK firm manufactured a range of very high precision engineering sub-components for sale to manufacturers of aircraft parts. This product range conformed to the relevant BSI (British Standards Institution) specification, and was sold in large quantities throughout the world on the basis of high quality and minimal reject rates. There was, however, one important country where market access was denied because of a local standard specification which the British products did not meet in one comparatively unimportant detail. There was little doubt that that standard had been arrived at in consultation with the local manufacturers with the sole object of keeping out the world-renowned British products. The British manufacturer was confronted with a choice: to produce a special adaptation of the range for that country, or to opt out of a substantial trade. The problem was solved and market access secured eventually by the acquisition of a local manufacturer.

- brands;
- distribution and sales networks;
- supply sources outside the company.

3. Set up wholly-owned assembly plants overseas to gain access and ship components in, where direct importation of finished goods is uneconomical (due to tariffs
and so forth).

■ **Market concentration and diversification**

Management is not, of course, concerned simply with the analysis of markets
and their typologies: management must construct some sort of plan to exploit
opportunities in country markets by some pre-set criteria which take account of
company resources as well as market access and potential. In general terms,
two alternative strategies have evolved over the past decade on the basis of a
survey of export practice (Piercy, 1982) sponsored originally by Barclays Bank
International. These strategies are:

1. Concentration of markets;
2. Diversification of markets.

One of the most important policy decisions management has to take is the
wise choice of foreign markets with which a company or a country is going to
trade. Yet, even today, some companies do not choose their country markets on
the basis of rational criteria, and others inherit areas which, though no longer
high in growth, are kept on through the persistence of a persuasive agent. Yet
at times when marginal talent and money are scarce, few companies can afford
the luxury of trying to develop trade in slow moving or credit risky countries. A
discriminating choice of country markets is more essential than ever, and criteria include:

1. Growth and continuity: is the market static or expanding; is it likely to repay sales
effort over the next ten years?
2. Is competition mainly on price or on other considerations?
3. Would the company's products be in demand, be well-received, and able to command a premium price?
4. Are currency problems, transfer of funds, repatriation of profits and local pricing
conditions difficult?
5. Is there scope for funding and developing effective agents or distributors able to
realise the full sales potential of the country?

The research cited showed that the distribution of country markets between
France, UK and Germany was as shown in Table 3.1.

It was found that only 20 per cent of German companies exported to more
than 100 markets, but 40 per cent of UK companies did so; 50 per cent of

Table 3.1　Number of country markets exported to regularly

Exporting country	Percentage of companies exporting to:		
	more than 100 markets	*50–100 markets*	*less than 50 markets*
France	32	30	38
UK	40	26	35
Germany	20	30	50

Source:　Adapted from Piercy (1982).

German companies exported to fewer than 50 markets, but only 35 per cent of UK companies did so. In short, the French and particularly the German companies displayed a higher degree of concentration than British companies. Indeed in the case of medium-sized companies, the research found the German tendency to concentrate on a smaller number of markets even stronger: only 11 per cent of these companies exported to 100 markets or more, but 36 per

---

CASE 3.8

A medium-sized Swedish engineering company manufactured fire-fighting equipment, but was incurring losses. In 1983 a new marketing director was appointed. After four years of work, turnover rose from £3 million to £10 million and profitability was restored, mainly on the basis of a complete reappraisal of markets and marketing policy.

The marketing director found that the company had been dealing with about 100 country markets, but many produced orders only in small quantities, and these intermittently. In total, the orders were a surprisingly small proportion of the turnover, but were just as costly and time-consuming to service as orders from the larger, steadier markets.

A careful process of selection showed that if the company concentrated more extensively on 50 markets its chances of progress would improve, and of these 50 some ten which looked the most promising were selected for constant and increasing attention; for example, visits were planned with increasing frequency. The company found that this core of key markets provided an almost ideal ratio, because where concentration is carried to the limit of five or six countries accounting for 75 per cent of trade, a contraction of business in those few countries could prove very harmful. Recognising important national differences among the ten key markets, the company was able to develop and deploy regional sales specialists to deal more effectively with local issues and customer contacts. Thus, by reducing the total number of markets, but retaining those with significant trade, the company improved its profit performance.

cent of UK companies did so. And some 60 per cent of medium-sized French companies exported to less than 50 markets; conscious of the fact that they do not possess the immense resources of their much bigger German competitors they tend to restrict themselves to a narrow front and deploy the bulk of their marketing resources accordingly. By contrast it has been found that UK companies, as a rule, have many more customers than their French and German competitors.

The advantages claimed for this policy of concentration on key markets can be summed up as follows:

1. companies which concentrate on key markets require less administration, gain in depth market knowledge, can compete better on non-price factors, and use resources more cost effectively for promotion.
2. The planning of marketing can be used more effectively for a few 'best' markets than it can over a wide range of differing markets.
3. Sales develop better through better staffing, better quality of selling and higher market shares.
4. Administration, logistics and supply can be organised more cost-effectively for fewer key markets.
5. Country market knowledge: restricting themselves to fewer countries, companies are better placed to acquire an in depth understanding of trade practices, customers' tastes, the requirements of agents and distributors, and the pricing policies of competitors.

Conversely, to deal effectively with, say, 150 markets requires enormous resources available to very few companies, and also the most frequent danger in market policy is dispersal of effort.

CASE 3.9

Tyrone Crystal Co. has always pursued a policy of market concentration. Tyrone is a producer of high-quality cut-glass crystal and employs some 65 people. 50 per cent of the output is exported outside the UK and Eire. The USA market has been penetrated by a link with an up-market retail chain. Hong Kong is serviced by mail order, and products are sold on the UK mainland by an independent distributor.

Now the other policy option of market diversification must be considered and compared to concentration on key markets. Whilst the latter offers the promise of market growth through penetration of anything from six to 20 countries, the alternatives of diversification may offer growth through market development by selling to more new markets.

CASE 3.10

A German printing and packaging machine manufacturer, with worldwide sales, analysed the positioning of different grades of machines on product life cycles across major trading regions. At issue was the extent to which the firm should continue manufacturing and marketing low-unit-value machines when, to retain its competitive lead in industrialised markets, the development of high-unit-value machines was essential. The life-cycle concept was applied to the entire range of machines, and while many low-unit-value ones were in the decline phase in industrialised markets, two salient features emerged:

1. These low-unit-value machines were still bringing in volume sales revenue in the maturity phase in less-industrialised countries.
2. In the highly industrialised markets, replacements of these older machines by high-unit-value machines in the growth phase need to be built into the marketing planning process.

While some rationalisation in the range of machines became necessary so as to increase manufacturing efficiency, this application of the life-cycle concept enabled management to apply a worldwide marketing strategy based on segmentation of markets by stages of the cycle. This has proved an effective strategy against low-cost competitors as well as ensuring competitiveness by innovation at the high-technology end.

CASE 3.11

A major UK carpet manufacturer has successfully differentiated its marketing between clusters or groups of markets (as opposed to the alternatives of concentration versus diversification). The company divides its foreign markets into three groups: (a) those which receive intensive individual attention, (b) those which are handled by distributors, and (c) those where orders are accepted, but usually only at premium prices. Such a policy of differentiation offers some of the advantages both of concentration and of diversification.

Other points to be considered in favour of market diversification are:

1. There are problems of market access and other obstacles to trade which mean that sales results can lag behind marketing expenditures, or occur only as a result of these cumulative expenditures.
2. Market concentration precludes the spreading of risks across many markets; indeed, dependence on a few country markets may be seen by some managements as a high-risk option.

3. Market concentration presupposes that the selection of markets has been made scientifically with full information, and in practice this is often not the case.
4. There is some research to suggest that product concentration spread over markets, rather than market concentration, can be a more successful policy, as indicated by many Japanese companies.
5. Product quality and design: it is highly likely that this is a prerequisite of successful market concentration rather than a direct result of it.

Some factors which managements can consider in deciding how far to adopt the option of concentration or diversification are shown in Table 3.2.

Table 3.2 Factors favouring diversification or concentration

Factors favouring diversification	*Factors favouring concentration*
Company factors	
Little market knowledge	Ability to pick best markets
Growth objective through market development	Growth objectives through market penetration
Product factors	
Limited specialist uses	General uses
Low volume	High volume
Standardised product	Adaptations required
Market factors	
Small markets – Specialised segments	Large markets – high volume sectors
Unstable markets	Stable markets
New or declining markets	Mature markets
Large markets are very competitive	Large markets are not very competitive
Competitors have large shares of key markets	Key markets are divided among many competitors
Marketing factors	
Low communication cost for additional markets	High communication costs for additional markets
Low physical distribution costs for additional markets	High physical distribution costs for additional markets

Source: Adapted from Piercy (1982).

■ Economic factors

Marketing opportunities exist in all countries regardless of the level of economic development. Analysis usually reveals far more market opportunities than a firm's limited resources can cope with.

A priority system is thus necessary to ensure that the available resources will not be spread too thinly. Such screening criteria may include:

1. Market potential;
2. Economic growth;
3. Political risk;
4. Available natural resources;
5. Available labour;
6. Trade barriers.

In assessing marketing opportunities, there is no single ideal criterion. Five key economic variables that should be considered are:

- GNP;
- Population;
- GNP per capita;
- Income;
- Personal consumption.

These now need to be looked at in some detail.

Gross National Product (GNP) is a measure of the value of all goods and services produced by a nation. As such, GNP in effect measures the size of the economy. GNPs range from a mere $30 million for the Maldives to $2 trillion for the United States. However, GNP alone does not accurately reflect market potential. India's GNP of $126 billion is almost twice as large as Austria's $65 billion, yet the larger number does not necessarily mean that India is a better market. A more valid indicator can be derived by dividing a country's GNP by its population. This gives a measure of market intensity – of the concentration of purchasing power. In the case of Austria and India, Austria has a GNP per capita of $8600 whilst India has a GNP per capita of $190.

Population is another general indicator of market size. On this score China is the foremost market as its population exceeds a billion. (Note that population size is a particularly good indicator of market opportunity for low unit-value products or necessities.)

Another indicator is GNP per capita. Since markets are dynamic, it is interesting to note that about 75 per cent of the world's people live in developing countries. However, it is inadequate to assess markets by relying only on each country's population, without considering its land area. From the marketing standpoint, the level of population density should be examined. While total population indicates the overall size of a market; over two-thirds of Indonesia's 160 million population live on Java, giving a population density of 740 persons per square mile.

Another clearly identifiable trend is that more and more people are becoming city dwellers. By the year 2010, half of the world's population will live in urban areas. Also, by the year 2000, all but three of the world's largest cities will be in the least-developed countries (LDCs).

The personal income of a country's citizens is also a useful indicator of a nation's wealth. Income can reflect the level of attractiveness of a market, because consumption generally rises as income rises. Consumers in LDCs may have low incomes but may still have ample buying power as the cost of living is usually comparatively low when compared to that of wealthier nations.

Per capita spending and how the money is spent will provide another clue to market potential. Food costs in Japan account for 25 per cent of disposable income (in the USA 15 per cent), so the Japanese do not have so much to spend on non-essentials. Income should never be considered by itself as the determinant of market attractiveness; China is the ninth largest economy in the world, yet its per capita income is only $350 (similar to that of Haiti and Guinea). One problem with per capita income is the assumption that everyone gets an equal share of the nation's income. To overcome this weakness, a marketer should examine the distribution of income.

Management should pay attention to the income elasticities of imports and also exports of target countries, because these coefficients indicate how imports and exports are influenced by consumers' income changes in each country. Typically the UK has a higher import elasticity than export elasticity, indicating that a rise in exports will be accompanied by a greater than proportional rise in imports, thus putting a strain on the balance of payments.

Income often indicates the extent of consumption because income and consumption are positively related. Although the effect of income is moderated by cultural preferences, it still indicates the degree of consumption for many products. Thus, a marketer should also observe per capita consumption of each product under consideration, since it can vary greatly from market to market.

In planning international market development it is useful to estimate geographical/customer concentration. The geographical concentration index is obtained by dividing the value of the country's merchandise exports to its main customers by the value of its total merchandise exports. The higher the index, the greater the concentration of exports to the main export markets.

Another useful indicator of a country's ability to endure the balance-of-payments problem is its compressibility of imports. A compressibility index is the value of a country's non-essential imports divided by the value of its total imports. A high index indicates that too much foreign exchange is being spent on non-essential imports. The country should then be able to compress its import bill in order to reduce the outflow of foreign exchange. Brazil's declining compressibility index, for example, is a reflection of its effort to conserve foreign exchange.

What is needed at this stage is an analysis of market typologies, market opportunities and company resources; and as a follow-up to the previous explanation of the diversification versus concentration, in Figure 3.2. Case 3.12 provides a short example of how to apply this analysis.

Market development strategies can be developed from the systematic assessment of other needs that the current product or services could satisfy. They include geographic expansion as well as entry into new market sectors. Product development, and finding new products for existing markets is a valid strategic alternative when advancing technology means that the product satisfaction can be improved, as in electronics.

CASE 3.12

A German metal manufacturing company was faced with capacity limitations and its objective was to market its limited output to the most attractive countries in the short and long term. Some 16 countries were assessed against the criteria shown below and nine chosen for strategic and tactical concentration. The criteria used were:

- acceptable country in relation to production capacity (quantified)
- adequate level in relation to investment and manufacturing costs (quantified);
- stable, consistent growth;
- resistant to substitution by other products;
- clear, stable distribution channels;
- potential for significant (quantified) country market share;
- sales potential in terms of location, access, buying power and trade prospects of customers;
- acceptable level of competitive supply and pricing.

Diversification is implied when companies enter new markets with new products; these are usually the highest cost and risk alternatives for a company because, by definition, least is known about either the market or the products which will satisfy it; increasingly diversification is now done by acquisitions.

■ Demand across countries and markets

■ Multi-country research

The development of overseas markets requires a sustained programme of research and analysis to assess demand and changes in demand trends; such a programme should be itemised along the following lines:

1. Existing and potential size of the market aimed at and what parts of the total population it comprises.
2. Attitudes to the product group generally, and to the main brand names and manufacturers, before and continuously after any introduction.
3. How the product itself (including any packaging) will behave in the territories concerned, how it appeals to consumers and how they are likely to use it.
4. The most suitable pricing policy to adopt.
5. How the distribution of the product is to be attained and, continuously after introduction, how it is moving through these channels (to distinguish always between the ultimate consumers' purchases and one's own current sales to distributors).
6. How best to advertise and promote the product, and hence the relative cost and effectiveness of different means of doing this.

In all the foregoing a careful comparison between one's own product and its competitors is obviously essential.

Multi-country research involves dealing with countries that differ not only in language, but which also have very different economic and social structures, behaviour and attribute patterns (see for example Moyes, 1968). It is essential that these differences are taken into account in the formulation of the initial design of a multi-country survey, and they may well necessitate variations in the research methods to be applied in individual countries. To ignore these differences in the interests of a spurious comparability is to commit the cardinal error of many researchers – both national and international – namely to take a technique rather than a problem-orientated view of their function. After all, the purpose of market research is to help in the solution of marketing problems, and the purpose of multi-country research is to help in the solution of multi-country marketing problems. There are, of course, a number of these problems that can be solved by using exactly the same sample design and asking exactly the same questions in all the countries under investigation; frequently, however, the imposition of a rigid research structure on a number of very different countries may defeat the very objective that the research is trying to achieve.

Moreover, the scope of research and analysis is also determined by two factors:

First, the position already reached by the company in the country market(s) concerned. Where it is exporting for the first time, the immediate need is for a straightforward market study to show the most profitable areas for attack – and hence to establish priorities and broad policy. While this research must be thorough, it is generally relatively simple and inexpensive. Only after the priority markets have been so chosen, using the screening process described in the previous section, does the more detailed research confined to these markets only, need to be undertaken. And at this stage some consumer research in the field may become necessary to establish the size of the market and shares of principal brands, thus bringing up to date or supplementing published statistics. Participation in a syndicated service (that is a shared questionnaire over a range of subjects), if provided by a reputable agency, can be an economical way of obtaining this.

Second, the type of product researched for overseas markets; clearly the research requirements for non-consumer or industrial goods (machine tools, aircraft, trucks and so on) are somewhat different than for consumer goods.

The users of industrial goods tend to be fewer and the methods of selling less sophisticated and more technical than for consumer goods. Industrial market research may therefore be more concentrated and without the need for large national samples and surveys, and therefore, in these respects, less expensive than research on consumer goods though the difficulties and need for care in planning and operations are just as great. Indeed the pilot desk research for an industrial study is on the whole far more lengthy and complex than for the average consumer study, and the interviews with the right people, though fewer, often difficult to obtain.

Even within consumer-goods research, the distinction should be recognised between the needs of high quality goods selling at premium prices, and likely to continue as viable exports (for example sports cars or branded knitwear) and mass market goods (for example toiletries) which for cost reasons soon have to be made in the country of consumption.

Multi-country analysis will, of course, also throw light on the differences in attitude and behaviour between one country and another; few manufacturers have the inclination or the resources to acquire this type of knowledge for its own sake. The objectives of most manufacturers embarking on a multi-country study are normally dictated by several practical considerations, such as evolving a product formulation likely to achieve acceptance in the maximum number of countries, or the adaptation of marketing and advertising strategy to differing local conditions. The purpose of most multi-country surveys is not to obtain information on basic economic and cultural differences: these differences should constitute the background on the basis of which a multi-country survey is planned; in other words, they should have already been understood and appreciated at the planning stage, since they are basic to the formulation of the initial design of such a survey. There is also the question of different universes to be considered at the design stage for such a survey. Completely different circumstances can result in a different universe having to be covered in each country.

CASE 3.13

A market survey was undertaken by the Italian Foreign Trade Centre (IFTC) to estimate the demand for a particular product: religious articles in the USA. The aim of the survey was to explain to Italian manufacturers of religious articles the demand situation in the USA and the export possibilities, and the means of organising such exports in the most effective manner. This survey was completed in approximately one year.

Research methodology: sampling was not used; data was collected by IFTC with the assistance of Commercial Officers in USA. The data provided through the survey comprised:

- the size in volume and value of the US market;
- selling prices in the the USA;
- details of American importers and department stores;

lists of architects specialising in religious architecture;

- lists of catholic associations and the religious press;
- customs duties and regulations;
- suggestions for the guidance of the potential exporter – various methods of production, landed US dollar prices, time limits for delivery and designs of products preferred, and other buying factors in the distribution chain.

CASE 3.14

In an eight-country survey amongst doctors on an ethical pharmaceutical product, it was found that in the Netherlands general practitioners are very restricted in the drugs they are allowed to prescribe, and there was no possibility of the product under examination being included in the Dutch national insurance list. Interviews were therefore limited to hospitals and specialists. In Belgium, general practitioners have considerable freedom in the drugs they prescribe, and most interviews were therefore carried out with this group. The problem was the same in both countries, namely to establish the acceptability of the product amongst the medical profession. There would have been no point, however, in interviewing general practitioners in the Netherlands, or concentrating on specialists in Belgium. Comparability at the interpretation stage was achieved in so far as the relative acceptability of the product in the two countries was established, but the methods of data collection were very different.

These considerations make it clear that multi-country analysis is a very different type of operation from single-country research. They also have an important bearing on the type of people or organisations that are able to carry out multi-country research. A researcher or research organisation that thinks in terms of one country only is unlikely to have the adaptability, knowledge and experience for the conduct of multi-country research. Researchers or research organisations operating on an international scale not only have to think internationally (and speak a number of languages), but also have to have considerable experience and knowledge of individual countries and international conditions. They must be constantly prepared to draw on this fund of knowledge or obtain new information when faced with a specific research problem. Moreover, they must be capable of using this knowledge as well as their knowledge of research techniques when designing a multi-country survey.

■ **Key factors in analysing demand**

In any analysis of foreign markets there are therefore a number of factors to take into account:

1. effective demand in the country;
2. market potential in the country;
3. market access into the country; and
4. competition.

These factors are considered further in this Section together with an assessment as to how market analysis can be used to,

1. screen markets,
2. select markets;
3. segment markets,

First, it is important to distinguish between three types of demand:

1. Demand in existing markets where customer needs are being served by existing suppliers and the main challenge is competition.
2. Latent demand where there is immediate market potential if the product were offered to customers at an acceptable price.
3. Incipient demand will lead in the longer term to sales if present market trends continue.

CASE 3.15

This survey of market potential was conducted on a cooperative basis between the business sector and the government foreign trade ministry; the product category was household electrical appliances (irons, cookers, toasters, fans, refrigerators, washing machines, vacuum cleaners, air conditioners and so on). Countries regarded as potential markets were Norway, Argentina, Pakistan, Denmark, Venezuela, Egypt, Saudi Arabia, Belgium, Peru, Nigeria, Spain, Chile, Canada, Turkey, Kenya and Brazil.

☐ Survey aim

These appliances were being sold mainly to South East Asia. The aim of the survey was to obtain an accurate grasp of market trends in the leading areas, in order for the full potential of these country markets to be exploited. However, only patchy data were available about these products which are closely related to people's living habits in these countries; this survey was aimed at filling this gap. By collecting data over an extensive region, it was expected that comparisons of market trends could be made and market potential accurately assessed.

☐ Detailed planning

In order to study the extent of popularisation of these appliances, the survey was conducted by classification into higher, middle and lower income groups, urban areas and villages and by fiscal year. Surveys were also conducted to ascertain the relation between energy consumption (electricity, gas, oil, LPG and so on) and income.

☐ Survey methods

The request for the survey was relayed to the government's trade centres in the countries concerned, and to agencies which actually conducted the survey. Data searches, interviews with suppliers and distributors were carried out, as was random sampling of consumers classified according to income.

The main challenge is identifying market opportunity, where initial success will not be through competitiveness but through the ability to identify and explore longer-term market development.

In the process of analysing overseas markets, therefore, management must assess market opportunities, identify and develop markets with potential, and undertake continuous market analysis.

There are three aspects to this overall task: market structure; factors affecting demand; and competition.

■ **Selective demand**

In international operations, markets must be assessed on a selective basis; this is usually done on,

1. a country-by-country basis, or
2. a sector-by-sector basis.

International market selection requires the use of a logical research sequence; this is concerned with,

1. sources of data,
2. interpretation of data, and
3. evaluation of data for both comparability and validity, all in relation to foreign markets.

It is also appropriate to distinguish between human sources (agents, or company executives based abroad); documentary sources (trade directories, or published market reports); and perception sources (local segmentation and experimental data)

In data analysis and interpretation, the most important aspect is the analysis of trends, and associating trends by comparing two or more series of data. Finding relationships by comparing series of data is an important step towards a full understanding by management of the forces at work in a market. And comparability of data is also an essential part of data evaluation in foreign markets.

These, then, are the principal phases of market research and analysis; the initial phase concerns demand analysis in foreign markets, and this is vital to the process of selecting markets. Also important is the interpretation of market trends and, using research methodology, the relationships between series of data and variables in order to understand the ways in which markets and in particular consumption patterns develop.

■ **Elasticities of demand**

In general terms, demand also depends on the size of the population. Other things being equal, the larger the population, the greater is the demand for all goods and services; and the smaller the population, the smaller the demand. But there are important exceptions to this, as where a rich minority in an otherwise poor country hold most of the purchasing power. An indicator widely used is the annual average per capita income: but like all averages, this can conceal significant differences in the distribution of incomes and in patterns of spending power across different market sectors or sub-markets. Moreover, one economic indicator alone is seldom a realistic guide to demand. If annual average per capita income is used, this should be adjusted for purchasing power which would take into account comparative tax and price levels.

Then there are demand elasticities and inelasticities to be considered. At the macro-level, governments concerned with the balance of trade typically find that the demand for exported goods is far more elastic than the demand for imports; export and import prices are both affected by exchange rate fluctuations, but many categories of imports such as chemicals, fertilisers, steel, components, produce and so on do not fall in volume if the price rises – the latter is passed on to distributors.

A more subtle and significant aspect is *cross-elasticities*, where fall in demand in one sector is typically accompanied by an increase in demand in another. Trade research in the UK has shown over many years that when consumers travel less and spend less in any year on holidays, they spend more on furniture, furnishings and so on for the home. And there are also interesting differences in per capita spending across countries. Similar research, for example, in the furniture industry has shown that on average German consumers spend, per capita, almost three times more on furniture and furnishings than their British counterparts.

The phenomenon of cross elasticities can be expressed algebraically as follows:

$$Q_H = f(P_H \cdot P_F \cdot P_T \cdot \ldots)$$

where

Q = quantity demanded
P = price
H = holidays
F = furniture
T = transport

Then there is the question of effective demand; put simply, people have money but are they spending it? The propensity to save has been shown to rise in conditions where consumers are uncertain or fearful of their future. Consumer confidence is known empirically to be adversely affected by unemployment, debt, uncertain economic prospects and so forth. In the United States this phenomenon is quantified by the well-established Consumer Confidence Index; this is constructed by periodic surveys of samples of households where consumers are asked about their actual spending on a range of goods and services,

Table 3.3   Economic factors influencing demand

The Law of Demand
The quality of product A

Decreases if price rises	Increases if price falls

The demand for product A

Decreases if:	Increases if:
• price of substitute falls	• price of a substitute rises
• income falls	• incomes rise
• price of substitute product falls	• price of substitute product rises
• price of product A is expected to fall in the future	• price of product A is expected to rise in the future
• the population decreases	• the population increases

and their spending plans six and 12 months in advance. Subsequent surveys establish whether these plans have been fulfilled, and, if cut back, for what reasons. This has applications in all industrial economies and is a key indicator of effective demand.

In international markets, there are further qualitative aspects to demand: preferences and acceptance. Preferences are an individual's attitudes (positive) towards goods and services. Of course preferences cannot be observed like income distribution and population size; economists assume that changes in preferences occur only slowly and so are not a critical influence on changes in demand. The question of consumer acceptance is also relevant; a product may be acceptable generally in different countries, market access has been secured, but consumers must accept the product as part of their lifestyle consumption and culture; the task of marketing and advertising is to ensure this acceptance and so exploit demand to the fullest possible extent. Table 3.3 illustrates some economic factors influencing demand.

However, the qualitative aspects influencing demand appear likely to have a deeper and more lasting impact than quantitative factors. Attitudinal and behavioural factors critically affect consumers' perceptions; this is psychographic research. One authoritative analysis researched demand and found that people with the same amount of money, education and status often have different priorities and spending habits (Hanson, 1986). For example, two men aged 30 might have the same income and status, but place a £3000 bonus in their hands and one will bank it in a pension-plan while the other spends it in Harrods and Fortnum & Mason. So instead of dividing up people by the traditional class and income categories, the psychographic approach is used to categorise people according to their attitude towards money, society, the media, and what they want out of life. The scope for inter-country comparisons of demand on this basis is enormous, and insufficient attention is paid to it by company researchers.

■ Conclusions

This chapter has covered controllable and uncontrollable elements in the international business environment, and has explained the strategies to cope with these. The approach to appraisal and scanning has been explained, together with the distinction between re-active and proactive approaches by companies. There followed a discussion of practical aspects such as access to foreign markets, and the importance of making strategic decisions about whether to concentrate on key markets or diversify across a much larger number of countries: the pros and cons of these strategies are explained. The managerial applications of research and research methods have been fully discussed in the last section, with a particular focus on demand trends, and the key factors management must take into account in assessing demand prospects, and especially key buying influences.

QUESTIONS

1. Discuss the contribution of environment analysis to improving communications between the company and its major constituencies.
2. Do you agree that it makes sense to base corporate strategy on worst case scenarios? Explain.
3. What do you understand by a company's political sensitivity; in what contexts can this enhance corporate performance in foreign markets?
4. What key factors influence (a) market access and (b) market demand in an international context?
5. What are the company-specific factors which would indicate whether a company should adopt market concentration as opposed to market diversification?
6. What criteria can management use to rank country markets in order of priority?
7. What are the implications for marketing management in identifying cross elasticities of demand among countries of operation?

CHAPTER 4

International business strategy

INTRODUCTION

This chapter builds on the foundations laid by the first three chapters by explaining the nature of competitiveness at the strategic and global levels. It discusses the formulation of competitive strategies in the light of environmental analysis and research, and against the background of the changing pattern of international trade; there is also a full exposition of how management should analyse competition. There follows an explanation of the *experience curve* and its implications and applications for global competition, especially opportunities for companies to adopt *innovator* and *follower* strategies. Some specific contexts in which management should consider changes of strategy are explained.

Technology factors are then analysed as an introduction to the important topic of technology collaboration and transfer; the various approaches to marketing technologies are then explained, in the context of the concept of the *technology life cycle* and its applications; there is another focus on technological advantage and its applications, as a *lead in* to the final section on competing internationally through innovation, design and manufacturing.

■ Developing competitive strategies and strategic options

■ Key strategic factors

Firms which succeed in implementing competitive strategy can gain competitive advantage: this latter improves the firm's competitive position, creates a barrier to entry, and enables a firm to change its competitive stance in response to market changes. Two constructs appear significant at this strategic level.

First, *distinctive competence*; this refers to activities which a firm does better than its competitors, but which require superior skills and resources. The latter are basically tangible assets such as the technology, the distribution network or superior resources; access to supply can also enhance the position. Distinctive competence can create barriers to imitation and help sustain competitive advantage; and superior skills and resources improve the firm's position when they can lower costs (through scale economies, the learning curve or capacity utilisation) or create value to customers. Organisation is another element of distinctive competence: a better organisational design and appropriate structure enables a firm to adapt more responsively and faster to changes in markets and the environment.

Secondly, *strategic fit*; in internal and external conditions this is relevant to dynamic competitiveness. Firms can achieve competitiveness only when management accurately identifies the skills and resources matched to strategic choices, including objectives, the target of market entry, and the quality of tactics and implementation. Some firms invest in unprofitable projects to establish a toehold in a potentially attractive market or technology in order to make a later move. Especially in the case of new technologies, the first investment often provides experience and useful information for making further investments. A first-mover strategy provides a competitive advantage, especially when ambiguity and a largely non-recoverable cost associated with entry are high. Uncertainty also affects strategic fit. When a market is volatile due to changing technology, political risk or economic uncertainty, a first-mover bears the risk and high cost of pioneering since new products can often be replaced quickly. This unstable condition requires a quick response. Changes in demand and competitive conditions in the host market also affect a firm's strategic flexibility.

Effective competitive strategy also depends on product and market characteristics, and types of products do influence the degree of standardisation. A standardised strategy is more applicable for consumer durables such as cameras, but less applicable for consumer non-durables such as foods which involves great differences in national tastes and habits. High-technology firms tend to use international diversification strategies since high-technology goods are more likely to have culture-free preferences, and only aspects of product design need to be customised. And expansion or switching strategic fit into a time horizon also affects competitiveness. An organisation's success depends on its ability to reshape strategies in response to changing global environments and markets.

■ The Changing Pattern of Competition

Two essential points must be made in this context, and they derive directly from the topics explained in Chapters 2 and 3.

First, the structure of competition is undergoing a profound change. Competitiveness is moving rapidly from a national to an international – indeed, global – scale; the oil and pharmaceutical industries experienced this years ago. It is clear that, even with government purchasing, fewer segments of industry remain defensible at the national level in, for example, consumer electronics, telecommunications, transport technology and power engineering; and there is a growing list of sectors where companies are experiencing the benefits of value-added from design to sales. In some sectors, it can be in terms of designing products for many markets, thus lowering production costs earlier than is possible for purely national forms (worldwide designs can cover 80 per cent of customer needs, with 20 per cent for local adaptations).

Secondly, competitive advantage, as the basis for strategy, must rest on some clear sustainable product or market factor, controlled by the firm, which is superior to what other companies can offer or deliver. This can relate to one or more of the following:

- purchasing and supply;
- research and development
- innovation;
- design;
- patents;
- production technology;
- quality and intensity of promotion;
- product/brand performance;
- pricing;
- delivery and technical support services;
- financial terms.

Of course, competitive advantage can also be based on market position: on strength in a particular sector or in some defined area of product/market operations. And a change has come about in the orientation of marketing management thinking in the last decade: there is now more concern with competitors and competitive strategy, compared with, previously, exclusive concern with customers. The building of competitive position and reaction to competitive attack are now accorded a prominent place in planning and plans, where a decade ago they would have been typically eclipsed by the focus on the customer.

The reality behind this change is simple: over-concentration on customers can result in a loss of competitive advantage by which to gain and keep customers. The strategy then is, equally, to gain and to keep competitive advantage, and thereby to secure a sustainable and profitable market position. At the same time, management must be ready to make country moves to prevent other firms from eroding this position; indeed, impeding a competitor can still bring greater relative gains, even though the firm's own performance may suffer in the short term. Lowering prices in a market where a competitor would otherwise make high profits can remove his funds from attack on some other front. The importance of some degree of international positioning is underlined by the danger of allowing a competitor to attack from a secure base (contrast, in this context, the failure of the British motorcycle industry and the success of the British ceramics/chinaware industry).

■ Competitive analysis by management

Competitive strategy requires, ideally, a process of scanning actual and potential competitors and planning competitive counter-moves to maintain market

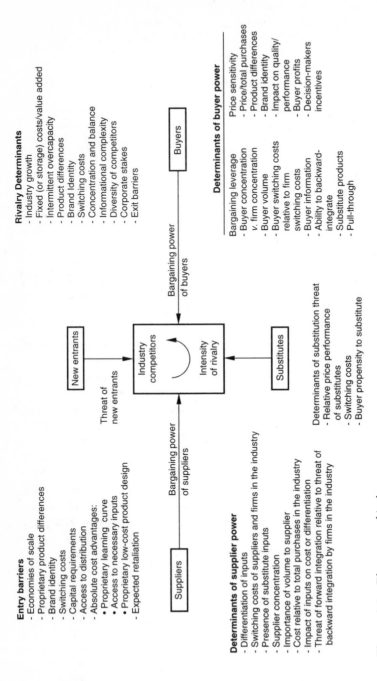

Figure 4.1 Elements of industry structure

Source: Porter (1985) *Competitive Advantage: Creating and Sustaining Superior Performance.*

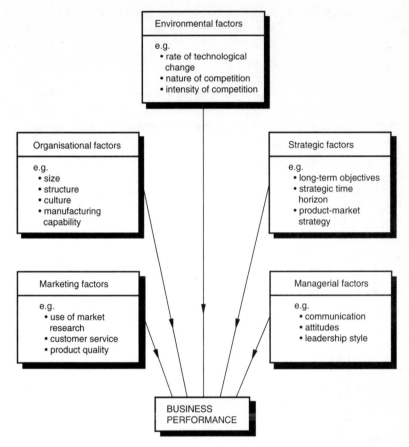

Figure 4.2   Factors influencing competitive success

position. Often the strongest competing company will make the first move (for example to introduce a new range of discounts), or counter-move (for example match, in expenditure and intensity, a promotional campaign). This means that in initiating competitive moves of its own, the medium-sized company should direct them at firms whose resources and profits are more closely matched to its own. Of course competitive opportunities or threats can arise from almost any direction, requiring a series of tactics rather than a single move. In general, management should endeavour to allocate resources to maximise the value of its competitive position. This is often easier said than done. Factors to be taken into account include: the closeness of a competitor's position in terms of product and market offering; the financial strength of the competitor and the nature of its speedy retaliation; and the distance of a competitor from a firm's own market position who appears likely to move closer and reduce the market boundary. Indeed, it is important that management does not draw these market boundaries too closely, but leaves some ground to be occupied by other firms who can then use this factor to counteract what is otherwise a competitive disadvantage.

Such a strategic planning process clearly requires competitive analysis by management as a data-base for setting up strategy. This involves several separate, though related, aspects. First, financial analysis: this refers to the link between competitive advantage and profit, and to the need to reinforce that position. Indeed, the competitive position becomes the company's most valuable asset, and it is this value that determines the worth of the business, not physical assets; volume of sales revenue does not guarantee competitive position in a declining market, the firm that can trade market share for high profits may well be increasing the value of its present position. Competitors' relative liquidity and borrowing capacity are also important in determining competitive threats. A high-cost competitor may still be an aggressive threat if it has the funds and determination to attack and overtake those who otherwise have the advantage.

One important study (Simmonds, 1986) has pointed out this very significant connection between profitability and competitiveness. A business that realises a

Table 4.1   Factors influencing average industry profitability

Influence Factor	Will lower profitability	Will raise profitability
Rivalry among competitors/		
Structure of competition	Numerous or equal size	One dominant
Growth	Slow	Rapid
Differentiation	Negligible	Significant
Fixed	High	Low
Capacity increments	Large	Small
Exit barriers	High	Low
Diversity of strategy	Significant	Limited
Ease of entry	Easy	Difficult
• scale thresholds		
• access to distribution		
• common technology		
Bargaining power of buyers		
Number of buyers	Few	Many
Purchase volume	Large	Small
Profitability	Low	High
Impact on end-product performance and quality	Unimportant	Important
Potential to back integrate	Significant	Not possible
Ability to switch to substitutes or other suppliers	Easy	Difficult

profit by running-down its competitive position would in its accounts appear no different from a firm that realises the same profit while building its competitive position. Yet when competitive position has been improved, it is very likely to have meant reducing accounting profit because of the cost of gaining on competitors. Conversely, increased profit can be a reflection of decay in competitive position as a result of higher prices or decreased quality; or through reducing advertising or any other reduction in spending that might have decreased the firm's relative competitive appeal in the market.

An examination of a competitor's portfolio of business and product lines can provide some indication of:

1. the importance and attractiveness of the business or the product line relative to the competitor's other businesses;
2. the financial and other resources the competitor may be able to draw on to support the business or product line.

This type of analysis can suggest areas of competitive vulnerability and future competitive actions and reactions.

CASE EXAMPLE 4.1

A company can be operating in the same business classification and yet not be competing directly; an example of such *non-competition* has been provided by Rolex Co. and Timex Co. Both companies marketed watches, primarily satisfying a need to tell the time. But their characteristics and competitive positions were very different.

	Rolex	*Timex*
Price range (UK)	£175+	£5-£50
Main mechanism	Mechanical	Electronic
Key sales points	Precision	Value for money
	Reliability	Features
	Durability	Choice
	Associated with success	Associated with fun
Social class	AB 35+	C–D all ages

Essentially, Rolex sold long-term, quality possessions, valued as much as things to have and display as time-pieces. Timex sold a cheap, functional, ultimately disposable way of telling the time (albeit a Timex quartz watch was probably as accurate as a Rolex chronometer).

■ The experience curve

One of the key issues in competitive strategy is the experience curve. Indeed, the competitive importance of any company's dominant position in world market sector(s) should be viewed in terms of cost/volume relationships (experience curves). It is necessary to view this initially in its historical context; a critical aspect of many industries' competitive development recently has been their demonstrated ability to lower a product's supply costs – especially in high-growth economies where firms have usually begun as internationally high-cost producers in most products, but in a few years have become very competitive. This competitive position of Japanese firms, for example, is only now being undermined by the rise in value of the Japanese yen and the growth of new low-cost volume manufacturers in other Asian countries such as South Korea and Taiwan.

On the basis of this and other industry studies, the experience curve has become widely accepted as a significant contribution to understanding changes in industry structure and competitive strategy. According to this concept, unit costs in many manufacturing industries, as well as in some service industries, decline with experience, or with a company's cumulative volume of production. The causes of this decline are a combination of elements, including economies of scale, capital–labour substitution and other cost-reduction investments, and also the learning curve for labour (the efficiency over a period of time by workers through repetition). The Boston Consulting Group (BCG) and other researchers have demonstrated, for a variety of products, that total costs per unit in constant dollars or other currency will decline by a characteristic amount (usually 20–30 per cent) each time accumulated production experience (total amount ever produced) doubles. The analysis illustrated in Figure 4.3 indicates a logarithmic relationship between real growth and the decline in annual costs.

This statistical phenomenon is observed in many regions including the USA, Europe and Japan; it is an accepted part of cost projection formulations, for example, in the aircraft and semiconductor industries. The cost–experience effect over time is more noticeable in new products. Such products have a small experience base and a high demand growth; accumulated production experience can double rapidly, and costs will fall accordingly. In mature industries the effects of inflation will obscure the decline in real dollar costs. To obtain an accurate picture one must factor-out inflation.

Given the relationship between cost and volume, an individual firm's cost position within an industry depends on its growth relative to the entire industry, that is on its market share. Conversely, an industry's ability to lower prices for a given amount of production experiences depends on the market shares of the individual producers, that is on the industry's concentration; with greater concentration, industry experience is spread among fewer producers.

The implication of the cost–experience effect for international competition is that growth directly determines a competitor's ability to accumulate experience

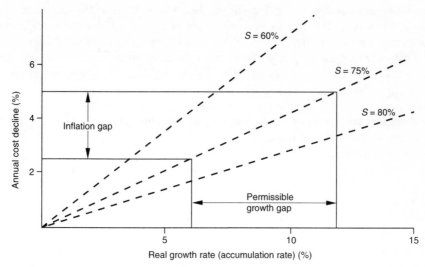

Figure 4.3   Real growth and decline of annual costs

Source: Rapp (1973)

Note: The annual rate of cost decline is equal to the mathematical slope of the experience curve times the accumulation rate. The mathematical slope equals

$$\frac{\log S}{\log 2}$$

where S is the slope of the experience curve. For a 75 per cent curve, $S = 0.75$ and the mathematical slope = 0.42.

and lower costs, and market share determines the ability to lower costs relative to competitors, domestic and foreign. The successful follower is therefore the firm that captures a dominant share of the world demand represented by its home market growth and subsequently by overseas demand.

■ Innovators versus followers

This analysis can be extended to competitive strategy by *innovator* and *follower* companies. For example, if a follower firm accumulates experience at 30 per cent per year, it will double its experience in less than three years, and will lower real costs by 20–30 per cent. If inflation in that firm's country is 5 per cent a year, the firm's current costs will decline between 5 and 15 per cent over the three-year period. If industry-demand is growing at 15 per cent per annum, and the industry growth rate has approached the industry-demand growth, the firm is capturing more than its share of incremental experience: it is gaining market-share relative to competitors and is improving its cost position. Once it is producing, though, the firm's ability to become internationally competitive is a function of its initial real production costs, the slope of its experience curve, its country's inflation rate, exchange rates, and the firm's accumulation rate.

Conversely, an innovator's ability to maintain price competitiveness and dominance in a product it has introduced depends on an appropriate combination of the following:

1. lower real start-up and initial production costs than the follower;
2. steeper experience-curve slope;
3. lower inflation rate;
4. declining value of the company's trading currency;
5. faster accumulation rate.

In reality, few of these conditions can be met simultaneously. The innovator usually has higher initial production and development costs than the follower, given a product's existence and the availability of production equipment and know-how, and the fact that the cost of transferring a given technology decreases over time. The follower need not accumulate equivalent experience to become competitive.

Actual international comparisons by the Boston Consulting Group have yet to show any appreciable slope differentials for the same product between leading industrial countries. Technological factors and industrial organisations at a given stage of development for the same product would seem similar, and cost-management by successful firms producing the product are roughly equivalent. The question of technology is tackled fully in a later section of this chapter.

Inflation and exchange rates are macroeconomic variables over which firms have little control. Nevertheless, it must be recognised that rising inflation rates can seriously affect companies' competitiveness.

Despite the above factors, innovators do have some control over follower firms' ability to capture world market share, to accumulate experience and to become cost-competitive. This is true even if they have not generally done so. Innovators usually have lower current costs when the follower begins production (even though start-up costs in real terms are higher). There is thus a minimum accumulation rate that a follower requires over some time period in order to become cost-competitive. The innovator can remain the dominant and low-cost producer if the follower fails to grow at this rate.

During the follower's initial production phase, the innovator can rarely accumulate experience as rapidly as the follower. The innovator is the initial producer and has a larger accumulated production base; consequently, he takes longer to double his experience. As the follower's smaller market is saturated, however, and as his experience base gets larger, further doublings and cost reductions become more difficult. The innovator must use his initial cost advantage, therefore, to participate in the follower's home market and/or shut off export development. This strategy may still require moving offshore later, but then production should be concentrated at the new location. Only in this way can the innovator deny the follower the growth necessary for fully competitive cost reduction; but his horizon is limited.

A useful way of assessing a follower's competitive requirement is to calculate the permissible growth (accumulation rate) gap allowed by differences in the follower's rate of inflation or by exchange rate movements. This gap equals the inflation or exchange rate differential divided by the mathematical slope of the experience curve. Given current costs and prices, if a follower's relative growth exceeds this permissible gap, the innovator's cost position is improving. A smaller inflation differential and/or a steeper product experience curve narrows the permissible growth gap long enough to become cost-competitive.

But many US and European innovators have not captured this required market growth. Thus, for many years, follower-firms in Japan and other countries have exceeded the permissible gap in many products. At stable exchange rates, this normally leads to large and persistent foreign exchange surpluses for the high-growth economy, owing to improved relative and absolute cost-positions. These surpluses can then be offset by tariff reductions, exchange rate adjustments or other measures. But even though total trade may become balanced, specific products and industries will continue to lose competitive position. Not all products have the same experience-curve slopes or are growing at the same rate.

CASE 4.2

Philips NV of Eindhoven has responded to the global competitive challenge in electronics, particularly from Japan, in a number of ways. First, it has invested heavily in R&D to maintain the expertise of its technology, since it is this that determines the cost and quality of components, and the price of the product.

Second, Philips has completed a massive programme of restructuring its production facilities (particularly in Europe), from factories producing for national markets to global production centres producing for world markets.

And, third, Philips has placed top priority on increasing its market position and production resources in the Pacific Basin (notably Japan); and the company has concluded joint ventures in Japan with a Japanese company for marketing the Philips data network system in Japan, and also for developing and marketing in Japan the company's interactive systems of small home computers.

■ Factors influencing changes in strategy

So far, special emphasis has been placed on: competitive advantage and the effects of the experience curve; the contribution of business analysis, in all phases, to an understanding of competitive position; the financial implications of competitive strategy; and international aspects, notably the different stances of *innovator* and *follower* companies. Having absorbed these policy aspects,

Table 4.2   Reasons for changing competitive strategy

Demographic	Changes in profile by age, sex, socioeconomic class or geographical location
Psychographic	Changes in the life-styles of buyers and the way these reflect upon purchasing habits
Demand	Fundamental changes in taste, usage patterns or consumption. Changes in the relative strengths and profitability of market segments
Technological	New processes on the one hand, obsolescence on the other
Market position	New forms of direct or indirect competition; changes in comparative market position (strengths and weaknesses in product, service, marketing, etc.)
Distributive	Changes in sales and distribution channels (either as an act of initiative or as a reflection of the way buyers purchase)
Price/profit relationships	Changes in search of improved results, for example low profit/high turnover versus high profit/low turnover
Regulations	Response to laws, codes, standards, regulations, inspectorates

management needs to be alert to two particular operating points. The first is the hazard of planning competitive strategy in isolation; that is, without sufficient regard to the company's resources and key management functions, such as finance and marketing, that are needed to implement it. In particular an inadequate data-base, especially on markets, can lead to incorrect strategies, and the pressure to innovate can push up costs with an adverse effect on short-term profits. The second point is that, at the same time, management must remain alert to signals that indicate a possible/desirable change in competitive strategy; these are summarised in Table 4.2.

■ An interactive approach

Case examples 4.3–4.5 serve to illustrate the necessity of having a complete integrated competitive strategy. Research and development alone is not enough; nor is salesmanship. For a competitive strategy to work, R&D, marketing and a sound organisational structure must function together. Both of the firms described in Case 4.3 have undergone major reorganisations in an attempt to coordinate these activities and make their strategies more effective.

CASE 4.3

By forging a global competitive strategy, Caterpillar Tractor Co. maintained its world leadership in the large-scale equipment business despite heavy competition. Caterpillar faced increasing pressure from Komatsu, Japan's leading construction equipment producer. Komatsu exported products from centralised facilities with labour and skill cost advantages. Despite this, Caterpillar gained a world market share through four defensive moves: a global strategy of its own, a willingness to invest in manufacturing, a willingness to commit finances, and a blocking position in the Japanese market.

How did Caterpillar implement this global strategy? The solution was in erecting two barriers to entry. The first was a global distribution system which served to block off competition; the second consisted of production economies. As a result, no competitor was able to match Caterpillar's production and distribution costs.

CASE 4.4

Chrysler is a US-based multinational, engaged in the manufacture of passenger cars and trucks. Honda Motors is a Japanese multinational which produces motorcycles, automobiles and power products. Both companies are the third largest domestic vehicle manufacturer in their home country. Both have been spending similar proportions of turnover on R&D (Chrysler 2.33 per cent and Honda 3.15 per cent). Yet the performances of the two companies has been far from similar.

During the 1980s, while Honda's worldwide sales were only 45 per cent of Chrysler's, its market share continued to increase, while Chrysler's fell. During 1978–81, Chrysler's market share dropped from 11.3 to 10.2 per cent. Honda's, on the other hand, almost doubled, from 2.4 to 4.6 per cent. During the same period, Chrysler suffered severe losses in its return on equity (ROE), while Honda's ROE averaged 14.7 per cent during this time. These performance measures were typical not only of these two firms at that time, but of the automobile industry as a whole, and they reflected the great contrasts between American and Japanese companies.

The answer to this disparity lay in the Japanese management style and its global strategy. This emphasised concepts such as quality-control circles and lifetime employment. It is this style that promoted participative management and a human-oriented approach, and it is this style that got results like those of Honda. Honda developed a comprehensive competitive strategy and an expanded product line to attract new customer segments. Also, Honda erected entry barriers with economies of scale by centralising manufacturing and logistics. The combination of these factors served as a strong competitive force in Honda's global strategy.

CASE 4.5

Texas Instruments (US) and Matsushita Electric (Japan) are MNCs in the consumer and industrial electronics industry. Both companies experienced phenome-
nal growth during the 1980s, and much of this success stemmed from their
firm-specific advantage in R&D. Matsushita also possessed worldwide marketing
skills and a unique (Japanese-style) management philosophy. For years, Texas
Instruments was known for its success in adopting a matrix structure along its
diverse product lines. More recently, however, both MNCs have experienced difficulties which are evident from their profit figures. For Texas Instruments, net
income declined (as a percentage of sales) from 5.8 per cent in 1976 to 2.6 per
cent in 1981.

Both Texas Instruments and Matsushita have been victims of their own success. Texas Instruments placed too much emphasis on R&D and ignored other
critical factors in an effective global strategy, such as an integrated marketing
effort and sound organisational structure. Instead, its strategy focused only on
technological innovations – the more the better. By constantly increasing the
amount of R&D, with inadequate regard for the marketplace, Texas Instruments
had to write-off very large investments in products that did not sell. Matsushita
made a similar mistake in relying on only one component of a successful global
strategy – salesmanship – only to be beaten by competitors.

The interactive approach is illustrated in Figure 4.4. The first factor is the
environment within which supplier–customer relationships have to be managed.
Furthermore, the structure of the different industries in which specific suppliers
operate points to the nature of the competition facing suppliers and to the
marketing tasks that have to be performed in order to operate successfully.
Finally, the size, growth rate and market potential of the different export
markets, together with the inter-country trade balances and exchange rate
movements, point to the relative opportunities and risks of each market. This
comprises the environmental background within which suppliers formulate
their sequence of approach to each market (or major foreign customers) and the
resources to be committed to each market or relationship.

The second major factor is the strategic offering for interacting with customers. One of the most important considerations for a supplier is the evaluation of the countries to which it will attempt to export and the customers with
whom it proposes to enter into relationships. This process is dependent upon
how the supplier-company executives perceive the opportunities, competition
and barriers to entry into export markets. This derives from their interpretation
of the environment. Obviously, for any interaction with customers to take
place, the supplier must have a competitive offering. A fey feature of industrial
marketing is the development of technological expertise and the application of

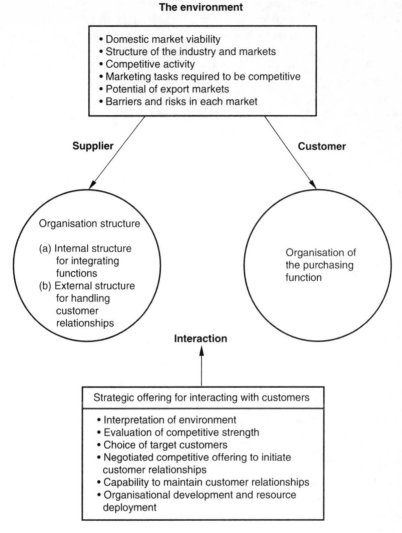

The environment

- Domestic market viability
- Structure of the industry and markets
- Competitive activity
- Marketing tasks required to be competitive
- Potential of export markets
- Barriers and risks in each market

Supplier

Customer

Organisation structure

(a) Internal structure
   for integrating
   functions
(b) External structure
   for handling
   customer
   relationships

Organisation of
the purchasing
function

Interaction

Strategic offering for interacting with customers

- Interpretation of environment
- Evaluation of competitive strength
- Choice of target customers
- Negotiated competitive offering to initiate
  customer relationships
- Capability to maintain customer relationships
- Organisational development and resource
  deployment

Figure 4.4   An interactive approach to competitive strategy

Source: Cunningham (1985).

this expertise to solving customers' problems. The competitive offering to accomplish this objective usually involves such elements as:

- the innovativeness of the product;
- its price competitiveness;
- the supply capability of the organisation as a whole; and
- the technical and commercial services accompanying the product.

It is this offering that will motivate customers to engage in an exchange process with suppliers. In industrial markets these usually have to be negotiated rather than being unilaterally imposed by the supplier. Even so, they may account for only short-term exchanges relating to a specific purchase or sale. They do not, of themselves, constitute prolonged interaction, nor are they necessarily the appropriate basis of an abiding relationship between a supplier and a customer. A relationship is really characterised by many more features. One essential feature is the relative importance of the exchange to both parties. Another is the social integration that occurs. A relationship will also consist of the inter-personal communications and adaptations between supplier and customer to achieve mutual benefits. Therefore, the strategic offering for interacting with customers can be considered as involving three interlinked behavioural and economic facets: first, the manager's perception of where market opportunities lie; second, the negotiated competitive offering to initiate relationships; and, third, the capability to handle all the characteristics of a satisfactory relationship with customers.

The third factor, which arises from the first two, is the supplier's organisation structure. This is the means by which suppliers actually handle their customer relationships. In the first instance, there is the internal organisation structure which coordinates and integrates the various types of expertise and functional specialisations in the company. This is in order to give effective direction and control over the interaction between these personnel and their counterparts in the decision-making unit of the customer organisation. Second, there is the external organisation structure, which is the channel of communication, sales activity and distribution between the supplier and the customer.

Relationships with customers, when handled directly through export staff or by agents or subsidiaries, demonstrate differing levels of commitment and resource investments by the supplier. They also permit different degrees of control over the interaction and the relationships.

The research study illustrated in Figure 4.4 covered the following industry sectors:

- Raw materials – speciality steels and speciality chemicals;
- Components – industrial components and automotive components;
- Capital goods – pumps, valves and compressors;
- Diesel engines;
- Other capital equipment.

The study grouped the ingredients of the competitive offering as a basis for initiating a relationship with a European industrial customer under the following headings:

- Product design and specification factors;
- Price factors;
- Delivery factors;

- Service factors;
- Quality reliability factors;
- Flexibility and adaptability factors.

And it found that the technical factors predominate both in frequency and criticality. These factors relate to the uniqueness of the product characteristics or its adaptation to meet customers' existing manufacturing processes; thereafter, security of supply, service facilities and price factors are of high importance.

■ Industrial market strategies

The study cited under Figure 4.4 shows five major competitive strategies adopted by UK industrial suppliers:

1. *Technical innovative strategy.* In nine instances, this strategy has been used in obtaining business from particular customers. It occurs where the supplier offers a specially-designed product which performs well, meets the customer's specification, but is also supported by high-quality and technical service. Price is of minimal importance.
2. *Product adaptation strategy.* Again, in nine instances this strategy was implemented. It occurs when the supplier's specially-designed product interests customers but some design modifications are insisted upon to minimise customer-inconvenience and conform to the specification. In order to be a supplier, the offer has to be supported by reliable deliveries, stockholding and service. Price is of secondary but significant importance.
3. *Availability and security strategies.* This logistic type of strategy was commonly used and occurred in eight instances. The customer is rarely innovative, or the products are well-established on the market. The supplier emphasises risk-reduction and reliability in his marketing approach. Quick and reliable delivery is of critical importance, but the product must still conform in all respects to the customer's specification and be at a competitive price. The supplier adapts his supply system to meet customers' requirements. Of vital importance also is an after-sales service network and ready availability of spares and replacements.
4. *Low-price strategies.* In six instances, this strategy has been used. Here the supplier initially prices his product lower than customers are currently paying in order to attract attention. The intention is to increase price once the business is well-established. The offer has to be supported by relliability of delivery, adequate quality and acceptable performance of the product on test.
5. *Total adaptation or conformity strategies.* This is somewhat less common and was found in only four instances. The supplier is considered as a second or third supplier only as a result of offering a product to match the performance of competitors and comply with customer-specification. Additionally, the supplier has to match competitors in delivery and price. This requires significant technical, commercial and administrative adaptation by the supplier.

■ Technology collaboration and transfer

■ Levels of technology

Technology factors refer to the level to which society in the target market has developed any technology in manufacturing and distribution. There is a close link between technology and demand. The extent of demand in a country market is determined by the stage of economic and industrial development achieved, and the technology which the country possesses to sustain this development. These may be very different from the home-base of the supplying, foreign company, and therefore technical and product adjustments may be necessary. Some analysts argue that the level of technology of a country is the most critical indicator of its market development. A company marketing an industrial product to a developing country may have to make manufacturing/technical adaptations to achieve sales as the following Case example shows.

CASE 4.6

Environmental/technology factor	Market response/technical change
Level of technical skills	Product simplification
Level of labour	Automation or manualisation of product
Level of literary	Remaking and simplification of product
Safety, health and noise	Use modifications
Level of interest rates	Credit, cost of inventories, margins
Level of maintenance	Changes in tolerances
Isolation (heavy repairs difficult and costly)	Product simplification and reliability improvement
Differences in standards	Recalibration of product and resizing of specifications
Availability of materials	Resizing of engine power and specifications
Power availability	Product redesign/innovation in specifications

These factors, itemised in this way, enable management to assess the levels of technology in their target overseas country markets, and so adapt their product and services to be the best possible fit from a technical viewpoint.

■ Transfers of technology

The development of new technologies, and the consequent need to develop appropriate marketing policies is illustrated in Figure 4.5 as a multi-country comparison. In this context, licensing has been increasingly significant: licensors

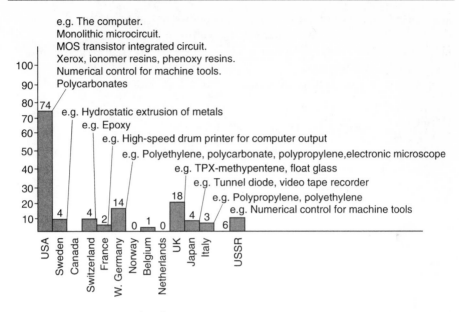

Figure 4.5 Gaps in technology

Source: OECD (1990).

are suppliers of technology, while licensees are the recipients; technology can be defined as any kind of know-how relevant to the solution of engineering and management problems. Many studies have explained the role of licensing in both the provision and the control of technology worldwide by manufacturers seeking to develop their international business operations with low risk and low capital outlay. What is indicated is the dominating position of the USA as an exporter of technology; the UK marginally in balance; and France, Germany and Japan as net importers. As regards government intervention, this usually takes the form of political and economic controls deemed to be in the national interest. In Western Europe and North America, licensing thrives mainly on private initiatives within a framework of competition law; among the technology-importing countries, the most successful example of controlled industrial development is that of modern Japan. Through its Ministry of International Trade and Industry, Japan has imposed a tight rein on foreign investment and technology transfer.

While the concept of the patent, and to some extent patent licensing, is relatively well-understood, some executives find it exceedingly difficult to extend their thinking to the wider aspects of know-how licensing. Generally, the more international a company is in its outlook and operations, the more likely licensing of technology (in and out) will emerge as a strategic option.

There are indications now that more companies seem to have discovered their technological know-how as a marketable commodity and profitable opportunity. Increasingly important are international technology transactions, often brought about by the mediation of governmental and private agencies, the increasing use of trade fairs and centres where technological know-how is traded, and state-financed facilities in many countries for bringing about industrial technology transfer. Five types of technology can be identified:

1. Mainstream technology (also by licensor);
2. Spin-off (by-product) technology (not generally used by licensor);
3. Hang-over technology (substituted by mainstream technology no longer used by licensor);
4. Stand-by technology (temporarily unused by licensor);
5. Up-and-coming technology (still in the development stage and/or not yet used by licensor).

Figure 4.6 illustrates the main steps in the licensing process based on the study of Hamman and Mittag (1985).

Target definition
↓
Technology identification
↓
Technology selection
↓
Determination of licensing entry
↓
User segmentation
↓
User communication
(inquiry by licensor, licensee or mediator)
↓
Pre-contract negotiations
(demand forecast-presentation-advance arrangements)
↓
Pre-selection of potential licensees
↓
Contract negotiations
↓
Selection of licensees
↓
Settlement of contract
↓
Fulfilment of contract
↓
Licensing audit

Figure 4.6   Stages of the technology licensing process

Source: Hamman and Mittag (1985), p.6.

It is clear, therefore, in the light of these developments, that companies must understand the process of technology marketing. However, decision criteria by which managements can judge how to identify licensable technology and when to license technology are by no means fully developed yet. While the first aim of effective technology marketing policy is to identify 'technology stock' in a company, definition is by no means straightforward. Certainly some indicators can be used such as, first, physical production facilities (for example machines and installations); second, information reservoirs; and, third, people. But the study illustrated in Figure 4.6 also points out that management faces the problem of rating existing, identified technology by its marketability, that is its economic prospects as measured by the number and scope of utilisations (for example the number of technology users, and the volume of technology utilisation). But, it is claimed, the aptitude of a technology for licensing is not stable over time, and it proposes the concept of the technology life-cycle (describing the ageing process of technology).

■ **Technology licensing**

Licensing in the early phases of the technology life-cycle (the development and trial phases) is usually difficult because the industrial applicability of technology is either not yet demonstrable or only guided by prototypes or pilot-constructions, and therefore its superiority over conventional technology is not clear. Moreover, the investment necessary to develop viable applications, the time required and the difficulties in estimating future profits may often deter possible users from licensing technology. Licensing in the later stages of the technology life-cycle (maturity and decline) phases may imply the disadvantage that in the meantime other companies have gained know-how from their own R&D so that the number of potential licensees decreases as the number of potential licensors increases. A license can also become unattractive because of its diminished technological and economic prospects.

The conditions to gain market access through licensing and to earn profits seem to be most advantageous at the growth-stage of the technology life-cycle. Interest in a technology increases drastically when it proves to be a viable proposition, and product marketing based on that technology is likely to be very successful. The licensing conditions are not only favourable because potential licensees want to enter the product market as far as possible, capitalising on the success of the innovator, but also because the technology opens opportunities for further development and for the advancement of their own technology. The proceeds from licensing normally achieve a maximum at this stage in the technology life-cycle; this is illustrated in Figure 4.7.

■ **Organisational aspects**

The transfer of technology to overseas operations, especially by MNCs, is typically done to build up a technical presence to serve as a base for the

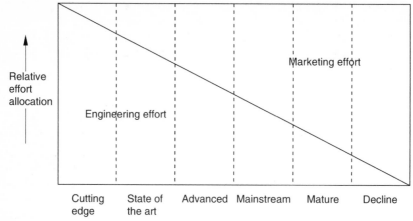

Notes:

Cutting edge
- technology marketed without specific application
- no target market
- sell on technology attributes

State of the art
- adopt cutting edge to meet wider market needs
- sell on technological benefits
- begin to sell on benefits

Advanced
- 'product' concept adopted
- sell on benefits

Mainstream
- low-cost, high-quality standard product
- sell on benefits
- segmented market

Mature
- reduced product differentiation (commodity market)
- shift from segmentation to customer service

Decline
- displaced by new technologies
- price competition

Figure 4.7   The technology lifecycle

Source: 'Industrial Market Behaviour and the Technology Lifecycle', *Industrial Management and Data Systems*, Nov/Dec 1986.

development of more value added research activities. One study (Kravis and Lipsey, 1971) of the internationalisation of R&D investigated technology transfer by US MNCs in Japan; it identified four kinds of foreign R&D units:

1. *Technology transfer units*, facilitating the transfer of the parent's technology to the subsidiary, and providing local technical services.

2. *Indigenous Technology Units*, developing new products for the local market, drawing on local technology.
3. *Global Technology Units*, developing new products and processes for world markets.
4. *Corporate Technology Units*, generating basic technology for use by the corporate parent.

CASE 4.7

The offshore oil industry is dominated by large multinational oil companies that weigh investment possibilities in the UK continental shelf against other opportunities worldwide. These MNCs hold about 85 per cent of known offshore assets, estimated to be worth about £40 billion by the energy consultancy firm Wood Mackenzie (a division of Nat-West Markets). Shell and Esso jointly have a stake worth nearly £6 billion through a longstanding collaboration agreement.

Organising technology collaboration, which helps to spread the commercial risk, has been a feature of North Sea exploration since the outset. The concept has been extended in recent years to pooling financial as well as technical resources, in both developing and operating oil and gas fields, in attempting to keep down offshore costs. For example, BP is working with Shell to develop a floating production system for the Foinaven field, the first oil find in the Atlantic waters west of Shetland to be declared commercial. This collaboration with BP is outside the area covered by Shell's partnership pact with Esso. Chevron and Conoco have also been working together on plans for the investment of £1.5 billion in the Britannia field, the North Sea's largest undeveloped gas field (given the government go-ahead in late 1994). The two companies have also set up joint logistical operations to share resources and services.

Leading offshore contractors have responded to this new way of working by gearing their operations to take over the project management functions which were previously handled by teams of oil company executives. Technology collaboration among contractors, without the need for every decision to be referred to oil company staff, have helped to reduce delays in project completion and contributed towards the target of reducing development costs by at least 30 per cent.

The handing over of project management responsibilities to contractors has often been accompanied by a transfer of technical expertise, leading to speculation that, in future, the technology to develop and produce fields will reside not with the oil companies, given legal responsibility for the safe and efficient operation of fields as part of the licensing conditions, but with the contractors. In this scenario there has been some suggestion that, eventually, the contractors could start competing for equity shares in licenses. This would mean that the main function of the oil companies would be reduced to financing the projects in return for deliveries of oil to use in downstream refining and distribution operations.

Source: Sunday Times, 6 August 1995.

Each type of unit was found to have distinctive linkages with the local sub-sidiary, the parent organisation and with local sources of technology. The study showed the options open to a company with a technology that is marketable worldwide. The previous Case example illustrates another aspect: organising collaboration in technology development between players in a global industry.

■ Technological advantage

The international flow of technology is, therefore, not restricted to a single format or channel; it is a multi-channel scenario. The motivations for tech-nology transfer are, of course, also linked to trade in goods or flows of capital. Basically, every firm seeks to secure its competitive position through technologi-cal advantage. This may be achieved in different ways: direct export (for exam-ple, of industrial goods), licensing worldwide, alliances or partnerships based on technology collaboration, investing in production facilities abroad, and the construction and sale of 'turnkey' plants. The use of these channels indicates a strategy, or at least a plan, to transfer or disseminate technical innovation. Yet much transfer of technology takes place in other, unplanned or unintended ways. Ideas for new products and processes spread internationally through scientific conferences and symposia, and personal communications (increasingly through shared data bases on E-mail and Internet) among researchers worldwide.

The important point is that unintentional transfers usually do not yield a profit to the firm, and may adversely affect its business; intentional transfers, on the other hand, are typically done as part of a competitive strategy and usually yield a return to the supplier firm. One form of transfer that takes place outside the control of the supplier firm is *reverse engineering*, a process widely used in the electronics, engineering and automotive industries where a competing manufac-turer buys, strips down and reassembles another's product. This can reveal technical designs and innovations, and can indicate manufacturing costs and competitors' profits. In some cases copies are then manufactured, but innovat-ing firms often try to guard against unplanned transfers of technology by patenting their products, registering designs, and taking other steps to keep key ingredients and technical processes secret. Obviously a company derives legal protection once a technology is patented (usually for a period of 20 years); but patent protection depends entirely on law enforcement which is weak and hazardous in some countries. Moreover, patents can be inspected by rival firms, some of which may try to launch a copy with minor modifications. And not all processes are patentable. If a company opts to keep its formulae and processes as trade secrets, it runs the risk that its innovations will not be protected by law if they are disclosed through industrial espionage.

■ Investing in innovation

In licensing, there is a contractual agreement to sell a design, a technical or scientific process, or the technology to manufacture a specific product under the licensing manufacturer's name or brand. Technical information is typically included under such an agreement, as are assistance and training, plant engineering and construction, and some advance notice of innovations under development. There are, however, usually strict limitations to what the licensee may do with the technology; these relate to the territory of operation, the period of the license, controls on price, and the quantity and quality of output. There are also limitations on the use of the technology in new products developed by the licensee, and an absolute ban on developing or making competitive products. In the case of the sale of entire plants, this is usually part of a larger management contract involving technical assistance, project management and other follow-up activities over a period: this is a typical arrangement in large-scale industries such as defence equipment, power generation and food processing; and in process industries such as cement, steel production, paper, chemicals, fertiliser and construction (for example dams, hospitals, ports and so on). Once the plant is built and tested it is handed over the recipient, but the management can be provided by the technology supplier (see Chapter 7 for a detailed account of contracting).

Firms investing heavily in innovation often opt to develop their technologies internally, and avoid licensing them or selling plants for innovations that they plan to exploit themselves. This raises the issue of investment in innovation and design, and the estimated pay back – the expected return on this investment over a given period. If market access in some countries is denied to direct exports, the manufacturer may have no alternative but to license local companies to make the product. But there is also a marketing aspect: licensing technology can give the innovating manufacturer market penetration quickly in key country markets when it would take much time and investment to sell direct. From the recipient or licensee's viewpoint, licensing may be an alternative to internal R&D or it may complement and enhance it. Foreign direct investment (FDI) is used where companies transfer the technology abroad by manufacturing in several host countries, selling locally using their subsidiary companies.

This enables the international firm to compete more effectively with local suppliers which have the benefit of local trade contacts and market know-how, and often the indirect support of the host government. FDI is of course part of the long-term global strategy of many MNCs. Indeed, when technology is transferred abroad through FDI, local firms may be involved through the provision of local inputs and services, or through some sort of joint venture with shared equity with host-country firms. The difference is that whereas with FDI transfers take place within the boundaries and under the control of the MNC, though across national frontiers, joint ventures give the MNC less control over technology and management than if it owned 100 per cent of the equity. But the MNC may contribute technology to a jointly-owned venture in return for access to a local partner's distribution network. Sometimes host-government policies encourage joint ventures precisely to promote such transfers of technology to local firms (see Chapter 6 for a fuller analysis of foreign direct investment).

As far as collaboration is concerned, there has been an increasing trend in the

1990s towards global alliances among large companies. These collaborative ventures are sometimes structured as equity joint ventures, extensive licensing arrangements, or as joint R&D projects. In many cases, collaboration comes about so that the technical skills of one firm can be combined with another, or to spread the risks and costs of technological development. In the very process of developing or selling a product jointly, global firms in different home countries effectively transfer technology to each other.

CASE 4.8

Spending-cuts and soaring costs are bringing about technology collaboration and rationalisation in the cross-border European defence industry. The consultancy firm Arthur D. Little has forecast that there will be a 50 per cent cut in the number of European aircraft manufacturers over the next 20 years, and similarly in other defence sectors. Collaborative pan-European funding is vital for main programmes with high development costs. For example, Matra Marconi Space, which includes the satellite business of GEC and Matra, is already in place; as is Messier Dowty, the Anglo-French venture that has created a market leader in aircraft landing gear.

The nature of this technology collaboration is changing from loose programme-specific, short-term ventures to structural, equity-based mergers that facilitate rationalisation, including cuts in duplicated capacity and R&D and the exploitation of regional centres of excellence: these must be capable of competing in world markets with US companies such as Lockheed Martin and developing world-class products.

The problem is that defence is a political industry: governments want to keep capacity for prestige or for strategic reasons. But the Ministry of Defence in the UK and its foreign counterparts are the only customers; defence is vitally important to the UK economy accounting for 7 per cent of GDP, but most governments are now cancelling or cutting defence programmes (or extending existing programmes over a longer period). This has put inexorable pressure on the major players to collaborate, not only in technology but in finance and management systems.

Source: Observer, 6 August 1995.

■ Competing internationally

■ Innovation

The development of new products and new technical processes is clearly critical to the long-term development – indeed, survival – of a company. The process is especially important for firms involved in medium and high-technology products or services. There are a number of different approaches worldwide to technological innovation, and they will be explored in this section.

Innovation policy is often closely linked to and indicative of the strategic intentions and direction of the company, explained earlier in this chapter. To allocate resources for innovation strategically, managers need to define the broad long-term actions, within and across operating divisions, that are necessary to achieve policy objectives. To start with basic principles, the strategies of innovation can be defined in the following terms:

1. *Technology-push innovation.* The momentum for the innovation is derived from a technical development (physical, mechanical and so forth). The innovation is developed to its full potential, and then management searches for sales opportunities and all possible alternative commercial uses for it.
2. *Market-pull innovation.* This type of innovation has been developed to fit a specific market need. The innovation is 'pulled' from the company by the needs of the market: the need is first perceived, and the innovation is then designed to fill that need.

The hazard that management must watch under the first of these is that the company may be tempted to develop what is technically interesting rather than what customers require: a technological innovation can appear to have such a lead internationally that the company is forced to pursue its development. Companies run by scientists or engineers are particularly prone to this hazard because technical elegance is more attractive to such professionals than market potential. Faced with a technological breakthrough, such a company tends to develop too-narrow a technological base to safeguard the competitiveness of the product range.

And the process of innovation is not simple; numerous studies have been carried out in an attempt to gain a better understanding of this important activity. Innovation has been compared to the blades of a pair of scissors. On the one hand it involves the recognition of a need, or more precisely, in economic terms, a potential market; on the other hand, it involves technical knowledge which may be generally available, although new scientific and technological information is often required. As we have seen, in the literature of innovation there are attempts to build a theory predominantly on the aspects of technology-push or market/demand-pull. Some engineers and scientists have stressed the element of original research and invention and have tended to neglect or belittle the market factor. Economists have often stressed the demand side – 'necessity is the mother of invention'. Like the analogous theories of inflation, these approaches may be complementary and not mutually exclusive.

It is not difficult to cite cases which appear to support one or the other theory. With regard to the atomic absorption spectrometer, for example, it was a scientist who envisaged the application, without any initial clear-cut demand from customers. Advocates of demand-pull, on the other hand, tend to cite examples such as synthetic rubber, or the photo-destruction of plastics, where a recognised need supposedly led to the necessary innovations.

And the process of successful innovation has been summarised aptly in an early study:

The idea for an innovation consists of the fusion of a recognised demand and a recognised technical feasibility into a design concept ... if a technical advance alone is considered it may or may not result in a solution from which there will be a demand.

(de Bono, 1978)

What is clear from the many studies on innovation, some of which are cited in this section, is the importance of innovation as the basis for sustaining competitive strength, and the need to ensure very close liaison by management between the marketing function, and the research and development, innovation and design functions. This management task is by no means an easy one in the face of increasing levels of specialisation, larger organisations and rapidly-changing international environments. Some steps that can be taken effectively to manage innovation in this context will be explained shortly.

So the main objective of innovation is to ensure that there is a continuous flow of commercially successful new products or services to meet changing or developing market requirements. This innovative task may produce products of essentially a breakthrough type, improvement of an already existing product, or simply a copy of a competitor's product. The most common innovations are of the second and third type, the second type being commonly referred to in research as process *innovation*.

A very large number of new product ideas never reach the market, and of those that do many are not successful. The criterion for a successful innovation is commercial; that is, it must obtain a worthwhile market share and make a profit. An interesting decay curve of new product ideas is given in Figure 4.8.

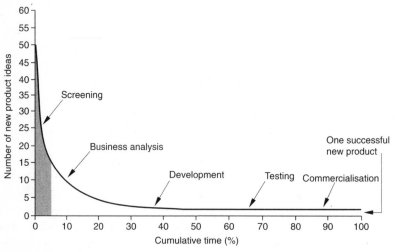

Figure 4.8   Innovation-decay curve and new-product ideas

The percentage decline from product idea to commercialisation is extremely high, and to achieve success a well-managed process of sequential steps is necessary, ranging from the generation of ideas to their commercial implementation.

Case example 4.9 illustrates the importance of the interface between innovation and marketing in competitiveness.

CASE 4.9

Nylon was the first purely synthetic fibre. It was used for making parachutes during World War II. Different applications of nylon – women's stockings, thread, rope, blouses, men's shorts, tyre cord, carpet and furnishing fabrics and so on – were made possible by the ability to process the material in different ways – by circular-knit, warp-knit, broadweave or textured yarns. However, polyester fibre made substantial inroads into these uses, largely because it was more adaptable in producing different finishes.

ICI had two polyesters: Mitrelle (silk finish) and Terinda (suede finish). Up until a major technical breakthrough by ICI Fibres Division in 1982, a number of markets were effectively closed to nylon because other synthetic fibres were more acceptable, particularly in the markets for lingerie (requiring a slinkier silk-like feel) and sportswear (requiring a more fashionable cotton-like feel). ICI has claimed that this technical breakthrough resolved the problem of changing the surface appearance and feel of nylon; it enabled ICI to compete up-market into more profitable price brackets, and to take market share from other synthetic fibres. The new product was first launched in the UK before entering European markets. ICI's Mitrelle was at the top end of the silk market and has sold in relatively low volume. The new silk-nylon does not compete directly with it, but it has enabled ICI to move volume in the quality end of the mass lingerie market. The aim with the easier-to-handle cotton-like nylon is to take sales from cotton in sportswear and skiwear. Because of the strong competitive position of continental manufacturers such as Adidas and Fila, the new product was offered to them first. According to an ICI Divisional Marketing Manager, these developments have in effect resulted in the rediscovery of the importance of marketing in the company's technical production approach.

■ **The role of marketing**

Every innovation in industry requires a combination of technical feasibility and economic demand; but some research has shown that successful innovation rests on marketing organisation and expertise. The Centre for the Study of Industrial Innovation surveyed a total of 53 industrial R&D projects abandoned for non-technical reasons in the electrical, mechanical and chemical industries: the most common cause of failure concerned the nature of the marketing resources of the firm. One of the report's conclusions was that there must be an efficient two-way liaison between R&D department and marketing.

These findings constitute some evidence of a failure by marketing management to involve itself in the research and development process, and by R&D management in understanding the functions of marketing and the potential contribution that can be made to successful innovation.

Innovation studies have stressed the importance of identifying a market need and establishing close coupling between functions, particularly marketing and R&D. Remarkably little attention has been paid to the importance and role of top (strategic) management in the innovation process. This would appear to be a major oversight, since one of the primary tasks of top management has to be the structuring of the company/environmental–product/market relationship. This task has to be carried out through the corporate strategic process, which is essentially a two-stage activity consisting of analysis/planning and implementation/control.

The implications of the foregoing are that, on the basis of high levels of innovation:

1. successful firms compete better and understand user/customer needs better;
2. successful firms ensure better linkage/coupling between specialised areas, particularly between marketing and R&D.

These clearly have significant implications for management in terms of improving a company's competitive position. The particular objectives that need to be achieved by management, can be summarised as follows:

1. Direct linkage of R&D, production and marketing;
2. Planned programmes of innovation related to market opportunities;
3. Effective technological management to contribute towards sharpening the overall competitiveness of the firm;
4. Short, or at least shorter, lead times;
5. Balanced use of scientific and technological resources over all stages of the innovative process.

Objective 4 has particular importance since the problems of long lead times have proved difficult to resolve. It is the commercialisation, the marketing of a new product or process, that provides the international competitive edge: shortening lead times by management can enhance competitiveness only by putting pressure on other suppliers in the market.

■ Characteristics of a successful innovator

It is now widely accepted that firms seeking to manufacture and market high-technology products must invest in R&D or accept that their products and processes will be overtaken by competitors from inside the industry or outside it. There remains one fundamental question, however: what management or policy indicators can be adduced to indicate which firms are likely to be more successful in innovating and competing than others? Some analysts claim that the drive or will of management in setting up an innovation strategy is all-important. Certainly, adopting a consistent, planned and positive competitive strategy is likely to be the foundation for success, as explained earlier in this Chapter. Certainly, too, generalisations about dynamism, teamwork and marketing have only limited value as exhortations to management to become more innovative.

The importance of an analytical study of management organisation and innovation is especially topical and provides a much needed synthesis based on empirical data, that is observed results, as for example Quinn, 1985. This study examined those practices/precepts most commonly found in large companies that successfully innovate, as follows.

1. *Atmosphere and vision.* Management understands innovation and develops the company's value system to support it.
2. *Orientation to the market.* There is a strong commitment to competitive marketing at the top of the company, and mechanisms to ensure interactions between technical and marketing people at lower levels.
3. *Opportunity orientation.* Entrepreneurial and innovative companies recognise that the necessary capital can always be found to exploit and develop good new ideas originated by their staff.
4. *Organising for innovation.* Managers need to think carefully about how innovation fits into their strategy, and to structure their technology, skills resources and organisational commitments accordingly.

Case example 4.10, summarised from this analytical study, amply illustrates how these important points can be put into practice.

CASE 4.10

Intel is a leading US company in semiconductor technology, and it is the declared intention of Intel's management to be the most outstandingly successful innovative company in this industry. Intel met the challenge of the last recession with what the management termed its '20 per cent solution': the professional staff agreed to work one extra day a week to help bring innovations to the marketplace earlier than planned. Despite the difficult times, Intel came out of the recession with several new products ready to sell (it also avoided lay-offs). In supplying highly-technical products to Original Equipment Manufacturers (OEMs), the firm has developed a strong technical sales network to discover and understand customer needs in depth, so as to have technical solutions designed into customers' products. Management has also organised an applied technology group working close to the marketplace and a cutting-edge technology group that allows rapid selection of available technologies.

■ Design

In the analysis of international competitiveness there is increasing awareness of the key contribution to be made by outstanding design. Companies must improve the quality of design in order to compete internationally; indeed, governments are concerned to improve the design of manufactured products by means of techniques known as *industrial design* so that companies can meet increasingly complex technical and other standards in competitive markets. Some standards are subject to international control, such as CENELEC (electro-technical products) and the Union of Agreement Boards (construction materials); also involved in standards are the Comité Européan de Normalisation (CEN) and the International Standards Organisation (ISO), the international harmonising body. There is scope, therefore, for companies to develop designs that meet the specifications of such bodies, as this can provide a basis for competitive access to wider markets. This latter consideration can also apply to the design specifications of national industrial bodies such as the West German DIN and Verband Deutsche Elektronik (VDE), where stringent product standards greatly enhance the value of customers' guarantees of performance and design quality.

This introduction to design, however, raises the question of what exactly is meant by the term industrial design. A detailed and authoritative definition has been produced by the United Nations Industrial Development Organisation (UNIDO):

Industrial design is tightly interwoven with and dependent on the socio-economic context in which it is exercised ... It is concerned with the improvement of usability of industrial products which forms part of the overall quality of a product. From the point of view of industrial design, a product is primarily an object which provides certain services, thus satisfying the needs of the user ... It is concerned with 'formal properties' of industrial products. Formal characteristics refer to the overall appearance of a product, including its three-dimensional configuration, its 'physiognomy', its texture and colour ... It is an innovative activity. It is one special type of technological innovation ... It is concerned with the marketability of the product in that it relates the produce to its market in terms of both raw material supply and product demand.

(Bonsiepe, 1973)

■ Managing the design function

Further analysis is required at this stage to show how, building on an understanding of the design concepts already explained, the total design function of a company can be effectively managed, and can be used as a competitive weapon. Case example 4.11 shows how German management has achieved this.

CASE 4.11

An exhibition of German design, 'Images of Quality', was held recently at the Science Museum, London. The impact of this exhibition was largely to show that design can be used as an economic tool, and not just as a cosmetic exercise. Indeed, the well-known phrase, *Vorsprung durch Technik*, used to promote Audi cars, indicates much about the role of design in German marketing. (Loosely translated, it means 'Advantage gained through doing things the best way'.) One such exhibit was a Messerschmitt-Bolkow-Blohm (MBB) video communications system (combined into a single office furniture module). This enables conferences to take place on a global scale using audio, video and fax transmission. The design brief was that this installation should not 'over-awe the user'; and, as a result, this new package in light-blue and white looks like an ordinary desk with two unobtrusive video screens let into it and a large TV screen placed in front. The overhead document-copying camera is no more obvious than a desk light. The implications of this piece of equipment are clear to the German designers: direct international communication without the stress and delay of long-distance travel. Of course, quality has always been paramount in the way Germans manage design: evolution, rather than revolution, protects German manufacturers from over-rapid obsolescence of their products at the hands of cheaper competitors. This is most clearly illustrated in the design of German cars, notably Mercedes-Benz. The cars exhibit not only quality but a family identity of models that goes back over 30 years. The company produces 600 000 units annually and three-quarters are exported. While substantial engineering improvements take place beneath the skin, vertical homogeneity is expressed in tiny incremental changes to headlamp and tail-light clusters, and to subtle alterations to the body profile which retain the essential character of the car and prevent any single model from suddenly appearing out-dated.

And in managing the design function, expertise not available internally can profitably be used. There are many consumer-goods sectors where the quality of a design (especially its aesthetic quality) is the leading factor in a product's attractiveness and competitive market position. These include:

- textiles, clothing and leather goods;
- ceramics, glassware and cutlery;
- furniture and household furnishings;
- housewares, kitchenware and gift trade items;
- jewellery, silverware and so forth;
- toys and games;
- educational products and paintings.

These sectors are highly competitive internationally, and there is a strong brand element in most of them; moreover, in each sector, the innovation element or originality of design plays a key role in the appeal of the product to the buyer. Mass-production techniques and unique packaging and presentation are of less importance than the design content of the products themselves. In this context, therefore, the management of design involves several discrete, but related, aspects or stages:

1. *Design for distinctness* – the development of innovation design (not necessarily technologically);
2. *Design for production* – to ensure that component parts are made easily and economically in the manufacturing process itself; here, the designer must be aware of the production processes, technology, alternative methods and their costs;
3. *Design for function* – value in use implies quality and reliability (the product must satisfy the customer in its prime function over the expected life period);
4. *Design for aesthetic appeal/appearance* – to appeal to the eye and attract customers;
5. *Design for distribution* – to facilitate easy low-cost packaging, and a reduction of handling and storage space.

Industrial Design
- Aesthetic knowledge
- Social and cultural backgrounds
- Environmental relationships
- Ergonomic requirements
- Visual trends
- Insight into aspects of marketing and production

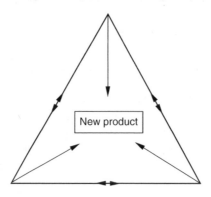

New product

Marketing
- Market research
- Market analysis
- Economics
- Distribution systems
- Promotion

Production
- Technical research
- Technical analysis
- Economic targets
- Production methods
- Ergonomic research

Figure 4.9   Management of design

■ Liaison with production and marketing

In managing these aspects to gain the best possible competitive advantage, the company must ensure that the designer's ideas are merged with those of the production engineer and the marketing department. So design must liaise with:

- production management, to maintain the scheme used for classification and coding; also to review manufacturing methods and investigate component parts proving difficult to manufacture; and
- marketing, to improve standards of finish and design quality; also technical aspects of customer requirements and requests for production improvements.

These linkages in the management of design for development of a new product are illustrated in Figure 4.9.

Case examples 4.12 and 4.13 show how sound management of design, including the use of some outside expertise, can bring about both improved design and market performance. A recent authoritative study (Bruce and Roy, 1991) has drawn attention to this important interface.

CASE 4.12

Allied International Designers (AID) researched a complete redesign for the Ever-Ready Co (now Berec) of a lamp for motorists. The old lamp was a solid square object designed originally to take a square battery. The designers could certainly have restyled that, by changing the colour, altering the handle and so on. The square batteries were not widely available, particularly in overseas markets, and because the lamp itself was bulky it was difficult to keep and was usually damaged by being knocked about in the car boot; also, new foreign products, cheaper and more compact, were beginning to take sales from the manufacturer.

What the designers did first was to redesign the lamp to take ordinary batteries, available everywhere. Second, at the expense of the swivelling beam, they made the lamp flat so that now it can be kept in a glove compartment; as an added attraction, the handle was made to move to form variable legs. Third, they simplified the manufacturing process to attack costs. The old lamp had 72 parts and 49 assembly operations: the new lamp has half the number of parts and only 28 assembly operations. It costs 25 per cent less to make, and even with an improved profit margin it meets the price of comparable products. Sales of the new lamp doubled in the first year and export prospects look bright. Interestingly, the company had already analysed the market before this complete redesign was launched; models were used to test the new proposition, and the company even value-engineered the product before tooling. So management knew how the product had to be positioned when the time came for investment. This is unusual in many engineering firms in the UK where technical staff are expected to develop new products, which production then makes, and only later, at a stage patently too late, are the international marketing staff involved in promotion and selling.

CASE 4.13

As part of the UK government's Funded Consultancy Scheme (FCS) through the Design Council, client companies have received design assistance and expertise ranging from a graphic design for tins, to an independent verification of the design calculation for an aircraft. All such projects must incorporate some contribution to national competitiveness.

One particular company, Servis, called on the help of Concept Development International (part of AID) to create a new style and range-signature for its household laundry appliances. The design brief was to reposition its range to cater to an increasingly fashion-conscious kitchen sector. The group redesigned the facias to tone in with that season's vogue colours, using soft grey with piano-key switches and toning blue lettering. In addition, a new control panel was designed which standardised all contact points across the 11 circuit boards and which allowed a single moulding tool to produce all the switch and control combinations. The benefit of the scheme is that it enables UK manufacturers to exploit market opportunities afforded by good design, to sharpen their competitive edge and to create genuine product value and benefits internationally.

■ Manufacturing

The management of all manufacturing operations (or operations management, as it is otherwise termed) occupies a critical role in maintaining the overall international competitiveness of a company. Many aspects of operations management directly influence this competitiveness, including output prices, labour productivity, cost-effective purchasing and supply, quality assurance, some phases of physical distribution, control of unit costs and efficiency of manufacturing and assembly operations. It is these aspects and their effects on competitiveness that are the subject of this section. Clearly, operations management in all phases has important interfaces with marketing management in servicing international customers cost-effectively and competitively.

These interfaces are sometimes a source of strain in management relationships, and therefore require some brief explanation. If the friction is unresolved it can lead to a deterioration in the company's competitive position. This is because marketing and manufacturing, in seeking to improve departmental efficiencies, can bring about operational conflicts which reduce the company's service to the customer; this point is fully explained below.

Also, the high costs of capital changes in manufacturing processes and the proliferation of automated operations can make it difficult to respond to changing market needs economically and promptly. The quickening obsolescence of many products, combined with the costs of redeploying plant facilities, make manufacturing changes difficult and can lead to declining competitiveness in a company's product/service offer. So managing the interface between marketing and manufacturing become all the more important in maintaining competitiveness. In this aspect of management the following areas require co-operation, but can be sources of potential conflict (Wheelwright and Hayes, 1985):

1. capacity planning and long-range sales forecasting;
2. production scheduling and short-term sales forecasting;
3. delivery, physical distribution and the level of customer service;
4. quality assurance at a competitive cost;
5. breadth of product line and variety reduction;
6. cost-control over operations relating to rapid response and high-quality service to customers;
7. introduction of new products and effective design management;
8. adjunct services such as spare parts, inventory support, installation and repair and the associated field service costs.

Where such conflicts arise, clear and specific corporate policies can go a long way to resolving if not forestalling them. For example, management can have a policy of full line production, emphasising only high-volume items or some other category of products. On the other hand, management can implement a planned programme of value analysis using the expertise of both manufacturing and marketing to improve product quality, to add product value and to sharpen product performance, while at the same time minimising/reducing operating costs. And a recent authoritative study has also drawn attention to the import-ance of the interface between marketing and manufacturing (St John and Hall, 1991).

■ Value analysis

The aim of value analysis is to examine products with the same care and atten-tion that work study has devoted to the activities of people; it is concerned with raw materials, components, work in progress and finished goods, placing the emphasis on the value of the design, and with the objective of reducing costs. The special role of value analysis (VA) in improving the competitiveness of the company's operations is shown in the following aspects:

1. The components of product value which include,

    - the fact that customers with money and unsatisfied wants comprise a market sector;
    - that 'utility' must be provided to such customers, and products must fit the sector;
    - scarcity or exclusivity, reflected in a limited range of high quality;

- total cost to the customer: this is an inverse component of value; given difficulty in attainment, the customer wants to pay the least for overcoming that difficulty;
- the customer's other options – competitors' offers.

The interaction of these components in value analysis is defined as the value of industrial products determined by the special relationship of utility to cost.

2. Identification of function in VA: function is that property of the product which makes it sell, and the most important step in VA is to identify the function of the product. Rarely does a product in international markets have only one function, although there will be a primary one; however, all its functions need to be identified during a VA exercise.

3. Management can also assess the kinds of value that determine the competitiveness of the company's output:

- use value – the price the purchaser will offer in order to ensure that the purpose or function of the product is achieved;
- esteem value – the price that is offered for the product over and above the use value on the basis of competitive advantage (in many cases this goes hand in hand with superior quality);
- exchange value – the conventional purchase price;
- market value – the price the purchaser will offer in the light of the scarcity of the product. Understanding market value helps to avoid reducing cost at the expense of customer acceptance.

Value analysis as a management process is summed up in Figure 4.10.

Clearly, management should seek to build its programmes round the operational strengths of manufacturing; an analysis of international customer segments must go hand in hand with an analysis of the company's manufacturing

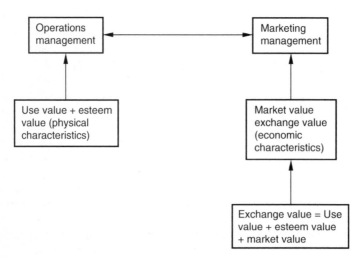

Figure 4.10   Value analysis

capability, so that marketing management understands its competitive strength and constraints. Some recent applications of this concept suggest that productive capacity can and must become more flexible in response to changing market conditions.

1. A modular approach means that the manufacturing function can provide substantial variety to the customer at limited cost by having products designed so that they can be made of interchangeable modules, resulting in greater cost effectiveness.
2. Improved competitiveness can result from managing and refining operations on a more limited scale to precise and quantified sectors of the total market, rather than adapting the volume output of a large plant. One large autoparts manufacturer, for example, committed itself to the construction of small (no more than 500 employees) plants designed around specific customer needs and production technologies.

■ The impact of new technology

The next step is to consider, critically, aspects of the impact of new technology both on manufacturing and on the operational competitiveness of the company. In this connection, Case example 4.14 is based on research at the Industrial Relations Research Unit at Warwick University.

CASE 4.14

Lucas Electrical (LE) drew on module production in order to increase international competitiveness. This is based on the Japanese concept of *Kanban*, and it also involves changing working practices by ending demarcations, and substantial investment in retraining and capital equipment. This research concentrated on one LE plant, BW3, which produces starters and alternators for the automobile industry. The Japanese-based system is a method of just-in-time production, where stocks and work in progress are closely monitored to exactly fit the production schedule – or a service of mini-factories within the factory based on a self-contained team of workers carrying out a complete stage of the production process. This system is intended to increase production and labour flexibility by reducing set-up costs, by reducing the number of defective parts and components by continually checking and controlling quality throughout the production cycle, and by transferring (indirect) work to sub-contractors. This methodology, in effect, replaces mass-produced items with little variety with a large variety of high-quality products in small volume, and it has been successfully introduced with major gains in productivity – up to 50 per cent in one case.

The company has set each business unit a competitiveness achievement plan, and the introduction of Japanese production methods is an integral part of the drive to beat international competitors, and especially to expand beyond the shrinking UK market into worldwide markets. Moreover, these changes have not been confined to the BW3 plant: the pace of change has been accelerating and has encompassed all the company's divisions.

Table 4.3   Stages in manufacturing's strategic role.

	Objective	Action
Stage 1	Minimize manufacturing's negative potential: *internally neutral*	Outside experts called in to make decisions about strategic manufacturing issues
		Internal, detailed, management control systems are the primary means for monitoring manufacturing performance
		Manufacturing is kept flexible and reactive
Stage 2	Achieve parity with competitors: *externally neutral*	Industry practice is followed
		The planning horizon for manufacturing investment decisions is extended to incorporate a single business cycle
		Capital investment is the primary means for catching up with competition or achieving a competitive edge
Stage 3	Provide credible support to the business strategy: *internally supportive*	Manufacturing investments are screened for consistency with the business strategy
		A manufacturing strategy is formulated and pursued
		Longer-term manufacturing developments and trends are addressed systematically
Stage 4	Pursue a manufacturing-base competitive advantage: *externally supportive*	Efforts are made to anticipate the potential of new manufacturing practices and technologies
		Manufacturing is involved up-front in major marketing and engineering decisions (and vice versa)
		Long-range programmes are pursued in order to acquire capabilities in advance of needs

Source: Wheelwright and Hayes (1985).

The above case history highlights the contribution of manufacturing management to improving a firm's competitiveness; indeed, superior overall manufacturing capability is widely argued to be the main factor underlying the commercial strength of Japanese companies. Furthermore, an industrial company's assets tend to be concentrated in capital plant and technical processes and equipment: changes to improve manufacturing, therefore, require investment decisions, and locating new manufacturing plant to maintain competitiveness is the biggest single investment decision a company is likely to have to face. One cited study (Wheelwright and Hayes, 1985), based on extensive research in the US manufacturing industry, argues that in making choices about investments in assets and in planning the manufacturing programme aimed at competitive advantage, management must grasp and act on four principal succeeding stages in manufacturing's strategic role. These stages are shown in Table 4.3.

While at stage 1 production can offer little contribution to a company's market success, by stage 4 it is providing a major source of competitive advantage. Clearly, the resources referred to earlier need to be utilised in a way that is planned to improve production's contribution to marketing. These include systems and quality control, plant and capacity utilisation, labour productivity, procurement and materials handling, physical distribution, process technology (where applicable), human resources (training and motivation), R&D and technical product development. Stage 4 of the table is of particular significance, in that the role of manufacturing is externally supportive in making an important contribution to competitiveness, particularly in process-intensive industries. There is a typology of companies operating at stage 4, which can be given in full:

1. They anticipate the potential of new manufacturing practices and technologies and seek to acquire expertise in them long before their implications are fully apparent.
2. They give sufficient credibility and influence to manufacturing for it to extract the full potential from production-based opportunities.
3. They place emphasis on structural (building and equipment) and infrastructural (management policies) activities as potential sources of continual improvement and competitive advantage.
4. They develop long-range business plans in which manufacturing capabilities are expected to play a meaningful role in securing the company's strategic objectives. By treating the manufacturing function as a strategic resource ... they encourage the interactive development of business, manufacturing and other functional strategies.

(Wheelwright and Hayes, 1985)

■ Conclusions

This chapter has explained how an understanding and analysis of the strategic options facing a company is a prerequisite for management to develop an effective competitive strategy. This requires a proactive approach to markets as opposed to reacting to events and changes. A number of differing strategic options for the company have been discussed: the choice of option clearly depends on many factors such as market opportunities, competitor strength, the company's resources and so on. The importance of understanding and where possible exploiting the experience curve has also been explained; examples of follower and innovator strategies illustrate the applications for management.

Competing internationally requires an understanding of the contributions of innovation, design and manufacturing, and ensuring that there are close and effective links among them; there is a focus too on value analysis and the impact of new technology.

QUESTIONS

1. Explain some company-specific factors which influence the level of innovation in new products or processes.
2. How can design and design management be exploited by companies seeking to penetrate foreign markets?
3. What is the contribution of the manufacturing process to international competitiveness?
4. How can management evaluate strategic options in sharpening the competitiveness of the firm?
5. Differentiate defensive, aggressive and innovative competitive strategies.
6. Compare the concepts of distinctive competence and strategic fit, in applying them to a firm's international position.
7. What are the main processes by which manufacturing companies transfer technologies to foreign markets?
8. Why and how has technology collaboration been adopted in industries worldwide, and in which industries do you see this process accelerating?

CHAPTER 5

Planning for international expansion: the link between strategy and operations

INTRODUCTION

This chapter deals with operational aspects following the consideration of strategic options in Chapter 4. Key criteria for setting and implementing corporate objectives and marketing strategies are discussed, as well as the key issue of how far to globalise operations across country markets. There is an explanation of how, to an extent, the operating or business environment can be influenced by the company. Following coverage of how best to implement strategies, there is a detailed analysis of international marketing planning, the adaptations needed to implement it across country markets, and the organisational requirements to make the plan effective, with a focus on the concept of interactive planning. Acquisitions and divestment policies are then explained and the growth of strategic business alliances is covered in the final section, explaining the factors for both success and failure.

■ **Strategy, environment and marketing planning**

■ **Long-term planning**

International strategy must be designed to meet clear objectives, and the strategic planning process must have regard to the interests of stakeholders such as shareholders, customers, managers and other staff, creditors, suppliers, bankers and distributors. Corporate objectives represent a statement as to what the company will achieve over a known time in terms of asset-management, return on investment, market positions and development of key business sectors in all countries of operation. These objectives must be expressed precisely.

Thus, if the corporate objectives prescribe building market shares(s) the marketing department must plan how to achieve this within the strategy. So the planning process becomes the operational means by which strategy is implemented.

Of course, in all marketing-oriented companies, marketing management will be involved in, and will influence the setting up of, strategy at both corporate and functional levels. This sequence can be described as follows:

- Develop long-term strategy;
- Determine objectives and timing;
- Design and develop plans to meet these objectives;
- Allocate resources for plans, and agree costs;
- Implement plans;
- Control, review progress and amend (within agreed limits);
- Evaluate the effectiveness of plans in implementing strategy.

There are certain key factors that management must take into account in setting and developing marketing strategy in the company's international operations. These include:

1. *Demand* – elasticities of demand; developments in taste, usage patterns and consumption; movement of economic indicators; demand stimulation and forecasting as an integral part of the marketing programme.
2. *Demographic factors* – changes in profile by age, socioeconomic status, population density and geographical locations of new business/industrial zones.
3. *Technology* – impact of microcomputers on purchasing and production methods; reformulation of products and the impact on life-cycles of products of new manufacturing processes.
4. *Competition* – new forms of direct or indirect competition; competitive strengths and weaknesses in product development; creativity in promotion and service provision.
5. *Distribution* – changes in channels and uses of logistics, and changes in customer uses of channels; purchasing and bargaining powers of key sectors of the distribution system.
6. *Finance* – profit implications of alternative marketing strategies; profit improvement projects; high turnover/low profit versus low turnover/high business profit, and the movement of margins; key financial ratios in alternative pricing decisions; control of direct marketing costs.
7. *Environment* – legal, cultural and political codes; standards and the effect of regulatory laws and inspectorates.

So long-term plans, also known as corporate or strategic planning, endeavour to assess future developments in the international environment and the marketing policies required to exploit them.

■ Planning criteria

The long-term plans of the company should be established and appraised on the following criteria:

1. *A precise understanding of the end purpose of the business.* This refers to the ultimate aim of the company, its scope, potential and character. If a company says that it makes breakfast foods, it limits its market; if it says it makes convenience goods, it enlarges its market; if it says it makes foods, it expands its potential still further. What can the company do better than other companies; what has it got, individually, that no other company can copy?
2. *The possession or acquisition of the means by which the company hopes to attain its objectives.* This embraces money, management, production facilities, the distribution system – the international product/service offer. It means above all the recruitment and retention of the right calibre of management at all levels.
3. *The organisation and management structure necessary to achieve company aims.* Of course if the right people have joined the company, the correct organisation and management structure will be developed by them.
4. *The ability to evolve operational controls required by the management.* This means among other things the ability to recognise, isolate and eliminate limiting factors, whatever they may be, in a management situation; limiting factors are usually directly concerned with personnel.

Management must, therefore, postulate its own long-term plans, since each company has its own characteristics. Common to all companies operating internationally, however, should be the following aims:

1. Profit growth to give increased resources for investment in international operations;
2. Increased earnings per share to attract new capital from international sources;
3. A higher, or more successful, achievement of certain management ratios, particularly,

    *   net-profit to net-sales (this indicates the competitive standing of the company and is a most important marketing indicator, especially in relation to competitors if this can be seen from inter-firm comparison figures);

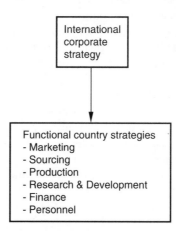

Figure 5.1   Development of strategy

- net-profit to tangible-net-worth (this shows the return of money invested in the business: if the figure is low, it can mean the money is invested in a stagnant or dying industry – what diversification steps should then be considered?);
- turnover rate of capital employed (a slow rate of turnover can mean that the company impact is small, and its penetration of the market weak: too much money has been invested in plant and not enough money in marketing);

4. Growth in sales, and growth in market shares overseas;
5. Growth in reputation and in impact and influence on overseas markets.

Strategy, while essential to future growth, is not enough on its own. It requires:

- programming, so that a commitment to the international operational aspects is assured; and
- an action plan, so that implementation and control are also assured across the spectrum of markets.

■ Globalisation

As international markets have developed, so management has to make policy decisions about the extent to which the company moves towards global marketing, as opposed to differential marketing across countries. Global marketing offers certain benefits such as standardisation of products leading to economies of scale, and better integration and control of industry marketing programmes; but management must also tailor the global marketing concept to fit the particular requirements of a business and its country markets.

Indeed, the policy of minimising country market divisions may not at all be the optimal strategy in many situations. The global marketing approach can pose problems of resourcing cross-country brand promotion and coordination which may not sustain a competitive position on a region-by-region basis.

So the concept of global marketing should not be viewed simply as one end of a spectrum, the other being complete localisation of marketing policy and control. A managerial approach to globalisation can fall anywhere along this spectrum, from full standardisation of marketing communications to a market-by-market programme of differentiated promotion and product adaptation.

Nevertheless, some MNCs view globalisation not just as a concept but as an opportunity: cultural and economic convergences have led to huge and expanding markets for the same or similar products, to new opportunities for economies of scale, and for standardisation of promotion and communications across regional markets.

Companies which find themselves at the forefront of global marketing are those that:

- have products that are similar across national borders;

- pursue highly-coordinated advertising and promotion across countries;
- benefit from scale economies in production, marketing and distribution.

■ Strategy appraisal

Management must, however, recognise that attractiveness of market opportunities overseas varies widely among industries as well as among individual firms: any strategy must therefore take account not only of corporate resources and industry prospects but of differences in levels of industrial activity and economic growth rates of overseas markets. There is also, of course, a wide variation in the capacities of individual firms to exploit foreign markets successfully. In setting up a strategy for international operations, therefore, management must:

1. assess opportunities in international markets for its products and technology as well as the potential risks associated with these opportunities;
2. examine the degree to which the firm can develop potential opportunities abroad in the light of its own organisational and managerial competence.

Where market analysis (explained in Chapter 3) reveals prospects of long-term market development and/or short-term sales opportunities, management must then determine the extent to which the company has the real or potential capacity to capitalise on these opportunities, and must set up the appropriate strategy for doing so. Clearly, this must take account of the fact that in all international operations the managerial task must be performed in diverse economic, cultural, political, technological and legal systems. Distant foreign affiliates must be continuously supported by the financial, technological and human resources of the corporate headquarters.

In the evaluation of alternative strategies, management must also ensure that there is some synergy of marketing, finance, technology and other resources which can be utilised for,

- market entry strategy,
- development of marketing strategy in existing world markets, and
- increasing standardisation of marketing operations on a global basis.

At this stage, therefore, using what we have already learned about marketing strategy, we can say that there are significant features of international strategy:

1. The strategy process is significantly more complex in multi-country markets, requiring a greater number of decision-areas.
2. The significance of assessing the relative cost position of the company's product range compared to that of international competitors and the degree of change possible in product technology and global economies of operation.

In making decisions about marketing strategy, management must set strategic objectives towards which the strategy must be directed. Here is some guidance in appraising corporate market objectives:

- Is there a detailed and up-to-date analysis of which global business or international markets the company is in?
- Are there clear profit and profitability objectives broken down into goals for each major international sector of the business?
- Have corporate growth rates been defined, and is there an optimal rate or size beyond which the company should not expect its international operations to grow?
- Are the corporate objectives practicable, specific, competitively advantageous and quantifiable to assure commitment by management at all levels?

CASE 5.1

Eastman Kodak Co. found its long established dominance in the world photo-graphic industry challenged by strong proactive marketing strategies of Japanese companies, including Fuji, Sony and Sharpe, which have been undercutting Kodak's prices on traditional products while providing quality. These companies have also made inroads into Kodak's market share by bringing out innovative products.

In addition, there has been a fall off in amateur photography (growth down from 13 per cent to 6 per cent in the past two decades) which has been the mainstay of Kodak's business.

Kodak is responding with new marketing strategies that include:

- expansion into new markets with non photographic products
- new emphasis on technological development;
- more aggressive marketing of film and photographic paper products to world-wide markets (particularly Japan, Germany, South-East Asia and the Middle East).

Underpinning these new marketing strategies is a keen understanding by Kodak's management of marketing opportunities and market forces, led by a newly-appointed director of marketing intelligence.

So here is some further guidance in selecting corporate marketing strategies:

- Have the selected strategies been evaluated to ensure their relevance to the global marketplace, the corporate objectives and resources, marketing operations and the international competitive situation?
- Have a company's strategies been checked and integrated into a cohesive approach which can be redefined or extended in the light of changing international conditions?

- Does the company have an effective procedure for considering and determining the corporate marketing direction?

How far a company should pursue global marketing strategy will depend, as we have seen, on a number of product, market and management factors. And, in particular, country factors: the parent company is, for example, likely to become more involved in marketing decisions in countries where performance is poor. But, performance aside, small country markets depend more on head-quarters assistance than large markets. Because a standardised international marketing programme is typically superior in quality to what country managers, even with the benefit of local market knowledge, can develop themselves, it is often successful. Large country markets with strong national managements are sometimes less willing to accept global programmes. Yet it is these country or regional markets that account for most of the company's worldwide investment. To secure their acceptance, the parent company should make global marketing strategies reflect the needs of larger country markets. The small ones are generally more tolerant of deviations from what would be locally appropriate, and are less likely to resist a standardised, global programme.

CASE 5.2

An important objective of Komatsu of Japan, founded in 1921, is to sustain a position as a world-class manufacturer of construction equipment, including bull-dozers, excavators, wheel loaders, dump trucks and motor graders. The company also manufactures industrial machinery such as presses, machine tools and industrial robots, and is rapidly expanding into machinery components including engines and hydraulic equipment. These lines offer promising growth, counteracting intensified competition and slow growth in global construction industry markets.

Komatsu's strategy of sustaining growth by global marketing is based on studying customer needs and strategic marketing to meet new areas of demand by diversification and refinement, particularly new technology, such as the robot press production system developed with Toshiba Corporation.

To achieve the above strategy, Komatsu continually strengthens its global marketing operations, particularly its worldwide sales and service networks, and improves developing products using advanced technology.

■ **Managing the business environment**

In Chapter 3, a full explanation of environmental analysis was given; in the context of strategy as a follow-up to this, management requires guidance as to the extent and feasibility of influencing or even managing the business environment. This is particularly relevant to market access and corporate promotion; it also touches on the proactive role of management in stimulating demand, or at least eliminating or reducing impediments to demand satisfaction.

The American Marketing Association has produced guidelines in implementing options for environmental management with particular emphasis on avoiding loss in host countries:

1. *Independent strategies*

   - Competitive aggression: company exploits a distinctive competence or improves its internal efficiency of resources for competitive advantage, e.g. product differentiation, comparative advertising.
   - Competitive pacification: company takes independent actions to improve relations with competitors for example helping competitors to find raw material.
   - Public relations: company attempts to establish and maintain favourable images in the minds of those making up the environment, for example corporate advertising to opinion-formers.
   - Voluntary action: company tries to manage and becomes committed to various special interest groups, causes and social problems, for example 3M's energy conservation programme.
   - Dependence development: company aims to create or modify relationships with external groups so that they become dependent on the company for example production of critical defence-related commodities, or providing vital information to regulators.
   - Legal action: company engages in private legal battle with competitor or anti-trust, deceptive advertising, trademark infringement or other grounds.
   - Political action: company tries to influence elected representatives to create a more favourable business environment or limit competition, for example corporate constituency programmes, or direct lobbying.
   - Smoothing: company attempts to resolve irregular demand; for example a telephone company lowers weekend rates, or an airline offers inexpensive fares during off-peak times.
   - Demarketing: firm attempts to discourage customers in general or a certain class of customers in particular, on either a temporary or a permanent basis.

2. *Cooperative strategies*

   - Implicit cooperation: firm adopts patterned, predictable and coordinated behaviours, for example price leadership.
   - Contracting: company negotiates an agreement with another group to exchange goods, services, information, patents, and so forth, for example contractual vertical and horizontal marketing systems.
   - Co-optation: firm absorbs new elements into its leadership or policy-making structure as a means of averting threats to its stability or existence, for example consumer representatives, women and bankers on boards of directors.
   - Coalition: two or more groups coalesce and act jointly with respect to some set of issues for some period of time, for example industry associations, or political initiatives of the Business Roundtable.

3.   *Strategic manoeuvring*

- Domain selection: firm enters industries or markets with limited competition or regulation and ample suppliers and customers, or enters high-growth markets, for example IBM's entry into the personal computer market and Miller Brewing Co's entry into the US 'lite' beer market.
- Diversification: company invests in different types of business, manufactures different types of products, integrates vertically or expands geographically to reduce dependence on a single product, service, market or technology.
- Merger and acquisition: two or more firms form a single enterprise or one company gains possession of another, for example the proposed collaboration between British Airways and American Airlines, or Philip Morris's acquisition of Miller Brewing Co.

Given the diverse and rapidly changing conditions overseas and the risks inherent in international ventures, the need for marketing strategy is self-evident: without it there can be no effective marketing planning or control of operations and market tactics.

■ Strategy implementation

There are three distinct stages that management should follow in setting up and implementing its marketing strategy in international markets:

- strategy formulation;
- programming;
- action/implementation.

The following check-list of questions can be used to evaluate the strategy of the company across all its markets:

1.   Is the strategy identifiable, and has it been made clear either in words or in practice?
2.   Does the strategy fully exploit the domestic and international market opportunities?
3.   Is the strategy consistent with corporate competence, resources and products, both present and projected?
4.   Does the strategy contain realistic and specific objectives stating how and when they will be achieved?
5.   Are the major provisions of the strategy and the programme of major policies of which it is comprised internally consistent?
6.   Is the chosen level of risk feasible in economic and personnel terms?
7.   Is the strategy appropriate to the values and aspirations of the key managers?
8.   Is the strategy appropriate to the desired level of contribution to society?
9.   Is the strategy reflected in an appropriate organisational structure?

Often it is the failure to develop long range international objectives, together with an underestimation of difficult and different operating conditions, that can lead to abortive and unprofitable marketing programmes.

CASE 5.3

In a large pharmaceutical firm, senior executives still held the opinion that foreign investment projects were inherently riskier than domestic ones. They therefore favoured domestic investment projects over their international counterparts. Every year the firm's international division was allocated a certain percentage of the total funds available for new investments, so that, according to one senior executive, safer domestic investments did not have to compete against glamorous but riskier international projects. Furthermore, the international division lacked a clear-cut policy to guide allocation of its funding between projects for expanding existing facilities and those for entering new (overseas) markets. Thus, decisions concerning the allocation of corporate resources within the international division were reached primarily through negotiations among various interest groups. One executive, noting the inadequacy of this method, commented: 'We take a great pride in being an international company, but we are far from achieving optimum allocation of resources on a global basis'.

While international marketing operations must be soundly based on strategy and planning, it is the heterogeneous environment in which the firm operates that requires both analysis and responsiveness: it is this environment that typically requires the firm to set its strategy so that, operationally, marketing components such as the communications-mix, the product portfolio and market coverage/concentration are modified for specific regions of the world to achieve the best possible fit. Indeed, the critical distinction between international and domestic operations derives from the fact that the differential international marketing environment makes it likely that some heterogeneous strategies will be required to achieve and hold substantial market shares. Most mistakes that have occurred in international operations derive from,

- the lack of a clear strategy (already discussed), and
- attempts to transport a marketing strategy that proved successful in one country, intact, to another country.

In addition, there are special factors relating to trade barriers which can frustrate the implementation of an international strategy; these barriers directly affect access to markets, and require as much analysis and interpretation as research into demand factors such as sales potential. The options available to management in tackling these environmental factors require analysis. For example, the international company can come to assume increasing control of

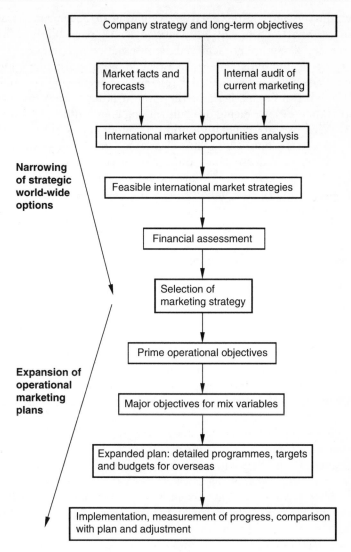

Figure 5.2   The link between strategy and planning

Source: L. Fisher, 'Industrial Marketing' (adapted).

distribution operations as it moves from exporting through joint ventures/ licensing to owning subsidiaries and manufacturing plants overseas. Whether such increased control is worth the higher initial investment costs will depend on such factors as sales potential, market access, the nature of the product, the resources of the company, competitors' policies and, of course, the long-term strategic objectives of the company itself.

The key question to be answered in evaluating management's strategy and operations is: what factors can be identified which particularly influence the level of success likely to be achieved in international operations? One apt research report (Simmonds, 1986) investigated both marketing practice and management attitudes, with particular reference to increasingly-complex international trading conditions. Perhaps the most striking feature to emerge from this report is that, despite facing difficult trading conditions in recent years, top marketing executives are generally optimistic about future business prospects. While any adverse economic climate clearly has major negative impacts on nearly all sectors of industry and commerce, there appear also to have been unexpectedly positive outcomes. Many executives report that improvements in organisational flexibility and market orientation have been generated by recent economic circumstances.

■ International marketing planning

It is at this point that implementing the strategy by marketing planning becomes the priority for management. Earlier in this section the relationships between strategy, planning and programming have been explained.

Now, it is appropriate to consider the planning process as it applies in international operations. The consequences to the firm of a lack of overall planning can be serious. Failure at the planning stage can result in sub-optimum deployment of corporate resources overseas and a consequent loss of the potential benefits of international operations. Lack of planning also frustrates a vital aspect of operations – timing. To exploit market and investment opportunities overseas, the timing of entry, negotiations, promotion and any acquisitions must be judged carefully, in a planned sequence. For instance, unless a firm can plan and time its entry into foreign markets with precision, it may be excluded from certain promising markets permanently because the first firm that undertakes local production overseas can often negotiate with the host government for preferred treatment and special concessions, including a provision to make subsequent entry into the market by competitors extremely difficult, if not impossible. Even without these negotiated benefits, the first entrant can often enjoy decided advantages over competitors because of the need for a long lead time to plan a foreign venture and to build a viable position in the market.

Furthermore, a lack of planning tends to restrict the flexibility of a firm's subsequent operations: initial agreements relating to licensing or exclusive distributorships entered into for short-term sales advantage are often found to seriously hamper subsequent overseas expansion. Some firms have found it impossible to establish their own production facilities in certain markets to take advantage of rapidly growing opportunities because of exclusive agreements made earlier without any planning or examination of the consequences. Second, ill-planned market entry is likely to lead to numerous operating problems after the foreign venture gets under way; lacking a plan to guide its moves overseas, a firm may postpone the decision to enter a given market until the last moment, thereby creating further problems.

All these aspects point to the need for management to initiate and implement the marketing plan as the operational focus for all the overseas markets. And it is logical that the analysis of the planning process should follow both Chapter 3, on research and analysis, and the earlier discussion in this Chapter of strategy and environmental management.

The research function and the planning function are to this extent inseparable. Accordingly, product, consumer, advertising and sales research are prerequisites to the formulation and implementation of the marketing plan, in all its phases of objectives, programming and operations, and in all key sectors of international markets where the company is already active, or is planning entry.

Aspects of the marketing planning process have been illustrated in Figure 5.2.

From the foregoing considerations, the managing director and his top management can now consolidate their objectives and intentions into a plan for action – the profit plan or the marketing programme, or, in more conventional language, the sales budget. Their time framework is, say, two years, with the first year spelled out in detail and the second year in outline terms, dealing with the main features of trading targets and concentrating on new product items and the market growth points.

The first year's plan or programme is an operating document, a tool of management action. Accordingly, it is laid out in relation to the firm's main divisions or departments, with the targets and control standards in line with the delegated centres of responsibility and accountability. Within the divisions, appropriate sub-sections again line up with operating activities, according to accountability for control: the production division does this by listing processing and finishing departments or sections, providing also for stores, packaging and transport; factory services are budgeted in standards of expenditure related to the planned volume of manufacture, and so too is provision for other overheads in supervision and production management. On the sales side, the subdivision is a cross-pattern of territories and product groups, such that each selling team or section knows what volume and turnover targets have been set for it in product-mix and in periods over the year; similarly, sales expenses and overheads are aligned in the budget, and the sales manager has his corresponding programme and budget for publicity and sales promotion. Provision is made for new product development activities, for research and development, and for the overhead expenses of managing and administering the firm, including such special activities as personnel services and the management development programme. All through, costs and expenses are budgeted in terms of standards for the planned pattern of trading activity, so that the variances can be thrown into relief in the control statements. The profit targets feature prominently in the main trading plan, and associated statements forecast the capital requirements and the expected cash flow.

■ The marketing programme

As an instrument of management, the international marketing programme has this same two-way application throughout the firm: it is the basis for briefing through executive instructions, because it sets out the objectives and the targets within a plan of action; and it is the basis of effective control, because it makes possible the comparison of what is actually happening against what was planned. In terms of documents and procedures, the marketing programme is the framework of the management information system by means of which control is attained: the periodic operating and financial statements are the sectional portrayal of what is happening, set against the targets, plans and standards in the programme. This is, perhaps, an argument in favour of the alternative term, the profit plan, which would emphasise the profit objectives towards which the firm is working and in terms of which the plans have been formed. In his periodic control meetings, the managing director uses as his instrument of control the feedback of actual attainment in comparison with the planned targets in the detail of the programme, both ways round: positively, in terms of sales turnover achieved and profits earned, and negatively, in terms of excess cost or expenditure incurred above standards budgeted. Review of performance is thus meaningful, the control of operations is effective, and both are supported by a single integrated management information system. Above all, warning signals can indicate potential dangers, be they in sales trends, advertising effectiveness, adverse price and cost movements, processing deficiencies or cash flow, and in which markets.

But top management must direct the business and provide the resources so that the company's international markets become the touchstone of company policy.

Commitment to marketing by top management means in practice that it has become a marketing-led business. The implications of this have been explained in this section: in short, the company's business begins and ends with the customers. The company must understand their real and perceived needs better than any other companies, and must then set out to serve those needs better than any other companies. The whole organisation should be geared to the achievement of these goals.

So once marketing staff have identified market opportunities overseas, top management's task is to direct the business, long-term, to offering a comprehensive product and service to cover the profitable and growing segments of the world market. Of course, marketing staff must use large-scale data continually to interpret market trends, as described above, as a basis for management action, and must design the marketing plan and subsequently execute that plan accordingly.

Case example 5.4 illustrates an effective approach by management towards marketing planning adopted by a rubber manufacturing company (Kravis and Lipsey, 1971).

CASE 5.4

Marketing plans are prepared annually in a manufacturing supply company, and in recent years have become more closely tied to the company's strategic plan objectives.

Marketing planning is preceded by the establishment of strategic objectives for each marketing division. Senior executives representing marketing, manufacturing and administrative services meet in formal planning sessions to consider progress against past objectives, the changing competitive and business environment within which the company operates, and forecasts relating to markets served. Updated and revised strategic objectives are arrived at, giving consideration to the following:

(a) profitability history of marketing units measured by net profit to sales, manufacturing costs trends and return on investment;
(b) market position history – an assessment of each marketing operation's current share position relative to competitors and progress against share objectives;
(c) long-range market growth prospects;
(d) product cost review – consideration of significant design or process improvement plans;
(e) manufacturing capacity – current and projected.

From these deliberations, strategic objectives are set stating sales growth, market share, and profit goals for each marketing unit. Sales divisions then prepare marketing plans designed to meet the targets stated in the strategic objectives. These plans do not follow a set format, but all include most of the elements listed below. Plans are prepared by the manager directly accountable for the sales operations covered by the plan. They generally include:

(a) a restatement of strategic objectives;
(b) analysis of these objectives' potential effect on future profits;
(c) a presentation of elements of the marketing plan: these vary depending upon the characteristics of the markets for which each sales operation is responsible, but may include:

- training – special training plans for field sales personnel and/or customers
- pricing plans
- identification of target markets or customers: these may be industries or individual accounts where improved sales penetration is required to meet objectives
- field sales programmes – identification of planned advertising and promotional programmes
- promotion programmes – identification of planned advertising and promotional programmes

- product plans, including new products: these include product design changes, product deletions and planned new introductions;

(d) a presentation in greater detail of selected key elements in the marketing plans;

(e) presentation and discussion of next year's sales budget, with some product detail and consideration of its fit to the strategic objective.

Marketing plans are presented in person to senior executives annually. Agendas for these market planning sessions include all marketing units, and are restricted to a consideration of each marketing operation's plan and its fit to strategic objectives. A summary of decisions made and actions required is prepared at the conclusion of the meetings.

■ Adapting the plan

While management has the responsibility of formulating the marketing plan in accordance with agreed, overall strategic objectives of the company, there are some important adaptations, both in management style and in plan implementation, that have to be made to take account of the diversity of conditions found in operating across political boundaries. Further complicating the marketing plan is the multiplicity of different types of marketing organisation that may be used simultaneously by the same international firm. The conventional planning sequence, therefore, used in mainly domestic marketing – resources audit, objective selling, demand and financial analysis, programming operations, review, evaluation and control – while valid in principle, requires differing applications for international operations in order to cope with different levels of uncertainty and diverse operating environments across foreign markets. Some of these special factors in planning for international operations might include the following:

1. *Regional specialisation.* Priorities among major economic regions must be determined in the light of exploitable market opportunities and the firm's own resources to operate globally.
2. *Timing and risk analysis.* Decisions in the plan have to be reached regarding both the timing of market entry to some foreign countries, and the time-scale of operations in other countries where the pay-back periods have to be estimated against some analysis of risks, both commercial and political.
3. *Nature and extent of foreign commitments.* This refers to what is probably the most important aspect of the international marketing plan: management's decision to plan for market concentration versus market-spreading, depending on its assessment of commercial trends and prospects in different regions and the resources of the firm to cover a given number of markets effectively.
4. *Degree of operating flexibility.* In planning the development of the firm's overseas

markets, management must assess the extent to which the firm's designs, product specifications, technical services and brand images should be changed to satisfy the requirements of different markets. This operating flexibility has to be built into the plan so that marketing programmes appropriate to each market can be resourced, implemented, controlled and evaluated effectively.

In incorporating all four of these essential elements into the international plan, management must pay particular attention to an analysis of the foreign operating environment, including an assessment of risk and evaluation of competition, both local and international. The research and analysis in Chapter 3 and these elements must be consolidated as a data-base on which management can construct the plan. Subsequently, in Chapter 8, various modes of market entry and operations will be analysed, and these must be viewed in their totality as the implementation of the plan with the broad objective of developing the firm's overseas business cost-effectively and competitively. The assessment of risk is emphasised because this is an essential part of planning, as opposed to intuitive management, which is still prevalent in many firms (particularly in industrial goods sectors), and which copes with crises and difficulties simply as and when they occur. While not all eventualities (for example retrospective import quotas suddenly imposed by a foreign government) can be foreseen, operational risk assessment can be and should be included in the plan; risks arise from certain inadequacies in indigenous technological and institutional systems, and from the scarcity of essential resources needed for the effective running of an industrial enterprise. While some political risks derive from minor bureaucratic harassment to outright expropriation, economic risks can take the form of unstable currency, poor foreign exchange position, severe inflationary trends or uncertain government economic policy.

The essential point for marketing management is that, with a sufficient data base, many of these risks can be assessed in the plan, and, more importantly, minimised or reduced by action in the plan relating to, for instance, negotiations with government agencies and other organisations prior to market entry, or prior to any major new investment in foreign markets where the firm is already operating. Therefore, while much research has been done on the complexities of international marketing planning, it is clear that these complexities arise mainly because the firm is operating in widely differing commercial environments and is adopting different modes of operation (such as direct exporting, contract manufacturing, and so on) to suit the requirements of foreign markets at differing stages of economic and industrial development.

The overall objectives of the international plan, therefore, must be:

1. To design programmes for national markets in order that the marketing mix will enable the company to adapt to each environment in such a way that its goals are achieved; and
2. To integrate all of these marketing operations into an effective worldwide corporate effort.

■ Interactive planning

There remains the question of whether there is any optimal form of organisation for the setting up and implementation of marketing planning across national markets; in short, who is to do it? Certainly it is arguable that lack of adequate information in many markets, particularly concerning customer motivations and attitudes, makes some marketing planning a subjective task that is best left to those more closely in touch with local consumer needs and trends; one leading analyst (de Bono, 1978) has maintained that because of this, 'responsibility for marketing planning must be carried out by those overseas executives who are most familiar with the local environment'; and, furthermore, in order to facilitate an understanding of locally-prepared marketing plans, headquarters should develop standard definitions and formats of presentation, at the same time supplying local management with important information at the macro-level, such as oil and chemical prices and trends in other world markets. The major advantage of this coordinating role by headquarters is that it enables top management to isolate markets offering opportunities for product and market rationalisation and extension. And the approach itself has been characterised as interactive marketing planning and, as such, superior to either centralised or totally decentralised planning. Headquarters still bears the major responsibility for searching out similar characteristics and unifying influences that provide opportunities for standardising elements of the global marketing plan such as product development and advertising programmes.

An international company planning and operating on this basis has some advantages over a company that allows its national managers complete freedom to plan and exploit their own local environments:

1. Within the global plan, such programme transfers enable a company to exploit successful practices, such as tried and tested promotional ideas, on a wider basis.
2. System transfers, such as planning budgeting and research systems, increase the efficiency of local operations and help top management to understand and react more accurately to the needs of local management.
3. Specialists, particularly in analysis and planning, can be assigned across national boundaries.
4. Headquarters management can ensure that no one national plan or policy will adversely affect another as for example in the case of a large customer who spans more than one market.

The interactive approach to international marketing planning can, therefore, combine inputs from the global and the local perspective, thus achieving a balance that approximates the objective of global optimisation as opposed to national suboptimization.

This interactive approach offers the optimal organisational and operational framework. In theory, headquarters staff would attempt to assess opportunities on the basis of world trends and then to break them down on a country-by-

---

CASE 5.5

In the ITT Corporation, headquarters staff develop plans for 400 operating units in 60 countries by first setting basic quantitative objectives and then reviewing the plans submitted by operating managers. Thus, central management does not make the plans: it merely reviews and coordinates them against basic quantitative parameters, and acts as a resource centre. This method is not without its problems, which arise principally because factors such as financial incentives, free competition, consistency of government policy, management skills, availability of market data and so on vary considerably from country to country.

---

country basis, with an indication of sales and earnings expectations for each. Within the framework of such guidance from headquarters, subsidiaries would then search for programmes that would achieve the specified expectations. These national plans would then be agreed with headquarters and integrated into the country-wide plan. Thus, headquarters would be responsible for strategic planning and would decide what resources to allocate, as well as coordinating and rationalising product design and the advertising, pricing and distribution activities of each subsidiary. The major advantage of this approach is that it recognises not only the major differences in the world's national markets, but also the similarities and common denominators.

The advantages of interactive planning can manifest themselves in the following ways. First, certain marketing information variables can be standardised in order to allow a comparison of performances in the planning process. Second, headquarters staff can present a market study in one country as a result of a similar study in another, or can suggest a new use for a product in one country based on experience in another, or can pass on any kind of useful knowledge gained in comparable markets. Third, a skilful manager with successful experience of problems in one country can assist in formulating plans to tackle similar problems in another market. Fourth, marketing plans and programmes can be tested in various forms in different markets. Finally, cost savings can result from developing intranational promotional programmes and product adaptations; for example, it may be possible to standardise product and promotional programmes for certain similar areas rather than allowing 50 separate developments to take place.

So this concept appears to offer the ideal solution to the problem of planning at headquarters; and the research cited goes some way towards showing that headquarters can play an extremely valuable role in the planning process, and that it is possible to realise synergistic benefits in an integrated international company.

Other important aspects of corporate organisation and management development for international operations are explored in Chapter 7.

Table 5.1   Corporate strategic audit

Setting and using corporate marketing objectives

1. Is there a detailed up-to-date analysis of what business(es) we are in?
2. Are there clear profit and profitability objectives, broken down into goals for each component part of the business?
3. Have growth rates been defined, and is there an optimum rate and/or size beyond which we should not expand?
4. Are the objectives practical, specific, where possible quantitative, timed, competitively advantageous and limited enough to ensure commitment?

Selecting corporate marketing strategies

1. Have the four major categories of strategy – market penetration, market development, product development and diversification – been investigated in turn and thoroughly?
2. Have the selected strategies been evaluated to ensure their relevance to the market-place, the corporate objectives and resources, the marketing activity and the competitive situation?
3. Have our strategies been checked and integrated into a cohesive approach which in turn could lead to a redefinition or extension of our objectives?
4. Do we have an effective mechanism for considering and deciding our corporate marketing direction?

■ Acquisitions and divestment

■ Acquisition policies

There are many different factors that bring about the acquisition of a foreign company; this section is concerned with marketing implications and outcomes of corporate acquisitions policies. The actual acquisition of a company overseas involves of course, the purchase of all or a majority of the shares of that company (otherwise the operation becomes a joint venture).

Any acquisitions policy presupposes that there are, in overseas markets, companies suitable and available for purchase, which is by no means always the case. There may also be further complications: for example, local government regulations and attitudes may make acquisition by a foreign company difficult. Some governments are anxious to develop new manufacturing facilities and technology under local ownership, and therefore may discriminate against foreign firms seeking to acquire local ones. The firm considering entry into a foreign market by acquisition is usually in a weaker position to negotiate with the host government than one planning to establish a new operation there. Indeed, foreign government grants of low-interest loans, tax holidays, tariff protection for infant industries and so on, so often offered to incoming investors in new plant, will not normally be available in the case of acquisition. And the benefit of time-saving sometimes claimed for acquisitions is not universally applicable:

CASE 5.6

Electrolux of Sweden, one of the first companies in the world to market vacuum cleaners, pursued its early international expansion largely to gain economies of scale through additional sales. The Swedish market was simply too small to absorb fixed costs as much as the home markets for competitive firms in larger countries. When additional sales were not possible by direct exporting, Electrolux was still able to gain certain scale economies through the establishment of foreign production (spreading R&D and other costs over additional sales and concentrating on standardised production). Electrolux has substantially expanded international operations by policies of investments and divestment. For example, US subsidiaries were sold-off in the 1960s, but Electrolux re-entered the US market in 1974 by purchasing National Union Electric (which manufactures Eureka vacuum cleaners). Since then, the company has expanded largely by acquiring firms whose product lines differed from those of Electrolux (to add appliance lines to complement those developed internally). Among 50 acquisitions made by Electrolux have been Facit (another Swedish firm, which already had extensive foreign sales and facilities), and (to gain captive sales for vacuum cleaners) cleaning service firms in France and the USA; in addition, Electrolux invested in Arthur Martin (French kitchen equipment manufacturer), Therma (Swiss home appliance firm) and Tappan (US cooking equipment manufacturer).

These acquisitions mostly involved firms that produced complementary lines (to enable the new parent to gain certain scale economies). However, not all the products of acquired firms were related, and Electrolux accordingly sought to sell-off unrelated business. In 1978, for example, a Swedish firm, Husqvarna, was bought because of its kitchen equipment lines. Electrolux was able to divest itself of Husqvarna's motorcycle line, but could not obtain a satisfactory price for the chain-saw facility; reconciled to being in the chain-saw business, Electrolux management then acquired chain-saw manufacturers in Canada and Norway (thus becoming, by investment, one of the world's largest chain-saw producers).

In recent years, Electrolux has announced a takeover of $175 million for Granges, Sweden's leading metal producer and fabricator, with 50 per cent of its sales of $1.2 billion outside Sweden; this has opened up the possibility of integrating Granges's aluminium, copper, plastics and other materials into Electrolux's production of appliances. It has also acquired Zanussi, the Italian electrical appliance manufacturer, giving Electrolux a dominant position in the European industry, but it has required substantial rationalisation of products and brands and manufacturing plants.

location and evaluation of potential candidates for acquisition are often time-consuming processes, and negotiations may extend over lengthy periods.

In particular, the broadening of the company's trading base, the search for synergy by acquisitions in new sectors, the need to find higher-growth sectors of business and the continuing drive to improve overall corporate profitability all have to be appraised on a multi-country basis. Analysis of such acquisitions reveals a situation in which policies are typically pursued by companies for a variety of reasons.

Some companies have a policy of seeking to invest in one or two medium-to-large strategically strong businesses to act as the core around which a new portfolio will be built. The current businesses are run down or sold off gradually over time, and further acquisitions or new ventures are added to the new strong core. The ultimate goal here is to change the nature of the company through investment acquisitions (that is, acquisitions made primarily on the basis of the financial potential of the stand-alone business). For successful implementation of such a policy, the typical situation would be a target company with fundamental strengths (high market share in certain key market segments, or highly differentiated products) which has shown poor performance often owing to extremely difficult market conditions. So where there is clear scope for improving operating effectiveness, the new parent company will also carry through divestment of marginal parts of the business, thus accelerating improvement in performance. If this is coupled with a recovery in key markets, the results can be dramatic. The problem that often arises is that companies with portfolios like the one described often do not have the resources to acquire a very large, successful business, let alone a series of them.

■ Strategic factors

The motivations behind international acquisitions can originate not only in the host country, but also in the parent, or source, country. These can be positive push factors or negative ones. Among the positive factors can be the desire to diversify risk by having earnings in a variety of foreign currencies, or the need to exploit particular strengths abroad which the firm has built up at home. In certain circumstances, the firm may have under-utilised resources which can be used at very low cost abroad and can earn a reasonable return. Examples of this may arise when internationally-skilled managers can be moved away from routine operations to managing the start, or growth, of foreign ventures recently acquired.

However, the principal strategic advantage of acquisition by total ownership is that it assures greater managerial control over a foreign firm than is possible under a joint venture arrangement. The acquiring firm can implement its own policy and standards in such key areas as financial management, product quality, selection of managerial personnel and the disposition of profit. So with total ownership, the basic conflicts of interest sometimes found in joint ventures are avoided. There are three further substantial operating benefits accruing to the acquiring company:

1. market entry and revenue earning are immediate;
2. the purchase price includes not only the production facilities but also an established marketing and distribution organisation, market knowledge and contacts, and some experienced local staff; and
3. the cash requirement for the purchase may be minimal, and it may be possible to issue shares in payment.
4. control of brand(s) with international sales

So an acquisitions policy can bring about timely entry into a market where sales potential can be exploited quickly through the established trade contacts and channels of the acquired company. By contrast, if the firm seeking a presence in the market were to initiate its own venture, a year or two of intensive development effort would generally be necessary before the affiliate/associate company became fully productive. Through acquisition, however, the investing firm can take advantage of managerial talents, technical resources, trade contacts and the labour force of the acquired company, thus avoiding some of the major difficulties of starting a foreign venture. The acquiring firm can also benefit from the sales network and goodwill among distributors and major customers cultivated by the acquired firm during many years of trading. Acquisition can also reduce high risks usually associated with foreign ventures, because the acquired firm possesses a familiarity with the particular industrial environment and competitive conditions in the market.

While there are, therefore, both constraints and benefits in embarking on an acquisitions policy, it is really up to the management of the company to determine what its policy is towards the ownership of foreign ventures/enterprises. Such a policy can be set up only on the basis of:

1. A comprehensive market data- base on which management can plan priorities in terms of overseas market entry through acquisition and the market potential; and
2. The determination of a set of marketing criteria and objectives by which investment decisions, operations and pay-back can be assessed in the light of demand, market access and long-term market development.

Of course, the complexities of international business often frustrate the best-laid marketing plans, but it is arguable that if the factors in (1) and (2) above do not measure up to the profit, sales and other criteria of the investing company in particular overseas markets, these should be bypassed in favour of those that do. Sometimes obstacles to trade make access to a promising overseas market practically impossible (for example duties making the landed price hopelessly uncompetitive) unless some sort of direct acquisition is undertaken. This operating difficulty is well illustrated in Case example 5.7.

CASE 5.7

IMI, the engineering group, is expanding its European plumbing and heating business with the DM300 million (£130 million) purchase of Heimeier, Germany's largest maker of thermostatic radiator valves.

The acquisition is being financed in part by the placing of 16 million IMI shares with investors at 298p per share to raise £47 million.

The German company had sales of DM209 million in 1994 and made operating profits of DM61 million. The acquisition, subject to approval by Germany's cartel office, will raise the turnover of IMI's building products division by a quarter, and IMI said that the deal would enhance earnings per share in the year to December 1996. News of the German deal follows the announcement this month of the closure of parts of IMI's titanium business at a cost of £20 million in the current year. IMI is already one of the larger manufacturers in Europe of copper tube and fittings for plumbing and heating, with factories in UK, Germany, France and Hungary. Gary Allen, chief executive, said that Heimeier brought with it modern plant and a low cost base. His plan is to expand the geographic base of Heimeier's sales by using IMI's distribution muscle to sell the German company's valve and thermostatic control products in the UK and elsewhere in Europe.

Heimeier sells 85 per cent of its product in Germany where legislation requires individual room temperature control in central heating systems. The legislation has proved a boon to the company's sales and IMI hopes similar legislation in the UK for new housing will provide a growing export market for Heimeier.

Source: The Times, 16 July 1995.

■ **Applying key criteria**

In the situation described in the last Case example, the company found itself in the position of having to resort to an acquisition in order to gain a market position in a particular country. There are, of course, many other applications of acquisitions policies, and it is important at this point to show how the management of an investing company should adapt these policies to serve distinct and commercially viable marketing objectives. Some of the significant criteria for management to apply include:

1. To secure the supply and/or improve the cost-effectiveness of procurement overseas (this has been a favoured policy in the UK wine trade among brewing, wine and hotel conglomerates seeking to control their supplies to UK and export markets by buying up wine properties and companies in France).
2. To acquire a manufacturing, processing or assembly plant in a potentially lucrative overseas market that would otherwise be difficult to service profitably or competitively owing to tariffs, quotas and other restrictions.

3. To obtain control of trade and distribution networks both within a particular market and among adjacent markets within an economically integrated region.

4. To buy out (that is eliminate) a competitor who, as a local supplier, has been taking out substantial business in an overseas market which it would otherwise be impossible for the acquiring company to obtain;

5. To secure complementarity of product range, service offers or technology (acquisition can offer a faster route to extending the product/service offer than investment in new plant or new product development to meet special requirements of some overseas markets).

6. To benefit from the goodwill, trade contacts, local expertise and promotional investment already available in a suitable acquired firm, rather than incur high initial costs of market development and heavy use of communications and media.

7. To use liquidity to secure the assets of an overseas company with a view to increasing the net international worth of the business, thereby strengthening the financial base and becoming a more attractive company for investors; there are also often tax advantages to be considered.

8. To apply an acquisitions policy on an international scale in order to reshape the business and move into new, high-growth sectors, in countries where it would otherwise mean massive expenditures and management time to set up new businesses.

9. To achieve a level of expertise and strength in managerial resources, and in technology, so that the group of companies thus formed or acquired can dominate or compete profitably in highly industrialised economies and in high-growth industries. The Hanson Group, for example, scrutinises and evaluates managerial performance and effectiveness in public companies in basic industries such as food and building materials. Where it identifies under-performance, under-utilisation of assets, deteriorating financial ratios, failure to grow with the market and/or stagnation of business policies, it will acquire these companies, put in more effective management, and sell off those parts in intensely price-competitive markets – all this in the expectation of increasing the net worth of the business.

As far as intensity of R&D operations is concerned, the important point is that the higher the technology on which the firm bases its asset, the higher is buyer-uncertainty and the more difficult it is to exploit the asset by means of ordinary market transactions; so the theory predicts that foreign direct investment by acquisition will be the usual strategy in technology-intensive firms. As for the degrees of integration/diversification, the latter is interpreted mostly as entry into new and little-known activities; and some research into this aspect clearly indicates that the more remote the new activities are, the greater the uncertainty and the more likely the firm is to pay for the greater security of market entry by acquisition (Boddewyn, 1983). A firm that follows a pronounced diversification strategy, therefore, will show a greater propensity to use acquisition as an expanding strategy than will other firms. This tendency will be stronger the more the diversification strategy means going into areas unknown to the firm, whether these areas are in the home market or abroad.

Of course, much depends on the extent of diversification achieved. It is

Candidates' attractiveness (quantified)

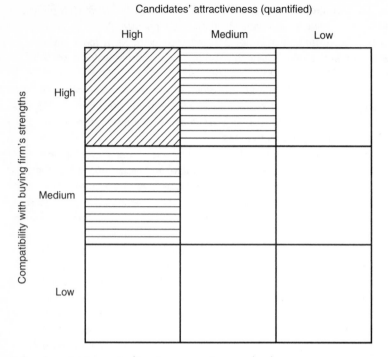

Figure 5.3   Acquisition – indicative screening method

Note: In this portfolio-management matrix for the screening of candidates, the diagonally hatched area indicates a prime target, and horizontally hatched areas indicate secondary targets; blank areas should be ignored.
Source: Majaro (1980) *Marketing in Perspective.*

arguable that repeated diversification by going into a new activity or a new country will decline the more diversified the firm already is, because there is an upper limit to the number of business areas that the firm can acquire.

It is the effective managing of both inter-firm relationships with suppliers, customers and so on, and the intra-firm relationships, particularly in the acquired company, that will determine the long-term success of acquisitions policies. And advantages associated with taking over an existing organisation and managerial personnel can, in part, be offset by the problems of integrating the acquired firm and its management personnel into the parent organisation. This process of integration is complicated by basic differences in managerial philosophy and orientation arising from cultural and environmental variations, and the climate of insecurity often found in acquired firms.

Case example 5.8 shows how a recent foreign investment was made both to strengthen market position in the USA and to achieve synergy in the newly-formed organisation.

CASE 5.8

The purchase by Unilever in the USA of Chesebrough-Ponds (CP) in 1986 for $3.1 billion came at a time when Unilever's US food business was thriving on its success in margarine, and its household products division was holding up well against rival Procter & Gamble. The significance of this investment is that Unilever's health, beauty and cosmetics interests can benefit substantially from the strong product and market positions which come with CP's renowned brands like Vaseline, Cutex and Q-tips. So there is a synergistic aspect to this investment. Also, the extra profitability of the new group is expected to fund a large new product development programme, and more than treble Unilever's health and beauty sales in the USA. CP will bring a heightened profile in US drugstores and supermarket personal care departments; also, its profitable packaged food division fits neatly into Unilever's branded foodstuffs business. The best fit of all is the skin-care market. Unilever's success with skin-care products like Fair and Lovely in India, and Dawn in South Africa, can now be complemented by the relative strength of CP's Vaseline brand (including Vaseline Intensive Care) in the USA and other Western markets. Application of the Vaseline brand to new products will also be considered; but, given the known difficulties of promoting internal growth in Unilever's weakest areas, the best option may be further acquisition.

At the same time, there has been divestment of businesses that do not fit the group's refined core-operations policy. Accordingly, much of CP's chemicals division will be sold-off, and footwear and sporting goods interests will also be disposed of.

CASE 5.9

US General Motors Corporation (GM) acquired Electronic Data Systems (EDS), a small competitor in the emerging robotics/production control industry. GM has gone to great lengths to maintain the strategic independence of EDS treating it purely as an investment acquisition, while at the same time providing it with major strategic advantages. GM created a special class of common shares to maintain the entrepreneurial spirit and incentive schemes for EDS's management. Thus, it is attempting to shield the flexible management style necessary to high-tech competition from the more entrenched traditions of Detroit. At the same time, GM's management intends to develop a communications standard for all computer-controlled production equipment to be used in GM facilities worldwide. EDS is expected to have a substantial share of that market, and thus will maintain its strategic independence while attaining enormous strategic advantage through market share expansion.

■ Divestment policy

CASE 5.10

The Exxon Co. of the USA invested heavily in establishing itself in the office equipment market. The motivation behind this investment programme arose out of the position of Exxon. The world's largest company found itself in markets that were generally stagnant or declining. Management felt a need to establish a position in high-growth areas, and an area that promised dramatic growth was the 'office of the future'. During the second half of the 1970s, Exxon acquired a number of small to medium-sized office equipment suppliers, many of which were reasonably profitable. The attempt to weld them into Exxon Office Systems immediately gave them a very high profile, and brought them into out-and-out competition with industry giants like Xerox and IBM. Even the formidable financial strength of Exxon could not offset the strategic disadvantages; late in 1984, Exxon announced a major write-down of its investment, and divestment of its office systems interests followed.

CASE 5.11

From 1990 to 1995 German companies have acquired British companies and property assets approaching £10 billion; in 1994 this process accelerated with Rover's purchase by BMW, and BASF Pharma's takeover of Boots' drugs division. In 1994, German companies paid a combined £2.6 billion for a dozen British firms. Only £1.2 billion had been spent on about 40 acquisitions in the previous two years. On top of these acquisitions there have been some significant joint ventures including Vickers link with BMW in 1995 for Rolls Royce car engine development and a deal in fibres between Hoesch and Courtaulds.

There are many reason why the Germans buy British:

- Japan's Toyota and Nissan and Korea's Samsung have shown that the UK is a good place in which to make things. In the marketplace German firms face competition from the products of Japanese and other foreign-owned UK plants.
- Having opted out of the European Union's Social Chapter, the UK has low unit labour costs.
- UK labour relations are among the best in Europe with fewer strikes than in most other EU countries.
- After Frankfurt was chosen as the venue for the planned European Central Bank, its big banks have felt free to locate their investment banks in London rather than in Germany. And Deutsche Bank last year decided to move its investment bank head office to London. Other big German banks are likely to follow; they recognise that London remains Europe's financial centre.

- British companies are easy to buy relative to companies in other parts of Europe. Boards of directors are more inclined to act in shareholders' interests.
- Anglo Saxon-style public companies and accounting standards mean more British companies are available to buy. There were almost as many new issues in London in 1995 as the total of German listed companies.

German businessmen have seen that they need to operate closer to their markets if they wish to build global companies. They can no longer rely solely on exports to ensure growth. And English is the second language of educated Germans and the language of the global business community. It makes Britain, with its long international trading traditions, an obvious choice for such transplant operations.

German takeovers in the UK have focused on areas such as financial services, pharmaceuticals, chemicals, motors, engineering and electronics where the pressure for rationalisation into fewer genuinely global players is intensifying.

Germans have also made inroads into financial services in recognition of the City's unique role. Germans own three merchant banks, Morgan Grenfell, the old Standard Chartered Merchant Bank and Charterhouse. In addition they have bought Thomas Cook, bullion dealer Sharps Pixley and half of fund manager Foreign & Colonial. German banks have to decide whether they want to go the consumer route like Citibank or move towards investment banking, as Deutsche Bank has done. If they choose the latter, they have to go either to the United States or the UK. Such acquisitions are not easy to integrate so it is probably better to do it closer to home.

The key driver behind the German invasion is specific industry logic rather than macro-economic factors. The industry pressures to consolidate in pharmaceuticals, chemicals, banking and maybe automotive suppliers are the real determinants of such corporate activity.

There are, however, situations in which investments in acquisitions or alliances fail to bring about the financial benefits and market dominance that management planned in the first place. Such an outcome is often followed by divestment. Sometimes the new parent company insists on rapid cash pay-back on its investment, thus weakening the long-term competitive position of the acquired business by preventing it from keeping up with growth in existing market sector(s). Alternatively, the new parent sometimes presses for growth from its newly-acquired business, generating high profits: the acquisition can then weaken its own market boundaries, sometimes moving from a dominant position in a sector to a weak position in the total market.

An investment policy also depends for its success on a realistic and up-to-date reading of the company being bought, particularly its competitive position *vis-à-vis* its market sector, and in the total market. For instance, the acquiring company must be alert to what may appear to be a dominant competitor in a market segment in reality being a weak competitor that has produced above-average performance by concentrating on those customers whom the truly dominant competitors have ignored. If that customer group were to continue to grow, or if growth in the overall market were to slow down, the truly dominant competitors would turn their attention to the neglected customer group. Profitability of the investment would fall precipitously, and divestment would almost certainly have to follow.

Foreign divestment can be voluntary, and consist of the closure or sale of all or a major part of an operation, or it may be involuntary. When the company is sold as a going-concern, and the assets and employment level remain more or less unchanged, the national authorities of the host country are likely to be more cooperative than in the case of a partial or full liquidation. Involuntary divestments such as nationalisations or expropriations, although they regularly capture the headlines, actually represent less than 5 per cent of all cases of voluntary and involuntary cases of divestment taken together. The distinction between voluntary and involuntary divestment is not always clearcut. The fade-out arrangements within the Latin American Common Market are an example. Although the foreign investor's participation in the subsidiary will be gradually diminished, the divestment occurs during a predetermined period about which one is normally informed in advance. There are also passive divestment strategies by which companies do not renew some of their past investments, or proceed to gradual lay-offs over a period of time; government measures about mass dismissals or collective lay-offs are intended to expose such policies, however.

Although it is likely that the relative proportion of divested ventures has somewhat stabilised, divestments are no longer regarded as accidents but have become a normal part of multinational business life. Management should have a clear policy in order to be able to deal with the internal organisational problems which result from divestment and to be able to cope with reactions from trade unions and host governments.

The generally expressed fear that in times of economic downturn MNCs fall back upon their home-country operations and are inclined to close down their subsidiaries in the host countries has not been confirmed in studies by the International Labour Office (ILO), which found that there appears to be no significant differences as regards divestment behaviour between exclusively domestically operating firms and MNCs or between European and American multinationals.

■ Contributory factors

Some other results from studies about divestment patterns and behaviour of MNCs are that:

1. Divestments occur more often in industries with a high level of competition, or more precisely in the so-called mature industries where technology has become more readily available and economies of scale have become less of a barrier to entry for new companies.

2. Divestments are more frequent in developed than in developing countries, mainly because,

   • new entrants will typically succeed in penetrating the mature industries first in the industrialised countries, and
   • potential buyers are relatively more present within developed countries.

3. In a very high proportion of the studied cases divestment consisted of the complete elimination of the subsidiary; this may be related however to the lack of information about partial and passive divestment:

4. A relatively limited number of companies were responsible for a high proportion of divestment cases.

For voluntary divestments it is to some extent possible to distinguish between offensive strategic decisions and defensive measures. The first group implies that a particular foreign subsidiary does not fit within the corporate strategy. In order to rationalise its global operations, the parent company may decide to disinvest on a selective basis those subsidiaries which tend to operate on the periphery of the corporate system and have few links with the rest of the group.

According to some studies, about one-quarter to one third of divestments actually were bad acquisitions, as they were based on poor pre-investment analyses or shortcomings in the original investment decision or acquisition process. A number of MNCs expanded too fast abroad and overextended their international division. This resulted in a lack of managerial fit and bad communications between the parent company and the subsidiary – and ultimately led to corrective action in the form of divestment.

A second group of divestment reasons are of a more defensive nature. Low profitability and losses are at the basis of most divestment decisions. Unprofitable ventures in a particular country are not to be discarded automatically, however, as they may be justified if they reduce the risk or increase the global yield of the corporate group as a whole. Divestment decisions are often linked with adverse changes in the environmental or external situation. Increased production costs because of rises in the price of energy, of raw materials or of labour may force a company to rearrange its operations on a global scale. Policy measures which make it difficult to transfer funds abroad or to borrow locally, and national policies which tend to favour indigenous firms, may also lead to divestment decisions.

Changing competitive situations, due for example to a relative decline in technological advance, often result in divestments by multinational corporations. The product life-cycle model may have some validity here. As products lose their competitive strengths and subsidiaries are approaching the decline stage of their product cycle, divestment may be the inevitable outcome, unless the parent company decides to introduce new products. This means that divestment does not necessarily imply management failure but can be seen as a stage of international business life.

CASE 5.12

Alcan, the Canadian aluminium company, plans to sell its non-core businesses in Britain, which have about 4200 employees and assets of almost £200 million. The sale represents the biggest opportunity in years to gain broad exposure to a wide variety of fabricated aluminum products, from household foil for cooking to aviation plate.

Alcan wants to sell the 12 companies in its downstream portfolio to a single buyer. A quick sale would enable it to take advantage of fairly strong demand and the long-awaited recovery in prices. A tonne of aluminium is now worth about $1800 compared with last year's price of $1200 or less. The companies up for auction block have combined annual sales of £400 million and trade from 35 locations in Britain, one in Ireland and seven in America. They include Alcan Consumer Products, the market leader in household foil, Luxfer Gas Cylinders, which makes high-pressure gas cylinders, Baco Contracts, an aluminium structures contractor, and Alcan Plate, a maker of alloy plate for the defence industry. The portfolio is said to be profitable, though industry experts think that it was likely that it lost money during the recession. British Alcan, which includes the larger smelting, rolling and chemicals operations, reported a pre-tax profit of £31 million in 1994 compared with a loss of £22.7 million the year before.

The sale comes as no surprise. In late 1993, Alcan announced that it would concentrate on its core 'up-stream' business – bauxite refining, smelting and manufacturing rolled products such as thin aluminium for beverage cans and cars.

Since then it has sold operations around the world, including Alcan Australia and a variety of building products, extrusion and distribution companies in North America. Charles Belbin, a company spokesman in Montreal, said: 'The United Kingdom companies are not in keeping with our new strategy of focusing on our core business'. When the sale is completed, British Alcan will consist of Alcan Smelting, which has three smelters, Alcan Rolled Products and Alcan Chemicals Europe. The group has 2800 employees and a turnover of £450 million. The sale will not affect Alcan's research centre in Banbury.

Source: Financial Times in 1995.

■ The role of subsidiaries

In order to be informed about the performance of their subsidiaries, companies need to develop a continuous evaluation process and control system. This implies that an operational description of the objectives of the subsidiaries is necessary. A central planning group should review operations not only on the basis of long term profit prospects but also in terms of management resources and the comparative industrial performance of the individual subsidiaries (life-cycle analysis). This corporate planning group should report directly to top management at the level of the group. If the discrepancy between the stated realistic objectives and the performance becomes too large, the subsidiary becomes a divestment candidate and a more detailed analysis should be under-taken. Before an eventual rescue attempt is started, the company should investi-gate the chances of turning around a bad situation without unduly straining the resources of the group. Subsidiaries will typically ask for additional resources to solve their problems or try to minimise them.

A suggestion to initiate a divestment study seldom originates with the sub-sidiary manager or the division president. The initiating force of the divestment decision is practically always located at the highest management level in the parent company. In most cases it is the president, the managing director, or the head of international operations who first suggests the possibility of the demise of a subsidiary from the group. The board of directors normally only gets involved at some later stage of the process.

When the divestment of a subsidiary is considered, the first question to be asked is how the value of the continued operation of the subsidiary (expressed in cash-flows) compares with its liquidation or sale value. The company must take into account the expected future profitability of its operation, the impact of foreign exchange fluctuations, and the policy measures of the host govern-ments, in order to estimate the expected future operating cash-flows. The amount of depreciation and other non-cash expenses and the eventual need for additional investments to continue operations should also be considered. When the cash-flows are discontinued at the marginal cost of capital they indicate the present value of the cash-flows of the subsidiary to the parent company. If this present value of the cash-flows of the subsidiary is lower than the divestment value, that is the proceeds provided by liquidation or sale of the subsidiary, the unit should be abandoned, unless other considerations receive priority. These cash-flow calculations should be carried out at on after-tax basis.

A complicating factor for this analysis is that the cash-flows in associated companies should also be taken into account. The liquidation of a subsidiary may decrease the total sales of the group over and above the sales of the sub-sidiary itself, especially if its production was complementary to other sub-sidiaries of the group or if there are shared marketing or distribution facilities. The divestment of a subsidiary may not necessarily decrease overheads or fixed costs for the other subsidiaries either, and it is likely to increase them for the other companies in the group. When, in cases of intra-group trade, transfer pricing favoured other companies of the group, the difference between the applied transfer price and the market price should be added to the future receipts of the subsidiary. To the extent that assets are specific to the MNC and the operations are highly integrated, the divestment value to potential buyers will be lowered. If the calculation of the discounted cash flows point towards divestment, top management must have good reasons to ignore these hard facts.

■ Implementation

The two main forms of implementing divestment are sale of the equity or closure of the operation. In both cases it is possible to go all the way (which means a full sale of the equity or closure of a division or product line), or part of the way (partial sale of the equity or closure of a division or product line). A recent UN Report (1994) 'Transnational Corporations in World Development' showed that out of 66 cases of voluntary divestment, a sale occurred one-and-a-half times as often as a liquidation, while full sales were about four times as frequent as partial ones. And in dealing with subsidiaries, this study noted that 63 per cent, or almost two-thirds, were divested by means of a sale. One-third were liquidations, and only 4 per cent were expropriations.

It is theoretically possible to sell a foreign subsidiary to competitors (both local firms or other foreign companies), to the local government, to the public, or to the workers. A sale as compared with a liquidation has the important advantage that it avoids or minimises social conflict. A sale to a local competitor may be preferred by those host governments which try to develop a national industrial policy. To increase the chances of a sale, local and international investment bankers should be asked to participate in the search for an interested buyer. The local government sometimes helps in the search for a possible buyer if a large number of jobs are involved.

As far as involuntary divestments are concerned, in theory no foreign subsidiary is safe from the nationalisation programmes (even in developed countries) or from expropriations. In most cases compensation will be paid by the expropriating countries. Many developing countries insist on domestication or indigenisation of their economies, and have set up total or partial fade-out formulas (for example the Andean Common Market).

In order to limit expropriation risk, some companies enter joint-venture arrangements with local partners or the local government. However, joint ventures may also be a prelude to forced divestment. Subsidiaries which are integrated with the rest of the multinational group and have achieved a technological advance, generally run less risk of being expropriated.

All major investor countries have created insurance programmes which allow companies to insure against expropriation or the inability to repatriate profits (for example the Export Credits Guarantee Department in the UK). Some countries have negotiated bilateral investment agreements with the governments of host countries which protect their investments and provide for an arbitration procedure.

So foreign divestment is certainly not a passing phenomenon. It is not necessarily the result of management failure, and can be regarded as the terminal stage in the development of a foreign subsidiary. When a subsidiary is faltering, its long-term prospects should be evaluated before a costly and ill-prepared rescue operation is set up. If the analysis points towards divestment it may be useful to carry out some changes in management and form a special divestment team to look after the implementation of the divestment in order to minimise side-effects and leave future options open. National governments and international organisations are increasingly intervening in the divestment process by obliging MNCs to notify their plans in advance and to enter into prior consultations and negotiations with workers' representatives. It is a real challenge to try to achieve a divestment package which will be agreeable for MNCs, national governments and the employees of the foreign subsidiary.

CASE 5.13

The decision by ITT in 1995 to break itself up marks the passing of an era. For more than three decades the giant American company has epitomised the faceless industrial conglomerate, buying up companies and fitting them into its own structure. The decision of the chairman and chief executive to divest, however, dealt the reputation of international conglomerates as vehicles of shareholder value a heavy blow. In the view of many observers, if even ITT has lost faith in the concept of bundling together different businesses into one giant holding company, the prospects for its smaller rivals are seriously questionable.

With sales of $24 billion (£15 billion), ITT was one of the world's largest conglomerates. Created in the 1920s in the Caribbean as a telephone company, it emerged as a powerful industrial force in the 1960s when its long-time chairman, Harold Geneen, bought up more than 250 businesses. It has been pruned in recent years – there have been more than 100 disposals – but it still has interests in industries such as gambling, hotels, automotive parts and electronics.

Now it will be broken into three: ITT Industries will include the manufacturing companies; ITT Hartford will inherit the company's insurance business; and new ITT will include the Sheraton and Ciga hotel chains and the Caesar's World casino group. Shareholders will receive one share in each of the three new companies for each share in the unbundled conglomerate.

And in Britain the traditional conglomerate is also under pressure. For the past five years many companies have focused more on stripping down their business to a single core than diversifying. There have been four big break-ups already – ICI, Courtaulds, Racal and BAT Industries – and the stock market has been seeking the next company to demerge: Thorn EMI saw its share price soar in 1995 on speculation that its music business would be broken away from the retailing side of the company, or that a predator would launch a break-up bid.

Such speculation has been fired by the often spectacular gains produced by companies that have broken up. BAT is still arguably a conglomerate, with a huge tobacco and financial-services business, but it is far less diversified than it was in 1990 when it also included high-street retailing (Argos) and paper manufacturing (Wiggins Teape Appleton). The combined value of all three companies is now £18.5 billion – £8.1 billion more than the combined company was worth at the time. Similarly, the ICI break-up – which has generated £5.7 billion of additional value – has been assisted by the takeover speculation that sent Zeneca's share price up in 1995.

Source: Adapted from *The Sunday Times*, 18 June 1995 (adapted).

■ Strategic business alliances

■ The development of SBAs

These alliances have been a growing phenomenon in international business: firms based in different countries engage in cooperative endeavours to pursue common goals. Such alliances have been defined as 'diverse interorganisational arrangements created by firms of different countries to obtain strategic advantages in their markets and environments.' Their predominant forms are licensing agreements, technological transfers and exchanges, research and development

Table 5.2   Strategic contributions of joint ventures

Risk Reduction
  Product portfolio diversification
  Dispersion and/or reduction of fixed cost
  Lower total capital investment
  Faster entry and payback

Economies of Scale and/or Rationalisation
  Lower average cost from larger volume
  Lower cost by using comparative advantage of each partner

Complementary Technologies and Patents
  Technology synergy
  Exchange of patents and territories

Co-opting and Blocking Competition
  Defensive joint ventures to reduce competition
  Offensive joint ventures to increase cost and/or lower market share for a
    third party

Overcoming Government Mandated Investment or Trade Barrier
  Receiving permit to operate as a local entity because of local partner
  Satisfying local content requirements

Initial International Expansion
  Benefit from local partner knowhow

Vertical Quasi Integration
  Access to materials
  Access to technology
  Access to labour
  Access to capital
  Regulatory permits
  Access to distribution channels
  Benefits from brand recognition
  Establishing links with major buyers
  Drawing on existing fixed marketing establishment

Source: Contractor (1986).

agreements and joint ventures. These alliances are a new strategic tool of firms operating in international markets in direct response to globalisation of industries as well as a rapidly changing international business environment. International alliances have been variously referred to in the literature as a strategic consortium, cooperative agreement, quasi integration and New Investment Form. International alliances have been situated at an intermediate position along a spectrum of inter-firm dealings between arms-length transactions at one end, and mergers at the other. International coalitions have become increasingly commonplace in industries like car, computer, robotics, air transport, biotechnology and carbon fibres.

The indicative benefits to be derived from business alliances and joint ventures can be summarised as follows:

1. Stronger market position to develop long-term sales potential, particularly in contracts and tenders.

Table 5.3 Types of cooperative arrangements

	Typical compensation method	*Extent of inter-organisational dependence*
Technical training/start-up assistance agreements	L	Negligible
Production/Assembly/ buyback agreements	m	
Patent licensing	r	Low
Franchising	r;m	
Know-how licensing	L;r	
Non-equity cooperative agreements in:		
Exploration	Pi:: f(Cv,Rv)	
Research partnership	Pi:: f(Cv,Ri)	Moderate
Development/co-production	Pi:: f(Ci,Ri)	
Equity Joint Venture	a	High

Notes:
a: fraction of shares/dividends
r: royalty as a percentage of turnover
L: lump sum fee
m: markup on components sold or finished output brought back
Pi: profit of firm i in nonequity joint venture
Cv,Rv: cost and revenue of the venture
Ci,Ri: cost and revenue of the firm i
Ri: revenues of the dominant partner
Source: Contractor (1987).

2. Sharing of financial and technical resources and risks, with better financing prospects and terms.
3. Increased direct participation in partner company's market through more control of sales and distribution.
4. Strengthen both technical and market competitiveness worldwide.

Certainly the increased use of alliances to achieve strategic marketing objectives has characterised the last decade. In many industry sectors companies cannot maintain their hold on a sufficient number of markets by themselves, and an alliance gives them the international coverage needed. For example, Siemens joined with Philips, each putting up $400 million and their governments another $400 million. The increasing costs of new technology and product development are going beyond the resources of even very large companies.

CASE 5.14

Unilever, the Anglo-Dutch food and consumer products group, and BSN, France's largest food company, have formed a joint venture to develop and market worldwide a range of new products combining ice cream and yoghurt.

Unilever is the world's largest maker of ice cream, with sales last year of about £1.6 billion in 30 countries, while BSN is the biggest producer of yoghurt, with sales of almost FFr24 billion (£2.8 billion) last year.

The venture appears intended to exploit growing demand among health-conscious consumers for new types of frozen desserts and snacks. Demand is strongest in the US, where sales of products such as frozen yoghurt have recently increased rapidly. However, the joint venture will focus initially on France and Spain, where it plans to launch products soon. Sales will be expanded to other countries later, and according to the two companies the worldwide market for the venture's products, described as 'combining the ideal properties of yoghurt and ice cream', could eventually amount to hundreds of millions of litres.

Marketing of the products is expected to rely heavily on the companies' leading brand names. Unilever's ice-cream brands include Motta in France, Frigo in Spain and Wall's in Britain, while BSN's main international yoghurt brand is Danone.

No figure has been given for the initial investment in the joint venture, which will be equally owned and use existing facilities provided by the two partners. Based in Paris, it will be headed by a steering committee of three managers from each company under a rotating chairmanship, while Unilever will provide operational management.

BSN has relied increasingly on alliances and partnerships to enter new markets, such as Italy, China and Japan, whereas Unilever has traditionally preferred to have full control of its businesses. However, the Anglo-Dutch group recently formed a joint venture with PepsiCo, the US soft drinks and snacks group, to sell canned iced tea.

Table 5.4 Evaluating the logic of collaboration

	Strategic Goals
Supply	Minimise transaction costs in product exchange
Learning	Develop new capabilities through technology transfer or joint R&D
Positioning	Expand market coverage and improve position *vis-à-vis* competitors

	Cost/Benefit Tradeoffs
Acquiring Capabilities, vs for example:	Yielding Control, for example:
Know-how and experience	Use of technology
Access to resources	Control over strategic inputs
Market presence	Market overlaps
New firm capabilities	New potential competitors
Government relations	Decision-making conflicts
Risk-sharing	Profit-sharing

	Alternative Options
Self-sufficiency	Alliance is cheaper and quicker, but implies dependence on outsider
Buying inputs or skills	Alliance gives access to capabilities embedded in firms, but may fail to internalise them
Acquisition	Alliance gives selective access to only what is needed, but implies sharing management with separate firm

Source: Casseres (1993)

■ Salient aspects of cooperative ventures

The forces that shape these changes in the economic environment help to explain the emergence of such cooperative ventures. They are:

- capital intensity in production processes;
- the high cost of technology development and innovation;
- the rapid phase of technological diffusion;
- the need for rapid and deep penetration of global markets both as a preemptive competitive strategy and to help defray the high outlay in technology development;
- the management of a technology portfolio through selective in-house development as well as through cross-licensing and cross-fertilisation with other companies; and
- the difficulties of foreign market access because of renewed protective and other measures already discussed.

Cooperative ventures reflect firms' accommodation to this changing environment.

From Table 5.5 it is seen that five major industrial sectors account for 87 per

Table 5.5   Characteristics of international coalitions

The pattern of collaboration

By regional distribution

Within EEC	0.8%
USA – Rest of World	4.2%
USA – Japan	8.4%
EEC – USA	25.8%
Within USA	8.4%
EEC – Rest of World	7.0%
EEC – Japan	10.1%
Other	5.4%

By industrial sector

Aerospace	19.0%
Telecommunications	17.2%
Computers	14.0%
Motor vehicles	23.7%
Other electricals	13.0%
Others	13.0%

By type of collaboration

Between two partners	81.0%
Between three partners	9.0%
Between buyer and supplier	14.0%
Between two competitors in the same market	71.0%
Between two firms making an entry into a new market	14.0%

By strategic rationale

Product development	37.7%
Product development/production	16.8%
Marketing	7.9%
Product development/marketing	2.9%
Production	23.3%
All three	66.0%
Production/marketing	5.0%

Source: Contractor (1987).

cent of all coalition agreements, and that the high-technology industrial group is actively involved in cooperative ventures. Furthermore, a large number of coalitions are formed to engage in product development (38 per cent), and if eventual production and/or marketing are included this figure rises to 66 per cent.

Cooperative ventures entail certain organisational and behavioural dynamics that are depicted in Figure 5.4. The driving force would appear to be need, and benefits to be gained from the venture. Each prospective party to the venture possesses certain resources and skills which serve as inputs to the venture. The

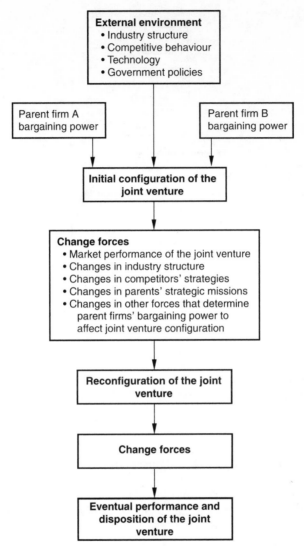

Figure 5.4 A dynamic model of joint venture activity

Source: Harrigan (1984).

bargaining power of the respective parties is directly proportional to their resources. But the greater their need to cooperate, the less will be their bargaining power in negotiating the configuration of the venture.

The venture itself is the result of the bilateral bargaining power of its parents. Its form, inputs, outputs and control mechanism are defined by a bargaining agreement. This agreement, which defines the venture domain of activity, specifies its output and sometimes its customers. The bargaining agreement

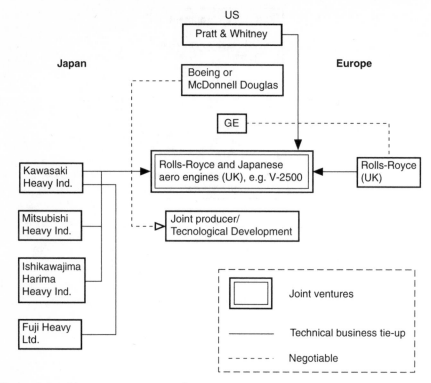

Figure 5.5   Air transport consortia

also specifies the inputs necessary for the venture to attain its objectives. The bargaining agreement also specifies the control mechanism to ensure that benefits accrue to the contracting parties, and serves to ensure the stability of the venture. Resources and need are therefore important determinants of cooperative venture formation. A firm with well developed distribution and channel networks which would complement the other partners' attributes usually brings strength to the negotiation. The desire to preempt competition through cooperation has also been imputed as a motive for venture formation. Cooperative ventures are also not without costs, as for instance the loss of control over certain resources surrendered to the venture; conflict arises over the use and sharing of resources, and there the management systems and culture of the partners prove incompatible.

■   **Other strategic factors**

One advantage of a coalition agreement is that it allows firms to spread costs and risks in product development through joint R&D. This incentive is especially attractive to firms that operate in highly R&D-intensified industries and where rivalry is keen and R&D expenditure are high. This is measured by average R&D expenditure as a percentage of net sales in the joint-venture industry. This variable typically has an apositive effect on coalition formation.

Access to foreign markets is also an important consideration to explain co-operative behaviour in international business. Research cited in this paper also indicates that new product development activity as reflected in high R&D expenditures is positively motivated by expectations of large markets both domestically and overseas. Coalitions in marketing with foreign partners also reflect the expectations that the foreign partners would provide the marketing support through established marketing infrastructure and distribution channels and local legitimacy. Tie-up with foreign partners would be especially attractive if such partners have strong international presence outside their home markets and the coalition entity decides to export beyond their respective local markets. The cooperation of a partner with a strong presence in another country market is a major incentive to forge an alliance.

Host nations' governments sometimes provide incentives for companies; such countries include Brazil, Japan, India and France. In the development of the V2500 20 000-pound thrust high-bypass engine in 1985 between the Japanese consortium and Rolls-Royce, Pratt and Whitney, MTU of Germany and Fiat of Italy, the Japanese government contributed US $62 million to the project. Host governments' policies and regulations in relation to incentive programmes typically have positive effects on coalition formation.

The size of firms in the UK parent industry, as measured by sales, is reflective of the hypothesis that larger average firm-size is associated with higher coalition rates. Size can be a proxy for the level of diversification of products by firms in the industry. It also reflects extensive distribution channels, financial capacity as well as innovative technological capacity; there is also the strategic rationale to increase market penetration, and to minimise risks associated with international marketing.

The higher the level of product differentiation in expansion into overseas markets, the greater the need for local assistance through joint ventures for the provision of local marketing know-how; this is because local product needs and usage are country-specific.

A high degree of industry concentration appears to be characterised by oligopolistic interdependence among firms in the industry; entry by coalition seems unlikely to invite retaliation or blocking moves by incumbents. Furthermore, since the number of firms in such industries is small (and hence the dearth of acquisition target firms), entry by joint venture would be encouraged. Industry concentration therefore typically has a positive influence on coalition activities. Industry concentration is measured by the percentage of an industry's share of the top six or eight firms in the industry.

■ Conclusions

This chapter has formed the link between the concepts and principles explained in Chapters 1 to 3, and the management operations covered in succeeding chapters. The strategies confronting international companies have been analysed and the criteria for implementation explained. This has led into a detailed coverage of the planning process, with the focus on long-term planning. The nature and organisation of acquisitions has been covered, with a number of Case examples showing recent trends in acquisitions policies. Finally, trends and developments in strategic business alliances, and the key influencing factors, have been explained.

QUESTIONS

1. What mechanisms can management use to ensure that an agreed strategy is taken forward and incorporated in marketing planning?
2. What strategies would you advise for a company facing increasing competition from local suppliers in its lead country markets?
3. What do you understand by interactive marketing planning; what are its benefits and its implications for management organisation?
4. Discuss the relative merits of acquisitions as distinct from business alliances as a strategy for penetrating key country markets.
5. What are the main factors behind management's decision to divest and how can this be done without damaging the parent company's business?
6. 'One of the main difficulties in operating successful alliances is that of control.' Discuss, with examples.

CHAPTER 6

Financial aspects

INTRODUCTION

Companies need finance to grow, and the raising of finance for international expansion is an important focus in this chapter. The first section deals with foreign direct investment (FDI), the criteria and the means of implementation and financial appraisal. The impact of FDI on host countries, and issues of control of R&D and technology are also addressed. There follows an explanation of the ways international finance can be raised, including an account of the Euromarket and other foreign exchange markets; the services of financial institutions are detailed too, together with an explanation of currency and credit management. There is particular emphasis on the importance of closer liaison between finance and marketing in pricing policy, credit and interest terms and currency management.

The next section deals with financial appraisal and project planning, particularly the general principles of project financing and how to cope with the various sources of finance available, the criteria to use and investor choices of risk and return. Finally, the significance of profit and performance-improvement is explained, the link between the two, with some Case examples showing what can be achieved.

■ Financing international operations

■ Foreign direct investment

Investing in operations overseas requires that capital be sent out of the home country either in money or in kind to finance or equip, for example, an assembly plant, and that capital cannot be returned except under strictly defined conditions. The phenomenon of foreign direct investment (FDI) has become a major influence on market entry and expansion, particularly for MNCs. FDI represents one component of the international business flow and includes start-ups of new operations as well as purchases of more than 10 per cent of existing companies. The other component is portfolio investment, the international purchase of stocks and bonds. Research by the Organisation for Economic Cooperation and Development (OECD) and the International Monetary Fund (IMF)

181

indicates that foreign direct investments have grown substantially in recent years (OECD, 1992). The total global value of such investment, which in 1967 was estimated at $105 billion, was estimated to have climbed to $596 billion in 1984, and in 1993 is estimated at $756 billion.

One of the salient features of FDI is the involvement of government, both direct and indirect, at both the levels of central and local government. After all (as explained in Chapter 2) governments are concerned to attract and retain large-scale foreign investment for industrial, economic and social reasons of state. The Indian Government, for example, now actively pursues this, and this represents a major policy change from the isolationist policy of self-sufficiency followed for decades after Independence in 1947. By the same token international companies seek out host governments which offer favourable fiscal and economic incentives to new investors, and also look to governments to protect their existing investments and assets in host countries. Indeed, FDI is seen by many companies as essential to maintain international competitiveness, especially in cases where:

- protective duties and measures to reinforce a weakening exchange rate can increase the cost of finished, landed products where they can no longer compete with local products;
- many industrial products require technical services to the point where local assembly becomes necessary; and
- the host country provides substantial operating savings in costs of materials and labour.

Indeed, some governments may well regard FDI as a strategic contribution to manufacturing capacity, particularly for export, and in attracting FDI such governments are concerned to maintain an attractive investment climate. Investor companies specifically seek, and expect, therefore:

- a 'fair wind' for private enterprise (with minimal restrictions on the movement of capital);
- tax and other fiscal incentives;
- an acceptable law-enforcement capability; and
- facilities to remit profits, dividends and fees.

Indeed FDI is seen by many governments as the principal means of developing industrial capacity and competitiveness in the newly-industrialising countries (NICs) and in the transition-economies of Eastern and Central Europe and the Newly Independent States (NIS) of the former Soviet Union; the OECD has urged these governments to 'play an active role in improving their economies as locations for FDI'.

CASE 6.1

DATAR is the French Government Agency responsible for regional industrial planning and development. The oversight body with policy control of all trade and investment promotion is the Direction des Relations Economiques Extérieures under the Ministry of Economic Affairs and Finance in Paris. There is also a link between DATAR and the Centre Français du Commerce Extérieur (CFCE) which does overseas market research for key industry sectors and regions with export potential.

DATAR offers French or foreign firms investing in new plant in certain designated development areas cash grants of between 12 and 25 per cent of the total value of the investment. Extension of existing facilities in those same areas attracts grants of between 12 and 20 per cent; subsidies are also payable for the cost of staff training (50 per cent) and instructor training (100 per cent). Other incentives available through DATAR include tax reductions and tax exemptions, and a proportion of personnel relocation costs. Local government bodies and other authorities offer additional assistance, including the sale of prepared industrial sites at less than cost, and standard factory buildings.

Figure 6.1 illustrates the principal factors and reasons for foreign direct investment, and these will now be explained in detail. Marketing considerations and the corporate desire for growth are a major cause for the recent increase in foreign direct investment. Even a sizeable domestic market may present limitations to growth. Firms therefore need to seek wider market-access in order to maintain and increase their sales.

A major cause for the recent growth in FDI is derived demand. Often, as large multinational firms move abroad they are quite interested in maintaining their established business relationships with other firms. Therefore they frequently encourage their suppliers to follow them and to continue to supply them from the new foreign location. For example, advertising agencies often move abroad in order to service foreign affiliates of their domestic clients. Similarly, engineering firms, insurance companies and consultants are often asked to provide their services abroad. Yet not all of these developments come about in this way. Often firms invest abroad for defensive reasons out of fear that their clients may find other sources abroad, and to preserve quality; Japanese motor manufacturers have urged more than 40 of their suppliers from Japan to establish production in the UK and the USA.

For similar reasons, firms follow their competitors abroad. Foreign direct investment permits firms to circumvent barriers to trade and operate abroad as domestic firms, unaffected by duties, tariffs or other import restrictions.

In addition to government measures, barriers may also be imposed by customers through their insistence on domestic goods and services, either as a result of nationalistic tendencies or as a function of cultural differences.

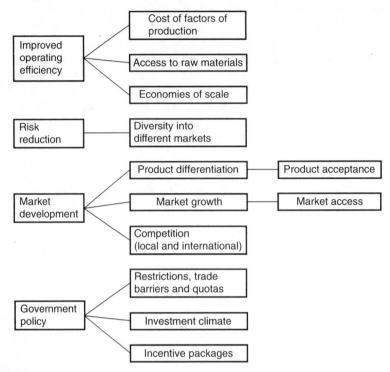

Figure 6.1   Reasons for foreign direct investment

Furthermore, local buyers may wish to buy from sources that they perceive to be reliable in their supply, which means buying from local producers. And then there are cost factors. Servicing markets at geographic distances and with tariff barriers has made many exporters' offerings in foreign markets prohibitively expensive. Many manufacturing multinationals have established plants overseas to gain cost advantages in terms of labour and raw materials. And FDI occurs not only horizontally by firms acquiring or establishing similar firms abroad, but also vertically. Some firms engage in foreign direct investment to secure their sources of supply for raw materials and components.

■ **Impact of FDI**

FDI by definition implies a degree of control over the enterprise. This may be unavailable because of environmental constraints even if the firm owns 100 per cent of the subsidiary. The general attitude towards foreign investment and its development over time may be indicative of the long-term prospects for invest-ment. In many countries foreign direct investment tends to arouse nationalistic feelings. Political risk has to be defined broadly to include not only the threat of

Table 6.1 Positive and negative impacts of foreign investment on host countries

Positive impact	Negative impact
Capital formation	Industrial dominance
Technology and management skills	Technological dependence
Regional and sectoral development	Disturbance to economic plans
Internal competition and	Cultural change
entrepreneurship	Interference by home government of
Balance of payments	MNC
Labour	

political upheaval but also the likelihood of arbitrary or discriminatory government action that will result in financial loss. This could take the form of tax increases, price controls, or measures directed specifically at foreign firms such as partial divestment of ownership, local content requirements, remittance restrictions, export requirements, and limits on expatriate employment. The investment market is also measured in terms of foreign currency risk.

FDI is typically the most important and sometimes sensitive issue in the interface between government and industry already discussed in Chapter 2. On the one hand, the host government has to appreciate the various contributions, especially economic, that FDI will make. On the other hand fears of dominance, interference, and dependence are frequently voiced and acted upon. The major positive and negative impacts are summarised in Table 6.1.

As far as the positive impact is concerned, capital flows are especially beneficial to countries with limited domestic resources and access to funds in the world's capital markets for projects for which local capital alone would not have sufficed. The impact of FDI can be seen on technology transfer, the importance of which was explained in Chapter 4; this includes not only the introduction of new hardware to markets but the techniques and skills to operate it. In industries where the role of intellectual property is substantial, such as pharmaceuticals or software development, access to parent companies' research and development provides benefits that may be far greater than those gained through infusion of capital. This explains the interest that many governments have expressed in having multinational corporations establish R&D facilities in their countries. An integral part of technology transfer is managerial skills, which are the most significant labour component of foreign direct investment. With the growth of the service sector, many economies need skills-development rather than expatriate personnel to perform the tasks.

The major impact of foreign direct investment on the balance of payments is long-term. Import substitution, export earnings, and subsidised imports of technology and management all assist the host nation on the trade-account side of the balance of payments. Not only may a new production facility substantially decrease the need to import the type of products manufactured, it may start earning export revenue as well. Several countries, such as Brazil, have imposed export requirements as a pre-condition for foreign direct investment. On the capital-account side, foreign direct investment may have a short-term impact in lowering a deficit as well as a long-term impact in keeping capital at home.

On the negative-impact side, although some of the threats posed by multinational corporations and foreign direct investments are exaggerated, in many countries some industrial sectors are dominated by foreign-owned entities. In France, for example, 75 per cent of the computer and data-processing equipment sector was dominated by foreign affiliates in the 1980s. In Belgium, oil refining (78 per cent) and electrical engineering (87 per cent) showed the highest rates of foreign participation.

Because foreign direct investment in most cases is concentrated in technology-intensive industries, research and development comprise another area of tension.

CASE 6.2

A leading international consultant, Dennis Brewster, has proposed a typology of country markets as a guide to management in assessing market access and FDI for local production.

Country A has for some time been importing the company's products and those of its competitors, but a series of protective duties and other measures (with the possible reinforcement of a weakening exchange rate) are steadily increasing its landed cost to a point where it becomes impossible to compete with local equivalents.

Country B has also been importing, and entry charges are not increasing to any great extent. Nevertheless, the company's product may be of such a type – either it has very high freight and packing costs, or it contains an inbuilt requirement for service and maintenance – that it becomes impracticable to go beyond a certain ceiling of volumes without investing in a local organisation.

Country C has also been importing and entry charges *per se* are not increasing. However, all shipments are subject to licences, or other restrictions (such as high import deposits), basically to conserve that country's foreign exchange; and these get turned on and off at unpredictable levels. Lack of availability, long delivery dates and even longer payment dates begin to affect sales.

Country D's FDI promises substantial savings in the cost of materials or labour for some products, compared with those in the home plant. On top of savings in freight and duty, this should enable prices to be reduced and/or volumes increased over the current level. This judgement may be arrived at whether or not substantial, or merely token imports have been taking place up to now.

Country E is a completely closed market, both now and in the past, for any of the reasons mentioned above. Even though the unit cost of production would undoubtedly be higher, it is judged that the market potential is sufficiently great to justify FDI, on what is after all incremental business.

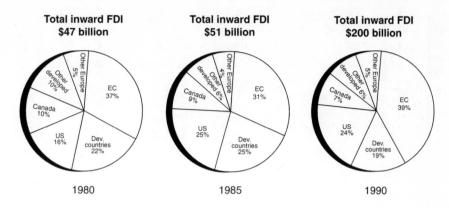

Figure 6.2   Worldwide distribution of FDI by recipient, 1980–90

Source: International Monetary Fund, *Balance of Payments Statistics Yearbook,* various years; and US Department of Commerce, *Foreign Direct Investment in the United States: An Update* (June 1993), p. 13.

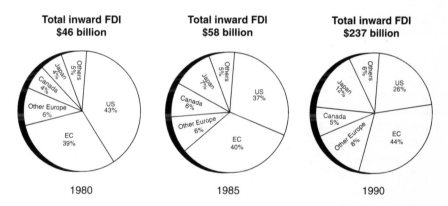

Figure 6.3   Worldwide distribution of FDI by source, 1980-90

Source: International Monetary Fund, *Balance of Payments Statistics Yearbook,* various years; and US Department of Commerce, *Foreign Direct Investment in the United States: An Update* (June 1993), p. 11.

MNCs usually want to concentrate their R&D efforts, especially their basic research. With its technology transfer, the MNC can assist the host country's economic development, but it may leave the host country dependent on flows of new and updated technology. Some governments have made a condition that research facilities are provided in their country; the result is that they can exercise more control. Western European nations, for example, have joined forces in basic research and development under the auspices of projects, such as

Table 6.2 Checklist of key questions for prospective investors

	Argentina	Brazil	Mexico
1. Are wholly owned subsidiaries permitted?	Yes	Yes	Yes (if of special interest to authorities)
2. Obligatory percentage of shareholding to be held by local citizens	None	No fixed percentage	51% (except as above)
3. Is there any minority protection provided from a practical viewpoint?	quorum and majority requirements for special resolutions – limitation of voting powers – special rights of foreign shareholders to examine books and nominate proxies	No	Yes
4. Can such protection be otherwise provided in the Memorandum and Articles of Association and by-laws?	Not known	Yes	Yes, charter can provide that 70% or 80% majority is for crucial decisions
5. Is there any limitation as to citizenship of shareholders?	No	No	No, but foreign shareholders do not invoke their government's protection
6. Is there any limitation as to citizenship of members of the board?	No, except for mixed companies where 'public' reps must be Argentinian	No, but they must be resident in Brazil	No, but a 25% minority has the right to appoint a director

7. Is there any restriction in repatriation of capital, profit and/or royalties?	No	No, provided contract or investment is negotiated with Banco Central
8. What, if any, is the obligatory proportion of national employees?	No requirement, except in case of mixed companies	90%
9. What is the minimum number of members of the Board allowed by law?	No legal requirement but usually 3–12 directors	One, but in practice a minimum of two is recommended
10. Are there restrictions of employment of foreign nationals assisting in building?	None	The 90% in Q.8 does not apply to directors and managerial staff
11. Is there an equal treatment taxwise for companies with foreign participation as compared with companies with only national composition?	Yes, except for dividends tax (see 12)	Some differences
12. Is there any dividend tax?	Only in respect of dividends paid to shareholders not resident in Argentina -12%	Yes (a withholding tax of 25% on non-residents' income applies) Yes
13. Enumeration of any industries (a) excluded to foreigners or (b) to private sector	Special legislation governing: petroleum, mining, banking and finance (some difficulties for foreign interests); however, (a) and (b) crude petroleum production and new refineries	(a) and (b) petroleum: electricity, basic petro-chemicals and telecommunications (a): forest products

Table 6.2 Checklist of key questions for prospective investors

	Argentina	Brazil	Mexico
	foreigners are not excluded from these activities; reinsurance is state monopoly		
14. Any types of business which, by law, exclude foreign voting control	None known except possibly where defence is concerned	Aviation, coastal shipping, fishing, the press and broadcasting, reinsurance	Transport, broadcasting, aerial photography, land settlement, films, advertising, insurance, banks, publishing, soft drinks, rubber and mining in general
15. Are there any tax incentives for new investments?	Yes – under certain promotion schemes, depending on location and nature of industry	Yes, in Sudene and Sudam area, and for the tourist trade, fishing and re-afforestation	Yes, for certain industries and in certain areas

EUREKA and RACE, which facilitate the pan-European pooling of resources to develop new technologies with both governmental and private-sector help. But some economic benefits of FDI remain controversial: capital inflows may be accompanied by outflows in a higher degree and over a longer term than is satisfactory to the host government. Furthermore, some governments see FDI as a disturbance to their economic planning. Decisions are being made concerning their economy over which they have little or no control.

■ **Raising international finance**

The next issue is the raising of finance for international operations; finance plays a critical role in securing overseas projects. Moreover, the terms on which a company obtains finance directly determine:

1. The competitiveness of the company's product/service offer in international markets, particularly the financial terms.
2. The pay-back of FDI: that is the period over which it is expected or required to re-cover the initial investment, and estimated ROI. Quantitative techniques to work out ROI and other financial controls are explained in the next section of this chapter.

On the importing and exporting side, exporters require pre-shipment finance for manufacturing and export inventories; importers seek finance to purchase goods. Overseas buyers frequently seek to place the financial burden and risk of trade on their suppliers, and if an exporter agrees to extend credit, he must obtain financial cover.

The complexity of international business finance, however, is reflected in the number of different sources of finance available almost exclusively for international business. There is, for example, self-financing, since a business can use its own capital or can withhold dividends so that profits can be ploughed back to develop the business. For retailers and manufacturers, trade-credit and financial assistance are available from export merchants and trading companies especially factoring companies which 'buy' a trading company's sales ledger in return for a commission to recover debts and collectables. This factoring can enormously improve the liquidity of the company by generating immediate cash flow (and profits). And in the case of MNCs, their subsidiaries may borrow from affiliated firms as well as from employee pension funds (though the latter is strictly controlled by law). Finally, the business may decide to raise equity capital by selling stocks, or it may depend on debt-financing by selling bonds (for example Euro bonds).

MNCs can also raise equity capital by selling stock or debentures both in their home countries and in foreign markets. Indeed, MNCs regularly raise capital offshore through international financial centres (for example London or Paris). There are other options too: a funding centre (for example Singapore) collects funds from outside a region for that region's internal use; a collection centre (for example Bahrain) on the other hand, takes in money for loans to the international banks to invest.

■ The Euromarket

One place where governments and business can go to borrow money of a desired currency at a competitive rate is the Euromarket. The international market of foreign currency deposits in Europe has no fixed boundary, though London is its main location. One unique feature of the Euromarket is its state-less financial system. Although governments place restrictions on the operations of their national money markets, such measures do not apply to the Euro-market. Indeed the spectacular growth of the Euromarket has been greatly aided by government regulations. Restrictions on lending and borrowing prac-tices in terms of ceiling rates, reserves, reserve requirements, taxes and so on have caused lenders to seek out opportunities abroad where they can earn higher yields. Much like lenders, borrowers with a good name and with large resources and demands have a good reason to tap the Euromarket. When MNCs need free access to hard currencies such as dollars, the money may not be readily available in, say, the United States, or the process may be cumber-some and time-consuming. So global money managers invest in such instru-ments as Eurobonds because of the dollar's stability and security as well as the interest rate advantages over similar mark and franc securities.

European banks (unlike American banks which accept nothing but US dollars for deposit) routinely accept all types of money, which do not have to be con-verted into any specific local currency. When a depositor needs funds and must withdraw them, no conversion is required. On the Euromarket, therefore, Eurocurrencies are traded, which the world's major banks bid for and use; Eurocurrencies are monies traded outside the country of their origin. The Eurodollar, just one of many Eurocurrencies, is simply US dollars deposited in banks outside the United States. The Eurodollar once commanded more than 90 per cent of the Euromarket, but it has now slipped back to about 70 per cent, with hard European currencies such as the German Mark holding the rest of the market.

■ Services of financial institutions

As far as financial institutions are concerned, international companies have several options in using institutions which have the capability of dealing in international finance. The common option is banks both domestic and overseas. In addition to the well-known banks that operate globally, there are many medium-sized banks that have international banking departments. The multi-national banks can make arrangements to satisfy all kinds of financing needs. Other than making loans, banks are also involved in financing indirectly by discounting letters of credit and bills of exchange. In the UK, companies have many institutions they can contact for loans. These include foreign banks, clearing banks, merchant banks, finance houses, investment trusts, pension funds, insurance companies, leasing firms and development capital and other specialist venture capital organisations such as 3i in the UK. In Germany, companies can obtain short-term loans from German and foreign banks, usually by overdraft.

The complexity of financing international operations is reflected in the many options open to companies requiring to borrow money to fund expansion. Because this is done across national frontiers, there are two elements which must be watched closely:

1. The exchange-rate risk exists regardless of the exchange-rate system used. Since MNCs have no fixed or floating rates, they must attempt to reduce their foreign exchange exposure by currency management (taking out forward contracts).
2. Varying rates of inflation exist among countries, and its impact on the value of the currency cannot be overlooked. For companies with assets in a high-inflation country, the value of their assets can be substantially and adversely affected. Yet MNCs can benefit from inflation if they know how to borrow money wisely. With regard to the timing of payment, money managers should lead in soft currencies and lag in stronger currencies. For the MNC with subsidiaries in many countries, reinvoicing can also be a well-advised strategy.

CASE 6.3

Late payers are a common problem among UK companies trading overseas, and payment delays by Europeans have been getting longer, averaging around 100 days to settle invoices, according to the Association of British Factors and Discounters (ABFD).

Phosyn, a Humberside-based manufacturer of trace elements for agriculture, exports 80 per cent of its products, but finds that overseas customers expect 60–180-day payment terms (as a matter of course, compared to 30-day terms in the UK). This means that the company carries a large amount of debt: 85 per cent of the company's sales are on an average of 120-day terms, so one-third of the annual sales overseas is outstanding at any one time. About £7.25 million of Phosyn's annual turnover of £8.5 million goes overseas; this means that more than £2 million is outstanding at any one time.

The company now factors its overseas business through the Lloyds Bank subsidiary, International Factors (IF). In effect, this gives Phosyn an additional overdraft facility; provided it has credit insurance on a customer, IF will advance 80 per cent of what is owed.

When Phosyn started exporting in the 1970s it used letters of credit; as soon as products were shipped out, it presented letter-of-credit documents and got payment straight away. Then in the 1980s as exports grew, it used discounted bills of exchange (through discount houses); but customers increasingly wanted long credit. Ultimately as exports began to form a larger and larger proportion of its business, Phosyn found it increasingly difficult to generate the cash needed to run the company on a day-to-day basis. It became essential to find a cost-effective way of getting a regular source of cash as and when the company required.

The use of factoring gives Phosyn 80 per cent of its debts straight away, provided it has insurance cover worldwide. The company can expand its international business because factoring enables it to take on more good contracts and develop some of the country markets it has not so far exploited. There is also more money to spend on developing products and markets which will sharpen the company's competitive position.

Source: Financial Times, January 1994.

■ Foreign exchange market

It is appropriate now to consider the operations of the foreign exchange market, and how companies should utilise it to improve both profitability and competitiveness. Companies needing to make payment for foreign transactions need the foreign exchange market for ease of access to large amounts of foreign currency. The market has no trading-floor where buyers and sellers meet: most trades are completed by banks and foreign-exchange dealers using telephones, cable, fax and E-mail. The Exchange is a worldwide market operating 24 hours a day, and it facilitates financial transactions in different ways:

1. It provides credit for firms engaged in international business through a variety of means such as letters of credit, bills of exchange, long-term loans and so forth.
2. It performs a clearing function similar to that of a domestic bank, clearing for cheque-account customers. Clearing is a process by which a financial transaction between two parties involving intermediation between banks is settled. In the case of international clearing, the funds are transferred on paper from a commercial customer to his local bank, from there to a London bank, and finally to a foreign bank abroad. The clearing process allows payments to be made for foreign goods without a physical transfer or movement of money across countries.
3. The market provides facilities for hedging so that businesses can cover or reduce their foreign exchange risks. Hedging is an activity that is used as a temporary substitute purchase or sale for the actual currency. This temporary transaction allows users to protect the price they secure from fluctuations, because it establishes equal and opposite positions in the market.
4. It can protect corporate profits against undesirable and unpredictable changes in currency exchange rates that may occur in the future. For this purpose the market operates two sub-markets: 'spot' and 'forward'. The spot market is available for immediate delivery at the prevailing or spot rate. More significant, however, is the operation of the forward market, whereby companies can protect themselves by

selling their expected foreign exchange forward. A forward contract is a commitment to buy or sell currencies at some specified time in the future at a specified rate. By signing a forward contract of (say) 45 days, a company knows precisely how many pounds if will obtain when payment, conversion and delivery occur after 45 days have elapsed.

The exchange rate specified in the 45-day contract is not necessarily the same rate as the forward rate of the next day, or the spot rate of 45 days later. The only rate which stays unchanged is the forward rate agreed between the bank and the company, even though other rates may change significantly: the bank receives neither financial loss or gain regardless of what the spot rate is after 45 days. However, if the forward contract is for delivery of a hard currency such as Swiss francs or Dutch guilders, there will be a small premium collectable by the company on the forward date agreed for delivery. This forward market is referred to again later in this section in a managerial context.

CASE 6.4

A collaborative agreement between the Bank of Wales and Banque Rivaud of France is helping British exporters speed up the collection of payments from French companies. Based on the LCR (Lettre de Change Relevé) system, the agreement effectively provides access to the French banking system which has a strict payment policy enforced by the Central Bank and a largely electronic settlement system. As LCR collections are subject to national law, judgements and enforcements can be made locally when necessary.

In practice, all the exporter has to do is add a simple clause to invoices stating that collection is to be made by LCR and send a copy to the Bank of Wales. The information is then transmitted electronically from Cardiff to Banque Rivaud which raises the documentation. The LCR imposes a duty on the buyer to effect payment within the agreed timescale. Should payment not be collected on the due date, the Central Bank is notified, a sanction most companies would wish to avoid.

One very important advantage of this system is the speed with which the debt is recovered. An electronically-collected LCR is also considerably cheaper and less work than a bill for collection. Bank of Wales takes responsibility for the entire process including all administration for a fee fully inclusive of all French bank charges.

This is thought to be the first collaboration of its type by a British bank specifically for collection as opposed to transmission, and if successful the concept will be expanded. France has a very progressive policy concerning the settlement of debts which constitute the biggest problem facing small and medium enterprises (SMEs).

Through this agreement British exporters can enjoy the protection of the French banking and legal systems, and avoid the problem of overdue payments.

Source: Export Today, December 1993.

■ Implications for management action

Those managers responsible for financing international operations of companies require not only a high level of expertise, but a willingness to work closely with the marketing function to exploit financial advantage. This is particularly so in utilising forward currency contracts, already described. This interface between finance and marketing can be highlighted from the following aspects:

1. *Pricing policy* – pricing research such as trade-off analysis to implement market-based pricing, and the relative merits of this approach compared to cost-plus pricing.
2. *Investment decisions* – the contributions of marketing in terms of demand-and-risk analysis, and assessments of pay-back and market access.
3. *Export credit insurance* and the use of credit policy as a key part of the marketing mix.
4. *Currency management* – the use of forward currency contracts to reduce both buyer-risk and buyer-resistance.

International credit agreements (Berne Convention) are intended to reduce the severity of credit competition; but in international markets the provision of credit is frequently more important than a competitive price – indeed the cost of very attractive credit terms is typically recovered by an inflated price bid. Matching the interest terms (the actual rate of interest and the term period over which repayments are completed) of Japanese companies has become a priority for their European counterparts.

CASE 6.5

A French company selling industrial chemicals to Latin America were on the point of winning a large contract in Argentina as a result of improved credit terms offered to a major customer by the resident export representative; the credit period was extended from 30 to 60 days after cabled approval had been received from the international sales director in France. When news of this contract was notified to the group financial controller, he refused to sanction it on the grounds that, given the cost of money, the company was close to giving the goods away. The financial controller took the resulting dispute to the group board, which decided to overrule the marketing staff. But the board immediately issued a directive on collaboration between finance and marketing which set out policy guidelines and credit procedures for securing future international contracts: the company lost the contract in Argentina.

Credit must be seen, therefore, as a key element, not only in the marketing mix, but as a way of safeguarding profit margins. But a sound corporate credit policy demands close liaison between finance and marketing and this can ensure that the company's credit terms are financially sound; it is not losing business because its credit terms are no longer competitive; and the cost of collecting debts internationally is fully taken into account in pricing policy.

Another important aspect of the finance/marketing interface is currency management, to improve both profitability and marketing impact by:

- selling or buying a foreign currency forward (as already explained);
- borrowing foreign currencies; and
- offsetting imports in one currency with exports in the same currency.

It is the responsibility of financial management to provide intelligence on currency interest and exchange rates to marketing staff to:

- up-date currency trends for costing and selling purposes;
- be briefed fully when quoting in negotiations with overseas buyers;
- quote in foreign currencies
- meet and beat foreign competitors' quotations; and
- reduce buyer resistance by quoting in the buyer's currency.

The benefits of currency management can be summarised as:

1. Depreciating value of book-debts (where inflation is higher at home than in other industrialised countries, the advantages of having receivables in currencies depreciating at a slower rate is self-evident).
2. Price stabilisation–cost escalation (in similar conditions to (1) export price rises can be minimised when invoicing in currencies with low inflation rates).
3. Additional flexibility (expertise in the forward market enables the company to quote a price based on a firm rate of exchange).
4. Buyer preference for own currency (this removes from the buyer any risks of currency conversion).
5. Additional profitability (where other trading currencies are at a premium to the home currency, this premium can make an additional yield on sales by the use of the market).
6. Additional flexibility in financial management (by invoicing in other currencies the exporter may be able to borrow that currency on the Eurocurrency market at considerably lower interest than his own currency, for example to obtain pre-shipment finance).

■ Liaison between finance and marketing

What are the implications of these points for finance and marketing? It is clear that management is having to operate under conditions of increasing uncertainty in overseas markets: political risks, commercial risks and the competition from

---

CASE 6.6

A British company should have helped its French buyer as follows. The exporter had sold to France in sterling, and the period from date of order to date of payment was approximately six months. The French buyer, wishing to cover his exchange risk, approached his bank in Paris in order to buy the sterling forward six months. He was told, however, that he was only allowed to buy forward up to two months and he was thus exposed to an exchange risk for the remaining four months. The British exporter, on the other hand, should have invoiced in French francs and sold forward on the London money market up to twelve months, if necessary: had he done so he would have secured the order in the first place, whereas in fact the French buyer delayed confirmation, with a resultant loss to the exporter.

CASE 6.7

Another case with a more successful outcome occurred when a British exporter, although requested to quote in sterling, was encouraged by his advisers to quote for a large contract in Germany in both sterling and D-marks. At the time, the three-year-forward premium on the D-mark was equivalent to no less than 15 per cent on the face value of the contract, and so the exporter was able safely to reduce his D-mark quotations by 5 per cent. Confronted by the two quotations, the Germans converted the sterling price into D-marks at the spot rate and were then surprised to find that the D-mark quotation was cheaper than the one in sterling.

---

newly-industrialising countries (NICs). Added to this are financial uncertainties, particularly in the movements of interest rates and currencies (see Chapter 7 for a detailed exposition of risk and crisis management).

These external factors alone demand the closest possible collaboration between the finance and marketing functions: the financial implications of alternative international strategies must be set out in terms of offering not only an attractive product range, but a competitive set of financial offers. Indeed, planning overseas marketing activities demands the most careful financial interpretation of the objectives and the means of achieving these objectives. This approach is essential to 'out-market' competitors with a superior 'total package', and to secure improved financial returns to the company.

The financial package offered by the company has become a vital part of its offers to customers; and there is some evidence that the nature of competition is changing and that management tasks and organisation need to be reappraised. Longer credit terms are essential to sustain a position overseas: this is an investment decision (tying up money) as well as a marketing decision. Furthermore, the financing of additional capacity or the setting-up of subsidiaries abroad means investment on a more substantial scale.

The net effect of these considerations is that international trading must increase demands on the company's financial resources under conditions world-wide where the profitable use of these resources is less certain. Of course, the effect can be offset to some extent by government services in making exporting more profitable through the provision of low-cost finance, remission of some internal taxes, financing of exports, credit insurance and facilitating inter-national transactions. But it is up to the company to organise its trading operations more profitably, and it can do this only if analysis and planning draw on the joint expertise in the company.

Consider, for example, the assessment of long-term prospects of an overseas market and the expected return on the company's investment over a given period, the impact of inflation on pricing policy, the relationship between major economic and financial indicators and market potential – these and other vital questions require both financial and marketing expertise to resolve; yet some manufacturing companies can improve the dialogue between finance and marketing staff. Companies should therefore consider setting up overseas-task-forces which bring together operational managers in key sectors such as marketing and finance (one might add design and supply), so that an integrated strategy to penetrate markets and to maximise profits and cash collection can be set up and implemented.

■ Financial appraisal and project planning

■ Project financing

An overseas project can involve substantial fixed assets and working capital investments. Purchasing a fixed asset such as a new packaging machine, or replacing an old assembly line with a technologically advanced one, require cash outlays. These facts suggest that when a firm invests in fixed assets and working capital for a project, it uses both internal and external funds. Deciding on the respective proportions of equity and external financing is a policy issue which is affected by:

- The availability of funds in the financial markets;
- Cost of these funds;
- The firm's ability to raise large amounts of external funds;
- The firm's optimal capital structure.

In addition, the management of overseas project financing involves a number of issues:

1. What sources of financing are available? In many countries, sources of funds are very limited.

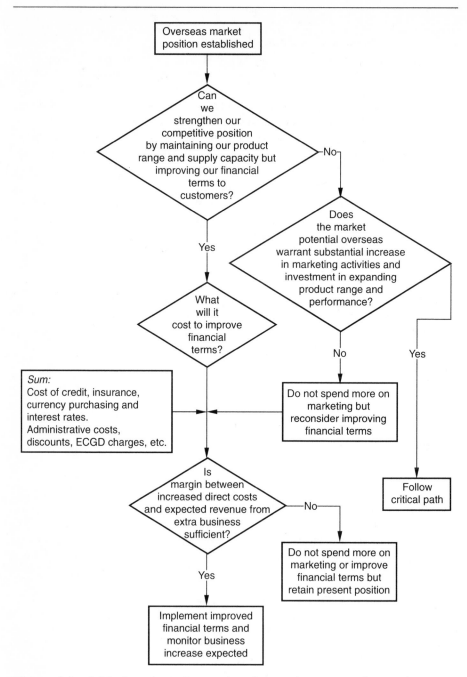

Figure 6.4   Critical path 1: Improving financial terms with no change in marketing or supply

Source: Adapted from Windle and Sizer (1985).

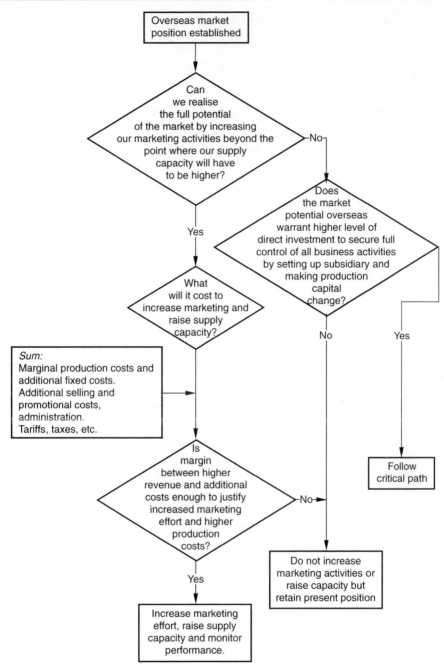

Figure 6.5 Critical path 2: Increasing marketing activities which require change in supply

Source: Adapted from Windle and Sizer (1985).

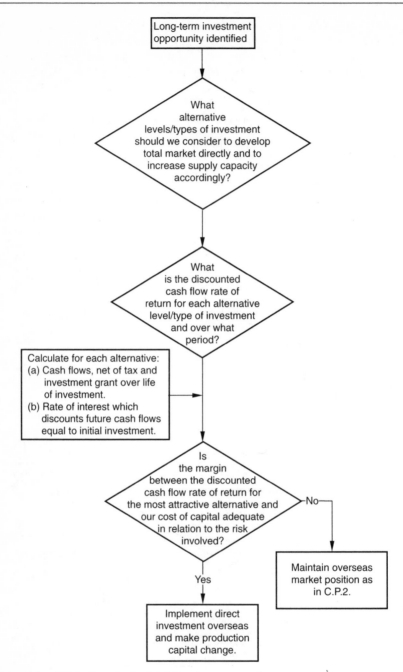

Figure 6.6   Critical path 3: Making long-term investment overseas requiring production capital change

Source: Adapted from Windle and Sizer (1985).

2. How long will the funds be required? Short-term needs such as working capital requirements should be financed by short-term loans because it is usually cheaper to borrow in the short term than the long term. It is, however, important that fixed assets be financed by long-term funds and that the total re-imbursement be completed well-ahead of the expiration of the economic life of the assets.
3. What are the trends in interest rates? Forecasting interest rates is not easy, but if rates are expected to rise, long-term borrowing at fixed rates is preferable. On the other hand if interest rates are likely to fall, short-term borrowings are more appropriate.
4. What are the operational consequences of different types of financing? Some sources of finance may place restrictions on dividend payments, asset purchases, management salaries and working capital levels. Restrictive covenants on bonds and loans are typical examples.
5. What is the company's cash flow likely to be in the future? If a company expects to be short of cash in the near future, repayment of loan principal should be scheduled out into the future in order to reduce the short-term financial risk to the project.

Once the total investment and production costs are determined over the life of the project, the project's financing aspects must be examined. The following four major aspects are particularly important:

- Means of project financing;
- Sources of financing;
- Financing plan and optimum capital structure;
- Financing terms and modalities.

Bearing these issues in mind, the decision on the means of financing must be in line with the objective of achieving the optimum capital structure and minimising the cost of capital. In ensuring this it must be remembered that while there are various financing sources, their availability may vary from country to country. A first attempt is made to determine the means of financing for the overseas project. It should be remembered that the project is still in the study stage and that there has almost certainly not yet been any contact with possible sources of finance. This contact will be made after acceptance of the project by the investors.

The means of project financing can be divided into four categories as shown in Figure 6.7. These are:

1. Project net worth (paid-up capital, preferred shares and internally generated funds);
2. Debt (short, medium and long-term credit);
3. Subsidies and grants;
4. Other means.

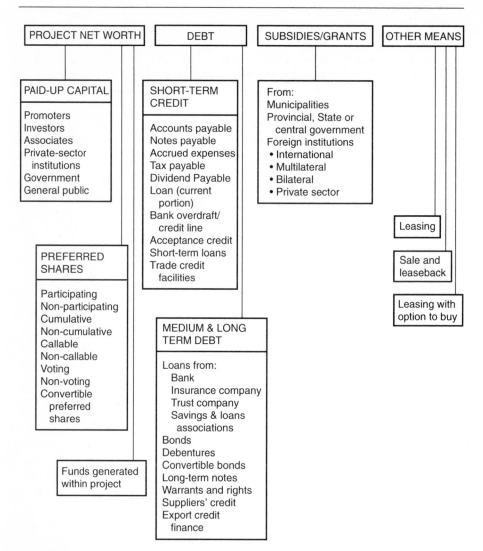

Figure 6.7   Means of project financing

Source: 1992 International Trade Centre UNCTAD/GATT, Geneva.

As far as project net worth is concerned, promoters, investors, associates, financial and governmental institutions and the general public usually participate in the paid-up capital or ordinary shares.

The participants in the capital will benefit from the success of the project or suffer financially if it fails. In short, it is to the shareholders that all future benefits and project profitability will revert. In case of failure, it is they who will have to bear the largest losses, as they assume the largest risk of the project. In

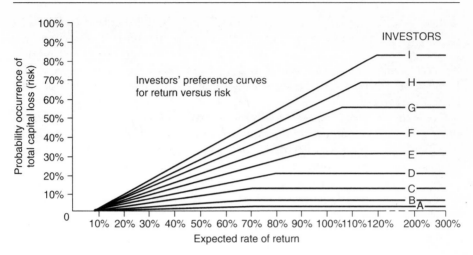

Figure 6.8 Investors' choice of risk versus return

Source: 1992 International Trade Centre UNCTAD/GATT, Geneva.

that respect, the investors' propensity to accept risk will vary considerably; some will shy away from assuming any risk, while others will accept high risk provided they are compensated by a high return. Thus return is always to be assessed in comparison to the expected risk. Figure 6.8 presents a group of investors ranging from the very conservative to the one seeking high risk and return. In small- and medium-sized projects where participants in the capital are limited in number, the participation can take the form of a lump-sum payment or instalment or the assignment or sale of an asset (such as land, equipment, patent rights, etc.) to the project. The number of ordinary shares in a company (paid-up capital) may run into millions for big projects. The public and/or the financial institutions (public and government) often take up shares.

■ Sources of financing

There are several sources of finance available to the company, both internal and external, and these are now explained. Preferred shares are usually subscribed by promoters, investors, associates or corporations. They are issued for investors who want to limit to a certain extent the risk factor. They are also issued for fiscal reasons (to reduce corporate taxes). They are privileged in comparison to ordinary shares in that they have priority over ordinary shares in respect of payment of dividends and priority for reimbursement in the event of liquidation of the project. Preferred shares can be cumulative: they have a priority right to the dividends not paid in the previous years, owing to lack of cashflow, over ordinary shares; or non-cumulative: they do not have the right to unpaid past dividends when the cash flow improves and dividend to the ordinary shares resumes. They also sometimes carry an option for conversion into ordinary shares to render them more attractive to investors, or of redemption by the management when interest rates in the market drop. They are generally non-voting, but otherwise have the same rights as ordinary shares unless these rights are revoked.

Other funds can be generated within the project: these result from the cash-flows generated during the production cycle. Then there is debt (short, medium, and long-term) to be considered. The interest charges on credit and loans must be paid on time for every period. Any delay in the payment of interest can expose the project to bankruptcy proceedings. Hence interest is an obligation and represents a fixed charge on the project. Short-term debt is to be repaid in less than 12 months, and this may include the following:

- Accounts payable;
- Notes payable;
- Accrued expenses;
- Tax payable;
- Dividend payable;
- Current portion of term loans;
- Bank overdraft or line of credit;
- Acceptance credit;
- Short-term loans;
- Trade credit facilities.

Medium and long-term credit and debts are to be repaid in a period exceeding 12 months; loans covered by collateral are available from financial institutions (for example a bank, trust company, savings and loans institution or an insurance company). These are generally formalised by documents of the following three types:

- Promissory notes, which formally commit the borrower to pay interest and repay the principal on time;
- Mortgage contract, which assigns collateral to the lender;
- The loan agreement, which stipulates the conditions that the borrower has to fulfil during the duration of the loan. These conditions include, among other things, the obligation to carry adequate insurance on the mortgage assets and to keep the assets in good condition.

The lender has the right to foreclose if the borrower fails to comply with any condition of the loan agreement. Foreclosure is ordered by a court of law, which names an administrator or liquidator who takes possession of the property and sells it. The proceeds go first to the court, then to the administrator, then to secured and unsecured creditors in order of priority. Financial institutions have limitations on the amount they can lend to any one borrower per project.

Sometimes they syndicate the financing to redistribute the loan risk while themselves complying with this fundamental rule.

■ Bonds and debentures

For big projects borrowing is effected by bond issues to the general public; there are a number of different types of bonds and debentures. A bond is a promise to pay interest, and to repay the principal, on fixed dates, formalised by a certificate which is purchased by the lender. Bonds are generally issued when large amounts have to be borrowed. In the United States they are of $1000 in denomination. They generally have the following features:

- They are guaranteed by a mortgage.
- They may be registered with the issuing corporation for protection against loss or theft, or they may be coupon (unregistered) bonds.
- They are sometimes sold to underwriters, who in turn sell them to the public.

The issuer can also select a trustee to represent the bondholders. His or her duties are to see that the company fulfils all the pledges in the mortgage contract (deed of trust) and to initiate foreclosure proceedings if necessary. Bonds can be callable (companies take advantage of this option when interest rates decline), or non-callable (in such cases companies can still go to the market to buy them back). In classifying bonds for the repayment of principal, the following methods apply: a portion of the principal may be reimbursed every year by retiring certain serial numbers; or a sinking fund may be created to repay the bonds at maturity. In this case, restrictions are replaced on the dividends on shares. Where no arrangements have been made for progressive retirement or to create a sinking fund, a new bond may be issued in replacement of the old one.

Bonds are secured by a mortgage or a lien, whereas debentures are unsecured and depend on the general standing of the company. Bonds can be secured by a mortgage or a lien on one of the following assets:

- Real estate (mortgage on a portion of or all the company's real-estate);
- Equipment (trust bond);
- Stocks and other securities;
- Accounts receivable.

A convertible bond is attractive in that it offers security in the initial years and profit participation when the project succeeds later on. Bond owners may exchange them for a predetermined number of shares when the share price reaches a given level. The option is generally not exercised until the ordinary share price reaches or passes the set level (profitable to the bondholder). They are generally offered when the survivability of the project in the initial years is uncertain. When bond interest rates are temporarily high and funds are

Table 6.3 Reimbursement of a loan under four different repayment methods

	Investment period US$ thousands		Total	Repayment period					Total
	1 Jan 1991	1 Jan 1992	31 Dec 1993	31 Dec 1993	31 Dec 1994	31 Dec 1995	31 Dec 1996	31 Dec 1997	
Amount of loan	400	600	1100						
Interest at 10%	84	60	144						
Loan and interest capitalised to 31 Dec 1992	484	660	1144						
a. Equal instalments of principal method:									
Outstanding amount of loan			1144	1144.0	915.2	686.4	457.6	228.8	
Equal instalment				228.8	228.8	228.8	228.8	228.8	
+ Interest charge (10%)				114.4	91.5	68.6	45.8	22.9	343.2
Yearly repayment amount				343.2	320.3	297.4	274.6	251.7	1487.2
b. Annuity reimbursement method:									
Outstanding amount of loan			1144	1144.0	956.6	750.5	523.8	274.4	
+ Current period interest				114.4	95.7	75.1	52.4	27.4	365.0
Total debt outstanding				1258.4	1052.3	825.6	576.2	301.8	
Equal instalment payments (principal and interest at 10%)				301.8	301.8	301.8	301.8	301.8	1509.0
c. Sinking fund method:									
Outstanding amount of loan			1144	1144.0	1258.4	1384.2	1522.6	1674.9	
+ Current period interest				114.4	125.8	138.4	152.3	167.5	698.4
Total debt outstanding				1258.4	1384.2	1522.6	1674.9	1842.4	
Payments to sinking fund (amount deposited annually)				301.8	301.8	301.8	301.8	301.8	1509.0
Interest earned (at 10%)					30.1	63.4	99.9	140.0	333.4
Total funds available				301.8	331.9	365.2	401.7	441.8	1842.4
d. Balloon repayment method:									
Outstanding amount of loan			1144	1144.0	1144.0	1144.0	1144.0	1144.0	
Yearly interest payment				114.4	114.4	114.4	114.4	114.4	572.0
Repayment of principal								1144.0	

Source: 1992 International Trade Centre UNCTAD/GATT, Geneva.

available from few institutions, two to five-year loan notes are issued to these institutions. They are also used to avoid the high cost of making bond issues and when dealing with substantial bondholders. These notes are usually secured by mortgages. Basically they are the same as bonds except they are issued to few lenders.

Warrants are sweeteners to a public issue of debt that is privately placed. Here the buyer gets the interest income of the debt and an option to purchase a share of the company at a pre-fixed price. Should the share market price rise to the stated level of conversion, the warrant becomes valuable and its price increases considerably (high). The main advantage for the issuer is that he or she can usually get a lower interest-rate charge. Issuing warrants is mainly important for projects with high credit risk primarily at the initial stage of the project, when funds are difficult or impossible to raise through other channels, such as supplier credits and export credit finance.

■ Debt servicing

Reimbursement of loans is also of considerable importance in the debt financing of an overseas project as it directly affects net cash flows. The interest portion of the payments constitutes the financial expenses of the project and is directly included in the cash outflows. Failure to meet the scheduled payments may force the company into bankruptcy.

Debt service involves two elements: interest payments and principal repayments. Interest payments are a function of the loan size and the interest rate. Interest rates vary with the maturity of the loan; a ten-year loan will normally have a higher rate of interest than a two-year loan, as the risk represented by the time factor is higher. In addition, they may be fixed or floating. The terms of repayment of a loan principal may vary considerably from project to project. The banker extending a loan will ensure that the repayment will be in accordance with the liquidity surplus appearing in the cash-flow statement for financial planning. Typically, management should try to strike a balance between deferring repayments of principal and the extra interest burden of deferred principal repayments.

■ Financial appraisal

Financial statements contain the fundamental information from which the viability of a project can be measured. The process of measurement consists of extracting different financial ratios revealing different viability parameters of the project. The financial ratios are tools and instruments of measurement essential to assessing project viability. However, it is important to stress that financial ratios taken by themselves are meaningless and might be misleading. The reason is that different projects have varying inherent levels of risk and

Table 6.4   Schedule for the financing plan of a project (including debt financing)

(US$ thousands or equivalent)	Total		Total		Total	
	Foreign	*Local*	*Foreign*	*Local*	*Foreign*	*Local*
I Equity capital						
II Long-term loan						
III Short-term credit						
IV Subsidies and grants						
Total						

return. Furthermore, an overseas project has to survive in a very competitive environment; hence, it is essential to assess its effectiveness in relation to other exporters/producers and to know its relative strengths and weaknesses over its life-span. The basic appraisal criteria are:

1. The relative profitability of the project in relation to the cost of capital and/or to competitors;
2. Financial ratios which signal the need for appropriate corrective measures if necessary.

Therefore, the internal rate of return (IRR) should be compared to the cost of capital (K_o) to determine the profitability of the project. Should K_o not be possible to obtain, then one of the substitutes mentioned earlier (average for the industry, etc.) may be used. The other ratios are to be compared to the industry averages published by one of the following financial services institutions: Standard and Poors, Moody's, Dun and Bradstreet, Forbes. Table 6.5 shows a typical example of industry groupings and yardsticks of performance currently in use. Comparison should be made from period to period to examine the trend of project results so that appropriate action can be taken to correct deviations.

The most important financial ratios to assess project viability can be grouped into five categories, namely:

- Profitability ratios;
- Liquidity ratios;
- Leverage ratios;
- Efficiency/rotation ratios;
- Risk assessment.

Profitability ratios assess the rate of return as well as the efficiency with which resources are utilised. The first subgroup of these ratios consists of discounted ratios. These are based on the time-value of money, that is, the technique of discounting cash-flows.

As far as discounted ratios are concerned, net present value (*NPV*) determines project viability by discounting cash flows at the cut-off rate desired by the investor. Where the *NPV* is positive, the project is yielding more than the discount rate and is thus retained; a negative NPV indicates that the project is not yielding the expected return. The cut-off rate applied is ideally the cost of capital. If this is not possible, substitutes (the rate of return obtained by competitors, or others as presented) are used. The advantages of *NPV* are that it discounts the cash flow at a rate desired by the investor, unlike the *IRR*, which assumes (specially in the case of a high rate of return) that the reinvestment will be at the same high rate throughout the project life; and it is an indicator of the surplus (in monetary units) above the cut-off rate. The weaknesses of *NPV* in mutually-exclusive projects are that it does not take into consideration the amount invested in each project; it does not take into consideration the life-span of each project; and its accuracy is dependent on the accuracy of the calculation of the cost of capital.

In mutually-exclusive and contingent project proposals, NPVR (net present value ratio) takes into account the investment cost and presents a profitability index by means of which the project with the highest ratio is identified and retained. Furthermore, when there are two projects having the same investment outlay and the same profitability index, one having a high cash-flow in the early years and the other with a high cash-flow in the later period, the first project will be preferred to the second. The reason is that the early cash-flow of the first can be used to meet budgetary needs.

CASE 6.8

As regards mutually-exclusive projects, it is also sometimes better to select two small projects taking up the full budget than to choose a large one leaving some unused funds, as is shown in the example below. This example assumes that total funds available for investment are $50 000.

Project	Investment	Profitability index	NPV	$
1	35 000	1.14	= .14 × 35 000	= 4900
2	15 000	1.12	= .12 × 15 000	= 1800
3	40 000	1.16	= .16 × 40 000	= 6400

The advantage of *NPVR* is that it ranks mutually-exclusive and contingent projects according to their rates of return. The weakness of *NPVR* if that it does not take into consideration the fact that two projects may have different time horizons.

Table 6.5 An example of industry groupings and yardsticks of performance

Yardsticks of management performance	Profitability					Growth					
	Return on equity			Debt as % of profit margin	Net profit margin	Sales			Earnings per share		
Industry	Rank	5-year average	Latest 12 months			Rank	5-year average	Latest 12 months	Rank	5-year average	Latest 12 months
Insurance											
Packaging											
Computers and electronics											
Conglomerates											
Paper											
Chemicals											
Automotive											
Leisure and recreation											
Construction											
Surface transportation											
Air transport											
Oil											
Heavy equipment											
Coal											
Metals											
All-industry medians											

Health
Electrical equipment
Food processors
Retailing
Food distributors
Banks and thrifts
Telecommunications
Aerospace and defense
Consumer products
Natural gas
Apparel, shoes & textiles

Source: International Trade Centre UNCTAD/GATT, 1992.

■ Internal rate of return

IRR is the rate of discount that will make the present value of all cash inflows equal to the present value of all cash outflows, at which point NPV = 0.

Two formulas can be used to obtain the benefit/cost ratio (*B/CR*):

1. Discounted cash-flow of all benefits divided by discounted cash-flow of all costs. If the ratio is higher than 1 the project is retained. This formula is mainly used in the appraisal of public-sector projects.
2. Discounted benefits less discounted costs. If the value is positive (higher than zero) the project is retained. This method is primarily applied in the appraisal of private and public-sector projects, and in the determination of minimum cost in the optimisation process of project appraisal.

After the net present value, *IRR* is one of the best tools for assessing the profitability of a project. However, it has its limitations and should be used in conjunction with a number of other ratios to assess the viability of a project. The advantages of *IRR* are that it takes into account the time-value of money; it indicates a ratio (return in percentage) on the basis of return on capital; and it can be easily compared to the cost of capital or its substitutes.

The weaknesses of *IRR* are that it assumes that for each year of the life of the project the rate of return will be the same. While this assumption is acceptable for average returns, it is not always true when profitability ratios are high. Also two projects having the same IRR may have different levels of cash-flow in the early or later years. In certain cases more than one *IRR* can be obtained if the cash flow turns negative and then positive during the life of the project. It gives the rate of return of the project itself and not the cut-off rate required by the investor, and hence can be contradictory to the result of the *NPV*, which reflects the return desired by the investor. This can be seen from the following example:

| | *Net cash flows* | | | *Net present value* | | | |
Period	*Year 0*	*Year 1*	*Year 2*	*At 15%*	*At 20%*	*At 25%*	*IRR*
Project A	100	80	59	14.18	7.63	1.76	26.6%
Project B	100	30	119	16.07	7.63	.16	25.1%

Should *IRR* be used, project A will be preferred to project B. However, if *NPV* is used and the desired rate of return is below 20 per cent, project B will be chosen. Above the 20 per cent cut-off rate, project A will be preferred.

The question here is what is the appropriate rate of reinvestment for each period, using this rate for discounting (or compounding for a terminal value). Thus, if a choice must be made, the *NPV* method is considered to be superior theoretically.

Consider the projected cash-flow in the following example.

Year 0	1	2	3	4	5	Discount rate	NPV	IRR
(450)	400	400	50	(25)	(410)	= 0%	(35.00)	—
						= 5%	(4.85)	—
						= 10%	10.12	6.25%
						= 15%	15.02	—
						= 20%	13.22	—
						= 25%	7.01	—
						= 30%	(2.04)	29.00%

Initially the *NPV* starts with a negative value, which becomes positive as the discount rate increases but finally turns negative. As for the *IRR*, different values are obtained which could be misleading. The situation is clearer when applying the *NPV*, where the investor can see that to retain the project, the cut-off rate has to be more than 5 per cent and less than 30 per cent.

■ Financial risk assessment

This is an important aspect of financial appraisal. The financial results of a new overseas project are forecast by extrapolating current conditions of business into the future. However, these conditions are not guaranteed to stay the same throughout the life of the project. Actual figures of sales volume, sales price, production and transportation costs may be dramatically different from the forecast figures. Moreover, the project is exposed to various risks and uncertainties, such as foreign exchange fluctuation, credit risk, changes in technology, entry of new competitors, shifts in consumer tastes and new substitutes for the product. Therefore investor and analyst alike need to have an idea about the conditions of uncertainty and risk (see Chapter 7 for a full discussion of these aspects).

Four basic types of analysis can be used to assist the planner in assessing conditions of financial uncertainty. These are the analysis of the pay-back period, break-even point, sensitivity, and the probability of risk.

The pay-back period is the time required for investors to recover their original investment outlay through the profit earned by the project. Profit is defined here as net profit (that is, profit after tax + financial charges + depreciation). Four versions of the pay-back period method can be used. Hence, care should be given to establishing which one is under consideration. The advantages are that it is simple and gives an estimate of the waiting time needed to recover the original investment. The longer the period, the riskier the project (as time increases, uncertainty increases). Therefore it gives a vague idea about the risk involved in terms of waiting time. In certain cases (for example in the microcomputer industry which is subject to rapid changes in technology, or in a project undertaken in an unstable environment) this waiting time would be the deciding factor. But this method neglects any profit or benefit accruing to the project once the investment has been recovered. Hence future cash inflow accruing to the project after the recovery of the investment is not taken into account at all. Furthermore, this method does not measure the intrinsic profitability of the project.

The four possible approaches to the measurement of risk by the pay-back method are:

1. Inclusion of the construction period in the time needed to recover the investment;
2. Elimination of the construction period from the time needed to recover the investment;
3. Elimination of the value of the land and the working capital cost from the investment cost on the assumption that these two amounts can be recovered at the end of the project's life. This method, while applicable under certain conditions, is not usable under other conditions;
4. Using discounted cash flow (instead of net profit) to take into account the time-value of money.

CASE 6.9

Here is a calculation of the pay-back period for a given set of data.

Year	Amount paid back from profit	Balance of total investment at year end
1. Construction period	—	$ 4 839
2. Construction period	—	$18 740
3. Production period	$2 878	$15 862
4. Production period	$4 049	$11 813
5. Production period	$5 219	$ 6 594
6. Production period	$6 002	$ 592
7 Production period	$6 002	($5 410)

In this hypothetical case the pay-back period is six years and one month. If the construction period is excluded the pay-back period is four years and one month.

■ Break-even point analysis

Since total fixed costs remain constant, irrespective of the volume of output (within a relevant range), it follows that their impact on unit product costs varies as output changes. Thus fixed costs per unit of product decrease as volume expands; consequently a reduction in unit costs can be obtained through greater utilisation of capacity.

However, by virtue of their being fixed irrespective of the volume of output, the existence of fixed costs implies that a minimum level of output is needed to cover them and to avoid operating losses through insufficient volume. The break-even volume of output is that level of capacity utilisation at which there is neither profit nor loss. The break-even point (BEP) may be expressed in terms of:

- Number of units to be produced;
- Total sales revenue;
- Percentage utilisation of plant capacity;
- Minimum sales price per unit.

The method of determining the BEP is as follows:

Let X = number of units
        P = unit price
        F = fixed costs
        V = variable costs per unit
        S = sales revenue
        R = sales revenue at full capacity
        C = percentage utilisation of plant capacity.

At BEP, sales revenue = production costs. Hence, at BEP the number of units to be produced is given by:

$$X = F/(P - V)$$

The total sales revenue is:

$$S = X \times P$$

The percentage utilisation of plant capacity is:

$$C = F/[R - (V{\cdot}X)]$$

The minimum sales price per unit is:

$$X{\cdot}P = F + (V{\cdot}X)$$

The following example shows the importance of BEP analysis. A firm has total fixed costs of $25 million. Its variable cost per unit is $0.9375. What will be the break-even point (BEP) at (1) a high unit sales price of $2.50, and (2) a low unit sales price of $1.25?

- BEP at a unit price of $2.50 = $25 million/(2.50 − 0.9375) = 16 million units.
- BEP at a unit price of $1.25 = $25 million/(1.25 − 0.9375) = 80 million units.

BEP analysis provides information about the level of risk and uncertainty inherent in the project through each one of the four indicators. By showing the minimum number of units to be produced, or the revenues or the capacity utilisation needed to break even, it indicates the closeness to the risk area (unprofitable area). The lower the level of each one of these measures the safer the project is.

The minimum sales price per unit is an excellent indicator of risk for projects involving products which are subject to considerable price fluctuation, such as basic materials (gold, oil, copper, aluminium, cocoa, coffee, grain and so on). With a knowledge of the level of that minimum it is possible to ascertain whether the project can survive if the price of the exportable product drops to levels previously experienced.

The margin of safety can also be found by deducting the break-even point from the expected total level of activity and calculating the remainder as a percentage of expected total production. Thus the margin of safety indicates the riskiness of the project by giving an idea of the safety-net remaining before the project becomes unprofitable. BEP must be used with caution, as the kind of analysis discussed here assumes a linearity of costs and revenues. In addition, the variable cost and sales price per unit change with the volume of activity (for example volume discounts for large purchases or sales). A further factor is that if different products are produced and sold and the product mix is changed, the BEP may also change.

■ Sensitivity analysis

The financial appraisal of an overseas project is an assessment of its future performance and survivability. To a certain degree the future is always uncertain. Sensitivity analysis involves the variation of certain parameters of the project, thus creating different scenarios and comparing the viability of the project under each scenario. The parameters subjected to sensitivity analysis may be cost of energy and certain raw materials, sales volume and the unit price, the investment cost, the entry of a new competitor or product substitute, foreign exchange rates, and so on. In this manner, a range of possible outcomes is obtained and the project is appraised on this range of outcomes rather than on one expected outcome. The scenarios for different outcomes would vary from one that is optimistic to one that is expected and one that is pessimistic.

It should be noted that sensitivity analysis should be applied only to elements with some probability of not materialising. Furthermore, when performing sensitivity analysis care should be taken to exclude overall pessimistic valuations for several components, as their inclusion will inevitably lead to the rejection of almost all projects. Rather, the approach should be conservative without being unrealistically negative or optimistic.

Sensitivity analysis involves a repetition of the calculation and presentation of projected financial statements and financial performance ratios. Therefore the calculation and presentation process substantially increases the required time and effort. Computer models are used to ease this burden. The advantage of using the computer is speed in the execution of the calculation process.

It should also be noted that a computer model does not correct for error or false data. Hence it is up to the analyst to ensure that the data processed by the computer are reliable, objective and rational. Furthermore, a feasibility study cannot be effected by a computer model; the latter only provides an accelerated means of executing the calculations. Errors of input will necessarily yield erroneous results.

■ **Probability analysis**

A project is subject to certain risks. If it is assessed on present and historical facts the results may mislead the management, and erroneous investment decisions may be made. Thus in appraising a project's future viability risk elements must be considered. However, risk elements vary considerably from project to project. Thus one or more of the project parameters could be made the subject of a probability distribution; from this, using the standard deviation technique, one can assess the risk in a project.

The standard deviation is the most frequently employed measure of dispersion around the central tendency of a probability distribution. The greater the standard deviation, the greater the risk associated with the distribution. The formula for the calculation of standard deviation is:

$$\delta = \sqrt{\sum_{t=1}^{n} (O_t - \mu)^2 P_t}$$

where δ = the standard deviation
 O_t = the tth outcome
 μ = the mean
 P_t = the probability of the tth outcome
 n = the number of possible outcomes

There are a number of variables that contribute to the risk of an export project, such as the sales volume, sales price, production cost, project life and so forth. In order to assess the total risk of the project, the risk inherent in each component variable must be determined. In this case, using a computer model becomes an absolute necessity to unify these separate risk variables into a general risk measure for the project as a whole.

Consider the problem of measuring the risk of a new project for which the probability distributions of anticipated future sales, production costs, required investment and salvage value are known. Since many of the data entries are not independent, appropriate tables of conditional probabilities should be prepared. As cost data depend on future sales projections, a high volume of sales

---

CASE 6.10

As an example, suppose we have an asset which will generate a cash flow as follows:

Outcome	Probability (P_t)
$1 000	0.3
$ 700	0.5
$ 500	0.2

The mean would be: $750.
Applying the formula, the standard deviation would be calcualted as follows:

$(O_t - \mu)$	$(O_t - \mu)^2$	$(O_t - \mu)^2 P_t$
$1 000 − 750 = 250	$(250)^2$	$62 500 \times (0.3) = \$18 750$
$700 − 750 = −50	$(-50)^2$	$2 500 \times (0.5) = \$1 250$
$500 − 750 = −250	$(-250)^2$	$62 500 \times (0.2) = \$12 500$
		$\Sigma = \$32 500$

which leads to:

$$\sigma = \sqrt{32\,500} = 180.3$$

The greater the standard deviation, the greater the risk associated with the cashflow.

---

would most likely produce higher costs. Let us suppose that the following data for the period t_1 have been determined:

Sales	Cash expenses	Net cashflow
20 (0.3)	15 (0.3)	5 (0.09)
20 (0.3)	16 (0.6)	4 (0.18)
20 (0.3)	9 (0.1)	1 (0.03)
18 (0.5)	13 (0.2)	5 (0.1)
18 (0.5)	15 (0.6)	3 (0.3)
18 (0.5)	16 (0.2)	2 (0.1)
15 (0.2)	10 (0.3)	5 (0.06)
15 (0.2)	12 (0.5)	3 (0.1)
15 (0.2)	15 (0.2)	0 (0.04)

The above data could be grouped into the following net cash flow distribution for t_1:

Net cash-flow	Probability
5	0.25
4	0.18
3	0.40
2	0.10
1	0.03
0	0.04
	1.00

To determine the net flows for future periods, repeat the same operation year-by-year throughout the project life to obtain a conditional probability distribution for each period.

Suppose the probability distribution of the following has been obtained:

- Required investment;
- Net cash-flows;
- Salvage value;
- Project life.

Using a computer we can calculate the *IRR* for each combination and array them in a frequency distribution. This distribution represents the relative probability that any one internal rate of return could occur, as presented in Figure 6.9.

The dispersion around the mean value of the *IRR* indicates the risk inherent

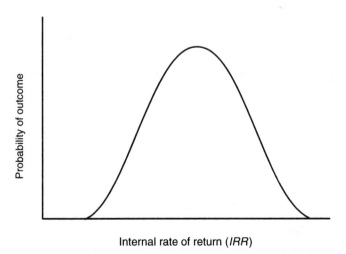

Internal rate of return (*IRR*)

Figure 6.9 Frequency distribution of probability of specific internal rates of return.

in the project. The formula for calculation of the standard deviation for the *IRR* is:

$$\sigma_{IRR} = \sqrt{\sum_{t=1}^{n} (IRR_t - IRR_{mean})^2 \, P_t}$$

where σ_{IRR} = the standard deviation
IRR_t = the t_{th} outcome
IRR_{mean} = the expected (mean) rate of return
P_t = the probability of the t_{th} outcome
n = the number of possible outcomes

Thus, if the distribution of *IRR* were determined as follows:

IRR	Probability
8%	0.3
9%	0.4
10%	0.2
11%	0.1

The mean of *IRR* would equal $(0.3)(0.08) + (0.4)(0.09) + (0.2)(0.1) + (0.1)(0.11) = 9.1\%$

The standard deviation of *IRR* can now be calculated as follows:

$IRR_t - IRR_{mean}$	$(IRR_t - IRR_{mean})^2$	P_t
8% − 9.1 = −1.1%	$(-1.1)^2 = 1.21\%$	1.21 × 0.3 = 0.363%
9% − 9.1 = −0.1%	$(-0.1)^2 = 0.01\%$	0.01 × 0.4 = 0.004%
10% − 9.1 = 0.9%	$(0.9)^2 = 0.81\%$	0.81 × 0.2 = 0.162%
11% − 9.1 = 1.9%	$(1.9)^2 = 3.61\%$	3.61 × 0.1 = 0.361%

$\sigma IRR = \sqrt{0.89} = 0.94\%$ or about 1% from mean.

The greater the standard deviation of *IRR*, the greater the risk involved in the project. Whether or not a high-risk project would be selected depends on the investors' risk preference.

■ Profit and performance improvement

Increases in productivity, particularly in sales and marketing, can improve operational effectiveness, ensure higher quality and increase customer satisfaction. These represent the ideal outcomes or situation for the company, and the contribution that research can make towards achieving this ideal is a substantial one, though one that is not generally recognised or given its due place in theory or in practice. Above all, performance improvement can generate more competitive advantages for the company. Marketing productivity itself is a measure of the profit responsiveness by segment to different levels of marketing investment.

An early research study (Sevin, 1965) defined marketing productivity as the ratio of sales or net profits (effect produced) to marketing costs (energy expended) for a specific segment of the business. This study indicates that performance improvement derives from increasing the productivity of marketing operations in any one of the five following ways:

- An increase in sales or net profits proportionately greater than a corresponding increase in marketing costs.
- An increase in sales or net profits with the same marketing costs.
- An increase in sales or net profits with a decrease in marketing costs.
- The same sales or net profits with a decrease in marketing costs.
- A decrease in sales or net profits proportionately less than a corresponding decrease in marketing costs.

Research can contribute two types of information towards the achievement of these five kinds of increase in marketing productivity. The first is the matching of marketing costs and revenues of segments of the business, such as individual products (this will reveal segments which are unprofitable, or where profit performance can be improved). Second, it is often necessary to know what would happen to sales and/or profits if marketing efforts were shifted from one segment to another (as from an unprofitable to a profitable segment); market experimentation is needed to obtain this second kind of information. Table 6.6 shows the different types of information needed to improve performance in specific marketing areas.

Information technology (IT) is also making increasingly significant contributions to decision-making in these and other areas of management. As the power of IT has become apparent, so more efforts have been made to extend its range of research applications, with particular emphasis on the degree of problem-complexity and the definition or quantification of explicit decision rules. In three categories involving quantitative elements of marketing, IT applications have been effective:

- Systems for developing marketing programmes, including statistical software for market research and analysis;
- Strategic planning systems, including systems for gathering and analysing marketing intelligence, forecasting industry trends and analysing competitors' market shares;
- Decision support systems, including numerous quantitative applications such as pricing/gaming models, decision-trees and new product/portfolio analysis systems.

IT has been adopted in these three areas not because the technology is mar-

Table 6.6   Information needed to improve performance in specific marketing areas

Area	Information
Basic data	
Sales forecasts	Long-term industry sales: • long-term 'own' product sales; • industry sales by segment; • 'own' product sales by segment.
Market share	Long-term projections of competing products' shares: • long-term projections of 'own' product's share; • projections of competing product's shares by segment; • projections of 'own' product's share by segment.
Product contribution	Product's direct costs: • long-term projections of product's contribution; • classification of product's direct contribution by segment
Refined data	
Relative market share	Absolute market share converted to relative share: • long-term projections of relative market share.
Value of market share	Value of market share computed: • long-term projections of relative market share; • estimates of market share value by segments.
Output data	
Product profitability	Product profitability statement present and future (2–3 years): • value of future income streams determining present value or cash flow for market share alternatives.

Source: Cosse and Swan (1986) pp. 92–102.

keting-specific, but because these marketing functions emphasise the collection and analysis of quantitative data. Market research, for example, demands the collection and organisation of large amounts of data, while market forecasting often involves extensive computation using research data. These, and similar tasks associated with risk-analysis and gaming models, are well-matched to the computational abilities of the computer. Quantitative systems have increased the range of analysis available, and presumably the quality of decisions by managers; and there are now available approaches to increasing productivity in key areas such as marketing, thereby improving overall corporate performance. Such approaches have the potential to provide significant competitive advantages through increased product or service differentiation, improved customer service and more streamlined operations.

CASE 6.11

The Digital Equipment Corporation (DEC) USA is one of the world's largest man-ufacturers of computer hardware and software, and was one of the first manufac-turers to market a computerised system to improve performance in sales and marketing administration. In 1985, DEC introduced an All-in-One System for sales and marketing, a general-purpose office automation package designed to operate on the company's VAX minicomputers. The system comprised three modules:

- a base system for storing and organising sales personnel information;
- a field reporting module that streamlined production of sales-call reports and sales intelligence reports, and generated summary reports for management;
- a lead-management module that updated prospect information, rank-ordering prospects and automatically forwarding leads to sales personnel.

Unlike some other software packages, DEC's All-in-One was designed to allow integration with third-party software, and DEC signed marketing agreements with some other system manufacturers.

There has also been substantial research in recent years on the key contribution of quality management to performance and profit improvement. A recent study by the Strategic Planning Institute in the USA using the PIMS data-base exam-ined customer perceptions of quality in 450 companies; the conclusion was: 'relative perceived quality, whether in service or product attributes, is the single most important element in determining a company's long-term profitability' (Buzzell and Gale, 1987).

The study found that several key benefits accrue to companies that offer superior products and services:

- stronger customer loyalty;
- more repeat purchases;
- less vulnerability to price wars.

More importantly, the study also concluded that, on average, companies with superior quality are able to:

- charge 4 per cent more for their product;
- grow at twice the rate of other companies;
- gain 6 per cent market share per annum.

This research provides hard evidence to support a strategy of service quality and customer satisfaction as a method of performance improvement, because of the strong relationship between perceived quality and profitability.·

Another recent and significant application of research to performance improvement is the *service quality gaps model*; this represents a concise conceptual framework of the service quality process, and readily identifies external customer research as well as the processes necessary to deliver service quality. Some service quality issues are externally visible to customers, while others are internal to the company but affect service delivery. The concept is applied through a form of gap analysis: where elements of service are not correctly acted upon, a service quality gap exists, which will detract from customer satisfaction (Berry, 1991). This research identifies five gaps.

☐ *Gap 1*

This arises when management fails to identify or understand customer needs. This occurs because:

- Market research may be poorly-orientated, so that the needs, wants and desires of customers are not determined. Management has little direct contact with customers and therefore a low awareness of customer needs.
- Poor upward communication will also prevent understanding of customer needs; feedback systems are important to bridge this gap.
- Too many management levels between the employees in touch with customers and top management can also lead to gap 1 arising.

Gap 1 should be measured by research into customer expectations, as well as into employee and management perceptions to determine what they think customer expectations are.

☐ *Gap 2*

This is caused by inconsistency between receipt of customer expectations and translation into service-quality standards, a management fault. This gap can be met by establishing clearly-defined service-quality goals, and committing adequate resources to the provision of these service quality standards, both of which should be performed by management.

☐ *Gap 3*

Gap 3 arises when the specified levels of service quality and actual levels of service quality delivered are not translated adequately into actual delivery to customers. This gap can be bridged by:

- development of teamwork and cooperation between all levels of the organisation;
- skill development to ensure that personnel can perform their job adequately, and with competence and confidence;
- control systems for management to evaluate and then implement rewards for performance.

This is one of the key areas for performance improvement.

☐ *Gap 4*

A difference between service delivery and what is communicated about the service to customers. This involves the ability of organisations to communicate to their external customers and highlight their service-quality standards. The importance of this external communication is that it matches the perceptions of what is promised by employees to what is actually communicated to consumers.

☐ *Gap 5*

This is the gap traditionally measured by marketing research as it is the difference between the customers' expectations of what they will receive and what they perceive they have received. This is sometimes referred to as 'the moment of truth' for organisations, where the company's perception of what constitutes service quality and the customer's perception of service quality are compared to see if they match, and thus whether the company's service-quality ethic has been effective in satisfying customers.

CASE 6.12

The most consistently profitable computer company in Europe is also a leading exponent of quality as a way of corporate life. ICL in April 1993 announced a revenue increase of 32 per cent to almost £2.5 billion; quality is, in fact, the secret of its success.

ICL's quality quest began in the mid-1980s when it introduced well-established quality practices to measure and monitor performance at all levels of the business – everything from delivery times and product faults to unused stock and staff productivity. The results were startling. In the first three years the cost of goods lying idle was reduced from £220 million to £138 million, on-time delivery and product-reliability increased significantly and output per employee leaped by nearly one-third. In the longer term, the ongoing quality process which involved giving quality training to everyone from the managing director to the shopfloor worker, has helped ICL to out-perform its rivals in one of the most competitive industries in the world and to defy the recession by remaining firmly in the black. Quality has been enshrined in the structure of the company since 1987, when it appointed a director of quality at board level. All 25 000 staff worldwide were trained in quality techniques and teams were set up to fix, and eliminate for good, problems in all areas of the company's business.

Today, ICL's quality focus has shifted away from getting its own house in order, to bringing extra benefit to its customers. The company has put its money where its mouth is by building special customer-care training into a comprehensive on-going quality-improvement programme estimated to cost more than £20 million a year. ICL sets out four rules for its employees to follow:

- exceed customer expectations, do not just meet them;
- aim for personal service;
- aim to become the first-choice supplier;
- measure customer care by what the customer says, not what you think he or she should be saying.

The message appears to have struck home. A recent IDC market research survey of European IT users, for instance, placed ICL at the top of the customer satisfaction league for mid-range computer systems. Quality attracts quality, bringing with it high-calibre customers. Marks & Spencer, for example, chose ICL to supply its point-of-sale terminals.

Fashion retailer Laura Ashley, whose chief executive introduced a new focus on the brand and the needs of customers when he was appointed in 1991, was also encouraged by the quality approach. It chose ICL to equip its stores worldwide.

The rewards for quality are more than merely financial. ICL holds a number of quality and training awards, and in 1991 the company became the first UK organisation to receive company-wide registration by the British Standards Institution to the internationally recognised ISO 9000 standard. Now the goal was to achieve similar recognition for its 70 international operations by the end of 1995.

A continuous-quality improvement process is built into ICL's operations. Called DELTA, its aim is to improve a thousand things by one per cent rather than one thing by a thousand per cent. ICL's policy is to compete with and win against the best in the world by exceeding customers' expectations: this is customer care.

The concept of 'moments of truth' for the customer is an integrated part of the customer satisfaction ethic often requiring a culture change within the company, so that the primary focus of the company is quality of contact between an individual customer and the company's employees who service the customer directly. Each contact with a customer ultimately determines whether a company will succeed or fail: it is the point where expectations and perceptions of quality meet, and therefore customer satisfaction is decided. Improving performance, therefore, rests on researching and orientating the company towards a competitive advantage. And handling these moments of truth determines whether a customer will walk away feeling better or worse about the company.

Mishandling this interaction can cost the customer's goodwill, his or her business and potentially the business of the people to whom he or she will recount the unhappy experience at the hands of the company. Managing this interaction, as the service model in Figure 6.10 illustrates, is a case of not just external but also internal factors for a company, and thus the value of employee motivation in providing service quality is apparent. Performance improvement to deliver service quality can provide a company with a source of competitive advantage by satisfying customers through the use of relationship-marketing.

The most widely used determinants of service quality are those shown in Figure 6.10, which suggests that the criteria used by consumers that are import-

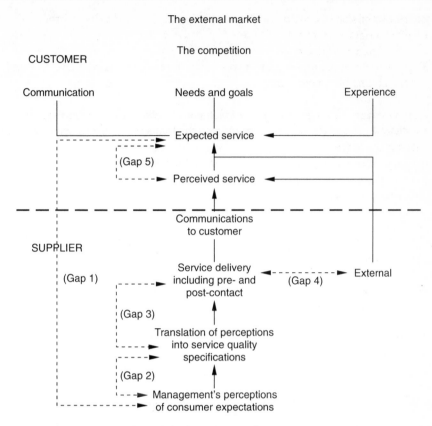

Figure 6.10   Conceptual model of service quality

Source: Adapted from Parasuraman, Zeithaml and Berry (1985), pp. 41–50.

ant in moulding their expectations and perceptions of delivered service fit ten dimensions, namely: tangibles, reliability, responsiveness, communication, credibility, security, non-competence, courtesy, understanding/knowing the customer and access. Subsequent research, analysis and testing by Parasuraman *et al.* have led to five dimensions of service performance, forming their model called SERVQUAL, the dimensions of which are:

- *Tangibles*—physical facilities, equipment, and appearance of personnel.
- *Reliability*—ability to perform the promised service dependably and accurately.
- *Responsiveness*—willingness to help customers and provide prompt service.
- *Empathy*—caring, individualised attention the company provides to customers.
- *Assurance*—knowledge and courtesy to employees and their ability to inspire trust and confidence.

This model, however, leaves out one very important aspect. It does not show the competition and market and what these contribute to customers' expectations. Since poor services lose customers, it is necessary to manage the customer relationship at the first point of contact. If quality is not built into the delivery systems, variations in the process are explained by customers as poor or inconsistent service at the front desk.

According to further research, three main factors act as barriers to quality and performance improvement:

1. Specifications of quality standards which cause difficulties owing to the intangible nature of parts of the service package and the management of customer expectations.
2. Control systems which do not include statements defining;
    *   what is to be measured;
    *   what the targets are; and
    *   how measurements are to be made and by whom.

CASE 6.13

The philosophy of performance improvement has been developed over 60 years by the Maritz Corporation, USA, which is a leading world consultant with a turnover of US$1.4 billion in 1990. Maritz Inc. designs and implements a range of services for improvement in levels of profitability and quality – quality offered by the client to its customers as well as quality in the package of benefits offered to the client's employees. The mission of the company is 'to serve clients as one unified, powerful agent for change and improvement'.

Maritz sets out the following performance improvement objectives for client companies:

*   Energise the entire organisation;
*   Organise efforts around work groups;
*   Clarify role responsibilities and training requirements;
*   Streamline internal processes;
*   Recognise and reward employees for improved performance;
*   Drive customer satisfaction and loyalty.

The market research division of Maritz is especially involved in analysis of the last of these, with the emphasis on tailor-made marketing solutions as a key outcome for clients in as widely-divergent industries as car manufacture, consumer food processing, banking, insurance and pharmaceuticals. So research is used not only for the information it provides, but as a tool to direct specific changes in a company.

The research and experience of Maritz strongly indicate that higher levels of customer satisfaction can lead to increased market share, higher profitability and differentiation from the competition, that is competitive advantage. And a 1994 survey conducted by Gallup among CEOs of top American companies to determine the most important quality issue in future performance lists customer service as the top-rated issue for 45 per cent of respondents.

3. Staff development that fails to make staff aware of quality objectives and fails to give them the capability to meet targets.

In seeking ways to improve productivity and quality of service, managers should be aware of some of the actions that can help in the specific areas of productivity. Input costs can be reduced overall through increased training of high-contact service personnel, and the use of technology to support those personnel and the service-delivery process.

■ Conclusions

This chapter has dealt with financial aspects of international business, and but has also explained the financial implications of business expansion and the financial criteria that management must adopt in evaluating and control business plans and operations. First, it has dealt with different ways of raising finance (both internally and externally) for overseas expansion. These considerations are particularly relevant to all decisions concerning foreign direct investment which were explained in the first section. The expertise available to firms from financial institutions has also been explained.

Currency management in all phases has been shown to be a crucial aspect of international pricing, and indeed marketing, by reducing buyer-costs and risks. A detailed exposition was also given of how overseas projects should be financed, costed and appraised for viability; particular attention being paid to debt-servicing, cash-flow management, key financial ratios and financial risk assessment. Finally the significance of profit and performance improvement has been assessed, together with techniques available and relevant Case examples.

QUESTIONS

1. Explain the main criteria that companies should adopt when making decisions about FDI.
2. What sources of finance are available to a medium-sized company planning to expand international operations?
3. Discuss and evaluate three measures of financial performance which are commonly applied to international companies.
4. What indicators/measurements would you use in judging the feasibility of a new project in a country market where the company has little experience of trading?
5. 'Financial risk can be a serious threat to a company's position unless effectively managed.' Comment and explain.
6. Discuss how performance improvement can be planned, and how in practice it can bring about some improvement in profit.

CHAPTER 7

Managing international operations

INTRODUCTION

The extent of the responsibilities and tasks of global management is addressed in this chapter, beginning with an explanation of what makes an effective global manager; Case examples illustrate some of the key points. The highly topical subject of risk and crisis management is tackled next; and the nature of both are examined and different managerial responses explained: clearly if either a risk or crisis is badly handled, the continued viability of the business many be in question. Different ways of effectively managing risk and crisis are discussed, with particular attention to communications once a crisis is in the public domain.

The next section deals with the management of subsidiaries, agents and associates, and explains the importance of communications and control in this process; the former must be: vertically between subsidiaries and headquarters and laterally among subsidiaries. It is important that control is not used by headquarters simply to impose targets and policies: consultation is also essential to planning. Similar principles apply to the management of agents.

The final sections cover international contracting, global 'make or buy' decisions and countertrading.

■ The global manager

■ Planning and control

Whatever worldwide organisational structure is adopted, for its effective management there must be a system of planning and control; where companies trade internationally to achieve corporate goals, control is simply the regulation and direction of operations to accomplish these goals. Control therefore involves:

1. establishing standards;
2. measuring performance against standards; and
3. correcting deviations from standards.

Control is closely linked to planning and organisation, and a lack of control in international operations is usually due to communication or delivery gaps. In order to close these gaps, and to minimise international and intercultural conflicts in business operations, there must be a centralisation of strategic decision-making, corporate acculturation, data management, staff management and resolution of conflict. To ensure that this approach to corporate planning and control is actually made operational, it is necessary to implement:

- a standard planning system;
- a standard reporting system;
- international control/review meetings/committees;
- business support systems;
- a rotation of personnel.

In marketing terms, for example, standards should be applied to all phases of controllable operations, including market research, sales, market share/position, market penetration, distribution, the communications mix and the deployment of agents. In expressing the outcome of operations in financial terms (profit, ROI), special account has to be taken of currency movements, management of debt, taxation, remittances and equity ownership, and these were explained in Chapter 6. Setting standards is, however, a complex task, and requires operating plans, reviews and personal contacts among different subsidiaries to minimise conflict. In other words, communication is the key in setting standards that are internationally understood and that will act as measures of both personal and corporate performance. Again, to take the marketing function as an illustration, two specialised measurement techniques available to management are:

1. The marketing audit – by which the total marketing effort is examined; and
2. Distribution cost analysis – which determines the profitability of different parts of the marketing programme.

In ensuring the development of the business internationally, there are three major aspects to setting up management systems for overall strategic control; these are shown in Table 7.1.

■ Management development

The question of management development to ensure implementation of operating systems has also to be considered. This applies, of course, as much to local managers as to expatriates: while the expatriate clearly has to be mobile, adaptable and dependable, and must remain motivated (sometimes in a difficult working environment), the position of the local manager is increasingly important in view of many governments' policies of localisation. The local manager

Table 7.1   Setting up management systems for overall strategic control

Data management	Staff management	Conflict resolution
Information systems	Selection of key managers	Decision and responsibility assignments
Measurement systems	Career paths	Coordinating committees
Resource allocation	Reward systems	Task forces
Strategic planning	Management development	Issue resolution process
Budgeting process	Socialisation and acculturation	Encouragement of creativity

will require intensive or accelerated training, and management experience perhaps outside his own country. Clearly, in both cases special attention must be paid to remuneration and reward systems, the costs to the company of employing expatriates, acclimatisation (linguistics and work ethic), special factors in local working conditions, relationships with host governments, the direction and level of investment put into the major overseas markets, and the operating aspects of corporate and business plans in different national environments.

Due to the diversity of the environments in which firms with overseas subsidiaries operate, staffing is subjected to a variety of influencing factors, both internal and external to the firm. These factors affect the choice of an effective management development policy and the subsequent implementation of the chosen policy. This can be seen clearly in the three stages of Figure 7.1.

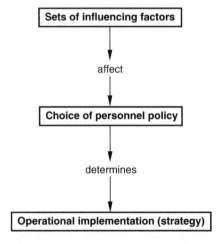

Figure 7.1   Management development policy

■ Company specific factors

Research and analysis of overseas operations over several years have identified a number of sets of these influencing factors. Foremost among these are the following company characteristics:

1. *Ownership of foreign subsidiaries.* A different policy, and indeed a different kind of person, will be required according to whether the investment is short or long-term. The investment that is expected to be short-term can be used either as a training place or as a final posting for those about to retire. The latter policy would overcome the problems of reintegration. Similar considerations may apply where minority holdings are concerned; but in joint ventures considerable powers of diplomacy and knowledge of the company may be required. Longer-term management policies are appropriate where the parent company has majority or total ownership. Many companies use skilled international staff in all of these situations.
2. *Industry group.* Policies will vary at least between manufacturing and service industries. The latter may depend more on intangible knowledge from headquarters, and so are likely to continue to employ expatriates, although this does not necessarily apply to banks, which employ local nationals for their knowledge of local business conditions.
3. *Technology.* The level of the technology in terms of sophistication, together with the amount of the research effort needed to sustain it, will affect the policies of both the technical and the marketing departments. This will apply particularly when the transfer of knowledge virtually requires the transfer of staff. There is some evidence, too, that companies operating in high-level technologies are more likely to transfer other personnel policies.
4. *Market influences.* If the market for the product is purely local and the techniques employed are well within the capacity of local management, expatriates or third-country nationals are much less likely to have a part to play than where global techniques are applicable in worldwide markets.
5. *Age of investment.* The older foreign subsidiaries are likely to have established means of staffing which are hard to change unless problems arise.
6. *Organisational structures.* Companies with product groups having worldwide structure are likely to have more expatriates; those with matrix organisations are almost certain to have some international management development schemes.
7. *Commitment to international business.* A company that does not have a substantial part of its business abroad would not consider the more elaborate schemes for international promotion.
8. *Cost factors.* These are debatable, and there is no formula for working out the costs and benefits of the possible programmes. The costs of expatriates of all types, especially third-country nationals, are increasing rapidly; but the benefits have also been shown to be so great as to make their employment almost certain under some conditions.

9. *The communication and coordination system.* This may affect staffing policies in many ways. One is the use of international transfers, meetings and educational programmes to facilitate communications.
10. *Style of management.* Companies will settle for a distinctive style which suits their business or their personalities. This style is likely to be culture-bound, however, and may cause difficulties.

CASE 7.1

The placement of foreign-born and/or internationally-experienced persons at the helm of the Dow Chemical company in 1992 might suggest the process of multi-nationalisation. For example Peter Drucker, a leading management authority, states that a truly multinational company 'demands of its management people that they think and act as international businessmen in a world in which national passions are as strong as ever'. A company whose top management includes people from various countries and with varied experiences abroad presumably is less likely to place the interests of one country above those of others, and supposedly will have a more worldwide outlook. Whether this is true is debatable. However, the experience of working abroad under some very different environmental conditions is very useful for grasping some problems that are not as prevalent in a purely domestic context.

That most executives of Dow have had considerable foreign experience indicates that international operations are an integral part of the company's total commitment. To bring international operations to this level, Dow had to gain a dedication to international business from a broad spectrum of managers. The company estimates that it took about 20 years to bring this about. Until 1954, only about 6 per cent of Dow's business was abroad, and of that, over 80 per cent was from its one foreign subsidiary in Canada.

Some dramatic steps were needed to convert the majority of managers to an international outlook. One method employed by the company's president has been to give international responsibilities to people who were widely perceived to be destined for top-level positions in the company. Thus the importance of international operations became readily apparent to the company's managers.

Although the emphasis so far has been on the importance of international exposure for top-level managers in MNCs, this is not the only management consideration. Companies also must attract and retain high-quality personnel within each country in which they operate. These are largely local personnel. To attract them, Dow feels it must give people from all over the world the same opportunity to reach the top levels. Local needs also change as corporate strategies evolve. For instance, Dow had to hire many more non-US scientists and technicians in the 1980s when the company was strengthening R&D in Europe and Asia.

Companies also must transfer people to foreign locations either when qualified local managers are not readily available or to upgrade the qualifications of the local managers. For many years, Dow had difficulty in convincing people to take foreign assignments because of bad experience in repatriating them to acceptable positions. Dow has reacted to this problem by:

- Sending some of its best people abroad so that 'everybody will want them when they come back';
- Assigning higher-level supervisors to serve as 'godfathers' by looking after the transferred employees' home-career interests;
- Providing each transferee with a written guarantee of a job at the same or higher level on return from the foreign assignment.

Because many managers have difficulty adjusting to foreign locations, Dow holds a briefing session with each prospective transferee to explain transfer policies and to provide an information package compiled by personnel in that host country. This is followed by a meeting between the transferee and that person's spouse and a recently repatriated employee or spouse to explain the emotional issues involved in the move's early stages. The couple is also given the option of attending a two-week language and orientation programme.

Source: Adapted from Daniels and Radebaugh (1995), pp. 746–7.

In the light of Case example 7.1, management development must take into account the characteristics of individuals who may be available. These include their life-style, their expectations and their ambitions, and can be listed as follows:

- qualifications and experience;
- record of previous performance;
- commitment to international business, including aspirations to international promotion;
- suitability for international business, including ability to adapt to new environments and to show sensitivity to new situations; family commitments.

■ Host country characteristics

These clearly have a significant impact on both the development and performance of managers. They can be summarised as follows:

1. *Level of economic development.* This naturally affects the ability of the company to recruit in a given country either for local or for international posts. On the other hand, there will be pressure on the company to assist the development process by the establishment of educational programmes to facilitate rapid promotion. Applications for permits for residents, wherever they come from, are likely to be scrutinised even more carefully in those countries that have most need of foreign management; the industrialised countries place less obstacles to the movement of managers across frontiers.

2. *Political stability and nationalist sentiments, including the propensity to nationalise or expropriate.* Similar considerations apply, but skilled and experienced management may be required to maintain a presence or get the best possible terms for a withdrawal.

3. *Control of foreign investment and immigration policies.* The control of ownership and the issue of work permits are usually the subject of negotiation, even where there are laws on the subject. If the company has international policies, however flexibly they have to be operated in practice, these will aid negotiations.

4. *Availability of qualified and experienced managers and the need to develop and promote local managers and technical staff.* These considerations apply in the same way as those already listed.

5. *Sociocultural setting.* There are clearly problems of adjustment across boundaries of culture, race, language and religion. There are equally clearly some boundaries that cannot be crossed; these are mainly political, and they sometimes prove impermanent. In general, these problems are the subject of many myths which are dispelled in practice. Some of the most difficult cultural boundaries are crossed successfully, and the myths are dispelled after brief examination. On the whole, if other considerations require that a manager move between two incompatible countries, then selection and training can minimise the problem to the point where they become tolerable.

6. *Geographical location.* As with the sociocultural setting, the location is obviously an important consideration, but it does not make for impossible difficulties for actions that are otherwise desirable.

These influencing factors are by no means exhaustive. They do include some of the more important factors affecting the rational choice of an international management policy. Within each set, variables themselves are interdependent. That is to say, a number of influencing factors within the host country may interact to affect strongly the choice of one particular policy rather than another. Also, each set of influencing variables interacts with the others. In choosing a management development policy, one set may be weighed by itself and, in comparison with the others, especially with a view to reconciling differences between the three parties involved: the company, the individual and the host country.

CASE 7.2

Effective country managers play three vital roles: as the sensor and interpreter of local opportunities and threats; as the builder of local resources and capabilities; and as the contributor to and active participant in global strategy. Howard Gottleib's experience as general manager of NEC's switching systems subsidiary in the USA illustrates the importance of all three tasks; his contribution to NEC's understanding of changes in the telecommunications market demonstrates how a good sensor can connect local intelligence with global strategy.

In the late 1980s, Gottleib was assigned to build the US market for NEAX61, a widely-acclaimed digital telecom switch designed by the parent company in Japan.

Although it was technologically sophisticated, early sales did not meet expectations. His local market background and contacts led Gottleib to a quick diagnosis of the problem. NEC had designed the switch to meet the needs of NTT, the Japanese telephone monopoly, and it lacked many features US customers wanted. In translating the needs of his US division to the parent company NEC, Gottleib had to convince his supervisors in Japan that redesigning NEAX61 was necessary, and in doing so he had to bridge two cultures and penetrate the subtleties of the parent company's Japanese-dominated management processes. He also had to instill a sense of urgency in several corporate management groups (for example, Bell operating companies were calling for quotes).

After convincing Tokyo that the United States would be an important market for NEC's global digital switch design, Howard Gottleib persuaded headquarters to permit his new engineering group to take part early on in the product development of the next generation switch – the NEAX61E. He sent teams of engineers to Japan to work with the original designers, and to verify his engineers' judgements Gottleib invited the designers to visit his customers in the United States. These exchanges not only raised the sensitivity of NEC's Japan-based engineers to US market needs, but also significantly increased their respect for their American colleagues. Equally, the US unit's morale rose.

As a builder, Gottleib used this mutual confidence as the foundation for creating a software development capability that would become a big corporate asset. Skilled software engineers, very scarce in Japan, were widely available in the United States. Gottleib's first move was to put together a small software team to support local projects. Though its resources were limited, the group turned out a number of innovations, including a remote software patching capability that later became part of the 61E switch design. The credibility he won at headquarters allowed Gottleib to expand his design engineering group from 10 to more than 50 people within two years, supporting developments not only in North America but also eventually in Asia.

At NEC Gottleib spent about 60 per cent of his time on customer relations and probing the market, and about 30 per cent managing the Tokyo interface. His ability to understand and interpret the global strategic implications of US market needs – and the software development group he built from scratch – allowed him to take part in NEC's ongoing strategy debate.

As a result, Gottleib changed his division's role from implementer of corporate strategy to active contributor in designing that strategy.

Source: Adapted from Bartlett and Ghoshal (1993).

■ Integrating key management functions

Management practice, as it has traditionally applied to international business, however, still tends to be fragmented. For example, the financial implications of marketing planning are not communicated sufficiently to staff responsible for developing overseas business; nor are the design and technical functions integrated early enough in the planning process. The importance and topicality of a task-force or integrated approach to markets by management has been stressed at the highest level of industry.

Management is itself insufficiently aware of international markets – and more particularly of how the design, engineering, manufacturing and selling disciplines have to be integrated if competitiveness is to be sharpened. A major task lies ahead for management in creating technically literate, professionally skilled and internationally experienced management at all levels in our companies ... The breadth and experience necessary to develop trade routes has to pervade all levels of a company so that its culture is international.'

(Corfield, 1984)

Management must seek to identify the extent to which European industrial competitiveness can be enhanced by an improved integration of management functions in overseas operations, particularly:

* operations management'
* research and technical development;
* design;
* marketing;
* supply; and
* finance.

Management is faced, therefore, with a number of options in bringing about integration to improve competitiveness:

1. Closer integration of key management functions, to bring about better-structured decision-making and longer-term planning in international markets;
2. Closer liaison between finance and marketing, to produce more competitive offers to international customers and to ensure higher levels of company profitability;
3. A task-force approach to international markets, to help companies penetrate markets and establish/sustain a long-term position of market strategy, rather than a short-term tactical presence based on individual countries or customers.

The main objective, then, is the identification and quantification of benefits in terms of increased international competitiveness through better-integrated management organisation for planning and business development. The focus is on effective management organisation as a competitive weapon for European industry. Under-manning in one vital sector, for example sales, is a direct consequence of inadequate management organisation to cope effectively with increasingly sophisticated demands of overseas customers in a competitive world.

■ The task-force approach

The question remains, how can management bring about better integration? Two practical options arising out of some of the research so far quoted are:

1. Setting up task forces which can be deployed in key overseas markets, and which are made up of sales staff supported by design and technical staff who can respond to customers' requirements as a team and present a package to overseas customers which is technically up-to-date, competitive in design and range, and so forth;
2. Assessing benefits of closer interfaces in all overseas operations, particularly between finance and marketing and technical development and marketing.

The entire concept of building task forces and setting up teamwork in international markets must of course encompass the financial as well as other functions. There are responsibilities for management to grasp in implementing the concept in it. For example:

1. The financial and marketing implications of export policy need to be set up in a coordinated way;
2. The typical management structure leans towards separation rather than integration of functions; and
3. Export marketing staff need to have greater financial expertise and support if they are to develop profitable business overseas.

Particular attention needs to be paid to the interface between technical development and marketing. New technology such as robotics and micro-computer-based designs and controls now make it possible not only to maintain volume production and quality but also to offer more varieties of products of consistent quality at comparable unit output costs. There is also the extent to which information technology (IT) is being used effectively by management for analysis and worldwide communications (for example accessing international product codes and data retrieval). The implications of these for marketing management's planning are significant and show the extent to which a company's competitiveness can be sharpened by integration. There is also the interface between supply and marketing: poor supply performance by UK firms reduces promotional effectiveness, and that this can be improved by more investment in new technology such as flexible manufacturing systems (FMSs).

CASE 7.3

A British company manufacturing prefabricated building materials and components for sale to the Far East, having previously used only sales staff abroad, decided to send out a senior designer to accompany the sales staff. The result was that customers' special requirements could be redrawn overnight, and new design concepts introduced and discussed on the spot, avoiding lengthy correspondence and consultation with the home base. Technical service and design quality for customers improved substantially, and within three years the company had doubled its export turnover in this region by penetration at the expense of competitors.

Management must assess the performance of these key tasks, with the focus on improving the terms offered to overseas customers so that the company's competitive position is strengthened and profitability is ensured. As the company's involvement overseas grows in the more successful markets, so investment decisions in new plant, direct representation and large-scale financing have to be made.

An early research study by the Royal Society of Arts (1976) highlighted the importance of the interface between marketing and supply, it singled out production problems as being often the biggest limitation to international sales growth. It reported supply shortfalls and an irregular flow of components as responsible for many bottlenecks, and cited instances where 300 per cent higher prices were being paid for imported components – to speed up orders to overseas customers. And management is having to operate under conditions of increasing uncertainty in international markets, such as political risks, commercial risks and competition from newly-industrialising countries (NICs). Added to this are financial uncertainties, particularly in the movements of interest rates and currencies.

■ The interface between finance and marketing

These external factors alone demand the closest possible collaboration between the finance and marketing functions: the financial implications of alternative export marketing strategies must be set out in terms of offering not only an attractive product range but also a competitive set of financial offers. Indeed, planning marketing activities for overseas demands the most careful financial interpretation of the objectives set and the means of achieving these objectives. This approach is essential,

- to 'out-market' competitors with a superior total package, and
- to secure improved financial returns to the exporting company.

Those responsible for management development should take steps to ensure that their companies gain from a policy of integration rather than separation. These steps can include the following (and each involves at least three functions):

1. Set out marketing objectives, methods of penetration, pricing and market follow-up, with their full financial implications.
2. Review the full sales potential of each overseas market, and determine investment in technical and design work beforehand, so that financial returns can be maximised and the company's market position or prospects safeguarded.
3. Analyse and remain alert to improvements in the price-thresholds perceived and accepted by overseas customers in the light of non-price benefits and of competitors' offers.
4. Study competitive design and supply capabilities, and improve both through integrated management action.
5. Critically review the competitiveness of trade terms (for example INCOTERMS) offered as part of the total marketing package.
6. Set up and maintain closer working relationships among financial management and export marketing staff and, where appropriate, export supply and design, so that the company has a controlling overseas project group responsible for total implementation, including major contracts.
7. Set up or buy-in management expertise so that the company can get and offer the best terms in foreign currency dealings, and know what it is doing.
8. Ensure that all marketing staff working abroad are better equipped – to understand their customer's business, to provide advice on business development, and to undertake negotiations successfully with overseas customers, using financial as well as sales expertise.

■ Managers versus professionals

The need for a forward-looking policy on management development, particularly for international operations, is given more immediacy by some new trends in management organisation. First, there is the challenge of the professionals; that is, those with specialised scientific, technical or professional qualifications whose career development is geared more towards internal and external consultancy than to traditional line-management progression. Peter Drucker, addressing the American Management Association (AMA) in 1990, warned of the coming domination of the corporation by two potentially conflicting cultures; that of managers and that of professionals. There is growing unease in many European companies over the rising presence and influence of new professional employees – engineering, computer, finance, design, research and other specialists. Professionals account for more than one-fifth of total employees in the EEC and one-third of those in the USA; and companies are cutting down on traditional managers and skilled, unskilled and semi-skilled workers who no longer fit in with new strategies.

In addition to cultural clashes, the advance of the professionals presents problems of organisation. Just where do the new professionals fit in? Who manages whom? What is the professional's pay in relation to the manager's? Pension schemes, performance rewards, management training and promotion policies are all having to be reworked. Those relatively few professionals employed in companies in the past enjoyed a certain autonomy, freedom from business management roles, and a status afforded by outside professional affiliations. Even so, managers conflicted with scientists over plans or budgets for new technical ideas; indeed, there is evidence leading breakthroughs often succeeded in spite of uncooperative managers. Such managers do not normally fit into 'the sub-culture that generates, without much discrimination, new ideas, and brilliant breakthrough'. For the most part, however, managers ran the businesses and controlled the workforce. The new professionals were often alienated, sometimes of their own choice. Companies needing to make better use of these professionals are those moving away from labour to capital – particularly in the banking, insurance, computer, TV and media, and other service sectors. There is some further indication that there is a negative impact on organisational effectiveness when proper integration between professionals and the rest of the organisation is lacking.

■ Project management

While many companies identify and develop more autonomous profit centres, a range of factors often makes it necessary to commission projects that affect the organisation as a whole. Common examples include: the introduction of new technology, change of corporate design, development of a new product or new market, an office move, a company takeover, or the design of a new building.

In many organisations important projects are used as a testing ground for junior or middle managers. Their potential is judged on their ability to define objectives and see these through. The key to this is recognising and reconciling the interests of everyone who has a stake in the project. This is often a highly-delicate process. In the introduction of a new computerised information service, for example, the project leader will have to take into account the views of senior management, who probably will not understand the technical complexities but will have strategic objectives. Departments within the organisation will all have different requirements. Staff who operate the hardware will need systems they can use easily, together with tailored training and support. Project leaders need to recruit a team drawn from different departments, functions and even countries. They need the skill to establish a common culture and commitment, drawing in members of the organisation who are not directly involved in the project but are concerned with its outcome. The task is therefore highly political. To succeed, project leaders have to develop close working relationships with the senior manager or director to whom they are responsible, and will have access to confidential information.

Some international companies are finding it difficult to adjust, particularly those in once-conservative industries that are now dependent on those with new professional skills – in particular, specialists in mergers, acquisitions, property, computers, international finance, food research and others. Head offices in these sectors are becoming staffed more by specialists who are playing their part in greater centralisation; and local branch management is losing its decision-making role and is responding to the centre.

Future prospects are likely to be increasingly coloured by this interface between managers and professionals. The companies are going to turn into the flexible-firm, according to a model developed at the Institute of Manpower Studies at Sussex University (1990). It will employ only a small core of full-time professionals, with project managers running everything from the centre; part-timers and contractors will serve its other needs.

So the role of senior management in bringing about close integration of key management functions is crucial in developing the international competitiveness of the company. All the evidence cited in this Section points towards this priority. What, then, are some of the specific tasks of management in this context?

1. Setting up an effective planning process on the basis of a clear international strategy.
2. Ensuring that planning is based on full and valid data, and involves all areas of management.
3. Allocating responsibilities to key teams or task forces, on the basis of the plan, to develop identified sectors of international business.
4. Developing the management organisation so that it is responsive to changes in key sectors of its market(s), particularly by the planned use of technical and professional inputs such as R&D, design, technical innovation and international sourcing.
5. Integrating in the management structure the growing roles of professional and project managers.

■ Risk and crisis management

■ Political risk

International business involves many types of risk: not all can be avoided but all can, to an extent, be managed. The same is true of crises, whether these afflict the company from external forces or whether they originate from problems within the company. First and foremost is political risk, because this affects the long-term viability of investments and assets overseas. This type of risk occurs through actions of the host governments, though it is not implied that these are common in most countries since they discourage any FDI; much depends on the political orientation and stability of the regime. Such actions are likely to be levied against foreign investments, though local firms' properties are not totally immune, and include:

1. *Confiscation* – this is the process of a government taking ownership of a property without compensation (for example the Chinese authorities' seizure of foreign assets when the Chinese Communists took power in 1949).
2. *Expropriation* – here there is generally some compensation, though not necessarily fair compensation. Frequently, a company whose property is being expropriated agrees to sell its operations – not through choice but rather because of some explicit or implied coercion.
3. *Nationalisation* – after property has been confiscated or expropriated it can be nationalised. Nationalisation involves government ownership and it is the government that operates the business (Burma's foreign trade, for example, is totally nationalised). A variant of this risk is domestication, where foreign companies relinquish control and ownership to the nationals. The result here is that private entities are allowed to operate the confiscated or expropriated property. (The French Government, for example, after finding out that the State was not the ideal organisation to run its banks, developed a plan to sell 36 banking houses.)

Another classification system (Root, 1982) identifies four sets of risk:

1. *General instability risk* – this relates to uncertainty about the future viability of a host-country's political system (the chaos following the Iranian revolution that overthrew the Shah is a classic example).
2. *Ownership/control risk* – this is related to the possibility that a host government might take actions (for example expropriation) to restrict an investor's ownership and control of a subsidiary in the host country.
3. *Operations risk* – this proceeds from the uncertainty that a host government might constrain the investor's business operations in all areas, including production, marketing and finance.
4. *Transfer risk* – this applies to any future acts by a host government that might constrain the ability of a subsidiary to transfer payments, capital or profit out of the host country.

The policies of host governments, therefore, directly influence the business climate: what international companies seek above all is some sort of policy stability, whatever the political complexion or philosophy of a particular government. Changes of government do not necessarily mean policy changes (there have been many changes of government in Nigeria, for example, but economic policies have not changed significantly for foreign companies). Of course, some changes of government can be accompanied by policy changes and this can create problems. On occasions, a government's attitude towards foreign firms can be volatile: the mood can change with time or change of leadership, and government policy formulation can affect business operations both internally and externally. Companies should be especially alert at election time and be fully conversant with the industrial policies of the opposition party or parties (should they be returned to power). Elections pose a special problem because candidates' activities and tactics can easily create an unwelcome atmosphere for foreign firms. (For example, when French politicians cited the fact that one French worker became unemployed for every five to ten Japanese cars imported, the government held up imported cars a few weeks before the election.)

CASE 7.4

A consultancy service to companies and banks operating internationally is provided by BERI Company's Political Risk Index (PRI). The objective of PRI is to gauge the business climate in different countries. The research focuses on sociopolitical conditions in the country by: creating a multi-component system with flexibility to weigh key factors; utilising a permanent panel of experts with a political science rather than a business orientation; providing data that can move independently of BERI risk measures, and using three periods – present conditions, +5-year conditions and +10-year conditions.

As a first step, the experts present conditions from 7 (no problems) to 0 (prohibitive problems). There are six internal causes of political risk: factionalisation of the political spectrum and the power of these factions; factionalisation by language, ethnic and/or religious groups, and the power of these factions; restrictive (coercive) measures required to retain power; mentality, including xenophobia, nationalism, corruption, nepotism, or willingness to compromise; and social conditions including population density and wealth distribution. There are two external causes of political risk; dependence on and/or importance to a hostile major power; and negative influence of regional political forces. And there are two symptoms of political risk: social conflict involving demonstrations, strikes and street violence; and instability as perceived by non-constitutional changes, assassinations and guerilla wars.

As one or more factors may have a very positive impact on the overall political risk, the research permits discretionary use of 30 points for the subset 'external causes of political risk' typically ±20 to a low-risk country and ±10 for moderate risk. This subset and the first subset 'internal causes of political risk' are also assessed for each of the +5 and +10-year period. The points awarded to a country under present conditions serving as a basis for changes in the future.

Four categories of political risk have emerged on the basis of this analysis:

- 70–100 low risk. Political changes will not lead to conditions seriously adverse to business. No major sociopolitical disturbances expected.
- 55–69 moderate risk. Political changes seriously adverse to business have occurred, but governments in power during the forecast period have a low probability of introducing such changes. Some disturbances will take place.
- 40–54 high risk. Political developments seriously adverse to business exist or could happen in the near future. Major sociopolitical disturbances are occurring periodically.
- 0–39 prohibitive risk. Political conditions severely restrict business operations. Loss of assets is possible. Disturbances are part of daily life.

Source: BERI Company (1990).

■ Managing risk

To manage political risk, there are these policies that an MNC can pursue:

- *Avoidance* – this means screening out politically uncertain countries. In this measurement an analysis of political risk can be useful.
- *Insurance* – this is a strategy to shift the risk to other parties.
- *Negotiating the environment* – the idea here is to develop an explicit concession agreement before committing the company to direct investment abroad. Such an agreement is used to define the rights and responsibilities of the MNC, the MNCs foreign partner, and the host-country government.
- *Structuring the investment* – the objective is to minimise the potential threats by adjusting the firm's operating and financial policies; once an investment is made, there are several operating policies that can deal with uncertainties. Such policies range from having local stakeholders and planned divestitures to short-term profit maximisation and a change in the benefit/cost ratio.

In this context there are some financial techniques which can be pursued as follows:

- Keeping the affiliate company or subsidiary dependent on sister companies for markets, or supplies, or both.
- Concentrating research and development affiliates and proprietary technology in the home country.
- Establishing a single, global trademark so that the host country can, at best, take away only physical facilities and not a product's intangible assets.
- Controlling transport.
- Sourcing production in multiple plants.
- Developing external financial stakeholders.

Political risks are also affected by the company's bargaining power. A subsidiary has little power when its technical, operational and managerial requirements are within a host-country's abilities; when this is the case, government intervention is likely to increase. To increase its bargaining power the company may want to take certain actions. As the sales of the subsidiary to affiliated companies climb, the MNC will exert a greater control over sales and will be able to deter intervention. Similarly, as the subsidiary engages more and more in exporting, the same effect can be achieved.

As far as risk-management is concerned, to cope with uncertainties it is possible to use strategies for exerting control and flexibility. Strategies for exerting control are used to keep the environment from adversely changing, some techniques include: using backward integration to control supply sources and forward integration to control markets, especially when some or most of the sources of supply and markets are outside the host country.

There are some actions by management in international business which, if they cannot eliminate risk, they can at least ensure that the firm is less suscept-ible to serious damage from risk and change. The importance of environmental analysis was explained in Chapter 3 in this context. Clearly, the influence that some firms, especially SMEs, have over government policy is minimal, though for large-scale projects MNCs can on occasion operate effectively with their home government in putting pressure on a foreign government not to damage bilateral trade, or to open up market access.

■ Managing economic risk

This is the point at which management should assess economic risk. Indeed it is on the marketing front that actions can be taken to make the firm's position more robust. These actions include using promotion to influence consumers and to gain product acceptance; selling products across country markets, and enter-ing into contracts with suppliers for inputs and buyers for outputs; forming business alliances and trading agreements, some of which may include competi-tors; and increasing flexibility of operations through:

- using general purpose equipment to produce multiple products so as to reduce dependence on a single product;
- resorting to more exporting, leasing, licensing, franchising and sub-contracting to reduce committing resources into fixed and durable assets abroad;
- avoiding long-term commitments;
- spreading risk through a multi-market strategy;
- using financial techniques to protect assets and eliminate risks in multi-currency trading; and
- implementing some system of marketing intelligence to ensure that management has data to utilise environment analysis and demand analysis across countries and markets (Chapter 3).

Management should also pay attention to the stimulation of the local econ-omy, as this can produce social and economic benefits both to the company and the community (for example by providing jobs for locals). One strategy may involve the company purchasing local products and raw materials for its pro-duction and operations. By assisting local firms, it can develop local allies who can provide valuable trade and political contacts. A modification of this strategy would be to use sub-contracting (this is discussed in a later Section of this chapter). Sometimes local sourcing is compulsory: governments may require products to contain locally-manufactured components because local content improves the economy in two ways:

- it stimulates demand for domestic components; and
- it saves the necessity of a foreign exchange transaction.

Table 7.2　Methods of uncertainty reduction

Methods	Conclusions	Examples
Prediction	1. When the uncertainty can be confidently reduced, using forecasting techniques 2. When markets are large and research costs can be absorbed over a large volume 3. When data are available and reliable 4. When the amount at stake is large and can easily absorb the research costs	Prediction of the consumption of a staple food item – e.g. dairy goods based on population trends
Control	1. When there are no ethical or government constraints to prohibit questionable payments 2. When there are no restrictions on advertising 3. When integration is not forbidden by anti-monopoly legislation 4. When integration is not precluded by the existence of many inputs and many outputs 5. When forward contracts are available for the time period, currency or commodity wanted 6. When contracts are likely to be honoured	Retailer with many suppliers and many clients cannot easily integrate backward or forward A company that markets clothes in Mexico uncertain as to sales and profits in the future is likely to use a forward contract
Insurance	1. Theoretically only risks whose historical probability is known are insurable 2. When the premiums are terms are reasonable	
Flexibility	1. When the technical nature of the business permits the investment to be split into viable parts 2. When subcontractors are available	Clothing company was able to subcontract out the stitching of jeans because the needed expertise was basic and readily available

Table 7.2   Continued

Methods	Conclusions	Examples
	3. When there are many sources of supply and many buyers for the firm's activities	
	4. When the need for effectiveness outweighs the benefits of economies of scale	
	5. When subcontracting is not likely to create a competitor	
	6. When licensing, franchising, and exporting are feasible	
Avoidance	1. When the bargaining power of the firm, or existence of government guarantees, allow the firm to transmit the uncertainty to others	Acceptance of payment only in hard currencies
	2. When the perceived risks are too high in the light of the foreseen rewards	

One strategy is to try to share ownership with local companies, by converting from a private company to a public one, or from a foreign company to one locally incorporated. Another strategy is to minimise exposure to economic risk by keeping a low profile; this is especially so where sharp disparities of wealth or pressing social problems presage a change of government or at least of industrial policy. It may be desirable for a company to become relatively inconspicuous (for example, in the 1980s Texas Instruments removed identifying logos and signs in El Salvador).

CASE 7.5

Black and Decker is one of the few multinationals known to actively manage its economic risk. The key to Black and Decker's strategy is flexible sourcing. In response to foreign exchange movements, Black and Decker is able to move production from one location to another to effect the most competitive pricing.

Black and Decker manufactures in more than a dozen locations around the world; these include major countries in Europe, Australia, Brazil, Mexico and Japan. In total, more than 50 per cent of the company's productive assets are based outside of North America. Although each of Black and Decker's factories focuses on one or two products to achieve economies of scale, there is considerable overlap. Moreover, on average, the company runs its factories at no more than 80 per cent capacity. As a consequence, most of the company's factories have the capability to switch rapidly from one product to producing another or to add a product. This allows what is produced at a given factory to be changed over time in response to foreign exchange movements. For example, as the dollar depreciated during the latter half of the 1980s, the amount of imports into the United States from overseas subsidiaries was reduced, and the amount of exports from US subsidiaries to other locations was increased.

According to the company, the ability to move production of a product in response to changes in foreign exchange movements is a source of competitive advantage. Black and Decker enjoys a much better long-term competitive position than one of its most significant competitors in the power tool business, Japan's Makita Electric Works Ltd. This is because 90 per cent of Makita's operations are located in Japan, and it exports heavily to the United States. Although Makita may benefit when the yen is depreciating, its margins are vulnerable during periods of yen strength. Black and Decker, in contrast, is not so vulnerable to appreciations in the value of the dollar.

Source: Arterian (1980).

■ The nature of crises

It is clear that some risk is unavoidable in international business; and the extent to which it can be managed has so far been explained. It is also clear that risk covers a broad spectrum: political, social, economic and financial. Some risks may be avoidable, others can be minimised; but what is certain is that there are some risks not predictable, even with the best intelligence, and this aspect provides the crucial link between risk and crisis management. Indeed, some risks (severe civil disturbances or natural disasters) are so serious as to provoke a crisis for the company. And here an important distinction lies: some crises impact on the company from outside, and others originate from problems within the company (for example, the source contamination that afflicted Perrier mineral water in 1990; the refitting fiasco on the liner Queen Elizabeth II that afflicted Cunard in 1994; the supply problem that almost put Farley's Baby Food Co. out of business in the 1970s). Some crises, if not wholly predictable, can be defused by an alert management before serious damage is done to the company. However, once the crisis is in the public domain through media exposure, the quality of crisis management in the company is severely tested.

In other words there are business-related problems (bankruptcy of supplier, strikes, hostile takeovers, cash shortages and so on) which can become crises if not dealt with promptly and robustly. But there are other crises arising from social, economic, political and other complexities of international business over which the company has no direct control, but which if not handled effectively can damage, on occasions fatally, the company's business. These include:

- Product hazards (source contamination, health concerns, safety and so forth).
- Natural disasters (floods, droughts or earthquakes).

- Civil unrest (riots, civil wars, bombings, strikes and so on).
- Hostile lobbies (campaigns by single-issue groups, animal welfare, environment – for example the loss of sales in 1995 in Germany following Shell's decision, later withdrawn, to dump an oil rig at sea – social justice or nationalism).
- Hostile targeting (product tampering, terrorism or kidnapping).
- Management failure (negligence, law-breaking or misconduct).
- Ownership battles (hostile takeovers or shareholder actions).
- Technology problems (accidents to employees, customers or in the local community).
- Crisis in the economic environment.

(Meyers and Holusha, 1986, p. 33)

■ Managing crises

The essential steps in this process are to at least define the extent of the crisis, if it cannot be avoided, and to respond promptly and firmly to the media once the crisis is in the public domain; and above all to manage or contain the crisis, with these objectives:

1. To ensure that the company's business is kept as a going concern and is not seriously or irreparably damaged by the crisis; this is damage limitation.
2. To put in place systems for predicting or at least for dealing with future crises to implement lessons learned in one country which may well have global applications.
3. To utilise the accompanying publicity positively to reassure the community and consumers of the company's control of the crisis and its commitment to service, quality and customer satisfaction; this is another aspect of damage limitation.

The definition of the crisis is not difficult but the fact there is a crisis means that the company is not in total control of events. The following must be ascertained: how much is at risk; where is it centred and who is involved in it and affected by it; how long is it expected to last; who is responsible for handling it in the company; and what are the implications of the crisis for relationships and communications with

- customers,
- government,
- the media,
- the community,
- suppliers, and
- stakeholders.

And lastly: is the crisis likely to interfere with normal business operations, cause a loss of confidence or affect the bottom-line? Defining the parameters gives management the data with which it must act firmly and speedily: speed is essential to counter false rumours, innuendos and distortions in the media and elsewhere which can be exploited effectively (and in some instances ruthlessly) by competitors. Nevertheless, it may not be possible, or feasible, to salvage everything in a crisis: it is essential to cope first in areas where quick intervention can make a difference (for example areas of high danger or high success potential); next the areas that can wait for intervention but where a difference can be made (low danger, or moderate success potential). In other areas much may be at risk but success potential is low, and provided that the running of the business is not fatally affected it is sometimes better for the company to cut its losses rather than dissipate resources, and try to salvage what can be saved in a reasonable time frame and at acceptable cost.

CASE 7.6

When time is short, the danger high, control insufficient, or options limited; this is the scenario where the chief executive should be personally involved. In 1982, Johnson & Johnson were faced with a product tampering crisis where an unknown saboteur put cyanide in Tylenol headache capsules causing the death of seven people in Chicago. This case is notable for the way in which the crisis was handled by a team directed by a marketing-led chief executive, Jim Burke. It acted in accordance with the Johnson & Johnson ethos which requires the first responsibility of all employees to be to the customer. Stock was withdrawn nationwide, despite the fact that testing revealed that only Chicago was affected. Costs of hundreds of millions of dollars were incurred and the package was completely redesigned; but Tylenol, and probably J&J, was saved. The company subsequently regained marketing supremacy by re-launching in tamper-proof packs – the first industry to do so. In this situation, one key executive took ownership of the crisis; such personal leadership is also a way of signalling the company's values – that avoiding harm to the public, for example, is the most important thing the leader can do.

CASE 7.7

In 1980, the discovery of the link between tampon usage and potentially deadly toxic-shock syndrome (TSS) threatened the survival of the US Tampax Corporation. It had marketed the first tampon in 1936 and dominated the market, but it was essentially a one-product company. If it had been implicated in the TSS outbreak it would probably have been the end of the product and the company.

Chairman, Russell Sprague, was not a marketer, and at the time the company was not marketing-led. But he was aware that the loss of consumer confidence in such a loyal market could lead to annihilation. He rushed into print to reassure loyal Tampax users that the risk was small, but informed them how to react to symptoms. He also offered the Centre for Diseases Control (CDC), which had reported the link, help in identifying the cause. The company funded Harvard Medical School research into TSS in line with the company's promise, 'Your health is important to us'.

In the UK, Tampax marketing director Alan Thornton took ownership of the problem. He increased advertising, made press enquiries a top priority, and put a senior spokesperson and top managers on 24-hour call.

In the US, the CDC established a link between TSS and Procter & Gamble's Rely tampon. P&G immediately withdrew Rely at huge cost. In the UK, the Playtex tampon received bad publicity and was banned from advertising by a leading publisher. It was eventually withdrawn.

Tampax emerged relatively unscathed in the US and the UK, largely because Sprague recognised it as primarily a consumer problem.

Source: Marketing Business, March 1995.

Action must, therefore, be combined with communication: the latter should ensure that facts, hard-information analysis, are communicated unambiguously to the company's major stakeholders, and in particular to the media and the government. But communication should also satisfy emotional needs among the public (reassurance, relief, sympathy, support and empathy for families). Communication should reinforce the values and invoke the symbols that keep the organisation together, and which give the company its public profile.

CASE 7.8

How well senior management assess and deal with crisis, even one that affects only one aspect of the business, can have major effects on the future success of the company. Gerald Meyers, former CEO of American Motors noted the difference between the denial mode of A. H. Robins and the 'responsibility' stance taken by Procter & Gamble in dealing with products found to have health risks.

A. H. Robins had problems with its Dalkon Shield, an intrauterine contraceptive device, from the outset. The evidence of injury and death was ignored at first and then denied. The company faced up to its product problems very late in the game – too late to save it from bankruptcy and loss of reputation. The crisis brought to light not only a serious product liability problem, but also a management style that could not confront such difficulties. Because of the crisis, subsequent managers are not likely to let anything like the Dalkon Shield incident happen again.

Procter & Gamble, on the other hand, reacted quickly and properly in withdrawing its Rely tampons when they became associated with toxic shock syndrome (TSS). Because it responded effectively, P&G's crisis passed quickly, and the company did not incur the damage suffered by Robins.

CASE 7.9

On 21 December 1988, Pan American Airways flight 103 was blown up over Lockerbie in Scotland, killing 270 people.

In the 1950s, Pan Am described itself as the world's most experienced airline and was admired internationally. By the 1980s, its image had gone into decline and it featured for five consecutive years in *Fortune* magazine's list of the ten least-admired corporations in the US. The company had retrenched and reduced corporate staffing with no external PR company.

Pan Am had handled crises before. A 1982 crash killed all 145 passengers on a Boeing 727 taking off from New Orleans. The company had a full-scale crisis procedure and every senior manager had a desk copy. Regular rehearsals and updates were also held.

Because the Lockerbie disaster was a terrorist attack, one might think that the tragedy would have been seen as beyond Pan Am's influence. But because of its inability to get control of the information-process and its perceived reluctance to display compassion and responsibility, Pan Am was faced with hostility and resentment. It is believed that managers' fear of legal retribution kept their humanity in check. However, there should have been a balance between the demonstration of concern and litigation fears.

The Pan Am experience demonstrates the pitfalls that can occur when attempting to manage a crisis. At the time of the crash, CEO Thomas Plaskett contacted consultancy Burson Marsteller, but this came to nothing because of the lack of time available for a briefing. Plaskett made the fundamental error of not appearing in public until eight days after the event. In retrospect, if he had taken the spotlight from the beginning, he would have been in a stronger position to safeguard the Pan Am brand.

Contrast this with the action of Sir Michael Bishop, chairman of British Midland Airways, following the crash landing of one of its aircraft on the M1 motorway in January 1989. He was seen on the first TV news bulletin, at the scene of the crash, with tears of compassion in his eyes. British Midland had always enjoyed a reputation as a caring airline, but the actions of its boss underlined this in its darkest hour. British Midland sales are said to have increased in subsequent months. This expression of concern was not something which could be applied because it was part of a business plan. It had to be heartfelt. The two are not incompatible.

Pan Am's crisis management manual said the role of the marketing department was to ensure that all advertising was cancelled, newspapers were removed from the next day's flights and next-of-kin were advised. These are all essential, but they are reactive, not proactive. In such a harrowing situation there can be little opportunity for brand enhancement, but in a leading service such as an airline, customer care, even beyond death, should be top of the list of priorities. Other mistakes were the result of a lack of trained communicators to control media and public enquiries.

Other shortcomings contributed to a sharp fall in bookings over the next few months. Six months later, following a hijack threat against US Airlines, business fell off even more sharply. In early 1991, Pan Am filed for Chapter 11 bankruptcy. Communications Vice-President, Jeffrey Kriendler believes that if Lockerbie had not happened, the company might have been attractive as a takeover candidate.

Source: Marketing Business, March 1995.

■ Lessons for management

There is no question that coping with both risk and crisis represents a rigorous test of the quality of a company's management. Companies less able to deal with crises typically have poor communications skills and little communications strategy, both internal and external, poor teamwork leading to fragmentation of response and internal conflict, and above all ineffectual leadership; this situation may also be symptomatic of a lack of confidence by staff in the company and its products, a feeling of insecurity leading to over-defensive reactions whenever the company is criticised or subject to media attention. Nevertheless, risk and crisis management is not an exact science: there is a vital and continuing element of learning by experience, and in the process improving performance and strengthening the company's position; this learning process is typified by:

- improved rational reactions to the unexpected (less emotion);
- better corporate communications (internal and external);
- capacity to robustly manage future eventualities;
- enhanced corporate values and culture on the basis of lessons learned;
- improved intelligence system;
- more effective handling of relationships with the media; and
- closer attention to prioritising events and situations by management.

■ Managing subsidiaries, agents and associates

■ Organising for international operations

There are many different forms of corporate organisation which have been developed over the years by companies operating worldwide, to develop in a planned way their international operations. The type of organisation operated will, of course, depend on many different factors, both internal and external. Every such company will have certain internal organisational strengths (and weaknesses): for example, a company can derive strength, organisationally, from some of the following:

1. Well-established and productive trade links in some overseas countries.
2. Organisational structure which both reflects and reinforces strong expertise in

managing particular types of overseas operations such as manufacturing or licensing.

3. Strong product positions in certain overseas markets and strong corporate image, both the result of consistent and planned investment in product development and communications.

4. Strong commitment to, and investment in, research and development reflected in the management structure.

Internal factors, therefore, are essentially all about resources: managerial, financial, technical and product. The essential point, of course, is that the external business environment is changing constantly, and what may have been organisational strengths two or three years ago in terms of international competitiveness, are now redundant as business conditions change; so new organisational strengths must be built up to combat these changes.

International trading involves a growing diversity of markets, products and countries and the company must ensure and invest in the appropriate management expertise for the organisation's effective control of business. Three factors are crucial in this context:

*   developing an organisational framework for developing international markets;
*   implementing control systems to ensure a coordinated strategy worldwide; and
*   setting and achieving financial targets such as ROI and profit improvement (see Chapter 6).

And some of the external factors influencing changes in every enterprise seeking to maintain competitiveness include some of the following:

1. Increasing levels of national indebtedness in the world economy, and the corresponding need to develop special financial expertise in the company to cope with the problems of non-payment, late payment for goods and deteriorating foreign currency reserves in many overseas markets.

2. Growth of local supply and manufacturing bases overseas, particularly in the designated newly-industrialising countries (NICs), requiring changes in management structure and skills which reflect the need for joint ventures, exporting improved technology, and productivity drives at home to maintain competitiveness with local suppliers and other foreign suppliers.

3. Growing price-competitiveness in international trade, and the impact of this on the company's organisation in terms of improved productivity, investing in new technologies, currency management and improvements in product/service quality, particularly the design function.

4. Growing importance of political, cultural and fiscal factors in opening up and maintaining market access in international operations, and the need to have these and related skills being reflected in an appropriate management organisation.

So a first step in organising effectively for international operations is the compiling of a management audit encompassing, in detail, all those internal and external factors, the latter having been explained in Chapter 3. The nature and extent of these key factors clearly influences and shapes the organisation and management structure of the company operating internationally. Furthermore, management must also be concerned with achieving strategic targets, and some companies have increasingly adopted the concept of strategic management teams operating globally to provide focus and coordination among operating subsidiaries.

In organising for international operations, companies must ensure that the management and overall corporate structure are shaped to ensure continuing competitiveness. Clearly, organisational effectiveness alone is not enough: planning and control have an important part to play in sustaining overall competitiveness within planned parameters, timing and targets. Planning provides the system and operating procedures, and control ensures that performance against targets is monitored and any corrective management action taken in good time. The organisation will be influenced by such factors as: the level of international expertise; the level of involvement in international markets; the number of markets the company operates in; the overall size of the business; the nature of the products and services sold; and the corporate goals set for the company in developing its international business. The essential aim of every organisation is to achieve *synergy*: but this does not come about on its own, and managers must make it happen by integrating the various functions and separate national operations into a coordinated enterprise. Whilst the principles of effective organisation are as valid in multinational as in domestic operations, special problems can arise in the former because of communication gaps.

■ Organisational modalities

There are a number of different approaches to international organisation reflecting different aims and conditions (as described above); there is clearly no one optimal form. The two basic alternatives are:

1. Separate/specialist approach – the international division.
2. Integration – the global approach for the world company.

The advantages of the international division approach are: centralisation of all specialist skills and expertise; a centralised focus and viewpoint to develop business; more effective allocation of resources; and a more objective and realistic analysis of market potential by major world sectors. The disadvantages are: sub-optimisation can result from dilution of corporate resources; growth of bureaucracy and inertia in the international division resulting in too much analysis and rigidity; management remoteness from front-line trading operations; and there can also be friction between international and domestic divisions.

The alternative integrated approach by the world company has the following major organisational characteristics: no distinction between domestic and inter-

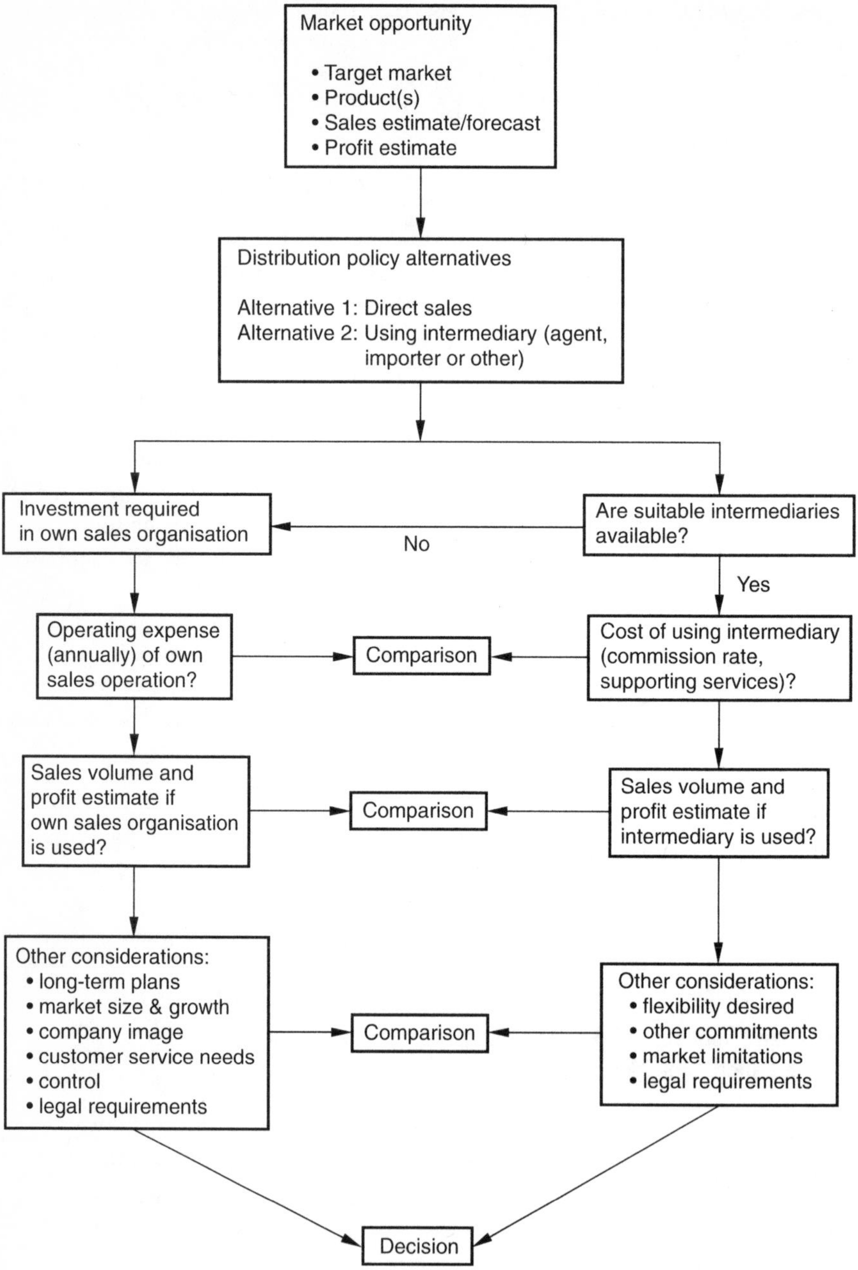

Figure 7.2 Decision model: direct export sales versus sales through intermediaries

Source: 1990 International Trade Centre UNCTAD/GATT, Geneva.

Table 7.3   Classification of market entry modes

Export entry modes
Methods of entry where the company's products are produced outside of the overseas market

Indirect exporting
Uses middlemen who are located in the company's own national market, and are responsible for undertaking the exporting

Direct exporting
Does not use home-country middlemen, but may employ middlemen based in the overseas market. Direct exporting can be subdivided according to whether entry involves: (1) direct agent/distributor exporting – where middle-men in the overseas market are responsible for marketing the exported goods; or (2) direct branch/ subsidiary – where the company uses its own sales organisations in the overseas market

Contractual entry modes
These may be described as non-equity associations between an international company (actual or emerging) and a legal entity in the overseas market, involving the transfer of knowledge, understanding and/or skills

Licensing
An arrangement whereby the company is prepared to transfer to the overseas entity for a defined period the right to use its commercial/industrial property (for example technology knowledge, patent, etc.) in return for some form of compensation, usually a royalty payment

Franchising
Franchising involves the right to use a business format in the overseas market in return for the franchiser receiving some form of payment

Other
These include technical agreements, service contracts, contract manufacture and co-production agreements (for example own-label supply)

Investment entry modes
Entry modes under this heading involve ownership of production units in the overseas market, based on some form of equity investment

Independent venture
These include overseas production facilities or outlets which are under the full ownership and control of the company selling into the overseas market. Such facilities may be newly developed, or acquired by taking over an existing operator in the market.

Joint venture
This mode of entry involves sharing the ownership and control of the overseas facilities or outlets with one or more local partners.

Source: Adapted from Root (1987), pp.7–8.

national business, the only discrimination being in terms of size of market; also, whilst there is great potential to optimise performance, potential efficiency and profits, this is rarely fully achieved due to managerial inflexibility.

Within these two main approaches there are also a number of different operating divisions which provide senior management with the following options:

☐ *Area structuring*

This approach which divides the world geographically into regions, appeals to marketing-oriented companies with a relatively stable product technology; for example pharmaceuticals and automobiles. The concept is illustrated in Figure 7.3.

The advantages of area structuring are: easy communications; grouping of expertise; quick identification and rectification of area problems; and the ability to exploit political and economic groups, for example the EU. The disadvantages are: some inefficiency and duplication in management (that is, several areas = several organisations); possible friction between areas and headquarters, and the emergence of gaps between countries in one area (increasing friction); and limited communication between areas.

☐ *Product structuring*

This approach entails global responsibility by product line, and it appeals to companies with diverse and unrelated product ranges, as in Figure 7.4.
The chief advantage of product structuring is flexibility: new divisions can be added easily. The disadvantages are possible conflict between divisions at board

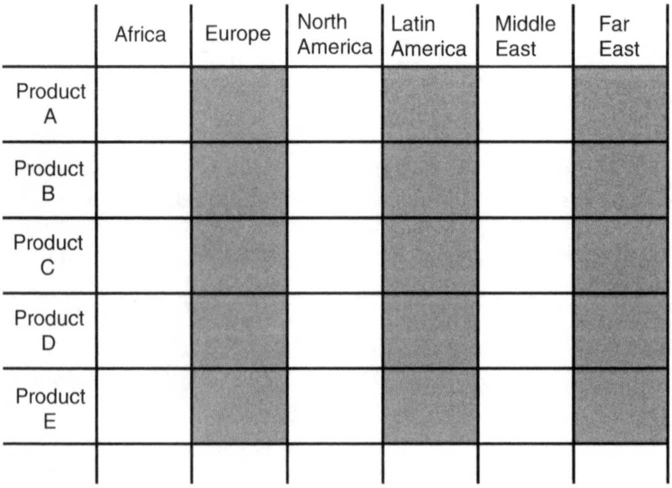

	Africa	Europe	North America	Latin America	Middle East	Far East
Product A						
Product B						
Product C						
Product D						
Product E						

Figure 7.3   Regional divisionalisation

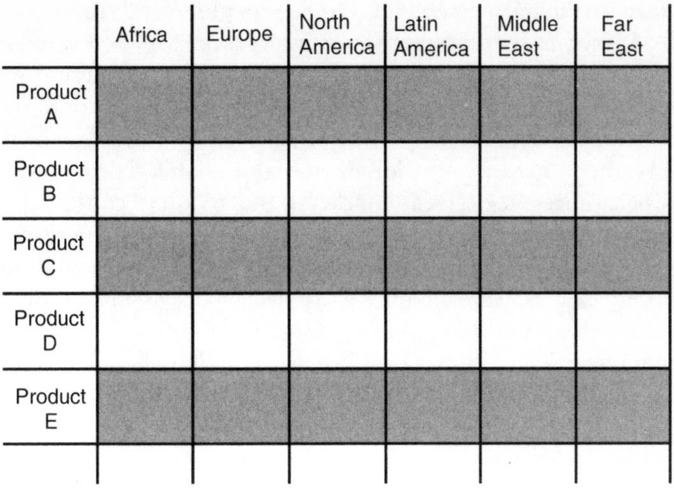

	Africa	Europe	North America	Latin America	Middle East	Far East
Product A						
Product B						
Product C						
Product D						
Product E						

Figure 7.4   Product divisionalisation

level; the structure is difficult to manage efficiently at board level, and effective coordination is complex.

☐ *Functional structuring*

This involves the top executives responsible for the major functions (finance, marketing, production and so on) each having global responsibility. This approach appeals to companies with narrow product lines where product expertise is not a variable, and where regional variations are not significant; but it is not an approach in common use.

Global problems with area, product, and functional approaches have led to more complex approaches, and in particular the development of the matrix organisation favoured by some multinational corporations (see Chapter 8 for marketing and business policy aspects). The matrix approach involves dual rather than single command chains and gained support in the 1980s, but it is not now so widely used as it is difficult to manage in practical terms.

There is, therefore, clearly no one ideal organisational format for international operations; some compromise is essential. After all, technology, size, mode of marketing operation and management, and so forth, are all variables. The objective is the format that best meets corporate goals, whilst minimising the organisational problems.

■ The role of marketing

The most important function discharged by an organisation operating globally is marketing: the analysis of demand across national markets, and the resourcing and direction of marketing operations to exploit and meet this demand profitably. Marketing involves managing the product/market strategy and the communications mix. In this respect, the organisational structure must ensure that management expertise and resources are transmitted continuously from headquarters to the regions: in particular, marketing should tend to be a decentralised rather than a centralised function. This is because it relates specifically to numerous overseas markets, and requires continual adaptation of the organisation to the needs of each market. Also, it is increasingly recognised that commercial success depends upon skilful marketing rather than just product attributes (see Chapter 8 for a full discussion of the marketing programme).

■ Relationships between headquarters and regions

If, therefore, the organisation is essentially about the division of labour in management of a company, then the issue of centralisation and decentralisation is about the division of labour in headquarters and field operations. In setting up and implementing marketing policies at the corporate level, headquarters has the following responsibilities:

- Setting objectives/policies for world markets;
- Playing a major role in planning;
- Acting as a focal point for the development of new ideas and back-up resources;
- Coordinating and integrating national programmes.

Under a decentralised organisation, the local subsidiary:

- Implements the plan within broad guidelines;
- Conducts market research;
- Has some initiative in product policy and pricing;
- Selects and administers distribution channels;
- Manages sales operations;
- Directs promotional programmes;
- Ideally has dual reporting – to local and headquarters management.

Depending on the size and complexity of the operations, some international companies prefer to centralise on regional offices rather than on one international headquarters. Regional headquarters have the following outline tasks:

- To service and coordinate individual country programmes;
- To report to and liaise with international head office;
- To give specific support to business development within the region;
- To ensure that the regional management benefits from decentralisation of marketing and control.

But, as noted in Case example 7.10, attempts by management to erase existing lines of communication and responsibility and to redraw them so that they converge on the centre are fraught with difficulty. The risk is not simply monetary: the company may also end up jeopardising the goodwill of key local management in the process. So to overcome this problem a number of multinational corporations are, in practice, looking at a compromise solution. Unable to choose between strong local organisations with autonomous marketing functions and a central marketing department responsible for several countries at once, management has increasingly settled on a compromise organisation, with the two systems in tandem. The reasoning behind this approach is that an international marketing department superimposed on the network of local subsidiaries will provide the best of both worlds. In practice, this does not always happen. While any kind of international advertising is impracticable with a

---

CASE 7.10

The Cinzano Company found itself, a few years ago, faced with an ageing customer profile, particularly in Europe, North America and Australasia. It was decided to apply the global remedy by appealing to the world's youth (emulating the worldwide strategy of Coca Cola Co.). Under Swiss-based management, all important marketing decisions were made centrally. This proved to be both costly and frustrating for the marketing managers in the regions. For example, consolidating research from a common data-base to achieve worldwide agreement and support was not easy: every idea or proposal from head office had to be bounced-off all the major markets for comment (usually by fax or telex). The real cost in terms of time, money and management effort was in the planning process and putting together the centralised marketing plan. The company has now dismantled this centralised structure and is considering other approaches.

CASE 7.11

American Express has been running international advertising for many years, mainly in magazines such as *Time* and *Business Week.* This has given its European marketing department considerable power. All marketing strategies are formulated at the centre, since it markets itself to a homogenous group throughout the world: local variations in markets are not wide. However, since charge/credit cards are at a different stage in their life-cycle in each country, local managers are allowed to use the strategy by adapting it to their own needs. So, for instance, there is a Europe-wide advertising strategy, but local companies can determine the execution of the strategy in their own countries. In Britain, therefore, Amex advertisements have used Roger Daltrey, while in France they have featured Michel Legrand.

central department that can mediate between various local/regional interests, its ability to do so is entirely dependent on its influence within the organisation and the extent of its control of budgetary allocations.

These hybrids of central and local marketing organisations take a multitude of forms; and these variations can be illustrated in the examples shown in cases 7.10, 7.11 and 7.12.

CASE 7.12

By contrast, in Unilever, the central marketing department has no operational budget of its own, and its role is therefore reduced to an advisory one. The company is highly-decentralised, with each subsidiary setting its advertising spends according to its own local targets. The central marketing department sees its main task as providing an information exchange, by picking up ideas from one country and relaying them to subsidiaries in another. While this system has worked for many years, it could prove a severe hindrance if cross-national campaigns needed to be implemented. With each subsidiary looking after its own interests, the difficulty for management at head office will be to decide who is to look after the pan-European opportunities, and, more important, pay for them. Management does not contemplate any major resources/organisational change for the time being; the argument is that having a central budget can create as many problems as it solves: if there is no central budget there is the problem of allocating the costs of international campaigns. If there is a central budget, this can create more and more pressure for international campaigns, because, effectively, the local companies benefit from free advertising.

■ The network organisation

It is so far clear that there is no optimal organisational structure for global operations, whether centralised, geographical or divisionalised; what is clear is that the format adopted must reflect:

- the company's decision-making and strategic direction;
- a company's spread of country markets; and
- the degree of control required to implement the strategy.

What has emerged in recent years is the networked global organisation (Figure 7.5); the network avoids the problems of duplication of effort, inefficiency and resistance to ideas developed elsewhere by giving subsidiaries the latitude, encouragement and tools to pursue local business development within the framework of global strategy. Headquarters considers each unit as a source of ideas, skills, capabilities and knowledge that can be utilised for the benefit of the entire organisation (for example, an idea for a new product design can

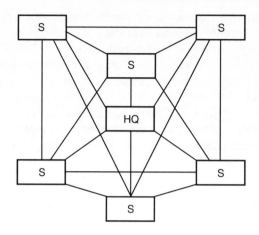

HQ = Headquarters
S = Subsidiary

Figure 7.5   Networked global organisation

originate in Latin America, be developed by R&D at headquarters, and test marketed in the Far East). The context of networking means that subsidiaries must be upgraded from the role of implementation and adaptation to that of contribution and partnership in the development and execution of worldwide strategies. Efficient plants may be converted into worldwide productive centres and leading subsidiaries groups may be given a leadership role in developing new strategy for the whole corporation.

The main tool for implementing the networked approach is international teams of managers who meet regularly to develop strategy. Although final direction may come from headquarters, the input has included the information on local conditions, and implementation of the strategy is enhanced because local managers were involved from the beginning.

CASE 7.13

Philips NV, of Eindhoven is one of the world's largest electronics companies with a main Board responsible for worldwide operations. In the 1980s the company found that its organisational structure of semi-autonomous subsidiaries and business units was increasingly uncompetitive. As a response, Philips created links throughout the geographic, business and functional areas of the company. These links were formed of international management groups or teams. The teams handle strategy development and implementation and headquarter–subsidiary relationships by providing the means to communicate corporate culture, develop a global perspective, coordinate the operations of the enterprise as a whole, and yet remain responsive to local market needs. These far-reaching activities are reason for describing the company as a global organisation. The teams meet quarterly, and larger, strategy-based meetings are held annually. The networked global organisation with its philosophy of sharing enables Philips to avoid purely national product lines and also the possibility of uncooperative attitudes among country managers where they are compelled to compete for resources. Although direction comes from top management, local considerations are incorporated into the decision thereby enhancing local commitment to the implementation.

So Philips has provided an example of the matrix organisation with five tiers in its global operations as follows:

- the Board;
- product divisions with global responsibility for R&D, production and marketing;
- service division with global responsibility for staff;
- regional bureaux with liaising responsibilities;
- country organisations with on-the-ground responsibility.

■ Managing subsidiaries and associates

At this point it is appropriate to clarify some of the terminology in this section. In English law a *subsidiary* is where more than 50 per cent of the voting shares are owned by the investing company; the fact that the latter chooses – or is compelled – to invite local partners to contribute up to 49 per cent of the equity does not make it any less of a subsidiary, since the investing company retains ultimate management control through its voting rights. Where such a large amount of new finance is required, it usually follows that a new manufacturing/distribution unit is being set up for the purpose. An *Associate* is where less than a controlling interest is exercised. There is, however, no absolutely clear rule about the level of ownership which constitutes effective management control. This is because there are many ways of exercising control and securing financial benefits in addition to royalties – for example, by royalties related to production or sale, by technical fees, supply of equipment and expertise and so forth. These are all regulated by contract between the parties.

The key points in the relationship between parent company and subsidiary are:

1. communication; and
2. control.

The quality of communications both ways between headquarters and subsidiary is crucial in determining the levels of coordination and motivation in implementing a global strategy, as shown in Tables 7.4 and 7.5.

There is a spectrum of relationships which can be described as running from open to closed in the degree of control exercised by the parent company over its

Table 7.4 Key problems identified by headquarters executives

	Rank (out of 182)	Score (%)
Lack of qualified international personnel		
Getting qualified international personnel is difficult	1	73
It is difficult to find qualified local managers for the subsidiaries	1	73
The company can't find enough capable people who are willing to move to different countries	15	60
There isn't enough manpower at headquarters to make the necessary visits to local operations	22	57
Lack of strategic thinking and long-range planning at the subsidiary level		
Subsidiary managers are preoccupied with purely operational problems and don't think enough about long-range strategy	3	71
Subsidiary managers don't do a good job of analysing and forecasting their business	5	65
There is too much emphasis in the subsidiary on short-term financial performance. This is an obstacle to the development of long-term marketing strategies	13	61
Lack of marketing expertise at the subsidiary level		
The company lacks marketing competence at the subsidiary level	4	69
The subsidiaries don't give their advertising agencies proper direction	8	63
The company doesn't understand consumers in the countries where it operates	8	63
Many subsidiaries don't gather enough marketing intelligence	17	59
The subsidiary does a poor job of defining targets for its product marketing	20	58
Too little relevant communication between headquarters and the subsidiaries		
The subsidiaries don't inform headquarters about their problems until the last minute	5	65
The subsidiaries do not get enough consulting service from headquarters	13	61
There is a communications gap between headquarters and the subsidiaries	31	51
The subsidiaries provide headquarters with too little feedback	33	50

Table 7.4   Continued

	Rank (out of 182)	Score (%)
Insufficient utilisation of multinational marketing experience		
The company is a national company with international business: there is too much focus on domestic operations	25	36
Subsidiary managers don't benefit from marketing experience available at headquarters and vice versa	28	53
The company does not take advantage of its experience with product introduction in one country for use in other countries	36	49
The company lacks central coordination of its marketing efforts	45	46
Restricted headquarters control of the subsidiaries		
The headquarters staff is too small to exercise proper control of the subsidiaries	8	63
Subsidiary managers resist direction from headquarters	17	59
Subsidiaries have profit responsibility and therefore resist any restraint on their decision-making authority	38	48

Source: Wiechmann and Pringle (1979).

Table 7.5   Key problems identified by subsidiary's executives

	Rank (out of 182)	Score (%)
Excessive headquarters control procedures		
Reaching a decision takes too long because we must get approval from headquarters	2	58
There is too much bureaucracy in the organisation	5	55
Too much paperwork has to be sent to headquarters	6	54
Headquarters staff and subsidiary management differ about which problems are important	17	46
Headquarters tries to control its subsidiaries too tightly	22	45
Excessive financial and marketing constraints		
The emphasis on short-term financial performance is an obstacle to the development of long-term marketing strategies for local markets	1	65

Table 7.5 Continued

	Rank (out of 182)	Score (%)
The subsidiary must increase sales to meet corporate profit objectives even though it operates with many marketing constraints imposed by headquarters	7	50
Headquarters expects a profit return each year without investing more money in the local company	10	49
Insufficient participation of subsidiaries in product decisions		
The subsidiary is too dependent on headquarters for new product development	13	47
Headquarters is unresponsive to the subsidiary's requests for product modifications	22	45
New products are developed centrally and are not geared to the specific needs of the local market	22	45
Domestic operations have priority in product and resource allocation: subsidiaries rank second	31	43
Insensitivity of headquarters to local market differences		
Headquarters management feels that what works in one market should also work in other markets	2	58
Headquarters makes decisions without thorough knowledge of marketing conditions in the subsidiary's country	12	48
Marketing strategies developed at headquarters don't reflect the fact that the subsidiary's position may be significantly different in its market	13	47
The attempt to standardise marketing programmes across borders neglects the fact that our company has different market shares and market acceptance in each country	27	44
Shortage of useful information from headquarters		
The company doesn't have a good training programme for its international managers	7	50
New product information doesn't come from headquarters often enough	22	45
The company has an inadequate procedure for sharing information among its subsidiaries	27	44
There is very little cross-fertilisation with respect to ideas and problem solving among functional groups within the company	27	44
Lack of multinational orientation at headquarters		
Headquarters is too home-country orientated	17	46
Headquarters managers are not truly multinational personnel	17	46

Source: Wiechmann and Pringle (1979).

subsidiaries. The most completely closed relationship occurs when the foreign subsidiaries are managed as if they were extensions of the domestic operations. Their autonomy is no greater than that of an operating unit in the home country and may well be less. At the other end of the spectrum there exists a purely investment relationship whereby the parent company is the sole principal shareholder in the subsidiary, but it is only interested in collecting dividends. Control is exercised solely through the annual meeting and representation on the board. The spectrum itself can be seen as a scale along which any given company, or given relationship within a company, can be placed.

The reason for this is that degrees of influence or authority have to be assessed, not just the position where a decision is taken. This can only be discovered by extensive research within the company, as the actual degree of authority so often differs from the perception of any one individual. The placing of a company is further complicated by the need to look at the information as well as the formal situation. In spite of the difficulties, enough evidence has come to light to permit some general observations.

A company does not usually have a very open relationship between some units, and a closed one between others. Some of the evidence for this assertion has already been widely established. A number of factors are expected to influence the relationship: these include the size of the subsidiary as well as its nationality and age. It is also frequently suggested that the relationship will differ according to the function, and the question of size is one that contains another paradox. Some companies argue that there is a closer relationship with the larger subsidiaries because of the effect that they can have on the well-being of the group as a whole. Other companies suggest just the opposite; that the large subsidiaries could look after themselves and close control was reserved for the small ones.

CASE 7.14

The Chairman and Chief Executive Officer of Nestlé heads both the board of directors and group management. In 1990, six corporate executive team members had geographic portfolios (USA, Canada, Asia/Oceania, Europe, Latin America, and Africa/Middle East); four had functional portfolios (finance/administration, R&D, technical and marketing); and three had product portfolios (chocolate and confectionery, pharmaceutical and other products). The Nestlé headquarters perceives itself performing essentially an arm's-length role in its highly-decentralised structure as exactly the opposite of the policy pursued by big American companies whose most important operations are generally located within the US, where their state-of-the-art factories and top executives are located, and where they make most of their profits. These executives have a natural tendency, of course, to want to export their methods, applying them to all their foreign subsidiaries.

With this decentralised structure, Nestlé's executive director-type affiliate heads have served as linchpins binding global management and locally-based companies; indeed the cohesion of the group has depended primarily on such relationships between the affiliate heads and holding company executives.

The Nestlé Group operating companies largely manage their own internal staffing and are encouraged to develop their own local managers. In making senior management appointments in the operating companies, Nestlé takes a pragmatic approach, promoting from within wherever possible, or assigning persons from other operating companies or headquarters. The Nestlé Group management staffing reflects the international character of the company. It seeks and draws upon talent not only from Switzerland but from as many markets as possible. Many of the headquarters staff (within which more than 50 nationalities are represented) have been assigned from the operating companies to develop an overall Nestlé perspective.

Nestlé has also developed an international corps whose role is to fill competency voids in operating companies, especially those companies in development phases, and to pass on their know-how to local personnel in these companies. For this corps, Nestlé recruits young persons with specific expertise in areas such as economics, finance, sales and engineering, and language. Personal requirements include maximum mobility, an open and enquiring mind and the ability to adapt.

In the late 1980s, the total number of expatriate assignments was 600; many were those from smaller operating companies who were transferred to Switzerland or larger companies to gain experience and later return to their country of origin to take up new responsibilities. Such international postings are a means not only of developing staff, but also of promoting Group 'cohesion and team spirit'. Indeed the Nestlé Group promotes a 'Nestlé Spirit' throughout the operating companies. When new companies are acquired, the task of promoting this has required special attention. Such integration is not only a matter of developing new knowledge and new skills within the Group, and of giving concrete form to the desired synergistic effects, but also of ensuring the perpetuation and enhancement of the Nestlé Spirit, sometimes called the corporate culture, which is essential to achieve the team spirit, so vital to the Group's success.

Source: Adapted from Humes (1992), pp. 215–16.

There is also a complex relationship between control in the sense of reporting and control in the sense of exercise of authority. There is a view and evidence to support it in domestic operations, that a substantial volume of reporting goes with decentralisation, with only a small amount of authority. It would seem logical to expect this, but it does not seem to happen in practice. The two most probable reasons why this should be so are, firstly, that a large amount of reporting from foreign, though not necessarily domestic, units forces conformity to head-office methods; and secondly that companies which exercise a close relationship with their foreign subsidiaries are just the ones that also develop elaborate control systems.

■ Developing relationships with markets and subsidiaries

The current variation in measures of control exercised by head office, particularly in Western industrialised countries, derives from four strategies which have evolved over the years.

The first of these is the exploitation of natural resources abroad. In Europe, this particular strategy has a long history going back to colonial times. The next strategy is international manufacturing, and includes companies which go abroad to made a wider use of their technical lead. The third strategy is commercial, and it is essentially defensive in character – the building of one or two plants abroad to counter threats to the market – and starts with an open relationship. The fourth strategy arises where geographical diversification is a main motive and where the parent company regards itself as the holding company. This is an investment strategy, and the contact between head office and the subsidiary may be really that of consultant to client.

Next, it is difficult to relate centralisation to success or failure since many other issues are involved. But two points are clear. One is that deviations from the norm are usually caused by companies being pressed by particular problems at particular times. The other point is that performance does not just depend on a variety of factors, but on a combination – the right combination.

Another major aspect is the head office's understanding or lack of understanding, of local market conditions. Lack of knowledge of basic market conditions is one of the major obstacles to the development of an effective control relationship between head office and subsidiary in international marketing. When head office commits itself to measure and evaluate subsidiary performance, the decision commits head office to participation in subsidiary planning. Measurement and evaluation of current performance are intrinsically involved in the planning cycle of operations and programmes in future time periods. In order to become effectively involved in this planning cycle, head office must understand the basic characteristic and conditions of the subsidiary market. If there is inadequate understanding, head office may adversely or inadequately influence the design of the country marketing plan for future periods and may misunderstand the significance of operating results in current periods.

The result of head office misunderstanding can involve major failures when head office succeeds in imposing an inappropriate plan on subsidiaries, or influencing subsidiaries to accept inappropriate objectives. Perhaps even more dangerously, head office misunderstanding can result in a failure of subsidiaries to achieve their full potential in a market. If head office does not understand the basic characteristics of a market, it will not be able to pinpoint subsidiary under-performance. The problem in international operations is the counterpart of the problem of managing product divisions in different technologies in a divisionalised company. In order to manage a product division, corporate management must understand the basic technology of the products being managed. If they do not understand the technology, divisional management virtually has free rein to develop its plan and explain its performance.

One often finds, when studying companies which are expanding, that a head office's understanding of foreign markets is enhanced in one important way; it is actively involved in the subsidiary planning process. This involvement ensures that head office executives learn about each subsidiary and region's market conditions. A few sophisticated companies are assigned approximately equal numbers of domestic and foreign executives to their international head offices in an effort to obtain an effective mix of home product and system know-how and international environmental knowledge in the head-office group.

The other issue is that of consistency. One of the difficulties of control systems in overseas operations is an attempt by headquarter's management to apply a consistent standardised approach to worldwide control. There is a view held by some managers that a well-run company should evidence the consistent application of tools and practices. If there is a best way to control international operations, should it not be applied on a universal scale?

There is no single best control system. There is a best way to control international operations only if these operations are homogeneous. Most companies that have extended themselves to more than one continent find their operations to be highly differentiated in terms of the kinds of markets they have, the length of experience of subsidiaries, and a host of other factors. The skilled and sophisticated international enterprise recognises this diversity, and develops control relationships with regions and subsidiaries based on the major variables influencing controls. If a subsidiary is large and has a highly developed head-quarters staff of its own, if the management of the subsidiary is highly confident, if the market in which the subsidiary operates is highly differentiated from other markets and requires a differentiated response to achieve company sales and profit objectives, then a differentiated control system is needed. If a company's technology, its size and position in markets, its communication relationships, its markets, and the competence of local management are uniform around the world, then a uniform control system is appropriate. Since these conditions are rarely if ever achieved, it follows that all control systems should be differentiated to respond to relevant differences. The secret of success is in developing systems that are responsible but not unique for each market.

■ Managing agents

The management of agents raises a number of issues, as they are not, of course, controlled by ownership of equity by the manufacturer, but work on the basis of a 5 or 8-year contract as agents for the principal (the manufacturer). However, there are variations on this theme, and it is not unknown for the manufacturer to take a small equity share in the agent's company, or more commonly, to support the agent in his territory by direct manufacturer-employed sales and promotion staff.

If an agent is to be used, once he/she has been chosen and has accepted the offer, the agency agreement needs careful consideration and expert legal advice is essential. One of the most important clauses will be the termination clause, which has to be set out in precise terms without any ambiguity. In some countries it is difficult to terminate agreements without substantial compensation, no matter what is written into the contract. The fact that the agreement is made subject to the laws of the UK does not always help, because sanctions can be applied which could make it difficult for the manufacturer to continue to trade in a country where he has gone against the local law when terminating an agency.

It is usual, but not essential, for the agent to be a national of the country concerned. He will probably operate on a commission basis, within a clearly defined territory. He will no doubt handle other non-competing agencies, but not too many. He may first sell, sending the orders to his principals for handling by them; or he may buy and sell in his own right, carrying stocks; or he could operate with a combination of both methods. He may also handle customer credit. However, although the most usual method of operating is still to use the services of agents, and although that method certainly has distinct advantages over the use of export houses, there can be problems involved. For instance, some agents tend to collect too many agencies, and then neglect those that bring in the least return.

■ Distributors

Many firms find it best to sell through sole distributors in export markets. This means quite simply that there is one customer only in the country or group of countries concerned, which stocks and resells the firm's products to others. In return for exclusivity, the sole distributor undertakes not to handle competitive products and often agrees to a minimum level of annual purchases. A country can be divided into regions, with a sole distributor for each region; or a few special or principal distributors can be appointed, each of whom gets favourable prices in return; for instance, for a minimum purchase commitment. There are a number of variations on the distributorship theme, and it could be wise, where there are several distributors in a territory, to have a local commission agent supervising these activities. In many instances this supervision can be undertaken by visits from head office; or the local agent's supervision can be reinforced by such visits.

Establishing a marketing or sales subsidiary is the ideal method of selling overseas if the scale of operations permits. A sound base is set up in the country concerned where stocks can be maintained if required, and the customers are presented with the easiest way of making contact with the manufacturer. This has advantages where spares and after-sales services are involved. Any such establishment inevitably involves the manufacturer in considerable problems of administration and control, and it is unlikely to be considered unless there is a well-established and secure market.

It is sometimes possible to establish a firm which, although not owned by the manufacturer, operates on a basis that gives very much the same result. For instance, some companies have found that the only way to be really successful in the US market is to sell American. To this end they appoint agents who are able to appear very much as a branch of the manufacturer. Prices are quoted in dollars for goods delivered to the customer's warehouse, and all invoicing is done through the agents and payments are made to them. Such an arrangement can work very well, and there are US agents who are expert in working for British companies in this way.

In addition, there are courses that lie somewhere between the scheme just described and the establishment of the firm's own office overseas. It is possible, for instance, to invest in an already-established business in the country concerned, or to join forces with other manufacturers as already described.

■ Factors influencing choice of intermediary

It is often difficult in practice to find new distributors or agents overseas who are effective and reliable. Manufacturers who adopt direct exporting will then have two main options:

1. to sell direct in the overseas market; or
2. to send their employees to travel throughout the market and obtain orders.

Both options are of course costly, particularly if overseas visits are frequent. Certainly, direct exporting has its limitations, particularly if the intent is to build up a strong market position; here the distinction between the company's own sales employees and self-employed agents or distributors overseas is important. A number of points arise for the company's management to consider in determining agency and other agreements:

1. The authority to be given to the foreign agent will have to be considered: shall the agent have authority only to procure and solicit orders that may or may not be accepted by the UK principal, or shall he, beyond that, be entitled to make contracts in a binding manner for the UK company?
2. The specific territory allotted to the agent and the goods he is to represent require careful determination.
3. It may be advisable to appoint the agent in the first place only for a probationary period; he may have other interests, and one can never be certain that he will live up to the principal's expectations.
4. The termination of the agency agreement should be laid down in the written contract which it is advisable for the principal to insist on, even if it consists of a simple exchange of letters. Many disputes arise when the agency relationship is dissolved, and the contract should be very specific on that contingency.
5. A number of countries, including Germany, France and Italy, contain protective legal provisions for some types of commercial agents, particularly of the smaller

group. These laws provide, in particular, for a goodwill compensation to which the agent may be entitled after termination of the agency relationship; while such a payment is not available in all cases in some legal systems, the principal cannot contract out of it.

In contrast to agency agreements, the main advantage of a distributor agreement is that it gives the exporter certainty to obtain a fixed turnover in the market into which he plans to direct his exports. It is, however, often more difficult to find a very suitable distributor than a self-employed agent. The exporter can conclude two types of contract with the distributor:

1. A basic contract containing clauses about the minimum amount of goods the distributor will undertake to buy annually, territory coverage, probation and termination, obligation of the distributor to sell the goods under the manufacturer's brand name (if that is intended), trademark arrangements, and so on.
2. A specific sales contract by which the above arrangements are actually carried out, providing for, among other details, terms of payment (whether cash or credit) and the agreed margin accruing to the distributor.

The exporter normally refrains from selling directly into the distributor's territory, except if there are reserved customers with whom the exporter was in contact before he entered into the sole distribution contract, and orders emanating from the distributor's territory are normally credited to him.

So sole agency or distribution agreements invariably provide that the agent or distributor shall have an exclusive territory. That exclusivity may contravene the fundamental concept of the EU, which is directed against the division of the territory of the Union into separate trading areas. However, the Commission has granted a block exemption to exclusive-agency contracts made with commercial agents. But the Commission's definition of agents is different from that in ordinary law. An agent is defined as a person who does not take the financial risk of the transaction (except in the case of a *del credere* agency); the text of the EC Regulation 67/67 goes on:

The Commission regards as the decisive criterion, which distinguishes the commercial agent from the independent trade, the agreement – express or implied – which deals with responsibility for the financial risks bound up with the sale or with the performance of the contract.

Thus, an Agent who keeps a considerable stock of goods or maintains, at his own expense, a service to customers, or has power to determine prices, is not covered by this ruling. What remains prohibited is any agreement preventing *parallel* imports and exports. This means that an exporter cannot impose an obligation on the foreign exclusive distributor not to buy the goods to which the contract relates in another EEC country, or not to sell them in such a country. He can prevent the distributor from advertising or offering them there, but he cannot prevent the actual buying and selling. In the use of foreign distributors and agents, it is common in some industries, notably pharmaceuticals and automobiles, for the manufacturing company to support the distributor (or agent) with some of its own sales staff in the market.

■ Export houses

There are other indirect methods of exporting which tend to be adopted by companies fulfilling overseas orders on a purely reactive basis, with little risk and no investment outlay. Export houses or buying offices in UK or overseas firms are the most commonly used. The former provide a wide range of services for manufacturers, although established exporters use them much less nowadays; as for the latter, manufacturers and foreign extractive industries often have equipment-procurement offices in the home countries of supplying firms. Also, some large-scale companies operate multinational buying for foreign operations through domestic purchasing. The situation concerning

---

CASE 7.15

The experience of United Biscuits (UB) illustrates how an analysis of competition underlines the need to have a direct stake in an overseas market. While UB was struggling to obtain an acceptable market share in Denmark, rivals Nabisco were taking 40 per cent of the Danish biscuit market through a local subsidiary, Oxford Biscuits. UB had depended on a distribution agreement with Copenhagen Bread Factories (CBF). CBF operated a bread van delivery sales force providing a daily covering of the smaller shops in Copenhagen, and claimed good access to the cooperatives and multiples through a small national sales force. But these arrangements quickly proved unsatisfactory. The small bakers did not have the volume market for biscuits, and CBF did not have entry to the large high-volume outlets, nor did it demonstrate the determination to gain entry.

Taking account of Nabisco's continuing success, UB took bolder action and set up its own subsidiary company in Denmark, United Biscuits A/S, which was to be concerned purely with selling (as opposed to selling and manufacturing). Even then, in its first two years of operations, the company failed to meet projected targets. This was due to incomplete utilisation of the company's limited resources and ineffective sales management (for example haphazard journey planning and excessive efforts expended on selling to small independent retailers). As a result, management changes were made, including appointing as managing director a senior executive from a major competitor in Denmark. Both administration and sales then improved in effectiveness; UB products are now handled by every wholesaler in Denmark, and its share of total UK biscuit exports to Denmark increased from 26 to 53 per cent in six years.

the British buying offices of foreign firms is somewhat similar; such offices can sometimes prove the only route of entry into a business. (A good example of this is provided by the London buying offices of American department stores.)

An export house is officially defined by the British Export Houses Association (BEHA) as 'any company or firm, not being a manufacturer whose main activity is the handling or financing of British trade and/or international trade not connected with the UK'. There are approximately 700 export houses in the UK, and they handle an estimated 20 per cent of UK export trade. The commission, or confirming houses, included in this definition are usually home-based and specialise in buying goods on behalf of overseas clients, paying the manufacturer and dealing with transport, payment, documentation and customs for a commission of from 3.5 to 8.5 per cent. Export merchants who buy and sell on their own account (acting as principals in the export transaction) also fall within the BEHA definition.

■ Evaluating performance

So in evaluating these modes of operations, management must have a well-researched data-base on which to base decision criteria; clearly, the management of a firm expanding international operations must assess the total control of operations conferred by ownership of a foreign subsidiary against the likely rewards and risks. Similarly, in evaluating a joint venture management must assess the value of the inputs, local market and technical expertise that the partner can bring, together with the lower level of risk and capital outlay involved. As already noted, many governments, particularly those of developing countries, make joint ventures with local capital a condition of market entry.

Furthermore, there does seem to be some relationship between full parental-control and market success. Evidence among small and medium-sized UK companies setting up a foreign production subsidiary for the first time suggests that firms with 75 per cent or more of voting shares in the foreign subsidiary have a markedly higher record of market success than those whose control is diluted; also small firms in particular have a low threshold of tolerance for joint decision-making, and agents (who often initiate moves towards some sort of direct investment) make bad partners unless consistently visited and supported. As already explained MNCs prefer to operate through wholly owned subsidiaries.

■ The role of marketing

Given that the commitment of companies to invest capital, resources, manpower and so forth in overseas operations has correspondingly higher risks than direct and indirect exporting, then this can only highlight the vital role of marketing. Market research, demand analysis, long-term market prospects and the assessment of sales potential, both in the overseas country and regionally, are all essential prerequisites to overseas operations. Marketing must provide a sound, realistic market data-base for planning and decisions. A knowledge level adequate for exporting must be increased and this will cost money; market knowledge of past and present trends and valid market projections must be extended.

In addition to research about the company's own products and supply capacity, there must be expert appraisal of the target country's financial and economic prospects. This staff work can be done internally by desk research followed up by some personal, investigative visits, or it can be obtained from outside consultants. (Even abortive studies can sometimes help to improve current marketing methods by the light they throw on market conditions.) And while there is always an element of hazard in market forecasting, the margins of error inherent in this exercise must be clarified at the outset of the research. Indeed, sensitivity-analysis should be made of the results in the light of an agreed range of options: should this range be greater than the possible limits of failure and success that the company is prepared to accept, then this will serve, on the first or second run of the complete data, either to discard the project before too much time is spent on secondary analysis, or to concentrate the analysis into market sectors (possibly different to those originally set out) that show a greater likelihood of success.

All these tasks are clearly the responsibility of marketing management, together with the actual implementation and evaluation of international marketing programmes, whatever mode of entry and operation is selected; and careful planning has to be balanced against the need for rapid market entry. Timing is often vital to pre-empt a competitor, or to secure a particular contract. Finally, the product range, technical expertise and marketing position of the investing company are themselves likely to be important in determining the viability of a subsidiary, and it is arguable that the foreign entrant should aim for the quality or luxury sectors of the market. Many investors are specialist manufacturers of producers' goods, and *quality* means producing abroad to at least the same or higher specifications as in the home market, for the following reasons:

1. The higher costs of producing abroad (initially at least) are more easily absorbed at the quality end of the market.
2. Good returns can be earned from a lower volume of production of a quality product (and this would be crucial in the earlier years of the foreign enterprise).

So a dilemma that faces a firm with a foreign subsidiary is the balance of advantage between centralising decision-making to achieve consistency between headquarters and subsidiary, and allowing local management the scope to exercise initiative.

■ Financial control

In terms of financial control, headquarters management needs to be well-informed of the activities of the subsidiary, otherwise capital, management-time and other resources can be wasted. This necessitates the regular submission of budget estimates and accounts from the subsidiary. As multinational corporations have long known, the existence of foreign subsidiaries allows greater flexibility in financial operations. These advantages can be wasted by naive foreign investors. A good example of this is transfer pricing policies. In many firms, internal prices are set on an *ad hoc* basis, rather than being oriented towards clear policy objectives. Often, a similar situation prevails in the choice between the repatriation of dividends and reinvestment in the subsidiary. Such decisions are strategically important and should be thought through at a higher management level.

The issue of control also arises with regard to the optimal number and nature of business functions that the foreign subsidiary should perform, such as marketing, purchasing, labour training and research. Here it is necessary to distinguish between strategy, which must be set by the parent in consultation with the subsidiary management, and contingent decision-making, which, within that policy, is usually best carried out by local management. It is achieving this division and balance that is difficult.

Each foreign investment is unique, but there are certain regularities in the problems encountered. Among the most frequently cited are: employment of workers, including training and supply; problems of control of foreign production, including quality control; managerial problems, including liaison problems with foreign partners, and the drain on resources in the parent company; and financial problems including taxation and generating sales in the start-up period.

None of these problems is uniquely an international problem, but all are exacerbated by difficulties of operation in an alien environment. However, a learning process is at work, and many firms that successfully establish a foreign unit are often able to put their experience to good use. Particularly important are lessons of *managing at a distance*, which often compels firms to formalise and systemise their decision-making procedures. Second, the importance of having the right man at the top of the subsidiary is often emphasised by small firms in particular. Third, lessons are learned on improvements in marketing; and evaluation by foreign investors is often based on the company's *sensitivity to local conditions*.

■ International contracting

■ Management contracts

A management contract has been defined as 'an arrangement under which operational control of an enterprise, which would otherwise be exercised by the directors or managers appointed or elected by its owners, is vested by contract in a separate enterprise which performs the necessary managerial functions for a fee'.

Such an agreement, usually valid for five to seven years, can be prolonged, and contract responsibility may be extended to various functions in the local firm, for example to manage production and sale of goods, introduce technical, financial and marketing programmes, and for skills-training or management development. The essential point is that it is the foreign firm that is normally responsible for managing and undertaking certain executive and technical functions in another (local) firm without having an equity shareholding. Other related forms of contract can include project management agreements, where the client brings in a contractor to carry out the design and construction phase of the projects, and technical service agreements, where the client draws on special kinds of operational know-how and advice available from the contractor.

Of course, a management contract is only one of the many options open to the firm operating internationally; furthermore, the boundaries between direct investment and other modes of operation discussed in this chapter, such as licensing, are often, in practice, not drawn precisely. Many market opportunities permit combinations, so that management contracts are frequently combined with turnkey projects or licensing agreements; and such a combination helps to ensure the success of the venture. In principle, therefore, the advantages of the management contract to the firm moving into a foreign market are: low-risk market entry, with no capital investment and no expropriation risk; and the fact that the contract capitalises on management skills and provides a guaranteed minimum income and a quick return. The disadvantages are that the local investor may seek to interfere with the way his investment is being managed, and the managing company may initially lack management resources and marketing expertise to exploit the local market fully.

Management contracts can be associated, therefore, with different modes of entry and operation, involving equity, technical know-how, managerial skills and so on; and the contract provides managerial know-how in a number of different arrangements, or else as the sole agreement, as illustrated in Figure 7.6. Indeed, direct foreign investment in some countries has in recent years become hazardous, if not impracticable, where governments have legislated directly to regulate the activities of foreign firms, even forcing them to withdraw from certain industrial or economic sectors (for example, Mexico, Nigeria, India and Malaysia); various obstacles such as foreign exchange restrictions have already been discussed. The management contract, therefore, has developed as an increasingly attractive mode to companies seeking to strengthen their international market position. It avoids direct confrontation with foreign governments, and provides a useful way of increasing cooperation with the local business enterprises to develop the market, whether they are in the private or public sectors. At the same time, any such contractual arrangement must be commercially justifiable compared with the profitability of other modes, such as direct or indirect exporting (discussed earlier in this chapter). Management

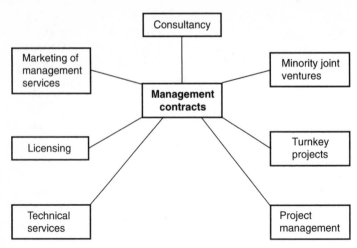

Figure 7.6   Management contracts

Source: J. Holly, 'Management Contracts', *Handbook of International Trade*, Vol. 1, Section 3.7(1), Macmillan, 1983.

contracts can guarantee a satisfactory rate of return to the contractor, even though a rigid comparison of the profit between direct investment and management contract would not be sufficient. In terms of allocating resources and developing appropriate management staff, it is essential for the firm operating internationally to devise some form of acceptable management control, as opposed to control arising from equity ownership; this is also necessary to meet marketing objectives and to minimise risk and uncertainty.

■ Market prospects for contracting

In analysing marketing prospects in particular, in having a management contract, the contracting company must take into account opportunities to sell machinery, equipment, technology and know-how in the local (foreign) country. There can also be opportunities to acquire market intelligence and trade contacts, as well as more advantageous local supply arrangements for materials, components, etc. And direct remuneration through fees from a particular contract should not necessarily be viewed as the primary goal; the realisation of broader, market-related, goals should be management's aim, and the longer-term value of the contract should be assessed in terms of such factors as:

• improved overseas market access, giving better competitiveness;
• realising a higher share of sales potential;

- local supply and distribution arrangements, bringing higher-quality service and cost-benefits to customers;
- longer-term development of a strong overall market position overseas, providing the means to generate/dominate new or key market sectors where demand prospects are high.

■ **Management aspects**

As has been pointed out, some management contracts do not separate management and ownership completely. This is an important point. Some companies and countries prefer the contractor to have some small financial involvement (1–10 per cent) or a minority joint venture (10–49 per cent) with a management contract, and the contractor himself may prefer a share in the action.

1. The foreign contractor makes no significant financial investment in the local firm.
2. In a minority joint venture with a management contract, there is limited ownership-related control of the local firm, and control is vested by the voluntary, temporary delegation of managerial responsibility by the majority shareholders.

Of course, joint ventures in which a minority partner is contracted to provide management are common throughout both the developed and the developing world. Management contracts, with a fixed term, are therefore used to ensure efficient operation, and to assist in the process of management development and the transfer of technology and marketing techniques. This type of contract is most commonly used either during the initial operation of new joint ventures or during the period after full or part nationalisation of a foreign company. Less often, it is used when a local operation overseas has run into difficulty and a foreign firm is invited into effect a turnround.

Many manufacturing companies are forced to sell-down their majority holding to a minority position by government policy. In order to protect their remaining equity, these companies endeavour to maintain control through several types of agreements, most particularly management contracts and technical service agreements. Such companies not only seek to maintain control through management contracts in order to ensure the good functioning of the former subsidiary and thus to receive returns from dividends, but they also seek to maintain the supply of goods from, or the sales of goods to, the former subsidiary. In these cases the function of the management contract is not just to obtain remuneration from the contract, but also to secure an overall strategy. The purpose of the management contract is to obtain profits by maintaining or obtaining a market rather than obtaining direct remuneration from the contract itself. In socialist countries, the contract ensures the maximum foreign control permitted.

■ Technology

Usually in a turnkey contract, the contractor has the obligation to deliver an operating industrial plant to the client without the active participation of the client in the various stages of construction. The contractor may also have to provide for technical assistance with training and operation of the plant for a short initial period (that is, the commissioning phase), and to assist with the marketing of the product manufactured. If the contract imposes on the contractor an additional guarantee as to the quantity and the quality of the production over a longer period (sometimes up to two years), the turnkey contract will become a turnkey-plus-management contract.

Where expertise is scarce, arrangements must be made to obtain trained and experienced operatives and managers. Technical assistance agreements and management contracts are, therefore, necessary if the transfer of technology is to be completed. Contractors can gain from the need for such agreements over and above a fee. The technology transferred can be tied into a foreign contractor's technology and become a captive sales market for intermediate goods and sophisticated technical equipment. Management contracts can arise in connection with the support of licences. The management is provided where the contract enterprise does not have sufficient know-how to operate a licence. In some circumstances there may be a failure of the licence agreement and the licensor may consider the operation valuable enough to assign management through a contract in order to ensure the continuation of the enterprise. Where the licensee does not exploit the licence effectively, then the licensor must either rescind the licence or devote more resources. Devoting more resources may be justified on several grounds, but two seem the most important: the fee that is derivable from licensing, and the access permitted to a particular market. In the absence of licensing, a firm may find that another company can exclude market entry at a later date, or can compete in certain markets through exploitation of the asset.

Management contracts may be associated with licensing in other ways. Few technologies can be transferred simply by transferring blueprints, documents and reports. The negotiation process itself is time-consuming and expensive, and must be followed by engineering, consultation and adaptation. The early stages of production are usually characterised by low quality and low productivity. Uncontrolled licensees may not exploit patents energetically enough, and a licensor's own management can effect higher sales because of better business know-how. A management contract may effect higher sales because of better business know-how. A management contract may then be used to ensure the efficacious application of a licence and a profitable rate of return.

Two Case examples below illustrate many of the key aspects of a management contract in operation.

CASE 7.16

This example concerns a Swedish firm, the Scandinavian Dairy Company (SDCo), which operates in the dairy and farming industry of Sweden. SDCo successfully defeated its rivals from Europe and the USA for a $40 million turnkey project in the Middle East by entering into a management contract; the company realised that the local firm lacked skilled personnel to establish and operate a modern dairy project. The management contract, moreover, gave SDCo an opportunity to establish a long-term business relationship with the local firm, which in turn helped it to win a much larger contract (worth $100 million) at a later stage for the supply of dairy and farming equipment.

CASE 7.17

Already established internationally through sales offices and subsidiaries, SDCo now acts as a turnkey contractor, assuming responsibility to do feasibility studies, technical and market research, and so forth; generally, SDCo supply directly only a quarter of the equipment installed in a turnkey project, and purchases the rest externally.

SDCo expect four major gains from this particular Middle Eastern management contract: (a) increased control over the mode of operation of the local firm and the use of the equipment supplied; (b) use of this management contract as a reference when bidding for turnkey projects in other developing countries; (c) additional business opportunities to sell components and accessories; and (d) improved capability to offer, worldwide, a complete dairy and farming system, including managerial services.

The actual project is located in an oil-rich country (though industrially backward with a scarcity of skilled workers). The overall contract incorporates an erection and construction contract; a materials supply contract; and a management contract, which is valid for seven years and makes SDCo responsible for the technical operation of the dairy farm and milk plant, and for providing management personnel to the local firm. SDCo receives its remuneration in three forms: (a) it receives a dividend on its financial investment; (b) it is paid a fixed management fee; and (c) it receives a tax-free payment (rising from 6 per cent in year 1, to 10 per cent in year 5 and thereafter) contingent on the results realised by the local firm. SDCo has also been receiving non-financial gains in the form of control, exports orders, market knowledge and trade contacts.

■ Contracting and marketing

The interesting aspect to emerge from these case examples is the importance of the management contract in the context of developing the company's international marketing strategy, specifically in some of the following ways:

1. The development and nurturing of a local enterprise into a flourishing business, coupled with a conflict-free relationship between SDCo and the local firm, is a source of potent and favourable public-relations activities for SDCo both in the country and the region.
2. There is a sharper competitiveness of SDCo's product/service offer: the company has developed new solutions and devised software to resolve extremes of climatic situations applicable to other projects in the region.
3. Market access has been opened up in many other countries with a potential for dairy farming and milk-production technology.
4. Long-term market development in such target countries is greatly enhanced by the evolution of system sales, and by the ability of SDCo to deliver firm-specific competence by differentiating the company's own solution from solutions offered by competitors in the market. (In practice, this competitive edge is more cost-effective by differentiating software than hardware solutions.)
5. Stronger market presence has been brought about by successful turnkey operations and the establishment of market leadership based on both technology and management expertise.
6. Such a project is valuable in strengthening the firm's base (managerial, technical and financial) to compete for other new turnkey projects.

These marketing aspects underline the wide scope of operations of management contracts in developing a firm's international business operations. For a firm newly entering an overseas market, high start-up costs can make it more expensive to bid for contracts; but the problem-solving and decision-making processes in the local firms (overseas) are likely to be similar to the corresponding processes in the foreign firms with which the local firm has had management contracts. Therefore, the former management contractor, in seeking new contract business, can generally reduce start-up costs at the margin and be more competitive in the market. So firms with previous experience of management contracts tend to have the competitive edge in terms of management expertise, technology transfer and the sale of plant, equipment and components to back up the project; and there is often a clear tactical advantage in securing new or follow-on contracts for the firm that won, and has completed, the initial contract. (Nor should the goodwill generated in the overseas market by the local firm be overlooked.)

■ Global make-or-buy decisions

The next issue for analysis in this context is manufacturing under contract where the level of technology is important. Many firms avoid subcontracting key technological items where counterfeiting or copying by competitors is a danger. However, for low technology items such as component supplies, control systems and so forth, there is much to be gained by using subcontractors for ensuring competitive supply terms. Here are some examples:

- A US pump company moved production off-shore, resulting in lower costs for operation to compete in world markets.
- A Canadian tools company subcontracted packaging to gain economies of scale, thus gaining a substantial price advantage.
- A US refractory manufacturer contracted-out sub-assembly and final assembly, thus avoiding some tasks which, when completed by union employees, would result in a very high cost to the company.
- A US components company moved production to other plants overseas and gained both cost and quality improvements by subcontracting some machined parts.

A taxonomy of different approaches to the make-or-buy issue is shown in the Table 7.6.

■ Strategic factors in sub-contracting

Clearly labour intensity and labour costs are key factors in decisions to subcontract; but there are other factors to be considered such as low energy costs in a country which can make it an attractive proposition for a processing industry (for example, alumina processed into aluminium and re-exported). Cost savings can also be achieved through reduced costs of raw materials and overheads as well as labour. Companies in industrialised countries seek to reduce overheads and fixed investment in plant and equipment; companies developing global production and distribution can use contract manufacturing through joint ownership of production in industrialising countries to minimise risk. The most crucial issue in the determination of the technology to be used is the size of the production-run involved. The break-point at which it becomes worthwhile to use the more capital-intensive technology will be affected by the going wage rate. (There are other considerations, such as the need for high precision.) The break-point can work in favour of a high degree of automation, as with aircraft parts, or against it, as with high-class cameras; for a short production run, any country will have to use simple technology. Production will therefore be labour-intensive, and, from a technical point of view, industrialising countries may be particularly well-placed for subcontracting, particularly for short production runs.

With MNCs, industrialising countries are no longer short of capital if the corporations decide to bring it in (in practice they may not want to for political reasons). Electronics is perhaps something of a special case: The future focus of the world market in videocassette recorders (VCRs) is in the Far East with its enormous populations. Philips intends to concentrate its world production

Table 7.6   Different approaches to the make-or-buy issue

Approach	Basis of approach	Examples	Problems or drawbacks
Operational/ cost-based approach	Decisions taken individually on the basis of cost-savings or operational advantage	Subcontracting transport, printing or peak-load manufacture	Failure to achieve all possible savings. No relationship to any overall company strategy
Business approach	Proactive approach to make-or-buy based on either a system of continuing evaluation or assessment based on broader cost criteria	Use of multifunctional team (materials, finance, legal), which assessed any departmental activity for cost-savings by buying in	Decisions may be based on short/medium-term cost-savings which are cyclical. Buying-in decisions may lead to strategic shortcomings
Policy approach	Based on an overview of the strategic direction of the company and its technological strengths and weaknesses	Activities based on single-minded concentration on cost/essential technologies	Difficulty in integrating business policy/technology strategy/purchasing operation

Source: Ford and Farmer (1990), pp. 54–62.

there, and the Far East already has 50 per cent of the world's production of transistor radios for the free-standing world market (that is, excluding markets such as Brazil, which are effectively isolated). By contrast, the United States produces very few radios or VCRs, and imports of televisions (often under domestic US labels) have a very large share of the total market.

It is also significant that those industrialising countries with sub-contracting do not impose severe fiscal or bureaucratic restraints on trade. Taiwan has the free trade zone of Kaoshiung to facilitate import and export, but even so companies complain of the difficulty of setting up operations there. Hong Kong and Singapore are essentially free ports, and Singapore in particular has its Industrial Development Board to assist potential investors. Singapore is famous for its honest and efficient administration: consultation delays are very short, and the Industrial Development Board provides technical data, arranges contacts with the Government, and assists with factory sites and the recruitment of labour. Elsewhere, international companies find that contacts with a government may be far from speedy and straightforward, and finding a factory site in a foreign country with complex land laws may be a difficult business. There is little doubt that the operations of the Industrial Development Board have greatly assisted in attracting investors to Singapore, but it would probably be wrong to concentrate on the cash value of any actual subsidies. Rather, a major factor has been the cash and convenience value of disincentives avoided.

Another topical issue is whether it would be better for industrialising countries if they could separately buy the items in the MNC package: capital, management, technical know-how, and marketing. In this context subcontracting can certainly take a wide variety of forms: one-off orders (for example, clothing), long-term contracts, and then varying degrees of technical assistance and capital participation right up to the wholly-owned subcontracting subsidiary of a large foreign firm. In practice it is arguable whether one sort of arrangement is always best for the industrialising country or for the investing firm. According to the type of product and the nationality of the firm giving the subcontract, firms may be more or less keen on wholly owned subsidiaries.

CASE 7.18

Contracting in the construction industry has been well-documented. Management faces uncertainty and risk in competitive bidding and tendering in this sector where subcontracting is widely used to give the main contractor the flexibility needed to complete on-site, customised projects. Thus the risks are spread among the subcontractors but the main contractor still has to tackle the problem of control, particularly the quality of bought-in components and systems. Where safeguarding production quality is especially critical, the main contractor has to either do more of the work in-house or exercise tighter and systematic control over the subcontractors. Studies have found that in general terms the level of subcontracting by the construction firm is an outcome of firms' strategic orientation and the management's choices with regard to structural elaboration and technology, as they respond to the volume and nature of work faced by the organisation. It appears to be the interplay between these variables that determines the level of subcontracting by the firm.

CASE 7.19

Subcontracting in the tannery industry was the subject of a study in Italy which explored the relationship between tanneries and their subcontractors. Among other things, the study found that purchasing firms rarely had the technology, size or personnel to carry out all the sequential operations required in the tanning cycle in-house. Moreover, the operations subcontracted were those of a physical character (such as pressing, nailing, stretching, gauging and so forth), which did not significantly influence the quality of the finished hide. Those processes that required relatively simple machinery but more personnel tended to be subcontracted, while the main contractor used more complex machinery where efficient utilisation depended on a steady flow of good-quality semifinished hides.

> It was determined that this sort of specialisation protected the main contractor to some extent against the risk of sudden and unexpected fluctuations in demand; it also enabled him to respond quickly to meet clients' widely differing demands and to adapt to changes in economic and market conditions. There were a number of general factors that affected decisions by management to sub-contract, including availability of product equipment, degree of machinery utilisation, comparative cost analysis, and availability of subcontracting companies. The key finding of this study was that 'the decision ... is always based on a strategy to expand and increase turnout of the end product while conserving size and features typical of small firms'.
>
> The study confirmed a 'mutuality of interest' between tanneries and subcontractors, particularly in the breakdown of production into two categories: chemical processing that tanneries performed themselves, and physical operations performed by subcontractors. Because the many subcontractors typically worked for several tanneries, they were closely linked to general demand trends and were well adapted to market contingencies.
>
> The study also found that subcontracting firms' comparative operational stability was a function of their high specialisation. This resulted in close technical and economic cooperation between the two parties.
>
> *Source:* Ford and Farmer (1990), pp. 54-62.

International subcontracting can therefore produce higher value inputs to manufacturing, but subcontracting companies must meet the following criteria:

- Offer design and manufacturing expertise in specialised fields superior to that of their customers;
- Test products and systems to standards that are customer- and industry-defined;
- Purchase and specify components;
- Have contingency plans to cope with handling sudden fluctuations in demand and other nonrecurring events

■ Licensing

This essentially entails the sale of a patent, technical know-how or processes on a contractual basis, by which a home manufacturer (licensor) grants a licence to a foreign manufacturer (licensee) and received royalty payments in return. Many companies in UK manufacturing industry (particularly in general engineering, paper, board and packaging machinery, food processing equipment, vehicle and vehicle parts, electronic testing and fire control equipment) operate licensing agreements as part of their plans to develop worldwide sales. The licensing system works especially well in more distant overseas markets where the extra costs and the logistics of shipping finished machines would make the products uncompetitive, or where the home manufacturer does not have the production capacity to meet overseas orders. Licensing can be a profitable approach to market entry and development, particularly if there are high tariffs on finished, imported manufactures or plant, high costs of setting up wholly-owned subsidiaries, and difficulties in the repatriation of profits and dividends (though this can also apply to the remittance of royalties).

The industrial or commercial expertise that is the subject of a licensing agreement can include access to design expertise and industrial designs; commissioning to achieve performance guarantees; product and process specifications; manufacturing know-how that is not the subject of a patent; technical advice or assistance (including the supply of components, materials or plant essential to the manufacturing process); management advice and assistance; and the use of a trademark or trade name. But before any decision to enter into a licensing agreement is made, the manufacturer (who would be the licensor) must check the following in overseas countries:

- the market potential and selling conditions;
- the copyright, and patent situations;
- the regulations on licensing agreements and royalty payments and on fiscal and exchange-control laws (the rate and remittance of royalties may be strictly controlled);
- the level of technical education and expertise available locally to manufacture and market the output (of the licensee), both in his locality and, possibly, to other countries within the region.

Ideally, licensing should combine the skills and expertise of the primary manufacturer (licensor) with the local knowledge, contacts and so on of the licensee overseas; the licensor there assigns to the licensee, for the royalty payment, one or more of the patent rights, trademark rights and so forth, in a particular overseas market or markets. In return, the licensee undertakes:

- to produce the licensor's products to agreed, specified standards;
- to market his output in the territories assigned to him; and
- to pay to the licensor a royalty payment, usually related to sales volume or profits.

There is often also an initial payment, payable as soon as the licence agreement is signed (often paid to cover the initial transfer of machinery, components or designs, or sometimes simply for know-how).

Clearly, the management of the manufacturing company must, therefore,

1. evaluate the relevance and benefits of operating licensing agreements overseas in particular situations relating to industrial competitiveness, technical developments and expansion of the business; and
2. if licensing is adopted, set up a control system as regards both operations and effectiveness, and the continuing technical back-up and support to maintain the necessary standards and quality in the licensee's production.

■ Evaluation and control

Much depends on market conditions and available local technical expertise: it may not be possible to identify a suitable licensee in the target country, and obtaining full and prompt payments/remittances may be difficult; costs of knowledge transfer may be high, and the licensor may consider that he is unwittingly creating a competitor. Any evaluation, therefore, should rest on an analysis of the benefits and disadvantages of licensing, leading to a well founded decision in each particular situation. The principal advantage to the licensor is market access: licensing provides entry into markets that are otherwise closed on account of high rates of duty, entrenched competition, import quotas or prohibitions, and high freight costs making any imported products uncompetitive. Furthermore, licensing requires little capital investment and should provide a higher rate of return on capital employed, with (relative to other modes) very low risks; this is especially attractive to firms short of capital or management time.

Many foreign governments favour licensing arrangements as infusions of new technology; therefore approval and operation are quicker and the licensor is not exposed to the danger of nationalisation or expropriation of assets. Local manufacture (under licence) can also be an advantage in securing foreign government contracts, especially defence contracts. And the licensor benefits in two further ways: because of the limited capital requirements, new products can be rapidly exploited on a worldwide basis before competition develops, and cross-licensing agreements can provide an additional way of avoiding excessive competition. The advantages to the licensee are access to new technology to strengthen the firm's competitive position; continuing support and advice from the licensor in quality control; promotion and product development; and the financial benefit of increasing profitability of incremental sales revenue (based on the fee or royalty paid).

As for the licensor, there are some negative aspects of licensing arrangements which need analysis. The licensor may be, indirectly, establishing and supporting his future competitor (when the licensing agreement finally expires). Furthermore, the licensee even if he reaches an agreed minimum turnover may not fully exploit the market, leaving it open to the entry of competitors, and the licensor then will inevitably lose direct control of the marketing operation. Again, strict product quality control is difficult, and the product will often be sold under the licensor's brand name. Governments often impose conditions on remittances of royalties or on component supply. As for revenue, license fees are normally a small percentage (between 2 and 7 per cent) of the licensee's turnover, and will often compare unfavourably with what might be obtained from a company's own manufacturing operation. Lastly, some arguments can arise, however carefully the licensing agreement is drafted, and a disaffected licensee can be a serious problem.

All these aspects, the last one especially, underline the importance of management control of the licensing agreement by the licensor, particularly as the licensee is operating under the licensor's brand name, using his expertise and developing the market on his behalf. This aspect encompasses a number of steps to be taken in a logical order. Regarding selection of the licensee, the manufacturer needs to have criteria against which he will screen possible licensees; companies should seek out and compare alternative licensees, and not just respond directly to an initiative from one foreign manufacturer. The licensing agreement should be drafted to protect the interests of both parties; the licensor must satisfy himself at first hand not only of the technical competence of the licensee but also that he has genuine up-to-date marketing knowledge and contacts over the whole of the area allotted to him.

The licensor should also endeavour, whenever possible, to maintain some degree of control throughout the duration of the agreement. He may, for example, retain the right to supply certain ingredients or key components rather than giving a licence for a complete package; alternatively, he may allow in the agreement for the acquiring of a sufficiently large equity interest to convert the operation into a joint venture (thus also avoiding the possibility of establishing a competitor at the expiry of the agreement). Control, however, must be combined with some motivation of the licensee. Such motivation is best ensured by encouraging and continuing interest on the part of the licensee by a steady flow of technical improvements and sales and marketing support and innovation: in this way, the licensee will always have something of value to gain by continuing with, and adhering to, the agreement.

CASE 7.20

A large manufacturing firm had relied exclusively on the licensing route to enter selected and growing markets in Western Europe and Japan because senior management believed that licensing allowed the firm to enter foreign markets with a minimum commitment of resources, while enjoying a guaranteed level of return. As time went on, however, the management became aware that many licensees overseas had developed extremely profitable business based on the licensed know-how, while the licensor's participation was limited to only a negligible royalty. The management belatedly realised that the direct investment route would have been much more suitable in entering and developing these growth markets. And the firm's position would have substantially improved, even under a licensing agreement, had it insisted on equity participation, rather than a straight royalty arrangement, in return for its technical know-how.

CASE 7.21

Van Heusen (VH), the Taunton-based shirt manufacturers, faced a market situation that practically excluded direct exporting techniques when trying to capture a sector of the lucrative Japanese market. In this case, the management (taking account, of course, of the local trading conditions in their sector of the industry) decided against setting up a wholly-owned subsidiary, and, after a lengthy period of screening and negotiating, opted instead for a licensing agreement with a Japanese company. The licensee appointed has proved active in utilising a large network of trade contacts and employs 60 representatives.

VH management recognised, through research and analysis of the market, that the company would make no headway in Japan without a licence agreement, because most retailers there, especially the large department stores, would not accept the product unless it was on a sale-or-return basis, and the company clearly could not cope with that condition on the basis of direct supply from Taunton. In fact, the licensee, Nissho-Iwai, produces about half a million shirts a year, and employs more marketing staff than the UK company. Yet it is this that now provides the back-up and market coverage essential in Japan.

■ Countertrading

■ Scope and applications

Countertrading is the term used in international trading to denote transactions by which goods and services are paid for by barter, or by other forms such as part-payment in kind and in cash. The various forms of countertrading, such as compensatory-trading, counterpurchasing-deals, switch-trading, parallel-deals, and buy-back arrangements, will be explained in this section. Countertrading has increased in recent years and it is more complex than is generally realised, even in the business community itself; it is becoming more widely used and is increasingly specified in many countries, and by many purchasing organisations, as a means of both bilateral and multilateral trade expansion.

There is ample evidence that countertrading is well-established in many markets, particularly in trade between OECD countries and other regions. Some companies in the countries in Eastern and Central Europe, for example, countertrade on most contracts; and China and many countries in the Third World recognise that establishing a market position in Western countries through countertrading deals is often as important as earning hard currency. Counterpurchase, for example, is used widely in these countries as a form of countertrade: in this kind of arrangement, the supplying company, say, in the European Union agrees to buy local products equivalent to a fixed percentage of its own deliveries. Sometimes the Western supplier is asked to take machinery in part payment for its goods and services; in these cases, other modes of counter-trading can be used by which the original supplier gets in touch with a third party which can sell the goods in the Third World, where technical sophistication is perhaps not as important as a low price. If the bought product from a country in Eastern Europe is one of the commodities, these are easier to offload in the West. The London Chamber of Commerce and Industry publishes lists of trading houses that will take such things as sugar, edible oils and metals; but the Western supplier still has to pay for the services of a trading house, and if such charges have not been included in the initial costings for the East European contract, it can result in the supplier incurring an overall loss.

CASE 7.22

Cadbury Schweppes has used its international group-purchasing resources as a means of entering and establishing a substantial market presence in East European countries. Its Swedish subsidiary manufactured tomato puree, and Schweppes in Britain accepted deliveries of Bulgarian tomatoes as part of a deal to sell its beverages into Bulgaria. And the company set up a HQ team, specialising in this sort of trading, which bought fruit pulp, juices, frozen fruit and aerosols from Bulgaria. These commodities were either used in Britain or sold to other members of the group in other countries. This approach has made it possible to open up a market far beyond anything that could have been achieved in Bulgaria on a direct export basis.

CASE 7.23

Hawker Siddeley (HS) successfully used countertrading to sell military aircraft to Finland. This country is not a centrally-planned economy and does not have exclusive strategic material with which to barter; but it used its defence purchasing as a lever, knowing that international competition in the sale of military aircraft is fierce. HS set up a Finnish Compensation Office, helping the Finns to use HS multinational group facilities to market a wide range of products in Britain and in third countries. Normally a foreign government would insist on a manufacturing involvement in such a deal – it is commonplace for aircraft components to be made locally, in order to reduce the hard currency cost of a defence contract and to enhance the buying country's maintenance and defence capability. However, in this case Finland had such small defence production facilities that the total value of the aircraft contract was set-off against a commitment by HS to arrange for pulp, paper, timber products, handing equipment and medical apparatus and other goods from Finland to be sold internationally.

While countertrading originated as straightforward barter trading (avoiding cash payment on the part of both partners), it has developed into a number of different modes, some of considerable complexity. It is important, therefore, to grasp that countertrading is no longer a *method of last resort* to encourage trade flows: some countertrade transactions can be used to generate new business in areas where cash payment is not easily effected. Indeed, barter trade (where there is only one contract between buyer and seller, and no third party is involved) was very much a feature of the immediate postwar period and is not at all common nowadays: this is mainly due to the increasing difficulty, in straight bartering, of matching the relative values of different commodities at times of widely-fluctuating inflation and currency exchange rates. And the inclusion of barter in an export deal can complicate financing and insurance arrangements: the Export Credits Guarantee Department (ECGD) can hardly cover the quality and resaleability of goods provided in full exchange for export products. Many firms in the UK have come to realise that there are market opportunities overseas which can be opened up by exploiting one or more modes of countertrading. Managers often find, on investigation, that their companies are buyers of materials or components from suppliers who are also potential customers for their products, and who could be influenced to enter bigger deals using the lever of their purchasing power.

The growing importance worldwide of countertrading has been highlighted in a US Government report (US Department of Commerce, 1985) which surveyed countertrading activities of more than 500 corporations; its major findings are as follows:

- The value of US corporations' countertrade with Europe has grown more than four-fold, and such obligations with Asia have more than tripled.
- Most of US countertrade, about 80 per cent, involves military components; however, non-military countertrade obligations have been rising steadily throughout the 1980s.
- Half of all UK imports resulting from non-military countertrade were shipped from Eastern Europe.
- The majority of US corporations surveyed claimed that they had derived benefits from countertrade, including larger and more efficient production runs, lower unit costs, increased capital formation and the development of new technology.
- Almost half of the goods and services imported under non-military countertrade were used internally by US companies that were party to the sales.
- Nevertheless, some businesses worried about the increasing competition emerging for technology transfer and local procurement conditions enhancing the strength of foreign suppliers.

■ Types of countertrading

It is now time to consider, in some detail, the various types of countertrading. Straightforward barter trading has already been described, and all the following modes really originated from it.

1. *Compensation deal.* This involves the exporter agreeing to receive full or partial payment (that is, compensation) in local goods produced in the importer's country. The countertrade ratio in this sort of deal really splits the transaction into a cash

portion (usually paid for immediately) and a barter portion (no money involved), and both these are fixed in one contract. Also, the exporter can, by means of a third-party clause, transfer his compensation commitment to a trading house or countertrade specialist.

2. *'Switch' trading.* This has developed out of type 1 but is more complicated, and can involve four or even five parties. It is still, basically, a means of offloading a commitment to take goods, instead of money, for part or whole payment of an export delivery. For example, an exporter may have agreed to accept £1 million of payment from Eastern Europe in the form of manufactured goods but can make use of only half of this amount within his own organisation. He sells his remaining credit to a switch dealer at a discount. The switch dealer finds someone who is in need of certain ranges of products that can be obtained from the Eastern European country, and the dealer offers the goods at a reduced price. The outcome is that the Eastern European country has obtained its imports in exchange for manufactures, the switch dealer has made a profit on the difference between the two rates of discount, and the buyer of the East European goods has bought them more cheaply than by going direct. The original exporter has completed his contract, but has had to finance the discount involved in doing so.

3. *Counterpurchase* or *parallel deal.* This is the most frequently used mode of countertrading today. The term indicates that two separate but related contracts are negotiated between two parties, each being a cash transaction. The first contract concerns the sale of Western products, for instance to the Middle Eastern importer (the export contract); in the second, parallel, contract the exporter commits himself to purchase countertrade (CT) goods,

   - amounting to a certain percentage of his export delivery (CT ratio), choosing products from within a certain range of CT goods;
   - over a given period.

   This latter part of the negotiations is termed *purchase-commitment* or *contract of obligation*; in case of non-performance of this part, the Western exporter has to pay a penalty to his Middle East partner. The attractions of this mode of countertrading are clear. The original export transaction is fulfilled by both parties to the contract, and the Western exporter receives full payment for the goods delivered. While his commitment to take goods in return may be stretched over a longer period, giving him more time to select and check quality, nevertheless, his purchase commitment results in a future payment to his Middle East partner, based on the separate (second) contract. And a known ability to buy goods from a foreign market can be a valuable lever in securing a big export contract. For example, a British firm with the intention of buying Czech machine tools might well approach a British exporter of cranes and suggest that the exporter includes machine tools in a counterpurchase deal. (The company in need of the tools can then specify in advance what it requires.)

4. *Buy-back contracts.* This mode of CT applies particularly in countries expanding their industrial infrastructure. It involves the seller of technology or equipment, or the supplier of a turnkey plant, agreeing to accept products manufactured in the

plant he has supplied as full or partial payment. For instance, a contractor selling chemical equipment is paid by the future output of the investment, that is chemicals. There is the commercial benefit to the buyer/owner of the plant in that he is enabled to pay the construction costs of the plant by using future cash flows earned by selling the resulting output. The supplier/seller of the plant, however, has to face waiting, sometimes for several years, between the erection of the plant and the beginning of cash inflows from product sales, which can be used to pay off construction costs. Also, there can be a difficulty in pricing future products when the market may have changed. A buy-back contract is illustrated in Case example 7.24.

■ Contributory factors and marketing implications

CASE 7.24

Japanese trading companies are able to handle a multifarious range of goods within the same organisation. C. Itoh of Japan gets the contract to set up a synthetic fibre plant in Poland and agrees to purchase back from Poland a proportion of the fibre that will eventually be produced. C. Itoh is, of course, one of the world's largest textile merchanting companies and can make such promises without too much difficulty. The attractiveness of such a deal to the buying country is obvious: it gets its new plant with the sure knowledge that it will increase its own exports and that the plant will earn hard currency to replace the cost of building it.

A UK government study (Department of Trade and Industry, 1985) has investigated the following factors accounting for countertrade (CT) expansion:

- Opportunities both to finance and to expand trade, which would otherwise not take place in the absence of sufficient commercial credit or convertible currency;
- The chance to exploit a buyer's-market position, which enables importers to obtain better terms of trade or similar benefits (assuming competitive bidding);
- The protection and/or stimulation of the output of domestic industries both to reduce manufactured imports and to earn hard currencies by overseas sales;
- An instrument for use in fulfilling political and economic policies by governments aiming at planning and balancing overseas trade;
- Maintenance of a country's own resources to protect its levels of domestic production and employment.

Furthermore, it is arguable that fluctuating exchange rates and unpredictable inflation and interest rates (together with hard currency shortages) have created the conditions that have forced government ministries and/or purchasing agencies

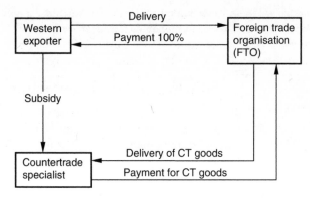

Figure 7.7 Counterpurchase/parallel deal

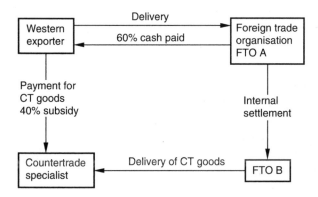

Figure 7.8 Compensation deal – quadrangular type

to stipulate some form of countertrading; the growing problem of international indebtedness has accentuated this trend. Iran and Iraq have policies of using their oil as a form of currency with which to purchase essential goods for industrialisation and health and welfare. Many such countries have realised, therefore, that the system whereby their purchases from abroad are restricted according to the hard currency they can earn from the West is highly unreliable, and that, to an increasing extent, CT can circumvent this problem.

As for the marketing implications of CT, it is clear from the evidence already cited that the exporter's willingness and ability to meet his customer's CT requirements is now, and probably more so in the future, a prior condition to the development of international markets. At the same time, another marketing aspect is in evidence: by means of one or more of CT modes, the initial exporter undertakes the marketing of CT goods, working as a kind of sales agent for

Table 7.7　Checklist of major points to take into account when deciding whether, and where, to invest in manufacturing abroad

Political

1. Political stability or uncertainty
2. Attitude of host government to private enterprise, and, in particular, to foreign private investment
3. Special inducements for foreign investors, such as tax holidays, grants, loans at favourable rates, tariff protection for newly-established industries
4. Membership of a free trade area, or trade agreements with other countries that might offer export opportunities

Legal

1. Legal discrimination against foreign companies or their expatriate employees
2. Percentage of company that may be foreign-owned
3. Patent protection laws and ease of enforcement
4. Trademark protection
5. Price-control legislation
6. Restrictive trade practice legislation

Cost

1. Cost increases resulting from a smaller scale of production, product modification to meet market needs, and so forth.
2. Wage costs – related to productivity
3. Additional labour costs (for example company share of social security payments)
4. Availability and costs of local raw materials and components
5. Availability and cost of transport services
6. Freight, packing and insurance savings (if product previously exported to the country)

Taxation

1. Existence of a double-taxation agreement between host country and parent-company country
2. Withholding of tax payable on remittances to parent company
3. Level of company taxation
4. Method of calculating depreciation allowances, stock valuation, and so forth

Exchange control

1. Restrictions on remittances to parent company (for example maximum percentage of foreign capital invested)
2. Restrictions on repatriation of capital
3. Convertibility of local currency

Finance

1. Local sources of capital (and interest rates payable)
2. Practicability of supplying capital from the UK
3. External sources of capital
4. Local accounting requirements and conventions
5. Rate of inflation

Table 7.7   Continued

Personnel

1. Availability of labour (skilled, unskilled or clerical)
2. Availability of local managerial talent
3. Percentage of employees that must be local nationals
4. Availability of work permits for expatriates
5. Living conditions for expatriates (housing, education, medical and so on)
6. Labour laws and regulations (especially regarding appointment and dismissal of staff)
7. Industrial relations, trade unions, worker participation in management. and so on
8. Existence of compulsory profit-sharing schemes for employees

---

his partner requiring the CT transaction. Indeed, there is a strong element of economic cooperation implicit in CT,

- in the field of international project financing, where CT commitments constitute essential parts of the different contractual relationships using primarily buy-back arrangements; and
- in joint-venture arrangements that involve close cooperation in a common business venture, where both parties participate in the risks and in the success (and profits) of the corresponding transactions.

In view of these complexities in CT, two types of transaction are illustrated in Figures 7.7 and 7.8. Finally, in Table 7.7, a checklist of factors to be taken into account in overseas manufacturing is given.

■ Conclusions

The changes occurring in the organisation of management have been explained: these are due to the changing nature of competition, and have given rise to the development of project managers, task forces and 'professionals' to cope with new systems and technologies. The quality of management is again the critical element in managing risk and crisis; the point is that management must take a proactive approach, learn by experience, and develop contingency planning; some Case examples have explained these points.

Organising for international operations is complex and companies must decide which forms of overseas representation and investment are most appropriate for their products and services in the light of market conditions and competition. These key factors have been explained in the context of managing subsidiaries, associates and agents, and in implementing and controlling licensing and contracting. There is clearly no one optimal mode: different approaches may be required to suit conditions in country markets. Finally, the significance of countertrading in expanding trade has been explained, again with Case examples.

QUESTIONS

1. Explain some of the organisational prerequisites for effective global control of subsidiary companies.

2. Discuss ways in which communications between headquarters and subsidiaries can be improved; what corporate benefits can be derived as a result?

3. Itemise some of the key aptitudes which you consider essential in an effective global manager, and say how these can be developed.

4. How far is it realistic to expect companies to manage crises which they cannot reasonably be expected to foresee?

5. Explain how the assessment of risks enables management to plan international operations and prioritise country markets.

6. Say what is meant by 'organic' growth in international companies; how should management ensure that this process remains sensitive to changing global conditions?

7. In what circumstances do companies which have traditionally used agents find that they need other forms of representation to develop markets further?

8. To what extent is a management contract a form of technology transfer? Discuss.

9. International subcontracting involves some loss of direct control of the manufacturing process; why then has it become more prevalent in global operation?

10. Give your views on the likely effects of the economic and political changes in Eastern and Central Europe on countertrading.

CHAPTER 8

Developing international marketing

INTRODUCTION

This chapter is concerned with the implementation of the global marketing programme: it follows logically from the research aspects discussed in Chapter 3, and the strategic planning aspects covered in Chapter 5. Indeed, throughout the text there is the continuing theme of marketing as the key discipline of the international firm. The matrix approach to both country markets and industry sectors is fully explained in the first section accompanied by numerous examples of companies which have implemented this approach, accompanied by a commentary on the benefits and drawbacks. Next the product portfolio is tackled, with the applications of the international product life-cycle; managing an international product portfolio is complex, and the sustaining of brand image across country markets is also addressed. The final section deals with the international communications mix, covering overseas representation, international sales, advertising and corporate promotion.

■ The matrix approach to products and markets

■ Applying the global approach

While there have been strong trends towards the globalisation of markets in recent years, it is not certain how far the concept will be universally adopted by companies operating across country markets. Here, the approach is explored on the basis of marketing strategy and, in particular, the management response of the matrix approach to products and markets in a global context. Indeed, the matrix approach is at least partly a response by companies concerned that operating and marketing globally, that is, minimising national market divisions, may not be the optimal corporate strategy in all situations. And the global approach does pose some problems of resourcing, control, cross-country brand promotion, communications and operations which may not sustain a competitive position on a geographical region-by-region basis. On the other hand, global marketing can yield benefits: standardising products can lower operating costs, and effective coordination can exploit a company's best product and marketing ideas.

Indeed there have been many references throughout this text on the importance of the marketing programme to the company's operations, and the contribution of marketing planning to achieving a high standard of customer service and satisfaction across countries. The marketing concept and the achievement of excellence are, therefore, the foundation and have been the subject of a recent and illuminating study by Hansen, Gronhaug and Warneryd (1990).

Global marketing should not be viewed simply as one end of a spectrum, with the other being complete localisation of marketing policy and control. A managerial approach to globalisation can fall anywhere along that spectrum, from full standardisation of brand promotion and advertising to a market-by-market programme of differentiated promotion and product adaptation. Understanding the globalisation is one thing: applying it flexibly in international operations is the basis of much of the matrix approach, where the industry's growth prospects and the company's competitive position can differ significantly from one country and one sector to another.

In applying the global approach and making it work, some adaptations to regional market conditions are essential. Managers need to tailor the approach they use to each part of the company's overall plan and marketing policy. For example, a manufacturer might market the same product under different brand names in different countries, or might market the same brands using different product formulas or advertising visuals. Also, the extent to which a decentralised multinational corporation will wish to pursue global marketing will often vary from country to country. Much will depend upon the company's competitive strengths and management organisation in markets of different sizes and types. Large markets with strong local managements are usually less willing to accept global programmes. It is arguable that, as these markets probably account for most of the company's investment, any completely standardised marketing programmes reflect the needs of large rather than small markets. Indeed, managements in the smaller markets depend more on their headquarter's assistance than those in large markets; and because any standardised marketing programme is superior in scope and quality to what the local executives, even with the benefit of local market knowledge, can develop themselves, they may welcome it, particularly if it requires resourcing beyond the means of the local organisation.

If global marketing is to be implemented effectively, it requires a planned appraisal of market priorities across the world in terms of industry attractiveness and competitive strengths; for the reality is that, whether or not some businesses decide to adopt a global strategy, many of their competitors will. This is because some companies view globalisation as not only a concept but also an opportunity: cultural and economic convergences have led to huge expanding markets for the same or similar products, to new opportunities for economies of scale and reductions in costs and prices, and for regional or standardised brand promotion and advertising programmes. Companies, therefore, that find themselves in the forefront of global competition are those that have products that are similar across borders, have low transportation costs, offer economies of scale in production and marketing, and have long lead-times and concentrated distribution.

Companies operating a global marketing policy are likely to have certain key characteristics, such as being technologically advanced, having significant economies of scale in manufacturing, having significant marketing skills, and producing at least one major worldwide selling brand backed by heavy, consistent investment. Furthermore, such a global marketing company is also likely to be capital-intensive and financially strong. (For example, the costs of designing a new aircraft exceed $1 billion; the introductory advertising budgets for Player's cigarettes and Diet Coke were over $30 million and $50 million, respectively.) Indeed, many companies selling on a region-by-region, or sector-by-sector, basis must increasingly compete with global marketing companies in order to survive in their domestic markets. Large imports of energy, advanced technology, products promoted globally to satisfy increasingly sophisticated consumer demand – all have to be met by successful operations on foreign markets. Economies of scale in production as well as in research and development in many industries require world markets for full exploitation, and world marketing requires skilful management. So a reduction in the obstacles to standardisation puts additional pressure on companies that do not participate in worldwide marketing programmes.

Furthermore, there are strong forces in the business environment today, driving more and more towards global marketing policies:

1. Demographic, cultural and economic convergence among consumer markets, and increasing homogeneity in the requirements of worldwide industrial customers (for example machine tools, plant construction);
2. The increasing investment in research needed to ensure long-term competitiveness, increasing lead-times involved to bring products to commercialisation, and the growing pay-back needed for this process;
3. Increasingly significant economies of scale on the supply side (purchasing, manufacturing and distribution and access to resources); also, the impact of technology on manufacturing;
4. Macroeconomic changes in regional economic cooperation, leading to freer movement of goods, labour services and capital (particularly for capital to invest in worldwide operations and market development); impact of technology on transportation and distribution;
5. The deregulation of national markets in airline transportation, banking and financial services, and the increasing signs of de-nationalisation of major industrial markets in the supply of telecommunications, power generation and transportation plant and equipment (especially in the USA and the EEC).

■ The matrix approach

In the light of these developments, the matrix approach to products and markets has become more significant in managing and developing international markets. The concept is not new, but it needs to be applied specifically and in a planned way if it is to prove of value operationally. Some examples of specific applications by companies will follow shortly, but in general terms, the matrix approach must be set up in two stages:

1. Global situation analysis;
2. Establishing the product/market matrix.

These are illustrated in Figures 8.1 and 8.2.

The advantages to management of adopting the matrix approach can be summed up as follows:

1. It provides a framework for prioritising key product sectors for development across global markets.
2. It permits the identification of major growth sectors where additional investment can substantially increase profits and market share.
3. It promotes better understanding and analysis of data needed for overall product/market planning.
4. It provokes greater sensitivity to the impact of external factors, particularly competition, on the success of marketing policies.
5. It permits the identification of products that are generating substantial cash in the short term, but are in long-term market decline, requiring 'harvest' or 'divestment' decisions by management.
6. It provides a framework for formulating both international policies and objectives by market sector/country.

In Figure 8.1 the matrix approach is developed in stages, beginning with an analysis of industry and market trends, and continuing with an evaluation of market attractiveness and competitive position. In Figure 8.2 these factors are ranked on a three-by-three matrix relating to growth, earnings and cash.

Understanding the matrix concept and the general benefits to be derived by management in using it is one thing; however, making it operational and specific in the context of a company's international marketing policies is another. And further reappraisal of the concept, as exemplified in the portfolio analysis of the Boston Consulting Group, has indicated that in international operations there are problems of definition and application. For example, a product globally evaluated as a 'dog' by the BCG may have a position as a star in a developing sector of the market; also products can be at different stages of the life-cycle internationally, and sector/market growth rates will also vary; so international applications will generally lead to considerations of multiple market entries/operations for a given product, and these are not readily accommodated in the

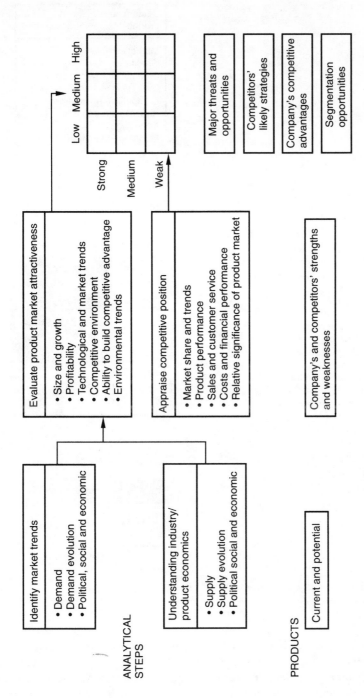

Figure 8.1 Global situation analysis

Source: International Trade Centre (1990) UNCTAD/GATT, Geneva.

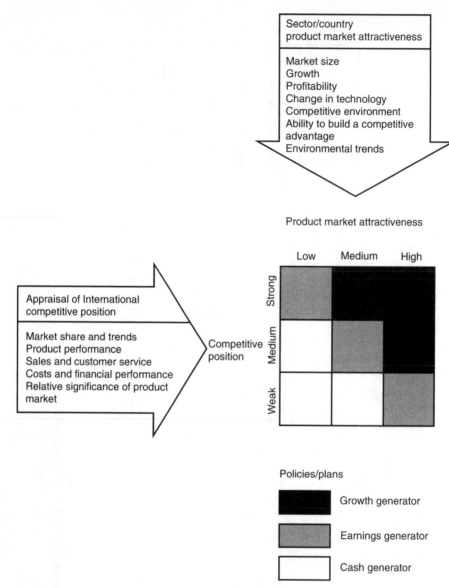

Figure 8.2   Establishing a product/market matrix

traditional BCG format. There are also difficulties of application brought about by differing levels of competitor strengths across global market sectors and some wide variations in cost structures of operating in different sectors, which may have similar market shapes and growth prospects, but where profit levels are significantly different.

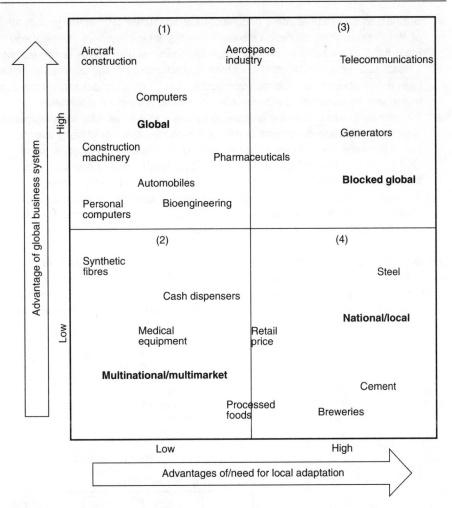

Figure 8.3   Matrix of trade-off – global versus national marketing policies by major industry sectors

Source: Henzler and Rall (1986).

The above analysis of global factors in managing multi-country markets demonstrates clearly how a matrix approach that breaks out of this stereotyped model can provide useful policy guidelines. In Figure 8.3 the matrix is designed to weigh the strength of globalising market factors and the advantages of globalisation against the advantages of local market adaptation. A four-cell matrix emerges, comprising the following cells:

1. Businesses where strong local adaptation is inappropriate and globalising forces can be exploited to great advantage. These are *global* marketing companies: computers and consumer electronics belong in this cell.

2. Businesses that require some degree of local adaptation and where globalisation of all functions offers no decisive competitive advantage, such as electrical equipment today. The world market for such *multinational* businesses is divided into several regions with different customer characteristics. Many of today's global businesses started with this polycentric structure – for example automobile and motorcycle manufacture, consumer electronics and production automation.

3. Businesses in which both the globalising factors and the need for local adaptation are strong. This group consists mainly of businesses that would be global from a purely economic point of view if they were not constrained by law or government purchasing policies to adapt their products. Regional telephone networks and sectors of the armaments industry are typical examples of such *blocked global* businesses.

4. Businesses such as food processing and basic chemicals, in which strong local adaptation is decisive for success and/or there are no major arguments in favour of globalisation. These are the true *local* businesses.

Further specific applications of the matrix approach have been developed by an increasing number of companies with global product/market businesses.

General Electric Company has developed a nine-cell *Business Screen* which is illustrated in Figure 8.4. Here the vertical axis is based upon a series of factors

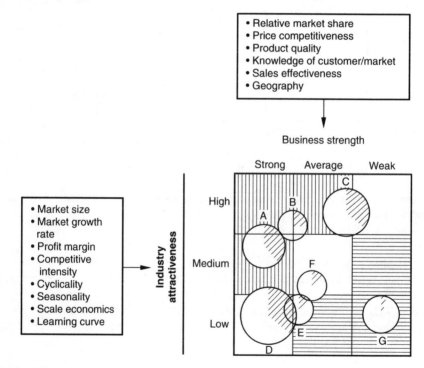

Figure 8.4   General Electric's nine-cell business screen

Source: Allio and Pennington (1979).

(each given a weighting) which represent the commercial attractiveness of each industry/market. The horizontal axis represents business strength or competitiveness. The area of the circles shows the size of the industry in which the business or product compete, with the shaded segments showing the company share. Both grids give additional and useful focus to management decisions on marketing objectives and policies.

Seagram Distillers Company, adapting the BCG concept, has developed a growth-share matrix applied to their portfolio of branded spirits. This is illustrated in Figure 8.5 and would seem to indicate that the brand portfolio is in

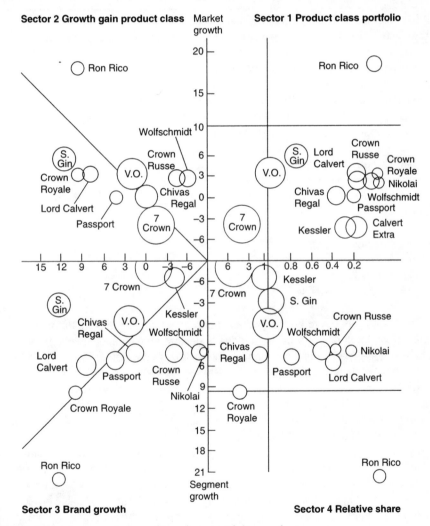

Figure 8.5   Seagram's brand/market portfolio analysis

Source: Allio and Pennington (1979).

need of upgrading. Since, on the matrix, the industry growth rate appears to be the same for all brands, the product class definition of the relevant market is used. Five Seagram brands are growing faster than their market segment, as in sector 3; moreover, using segment growth in place of product class, growth in the growth/share matrix (sector 4) reveals that six brands are leaders in their market segments (of these, five are cash-cows and one is a star).

CASE 8.1

Shell International Chemical Company has developed a portfolio analysis approach to help top management decide which product/market sectors they should be in and which ones ought to be phased out. Shell believes that the development of an optimum corporate strategy demands some structural and preferably quantifiable method of analysis. Its tool for achieving this is called the Directional Policy Matrix (DPM) and is shown in Figure 8.6.

In this figure, the horizontal axis shows the prospects for profitable operation within the particular sector under investigation, while the vertical axis measures the company's present competitive position against other companies. The matrix is then divided into a series of boxes and, depending on its position on each axis, each product is categorised.

In chemicals, Shell has decided that there are four main criteria which need to be used to place products on the horizontal axis:

1. market growth rate;
2. market quality;
3. feed stock;
4. environmental aspects.

DPM is considered to be more widely applicable than the Boston Matrix, since criteria can be chosen for different industry sectors and situations where market share is not of paramount importance. The technique developed by Shell for deciding how to place products within the DPM uses a system of stars and grading.

Under growth rate, a product will be accorded from one to five stars. Thus, if it is a product for which demand will grow only as fast as the chemical industry average, it will attract three stars, with more stars (up to a maximum of five) for a faster growth rate and less for a slower one.

Under market quality, the ability of new products to achieve a consistently higher or more stable level of profitability than in other sectors is assessed. For example, the analysis will cover whether margins can be maintained at a time of excess capacity, susceptibility to commodity price behaviour, availability of technology to competitors, the number of market suppliers, the power of customers and the risk of substitution by other products.

The availability of feed stock and the likelihood of environmental restrictions on the manufacture, transportation and marketing of a new product are also considered, and stars similarly awarded.

The stars are then converted into points and totalled so that the position of the new product along one arm of the axis can be determined.

In the analysis of the company's competitive position in a particular sector, three criteria are used:

1. market position;
2. production capability;
3. product research and development.

If a company is in a pre-eminent position in a particular market (likely to be followed by others in pricing) and with acknowledged technical leadership, it will probably award itself five stars. If, however, it is one of a number of major producers, it may mark itself down to four; if only a minor producer, it may mark itself two. In assessing production capability, factors such as whether the process used is modern, whether the plant is big enough for market share to be maintained, the degree of security from breakdowns or industrial action, and logistics to principal markets are considered. The research and development assessment will take into account product range and quality, technical service and applicational development.

When the points under each heading (on a 0–4 scale to correspond with the 1–5 stars) have been added together, the position on the other axis become clear, and by cross-reference to the horizontal axis the position of the product on the matrix can be obtained.

Within the matrix, the boxes have been given labels to indicate the significance of the position in which products find themselves. If a product is in the *leader* box, it will have scored five points on each axis, and the implication is that the company should give priority to its development, devoting all the necessary resources. The *try harder* label is meant to suggest that with the right allocation of resources the company could build on a number-2 position in which the product finds itself. The *double-or-quit* zone is seen as the area from which products that are destined to become future bright prospects should be selected. Elsewhere in the matrix, the *custodial* position – the zone where most of any company's products are likely to fall at any one time – suggests a strategy of maximising cash-generation without further major commitment of resources. Where products are in the *growth* position, the indicated strategy is to allocate resources sufficient to enable the product (which will probably be generating the funds itself) to grow with the market.

The products in the left-hand column will be those with poor prospects, where perhaps a new product is taking over. It remains possible, however, for companies with a strong position in this sector to earn satisfactory profits which can be used to finance faster growing areas. In the *disinvest* sector, products will probably already be losing money and the correct strategy is probably to dispose of the assets as quickly as possible.

There are now examples of the DPM being applied to companies such as Rolls-Royce, the National Freight Corporation and Arthur Guinness & Co. It has been found that the concepts of market growth, quality and supply are generally applicable, although certain specific criteria have to be changed for particular businesses. The competitive concepts of market share, supply and support which underlie the Boston Matrix raise problems, particularly that of market share. The criteria chosen for the competitive axis do become more widely applicable if the concept of 'market leadership' is used, and this includes viable and minor producers, as well as leaders and majors.

Some analysts see great value in the use of DPM as a behavioural technique in that it encourages analysis, helping managers to think as a group about their international markets, the competition and the relative strategic value of particular portfolios to the company as a whole. Finally, it provides a useful way of communicating strategic guidelines to different business units.

In the objective appraisal of alternative markets and products, management should assure itself not only that there is some synergy of marketing, production, technological or other expertise which can be utilised for successful entry, but also that it has the general creative capability and capacity to manage the new business, particularly if unforeseen problems occur at a time when there is pressure on the existing enterprise. The greatest shortage will commonly be in competent management.

CASE 8.2

Using such a matrix approach, a company in the security industry defined its desired profile thus: 'to become a major, technologically advanced, competent and responsible supplier of fire, property and personal protection'. The management then specified what each of the words meant, for example 'major' meant the segment of the top three suppliers in each selected market segment holding a minimum of 25 per cent share. Such a strategy could therefore be used as a basis for more specific target setting, not only in terms of sales and share, but also to set communications goals for promotional activity.

Furthermore, using the variables in Figure 8.7, and given some scheme for weighting them, the company's country markets can be classified into one of the nine cells in the 3×3 matrix depicting market investment opportunities or other strategies indicated as described in the cells.

For management, therefore, portfolio analysis of markets provides a global view of international competitive structure; competitive positions which are thought to be dominant and secure when the analysis is limited to a single country market (or a restricted group of countries) may in fact be threatened in the long term when considering the growth and structure of other international markets.

Business sector prospects

	Unattractive	Average	Attractive
Weak	Disinvest	Phased withdrawal	Double or quit
Average	Phased withdrawal	Custodial	Try harder (Avis)
		Growth	
Strong	Cash generation	Growth	Leader
		Leader	

Company's competitive capabilities

Figure 8.6   Directional policy matrix

Source: Shell International Chemical Company, London.

It provides a guide for the formulation of an international strategy; by considering country markets on the basis of investment units, generators or users of cash, this approach places the emphasis on the strategic issue of allocating scarce resources between countries to attain a stable long-term growth in sales and profits. It provides a framework for analysing long-term market opportunities, competitive threats and the flow of resources needed in the formulation of global marketing strategy. It also provides an opportunity to build an analysis of other aspects such as regionalisation of world markets.

It serves as a guide for the formulation of marketing objectives for specific international markets. For example in some fast growing markets management may limit expansion because of limited cash resources or in order to show profits which are more in line with company norms; in other countries the high level of cash generated by a mature product may be spent on extensive promotional or product differentiation policies to try to generate some growth.

And it helps to determine the primary role of each specific country in the

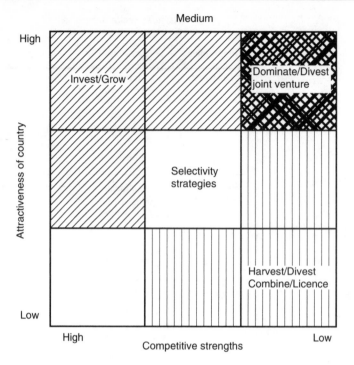

Figure 8.7 Market portfolio analysis: a country attractiveness/competitive
■■■■ strength matrix

Source: Harell and Keifer (1981), pp. 5–15.

international context; this role may for instance be to generate cash, to provide
growth, to contribute to production volume or to block the expansion of competition. Once this role has been defined, objectives can be determined for each
country to ensure that country strategies are coherent with global marketing
strategies. Whatever the strategies or combinations of strategies selected,
management should carefully review them to check if they are implemented
successfully.

1. They must satisfy the needs of the various precise target groups at which they are
   aimed – consumers, distributors, customers and so forth.
2. They must achieve the corporate marketing, financial and growth objectives.
3. They must give direction to the various elements of the marketing activity –
   products, prices, distribution and promotion.
4. They must be congruent with each other, and the fulfilment of one strategy must
   not adversely affect the achievement of others.
5. They must capitalise on the corporate strengths and minimise the effect of any
   weaknesses.
6. They must give a competitive advantage which is difficult to match or surpass.

7.   They must be within the competence and resources of the company.

The matrix approach to products and markets reflects management's need to respond to increasingly complex and competitive international markets. And in assessing the resources required for existing product/market policies, as against resources needed to originate and develop products, a matrix approach more complex than BCG is increasingly required. Priorities must be determined, for example, for investment in resources that ensure intermediate and long-term growth, market penetration and technical development, so that product/market prospects can be exploited to maximise price–earnings ratios of the business. Hence the importance of prioritising market prospects and product development by sectors, and for this the matrix approach is proving to be a powerful planning and control mechanism.

■ The product portfolio

■ Key issues

The process of developing and managing a product portfolio for international markets is increasingly complex. The strategic question to be resolved is, how far should a standard product portfolio be marketed worldwide, and how far should different portfolios be adopted for trading regions at different stages of market development? There are tactical decisions to be made: targeting product lines in countries where the product life-cycle is operating at different stages, and developing brands and brand images to exploit short-term market opportunities, while at the same time investing in longer-term brand development across national frontiers. Then there are substantial economies of scale to be derived from volume sales of world brands. But how are such volumes to be sustained by Western manufacturers in a world where low-cost volume manufacturing is increasingly moving eastward to the Pacific-Rim countries of South-east Asia; and is the pursuit of niche product marketing on a worldwide basis likely to provide a viable alternative strategy? These and other important aspects of managing the product portfolio will be addressed in this section.

■ International product life-cycle

By far the most significant factor for management to consider at the outset is the product life-cycle. While the concept is not, of course, new, it has special applications in international product management. In the first place, there is a link between the life-cycle and international trade: management needs insights into the overseas sales potential of its products as well as predictors of which products are most likely to be threatened by import competition. Nevertheless, macroeconomic theories abound. The theory of *comparative advantage* states that, ideally, every country will market those products that use the country's most abundant production factors. As such theories have been found to have only limited use at the micro level, increasingly, research has concentrated on managerial applications of the trade cycle, and its relationship to the product life-cycle. According to one early study of US industry, the trade-cycle concept means that many products typically follow a pattern that can be divided into four stages:

1. Export strength is based on heavy investment in manufacturing and a large body of high-income consumers.
2. Foreign production starts as demand builds up overseas and volume sales bring down manufacturing costs in countries formerly importing.
3. Foreign production becomes competitive in overseas markets as unit labour costs undercut those of original manufacturers.
4. Import competition begins as foreign manufacturers optimise mass production based on home and overseas markets, further lower their unit costs, and capitalise on newer plant.

These stages at the macro-level correspond to the four stages of the product life (the micro-level), which, of course, are: introduction, growth, maturity/saturation, and decline. So this trade cycle infers that many products, too, go through a cycle during which high-income, mass-consumption countries are initially exporters, then lose their export markets, and finally become importers of the product; other industrialising countries also make corresponding changes from importing to exporting, and this pattern is followed in the final stage by the developing countries.

In principle, therefore, management must ensure that its product portfolio is soundly-based for international markets; that it is developed at stages of the life-cycle to exploit the macro-market factors already referred to. Indeed, at different phases in the trade cycle there must be variations in the makeup of the product portfolio. Apart from the implications of profit planning through the building-up of the portfolio (referred to later), life-cycle analysis can also identify the critical stages through which a product is passing, thereby indicating some appropriate options for strategy.

Early research (Mickwitz, 1959) has also indicated some hypotheses about the elasticity of several marketing variables at each major stage of the life-cycle, as shown in Figure 8.8. While there is little doubt that, in different marketing environments worldwide, different elasticities will apply, the analysis highlighted in this research is of importance in setting up marketing strategy. It is interesting to observe here how the elasticity of product quality (q) has the major impact on sales in the introductory stages of the life-cycle, where the X-axis represents sales responsiveness and the Y-axis increasing marketing costs. In the stages representing growth and maturity, the sales curve become much steeper, with sales growth slowing in stages 4 and 5.

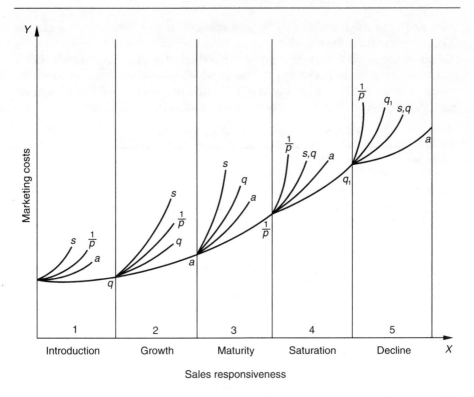

a — advertising; q — quality; q_1 — quasi-quality; s — service; $\frac{1}{p}$ — price inverted

Figure 8.8   Elasticity of marketing variables at each stage of the product life-cycle

Source: Mickwitz (1959).

Referring again to Figure 8.8 it is clear that, in developing and managing a portfolio of products, sales become more volume-sensitive, in that increasing inelasticity means that proportionately higher sales costs are incurred to bring in incremental sales revenue. The precise levels of elasticity will, of course, vary at each stage of the life-cycle in different national markets. This highlights the need for management to assess the positions of products within its portfolio in different markets, and to compare the costs of maintaining sales by marketing expenditures: this will reveal in which markets the portfolio can be maintained at its most profitable position.

The development and extension of the portfolio in terms of profit enhancement is also important. It is sufficient to note, at this stage, that the relationship between total sales volume and net profits varies among different markets in the course of the life-cycle. The peak of net profits is usually reached much earlier than the peak of total sales volume; this is because, from a certain point onwards, additional sales can be realised only through a reduction in the selling price and/or through additional, but less cost-effective, expenditures on marketing, as is clear from Figure 8.8.

And by the saturation stage there emerges the factor that this research cites as *quasi-quality* (such as packaging changes), which has some effect, but much less than the original force of quality, and the responsiveness of sales to all marketing variables becomes consistently more inelastic as the cycle progresses.

Table 8.1   Product portfolio through the life-cycle

Characteristics	Introduction	Growth	Maturity/saturation
Technology	Rapidly changing and adapting to consumer preferences	Few product variations of importance with various degrees of refinement: process innovations critical	Both product and process stable; no major design innovations of importance
	Closely held by innovating firm; no licensing or sale	Patent variations decrease monopoly of technology; some diffusion and licensing	Readily available and transferable
Production	Product-centred	Shifting to process	Process-centred
	Short runs; prototype manufacturing	Larger runs; mass production introduced although techniques may differ	Long runs; stable processes
Capital	Low use of capital; multi-purpose equipment	Increased utilisation	High investment in specialised equipment
Industry structure	Innovating firm leads, with others entering field to capitalize on success	Large number of firms; many casualties and mergers; growing integration	Number of firms declining with lower margins
	Know-how principal barrier to entry	Financial and production management necessary to reduce costs	Unskilled and semi-skilled labour; marketing
Marketing and demand structure	Sellers' market	Balanced market	Buyers' market
	High introductory marketing effort in communication and awareness	Beginning product differentiation; distribution critical	High brand and product differentiation may appear through various means
	High monopoly prices	Increased competition reducing prices	Lower prices and margins

Source: de la Torre (1975).

These applications of demand elasticities to the stages of the life-cycle clearly have important implications for international markets. Because of differences in the levels and quality of consumer spending, and in the stages of industrialisation and urbanisation, similar products, worldwide, are likely to be at very different stages of the life-cycle. These considerations apply more, today, to industrial and technical goods than to consumer goods: the latter are increasingly subject to worldwide branding, and will be discussed later. Clearly, although there are many industrialising and developing countries where relatively low unit labour costs and proximity to supply sources combine to keep low unit medium-technology products in the maturity and saturation stages, in the most advanced industrial countries these products have long since gone into the decline stage, to be replaced by high-technology products in the growth stage.

Further research has also been undertaken on the analysis of the life-cycle as an indicator of specific global marketing policies, taking into account some of the basic assets of the business (capital, people and so on) and adapting these to changes in demand and market structure at each stage of the cycle. The results of this research for the first three phases are summarised in Table 8.1.

■ **Product policy**

What is defined as a company's optimal international product portfolio is very much determined by the company's basic objectives.

1. If the basic objective is profit maximisation, then the optimal product portfolio has been achieved when no addition, deletion or changes will lead to increased total profits.
2. If the basic objective is worldwide sales growth, the product portfolio is optimal whenever any change will lead to a lower rate of growth of total sales.
3. If the basic objective is stability and security for the company, then the optimal portfolio guarantees stable sales volume, cost-levels, profits and cash flow.

In practice, it is more useful and realistic to seek situations and conditions in world markets that indicate that the product portfolio is less than optimal, rather than to seek standards/criteria for the ideal situation, which will be difficult to achieve. Typical indications that the product portfolio is not optimal include the following:

1. There are wide variations in utilisation of manufacturing capacity supplying important overseas markets over a set period.
2. A small proportion of the portfolio has a very high share of the company's worldwide sales and/or profits.
3. The company's overseas marketing and sales organisations are not fully occupied with the existing portfolio.

4. The markets services by the company are expanding into product types not currently marketed but for which production capacity could be adapted.
5. Sales volumes and profits relating to a significant part of the portfolio are steadily declining.

In international operations, most companies now recognise that their survival and financial security depend on growth; it is only through growth that sales volume and profits will increase steadily. The development and extension of the product portfolio is essential to growth in this highly competitive international environment. Case example 8.3 illustrates this aspect.

CASE 8.3

Back in 1975, Dunhill Co. had annual sales with a retail value of about £35 million, of which three-quarters was cigarette lighters (most of these being sold in Japan). Today, Dunhill sells a portfolio of branded luxury products, from pipes and pipe tobacco to watches, pens, menswear and women's wear, with a retail sales value in 1985 of £450 million (with profits rising from £5.9 million in 1983 to £15 million in 1985). Dunhill's management has shown how to drive up corporate profits by exploiting a portfolio of products under a luxury brand name. While other companies have done it with individual brands (for example Cartier and Gucci), only Dunhill has assembled a portfolio of products in a holding-company structure. This has been done on the basis of exploiting the Dunhill name with a wider portfolio, and using the company's cash balances to fund expansion; at the same time, some other companies have been bought-out to round-out the portfolio with the addition of new brand names: Lane (US pipe tobacco), Montblanc (German quality pens) and Chloe (French luxury women's wear and perfumeries). Then, the Varsity clothing range has been promoted. All this portfolio development has also been combined with rationalisation in pipe manufacturing, thus also sharply improving return on capital employed.

Clearly, a product portfolio must be developed to produce a specified rate of return while at the same time minimising risks in worldwide operations.

■ Portfolio analysis

The computation of rate of return and risk is complex because of the difficulties in estimating the expected rate of return for each product. So portfolio analysis is concerned with the relationship between risk and return, and the products in a company's portfolio will therefore have varying degrees of risk and return associated with them. Four possible combinations are attainable, and these are depicted in Figure 8.9.

	Return	
	High	Low
Risk — High	1	2
Risk — Low	3	4

1: High risk, high return
2: High risk, low return
3: Low risk, high return
4: Low risk, low return

Figure 8.9   Product portfolio analysis

It should be possible to represent a product mix on such a matrix (using the four coordinates against risk and return), thus ensuring that the performance of the product portfolio is continually monitored.

Indeed, product portfolio analysis can also be used to develop profiles of different products in terms of their suitability for global marketing, which is to be discussed shortly. For the assumptions underlying all global product marketing are that the investment costs in promotion and education worldwide, and in manufacturing worldwide, are all justified by researched evidence of demand/ sales potential. In this analysis, the competitive position and strength overseas of the product portfolio, and the extent and strength of significant market differences (economic, social, cultural and so forth), are two significant factors to be taken into account. Much will depend on the nature of the product: some consumer products are heavily branded worldwide to the same specifications, and appeal to an international taste (for example, the global campaign for Camel cigarettes); but specialised industrial products are by definition severely limited in their scope for global marketing, since they are designed to meet specific technical requirements in different markets.

One interesting and topical analysis (Gur-Arie and Taylor, 1982) of the spectrum of opportunities and risks shows how different product portfolios can be assessed by management. This analysis goes on to explain some significant differences:

A major difference between companies in quadrants 1 and 2 is that those in 1 typically have a competitive attractiveness that is based on both product and marketing communications superiority, whereas those in quadrant 2 might rely more on marketing communications superiority only. Companies in quadrant 3 sell, for example, standardized products in the maturity phase. From a marketing point of view these products are difficult in all markets ... Companies in quadrant 4 expose themselves to large risks; they do not have any real competitive advantage and they are perceived to be different from what the market is used to ... these are innovative companies ... and companies which have made unrealistic evaluations of resources needed, competitive pressure, and consumers' willingness to adopt differences in foreign markets.

(Gur-Arie and Taylor, 1982)

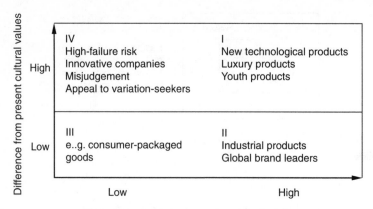

Figure 8.10   Matrix of product opportunities and risks in foreign markets

Source: Martenson (1986).

Figure 8.10 also illustrates some other approaches to the analysis of the product portfolio in terms of competitiveness, risk, return and adaptability to global marketing conditions. Management must ensure that this sort of analytical approach is used, particularly in evaluating global aspects of product development and branding.

■ **The development of global brands**

While the concept of global branding of products has been recently widely documented, in practice it is not in all cases an appropriate marketing strategy; indeed, it should be seen as only one of a number of options, among which is the development of regional or national brands as distinct from global brands. In evaluating these options a useful classification for management has been proposed by Pitcher (1985) and is shown in Table 8.2. This classification leads further to an assessment of characteristics to identify global brands, and this assessment is quoted in full from the study cited:

1.   How widely available is the product under consideration?

   ●   Are distribution channels common around the world?
   ●   Are the pricing structure and the margins similar?
   ●   Are there differing legal constraints on the product – ingredients, attributes, etc.?

2.   What is the competitive climate, country by country?

   ●   How many brands compete?
   ●   What is their ranking?

Table 8.2   A classification of international branding options

	Product	Current positioning (point A)	Desired positioning (point B)	Strategy	Execution
Global product	Must be same	Not applicable	Not applicable	Not applicable	Not applicable
World brand	Must be same	Optimally same	Must be same	Optimally same	Optimally same, including name and packaging
Regional brand	Same or different by region	Reflects existing consumer perceptions	Different by country	Usually different	Usually different
National brand	Same or different by country	Reflects existing consumer perceptions	Different by country	Usually different	Usually different

Source: Pitcher (1985).

- Are there strong local entries?
- Is the brand in the same product life-cycle stage around the world?

3. What consumer usage segments support the brand?

- For what reasons?
- What are their attitudes towards the category? the brand?
- How is the brand used by consumers?
- Are consumer segments consistent on life-styles and values across borders?

4. What is the brand/s advertising history around the world?

- Are there any commonalities of strategy, execution, etc.?
- What has been the role of advertising in promoting the brand?
- What media are used?
- What is the competitive advertising activity?

5. What is the advertisers' organisational structure, and can it 'support' world brand orchestration?

- Centralised v. decentralised?
- Recent history of (worldwide) growth?
- Sophistication of temperament to deal with the exigencies of international marketing?

■ Brand values

While this assessment is clearly of value to management at the micro-level, there are other macro-aspects of global branding which must form part of the overall analysis of options. These macro-aspects essentially concern long-term market trends worldwide, rather than short-term market prospects; so they are on the one hand negative, and on the other, positive. Negative factors can be overcome by manufacturers seeking to market global brands, but they require increasingly heavy investment in new manufacturing technology, distribution and brand promotion; they include:

1. the growing influence of the retailer in many parts of the world, bringing a diversion of marketing funds to the retailer and away from the consumer;
2. depressed or static economies, creating increased competition for market share;
3. continuing pressure from low-price or generic brands in many basic packaged goods categories;
4. product quality converging with increasing technological parity among major marketing companies;
5. continuing government restrictions on brand marketing, including regulation of advertising copy and media;
6. growing marketing expenses as manufacturers respond to the even higher costs of reaching the consumer.

Against these, of course, must be set some significant and positive factors which favour the development of global brands. Foremost among these is the value of a brand franchise. Recent research has shown that leading global brands, backed by consistent investment in promotion, advertising and any other form of image-strengthening, not only hold their own, but actually benefit from the weakening position of the lesser brands. This is especially noteworthy in view of the growth internationally of retailer brands (see Table 8.3).

Certainly another significant point is that consumer convergence in demography, habits and culture is increasingly leading manufacturers to a consumer-driven rather than a geography-driven view of global markets for products. Demographic convergence is the single most important factor in brand development in industrialised markets: it derives from such factors as ageing populations, falling birth rates and increased female employment. On the economic front, too, many of the negative factors already referred to have actually underlined the economic logic of world brands; continuing cost-inflation, and the competitive intensity of maturing packaged-goods markets have reinforced management's opportunities for international economies of scale as the basis of long-term strategic market development and security; indeed, the continuing competitiveness of a global brand depends critically on skilful management of these economic aspects.

The final component that management has to consider, therefore, in developing brands as part of a worldwide product portfolio is the measurement and

Table 8.3   The value of international brand franchises

| | Market share (%) | | | |
| | UK | | USA | |
	1985	1990	1985	1990
No. 1 brand	32.6	30.9	31.4	31.9
Other manufacturers' brands	46.7	44.2	44.8	42.7
Retailer brands	22.1	20.7	25.2	23.8

Source: International Advertising Association 1995.

enhancement of *brand character*. (Brand-image and brand-personality are other widely used terms to denote this concept.) Measuring brand character world-wide can be hazardous, owing to differences of local customs, language, media availability and so on; nevertheless, four basic components of brand character can be identified:

1. Functional attributes (such as cleaning and decay-prevention for dentifrices);
2. Emotional attributes (such as 'confidence-inspiring', 'old-fashioned and reliable', 'modern', 'cheerful', and so forth);
3. Market status (is the brand perceived as the outstanding leader in its field, one of the number of acceptable choices, or out-of-the-running?);
4. Badge-status (what kind of people use the brand, and what does it say about them?).

Some assessment of these factors is essential for the management of global brands.

Saatchi & Saatchi developed the Brand Character Index (BCI) on the basis of research initiated in their New York agency. BCI provides a structure that allows management to assess decisively the extent to which any particular brand lives up to the company's chosen central positioning strategy for that brand; this research means that the apparently ephemeral subject of brand character can be managed by objectives in the same way as most other aspects of an efficient company's business. So BCI would enable a multinational company to measure the extent to which a brand's character differs across national boundaries: the key point of reference in the development of an international measure of brand-character is the clear definition of the desired character for the brand. So there is a two-way interaction, between the actual position of the brand's character as revealed by market research, and management's perception of where the brand's character should be, even if the product is not quite perceived in those terms by the consumer. So BCI measures the gap between actual and optimum brand character.

Case examples 8.4 and 8.5 illustrate the potential, in penetration and power, of developing clear and consistent brand personalities.

CASE 8.4

One of the leading European manufacturers of electrical domestic appliances is the Italian company Zanussi, which as IAZ International has been trading in the UK for many years. A few years ago, this company was among the first successfully to develop a new clear brand personality encompassing its complete range of appliances. Two points are noteworthy: first, the brand personality comprised the concept of 'modern scientific man' utilising the very latest technology, made available (of course) by the Zanussi company; this was a radical departure from the mundane kitchen-centred brand advertising being adopted by its competitors. Second, this personality was consistently and clearly projected in the company's TV advertising by skilful use of impact camera work showing the sudden appearance of the newest machine in the range, with the smart slogan reinforcing the concept: 'Zanussi – the appliance of science'. Research in the UK has shown that this strong 'scientific' personality has made a longer-lasting impact on European consumers than the more pedestrian images of Zanussi's competitors.

CASE 8.5

Suntory Co. is Japan's leading distiller, but it is a relative newcomer in the Japanese beer market; its market share remained at about 6 per cent, and the company had difficulty in achieving distribution in the face of competition by the established market leader, Kirin, which had 70 per cent market share. Suntory initially focused on improving the formulation of its product by concentrating on canned beer for home consumption, and on 'authenticity/purity' in non-pasteurised or draught beer, both aimed at young drinkers. Management's next step was to devise a character-based campaign to attract older drinkers and their families. Utilising the initial appeal of an existing commercial with dancing penguins, the company made three animated penguin commercials based on well-known movies: *Casablanca*, *Rocky*, and *Brief Encounter*, all with a romantic and sentimental theme. Not only did Suntory beer sales move ahead in the low autumn season, but penguin-cans became an integral part of brand marketing, with the symbol appearing on cans, and a hit song and an animated film reinforcing the penguin character. Suntory's market share has already doubled. Moreover, research has shown that 90 per cent of all sectors of the population, irrespective of age and sex, are enthusiastic about penguins, and therefore that this characterisation has achieved remarkable 'across-the-board' appeal.

■ The communications mix

■ Communications with key constituencies

The management of an international company has special responsibilities for developing effective communications with important sectors of each country in which the company has business interests. Foremost among such sectors are consumers/customers (depending on the nature of the product or service). Much of the communications mix directed at these will be media advertising and other forms of promotion (these aspects will be discussed later, and in particular the impact of new technology); personal influence is also an important factor. But the first step for management, before any detailed planning of media advertising is done, is to determine the direction and development of the communications mix, in its totality, in regions of operation.

Different forms of communication must be used to develop relationships with the major 'publics' involved with the company's operations. These sectors, with some of the appropriate communications methods, can be summarised as follows, together with expectations/requirements as perceived by both company and stakeholder:

1. *Customers* (consumers and/or industrial) – expect quality, value, service, satisfaction, reassurance and reliability; in return, the company expects goodwill, loyalty, satisfaction and favour. Communications modes: advertising, sales promotion, personal selling, trade fairs and missions.
2. *Suppliers* – expect reliability and efficiency, fair credit treatment, financial dependability; in return, the company expects service, value, reliability and loyalty. Communications modes are via personal communications and some promotion/public relations.
3. *Government* – expects the fostering of job provision, legal operations, productivity and public-spiritedness; in return, the company expects understanding of business needs, a favourable business climate and infrastructure. Communications modes are through personal communications, public relations, public-opinion forming, political lobbying, corporate advertising and trade missions.
4. *Employees* – expect fairness, rewards, job satisfaction/security and being kept informed; in return, the company expects loyalty, honesty and effort. Communications modes are through internal promotion, personal relationships and training programmes.
5. *Trade/distributors* – expect product quality, service, profits, value and marketing skills; in return, the company expects trade support, goodwill, loyalty stockholding, customer access. Communications modes are via trade promotion, personal contacts, selling, trade symposia and fairs.
6. *Local community* – expects employment, clean environment, social activities and trading prosperity; in return, the company expects local infrastructure, labour provision and social support. Communications modes are through personal contacts, public relations, open days, sponsorships and training.

7. *Bankers and creditors* – expect sound management of markets and assets, credit-worthiness and realism in risk analysis; in return, the company expects financial support and expertise, understanding of the company's business and trust. Communications modes are through regular personal contacts and corporate advertising.
8. *Media organisations* – expect openness, professional briefing and de-briefing, information and planning on marketing policies; in return, the company expects integrity, expertise, reliability, favourable coverage/comment and effective control. Communications modes are through briefings, presentations prior to and during media campaigns to selected markets.
9. *Shareholders* – expect sound financial management, integrity, profits and corpo-rate growth; in return, the company expects support, trust, satisfaction, increasing investment and recommendation. Communications modes are through direct mail, presentations, personal contacts, public relations (particularly regarding institu-tional shareholders), and corporate advertising.

■ Communications planning

The management of the total communications mix entails a continuous and complex set of tasks leading to the establishment of an overall communications strategy, so that the component parts of the mix can be both integrated to serve that strategy, and targeted to meet specific objectives for each of these major market sectors. Clearly, certain parts of the mix are directly concerned with the marketing of goods and services to customers in different national markets, particularly sales and sales management and media advertising. These two aspects of the mix will be discussed specifically later in this chapter; at this stage, two significant points must be noted by management:

1. There is a close link in both concept and implementation between the total com-munications mix and environment-management; that is, the role of management in using specific parts of the mix (for example political pressure or public-opinion forming) to manage or at least influence the company's trading environment.
2. The planning and implementing of those parts of the mix that are the responsibil-ity of marketing management, particularly selling and media advertising, must be done in the context of an agreed strategy for the company's total communications mix, as outlined above. This approach is essential to ensure consistency and quality in all communications with these major sectors. Public relations, public-opinion forming and corporate image building, for example, should all be directed to maintaining favourable attitudes to the company and a favourable business climate in which selling and advertising themselves can work most pro-ductively.

Both of these aspects are touched on in Case example 8.6.

CASE 8.6

The Esso Petroleum Co. in South America (which became Exxon in North America) was faced with a difficult situation. The assets of the company had been expropriated in Peru, and management had to decide what stance the company should adopt in other South American countries. Rather than embark on divestment and damage-limitation, the company adopted a strong, positive profile. In particular, it contrived to project a better image in Columbia by organising a comprehensive collection of Colombian art and sponsoring its presentation in the USA. The acclaim this received created a better understanding of South American culture, and led to the company being awarded the Colombian government's highest decoration. This initiative helped the company to secure its market position as well as creating a favourable public image throughout South America.

■ Overseas representation

The management of the communications mix is closely bound up with the quality and consistency of the company's overseas representation. How effectively a company operates overseas clearly depends heavily on planning and on the quality of the company's communications. Sales and sales management, for example, are the operational means by which products find customers, and so a large part of the communications process is to create and sustain demand. And, indeed, the various methods of ensuring effective representation overseas are by no means mutually exclusive. Many companies find, for example, that the overseas agent can be made more effective in sales coverage and promotional impact if supported by some form of direct sales organisation. As mentioned earlier, many firms conclude that, as sales develop, it is time to establish their own sales office in the market; there are two main reasons for this:

1. Companies relying heavily on agents risk losing control of the selling process; agents often prove less flexible than direct sales staff in coping with competition and are relatively expensive in areas where sales volume is high.
2. Productivity and performance of agent's staff are generally lower than a company's own staff in terms of obtaining orders, handling customer problems/complaints, product knowledge and technical support and demonstrations.

So on-the-spot sales representation can make the agency system work more effectively for the manufacturer selling overseas: the agent ensures specific expertise in knowledge of the language, local competitors, trade regulations and contracts in the localities, while the company representative promotes the firm's sole interests, ensures that the agent is giving priority to its products, and provides local agency training.

CASE 8.7

An Italian paint manufacturer with worldwide sales treats its agents as an extension of its own sales force. Sales offices abroad and agents alike are expected to submit monthly progress reports, which are put into a computer for analysis, and a video display system enables the company's management to check what stocks key customers have bought and the price paid: if an agent's sales fall off, management can quickly identify the problem area and send one of its senior staff to investigate, and support the local agent.

■ International sales

Companies in industrial sectors particularly favour direct selling internationally, especially where market growth is slow or where negotiating with key clients is a necessary part of the sales process. Advantages claimed by companies doing this include:

1. a close relationship with customers who prefer to deal direct with manufacturers;
2. increased confidence in the supplier where technical problems can be sorted out directly with technical sales staff;
3. a sounder base for longer-term market development and sales planning; and
4. more accurate and fuller reporting back to the company of price levels, competition and changes in specifications or buyers' organisations.

In many countries, personal selling takes on special importance where restrictions on advertising and lack of media availability restrict advertising; again, low wages in other countries enable the company to hire a much larger local sales force than at home. Although there is no substitute for the trained and experienced home-based sales representative, a local force of sales assistants *can* cover a local market effectively; this is the sales organisation favoured by some major cigarette manufacturers in developing countries.

Depending on the type of product, sales support staff are often drawn from nationals of the overseas country. Some manufacturers use national representatives in each of its markets; whereas in the case of sales to large retail or wholesaling organisations, which handle their own important arrangements, it is common for the manufacturer's sales representative to sell across national boundaries. However, if it is the company's policy to have local sales assistants who are nationals working under the overall direction of senior home-based sales staff, either directly or through an agent, the management of such a force will have to be largely decentralised to each national market, with home-based staff acting as sales trainers and advisers to national operations, contributing guidance and direction because of their special product knowledge and experience.

Table 8.4 Sales profile analysis

Environment	Extent and topography of area to be covered Requirements of distributors as to sales support Expectations and attitudes of key customers to selling methods Language
Competition	Competitor sales audit Key points of effectiveness of competitors Competitor information on market prospects including strengths and weaknesses
Institutions	Organisations that support and/or recognise the value of salesmanship Contract/task sales forces Study of purchasing institutions Training (e.g. languages) institutions
Legal System	Laws relating to selling practices and transfer of goods and services
Economics	Market growth rates and other business indicators (e.g. stock levels) Credit terms; expected levels of trade solvency
Technology	Applications of microcomputers; extent of 'remote-access' buying; communications levels

In setting up and running an international sales force, the company's management should undertake a Sales Profile Analysis of the market (and should update it as appropriate) as in Table 8.4.

Such a sales profile analysis is a vital, yet often ignored, step in establishing (and updating) realistic views of the sales potential (growth prospects and competition levels) of an overseas market. While it will not answer all problems, and in particular lacks the sophistication of demand-forecasting techniques now used (usually with computer applications) by many multinational corporations, it does at least guide management as to the most relevant and effective sales organisation required by a particular market.

■ Sales management

In managing an overseas sales force, two problems can arise:

1. Selling is a low-status occupation in some countries, and therefore quality of training and competitive pay are vital in attracting high-quality sales recruits.
2. Finding people with the requisite educational and technical (and social) accomplishments is often difficult and time-consuming for management.

Differences of culture, environment, status and economics have similar impacts on management's methods of remunerating, motivating and controlling the sales force overseas. Clearly, non-monetary rewards such as status, foreign travel and recognition will have greater pull in some countries than in others. (Philip Morris of Venezuela publicises the achievements of its best sales staff.) A mix of monetary (salary and/or commission) and non-monetary rewards appropriate to each overseas market must be set which will take account of these local values or norms. Further, where the sales profile analysis is carried out, and other well-proved sales management ratios used and updated for each market, comparative evaluation of the performance of each overseas sales force becomes standard practice (the comparisons must be among groups of similar countries); and performance can be improved overall (particularly where some innovation is put in hand) by learning from experiences in the company's other markets.

CASE 8.8

NCR Company has been in Japan for over 70 years, but only in the past two decades has it been able to recruit college graduates; selling was considered low-prestige. Today, however, 80 per cent of its sales force are college graduates as a result of targeted, planned promotion of the company in higher education, and the design of management training programmes linked to career development plans.

CASE 8.9

A joint venture between 3M Company and Sumitomo has developed a sales training programme that has drawn much interest from Japanese firms. This programme involves initial training, dealer training, marketing seminars, training for experienced sales staff, sales manuals and national sales meetings. New sales recruits from Japanese universities have two months' intensive training followed by ten months more of general marketing and field training.

All such programmes (for agents and sometimes for licensees) must, of course, be part of the company's planned communications programmes, usually supported by a home-based resource team. Indeed, as the company finds new product applications, or enters new market segments, the sales tasks will have to be changed or sharpened, especially in such sectors as computers, chemicals and technical equipment. Much will depend on management's assessment of the competitiveness of the company's sales operations; and this will depend on factors such as the productivity of sales representatives and agents. Overall, the development of a plan for this sales component of the mix requires attention to the following:

1. Key markets and key customers overseas, to be targeted in the light of research and analysis;
2. Task-force selling in appropriate markets where strength of competition requires it; this means supporting all sales staff with technical, design and financial expertise to negotiate and develop sales from key customers;
3. Constant review of the productivity of overseas sales operations in terms of unit values/profits and levels and quality of manpower.

■ **Advertising and promotion**

The effectiveness of international sales operations is determined by the quality of management, and by the impact and organisation of the company's advertising and promotion; these must be targeted in overseas markets and must create and sustain the demand which sales can then exploit. Particularly important, therefore, are the links between media advertising, sales promotion, publicity and public relations.

As has been pointed out, the scope of the communications mix is wide, requiring the planning and implementation of many interlinked activities; these include (apart from sales and media advertising) promotional activities such as trade fairs, trade missions, store promotions, trade symposia, sponsorship and endorsements, and marketing weeks in trade centres. Reference should also be made to those other aspects of communications, including influencing opinion-formers, political lobbying and other forms of PR. All these parts of the communications mix have objectives that, tactically, are by no means the same as sales operations (to obtain contracts/orders): they are designed and planned in the context of:

1. long-term market development;
2. creating a favourable international image of a company;
3. setting up conditions conducive to business deals/contracts;
4. communicating with key sectors of business and governments overseas about the benefits of the product or service.

So, while public relations is concerned with creating and maintaining favourable relationships between an organisation and its 'publics', media advertising encompasses persuasive communications paid for by the advertiser and transmitted through one or more media, designed to secure purchases or other behaviour by customers favourable to the advertiser. Media advertising therefore occupies a central role in the total communications mix, and in terms of investment represents one of the major sets of decisions in international marketing planning. The first steps in researching advertising, therefore, are as shown in Table 8.5.

Table 8.5   Advertising profile analysis

Environment	Culture; literacy levels; readership details; response to symbolism; general attitude to advertising; details of buyer, decider; influencer patterns; market segments; demography
Competition	Identification of competitive advertising practices; their expenditure and ratio to sales over a period Research into strengths and weaknesses of competitors' advertising policies
Institutions	Total advertising expenditure in country; media available and growth in expenditure patterns; technical facilities (e.g. colour) Media details – circulation, readership and segments, media costs, frequency; code of advertising
Legal System	Trade description legislation; special rules pertaining to various products (e.g. cigarettes, drugs, fertilizers) Law limiting expenditure
Economics	Levels of consumption; disposable incomes; ownership of radios, TVs, etc.; readership of newspapers, magazines; socioeconomic class structure Degree of social mobility
Language	Translation and 'back-translation' of copy, etc.
Technology	Availability of satellite/cable communications etc. and levels/organisation of research methodologies; microcomputer applications

The setting-up of advertising objectives in relation to market opportunities and company resources is summarised in Figure 8.11.

■ Organisation and implementation

The next steps are, of course, concerned with the actual implementation of advertising plans through media campaigns. These involve the appointment, briefing of, and establishment of working relationships with advertising agencies in overseas markets, or the coordination of an international advertising campaign by one agency headquarters through subsidiary/associated companies in the countries concerned. Operations involve creative work – origination and design – to agreed briefs; media planning, buying and scheduling, control and evaluation of media campaigns; and financial aspects.

In briefing and evaluating the advertising agency, management can refer to the following useful set of guidelines.

1. *Market coverage* – does the particular agency or package of agencies cover all the relevant markets?

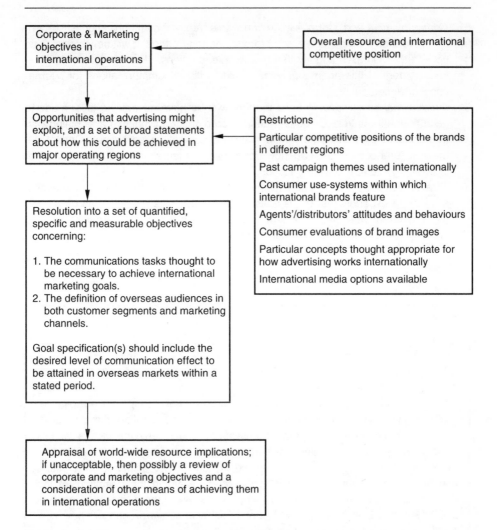

Figure 8.11 Development of international advertising objectives

2. *Quality of coverage* – how good a job does this package of agencies do in preparing advertising in each market?
3. *Market research,* public relations, and other marketing services – if the firm needs these services in world markets, in addition to advertising work, how do the different agencies compare on their offerings of these facilities?
4. *Relative roles of the company's advertising department and the agency* – some firms have a large staff that does much of the work of preparing advertising campaigns. These firms require less of an agency than do companies that rely on the agency for almost everything relating to advertising. Thus, a weak company advertising department needs a strong agency, and vice versa.

5. *Communication and control* – if the firm wants frequent communication with agencies in foreign markets and wishes to oversee their efforts, it will be inclined to tie up with the domestic agency that has overseas offices. The internal communications system of this agency network would facilitate communications for international arrangement.

6. *International coordination* – does the firm wish to have advertising tailor-made to each national market? Or does it desire coordination of national advertising with that done in other markets, and/or with the domestic programme? One of the major differences between agency groups will be their ability to aid the advertiser in attaining international coordination.

7. *Size of company's international business* – the smaller the firm's international advertising expenditures, the less its ability to divide its expenditures up among many different agencies. The firm's advertising volume may determine agency choice to ensure some minimum level of service.

The Martini Rossi Co. for some years ran a European TV campaign for Martini with the slogan 'The right one' (German translation, *Dabei mit*). The basic advertising concept was the presentation of the brand as a pleasant, refreshing and smart drink for the young professional classes. These people have an active, socialising life-style, and the brand is promoted as being just-right in that context. While this concept was put across consistently and clearly, the actual visuals used in the commercials were specially designed for German, UK and Italian audiences: car-racing scenes were filmed in Italy as the backdrop to a young couple drinking Martini and watching the race (reflecting the popularity of the sport in Italy). German consumers typically like to know more about the product and how it can best be used, so mountain ski scenes were used to show how Martini is an especially refreshing drink for skiers. In the UK, TV viewers have become more accustomed to complex visual images, and so fantasy sequences are popular and are increasingly used by advertisers: in this case, ballooning sequences over castles in mid-summer followed by a drinks party for the balloonists were used. Interestingly, the advertising in France was initially unsuccessful and had to be changed: the first visuals showed a hunting scene with riders enjoying Martini *apres la chasse*. This proved unacceptably *exclusif* as a concept, with connections to *le snobisme*: the visuals were changed to show young people enjoying Martini in a fishing village. These campaigns were successful in terms of both increasing sales revenue and establishing a clear advertising concept for the brand.

(Agency: McCann Ericson)

CASE 8.11

Rank Xerox undertook a European advertising campaign for a new model of office photocopier some years ago. A new typeface was designed (common to all countries) to illustrate the clarity and quality of copy and visuals in newspaper and TV advertisements. Again, different visuals or variations on a basic picture were used in press advertisements throughout Europe. Within Germany a photograph of a child was used to appeal to the executive secretary in German companies (usually female) who would make or influence the decision to buy. In the UK the appeal was to a traditional game: a group of footballers! In another series of advertisements the concept was problem-solving and office efficiency: two office products (including the new photocopier) were pictured, together with a teapot for UK customers, with the copy, 'These three products solve all office problems: Rank Xerox make two of them'. Coffee pots replaced teapots in France and Benelux countries (though even here the designs of pot differed); but these were considered too flippant for the practical Swiss and German markets, so a telephone was substituted. This pan-European campaign soon established the product as the best-selling office copier throughout Europe.

(Agency: McCann Ericson)

CASE 8.12

The Timex Corporation designed and implemented a marketing policy in Germany by coordinating the mix as follows:

(a) *Products.* The company studied the competitive situation and found existing producers selling primarily high and medium-priced watches – as status items. There were also sales of low-priced, low-quality watches, sold without guarantee and with the initial repair costing more than the price of the watch. The company felt that its products filled a gap between these two segments, as to both price and quality.

(b) *Service.* To beat the low-priced competition and to meet the high-priced competition, Timex provided service arrangements at moderate cost. Service was free during the guarantee period. After that, a new movement could be purchased for one-half to one-fourth the price of the new watch. This helped upgrade the image of the inexpensive or cheap watch.

(c) *Guarantee.* The company offered the first inexpensive watch with a guarantee. In fact the guarantee was as liberal as those on high-priced watches, with free service or repairs during the first year. This was important in persuading a sceptical public about the quality of the inexpensive watch.

(d) *Price.* Timex stressed its low prices but at the same time emphasised the quality and the guarantee. The company's prices were generally a step above the low-priced competition, but well below most of the high-priced competition. Other pricing decisions were to maintain price levels and to give retailers the same margins as on high-priced watches (33 per cent).

(e) *Distribution*. Distribution strategy was one of the major elements in the Timex programme in Germany. Since jewellers sold 75 per cent of the watches, Times needed that channel. However, the company also felt it necessary to use the large department stores and mail-order houses. Others who had tried this earlier had been boycotted by the jewellers. Timex was successful in persuading jewellers that its business was too profitable to ignore. The elements of persuasion were:

- giving the same margin as on expensive watches;
- saving repair work by having the watches sent to the Timex factory in France, while giving the dealer 25 per cent commission on the charges to the customer;
- a heavy publicity and advertising campaign (more than twice that spent by the German competition); this made Timex the best-known watch in Germany.

(f) *Promotion*. A heavy advertising campaign, double the total competitive outlays, initiated the hard-sell approach. Dramatic torture-tests were used as the advertisements. Competitors called these undignified, but later on some began to imitate them. Eighty per cent of the marketing budget went on television advertising because of its coverage and dramatic effect. In a separate promotional effort, a missionary selling force toured Germany, explaining to retailers the advantages of handling Timex.

■ Corporate promotion

This is basically concerned with the communication of positive and consistent messages about the MNC to both internal and external audiences, and particularly to opinion-formers. It is very much related to corporate image and identity, and to the effective projection of policies and actions by the company consistent with that image. It encompasses arts and sports sponsorship, corporate hospitality, publicity and public relations, internal promotion and any targeted communications to those stakeholders defined above. The essential question, of course, is what to communicate: corporate promotion can work effectively only if the company has at least some clear corporate objectives. With regard to the examples that follow, management should not consider adopting all, but only those that are internally consistent and accord with overall strategy. In setting up any policy or plan of corporate promotion, management of a large corporation or MNC would be well-advised, on the basis of the analysis and experience offered in this section, to adopt the following steps, in logical order:

1. Establish which public sectors are of importance to the company, in which countries, and why.

2. Assess the perceptions, attitudes and behaviour of these key sectors *vis-à-vis* the company, by verifiable, valid research methods.
3. Set corporate communications objectives, and criteria by which promotional impact can be judged.
4. Assess what changes or improvements are needed in the way the business is run.
5. Do an audit of the company's current reputation, and determine whether steps 3 and 4 above are reinforcing the reputation that management seeks.
6. Choose communications methods, and ensure, as far as possible, that they are appropriate to steps 1, 3, 4 and 5 above.

On the basis of the above, then, corporate promotion can be put effectively into action to: increase awareness, project truths, correct false impressions, establish a favourable business climate, develop influence and enhance morale.

CASE 8.13

Here is a corporate mission statement which typifies the responsibilities and views of a successful global company:

1. To be worldwide in scope; not just to sell in every country in the world, which, through distributors, the company is already doing, but to think internationally, to consider operations in any country, and to arrange the organisation and activities of the company on a basis where there is no distinction between home and foreign operations;
2. To increase profitability and earnings per share each year by improving the company's added value, not only as a proportion of sales income but also in terms of the average amount generated by each employee;
3. To be an integrated producer; not only will the company seek control over the manufacture of its products, but it will progressively arrange for the manufacture of components at such locations worldwide as will give the company real flexibility in sourcing or assembling finished products at points were costs, tariffs and demand may dictate. This is to be a prime factor in the company's strategy, and the means of regulating total corporate activities;
4. To be flexible and not to depend too much on any one product, customer or market sector; to continue to broaden the base of the trading activities of the company worldwide; and to maintain an efficient research and development policy so that opportunities can be quickly recognised and exploited;
5. To remain an independent public company with a distinctive management style; to give executives the maximum freedom of action, and to encourage them to make the fullest use of it, so that they can personally influence profits;
6. To pay the best wages and salary rates that the company can afford, and to ensure job satisfaction for all employees through enlightened management. To improve working conditions in all countries of operation, and to take appropriate steps to ensure the health and safety of all employees. To promote the

best possible human relations and a situation in which people really enjoy working for the company;

7. To continue to encourage employee-participation in the ownership of the company (the group profit-sharing scheme is an important step in this direction);

8. To benefit the local community in every country of operation whenever and wherever the company can afford to do so, and to preserve the quality of life and of the environment.

CASE 8.14

The Esso Petroleum Company, part of Exxon Group, USA, recently took the initiative to promote woodland conservation as part of the European Year of the Environment. Esso has joined with the Nature Conservancy Council (NCC) to launch, in the UK, the Ancient Woodlands Project to halt the cutting down of medieval woodlands. (Since 1945 in the UK, 10 per cent of the remaining 500 000 hectares has been cut down.) This sponsorship by Esso has been featured in national newspaper advertisements under one caption, 'On guard', with the Esso logo shown underneath with the other caption, 'Quality at work for Britain'. This corporate promotion is clearly intended to project the image of a successful international company, aware of and acting on its responsibilities to protect the environment.

Corporate communications are therefore a means to an end, and not an end in themselves; with clear objectives, they can be used to best effect to promote the interests of the company. Indeed, the growth in the communications industry in the last few years indicates the importance that MNCs are now attaching to their image; management is increasingly using identity, corporate culture and reputation as a means of improving profitability (as some of the case examples in this section show). The way an organisation is perceived by its customers, shareholders and analysts, financiers and the media will directly affect both its market position and prospects, and its profitability. This is the company's external market-place, and it must be communicated with effectively, professionally and regularly. But there is also the internal market-place (for example employees, distributors and so forth) which requires attention, and where the objectives of the company need to be spelt out just as clearly as to the external stakeholders.

Corporate promotion in Case 8.15 has proved to have had a high impact both on perceptions of ICI as a technically innovative and environmentally sensitive company among industry and the trade. It has also opened lucrative new market sectors for the Paints Division (for example camouflage coatings, and temporary road and construction markings using Tempro coatings).

CASE 8.15

The Paints Division of Imperial Chemical Industries (ICI) has recently shown how corporate promotion can be used effectively both to demonstrate positive concern to reduce atmospheric pollution, and to generate profits. Car painting operations are thought to be one of the many contributors to the growing amount of volatile compounds discharged into the atmosphere. (In the process of painting one car, some 12–15 litres of organic solvents are released.) This is a matter of concern for motor manufacturers because the quality of the car finish has become a major selling feature. This presented ICI, as a paint supplier, with a technical problem, and at the same time an opportunity for corporate promotion and profits. The outcome of lengthy research was a waterborne paint, Aquabase (wherein the solvents had been replaced by water), which, while maintaining the quality and appearance of existing paint finishes, reduces very substantially the overall emissions. ICI has also developed an emission-free protective material, Tempro, to replace the traditional wax car finish (which emitted up to 3 litres of solvent per car).

CASE 8.16

H. J. Heinz Co. Ltd have a policy of promotion through sponsorship which is by no means always linked to the promotion of a product, although the benefit the company derives from public esteem and increased sales is, of course, most apparent when the support the company gives an event is related to a specific promotion. But the company's support is often given for reasons of good-citizenship or social responsibility, provided there is some relevance to the company's business. So the company's recent support for the World Wildlife Fund (WWF) through its Guardian of the Countryside programme reflects the company's concern to improve the quality of life for the community.

But both this theme and its timing were relevant to the company in 1986. Management was then considering how to follow up a series of successful charity promotions and to enhance its reputation of a caring company. Also, 1986 was the centenary of the first Heinz sale in Britain, and WWF sponsorship provided an ideal opportunity to mark this anniversary. (The Guardian of the Countryside programme encourages adults and children to become involved in a whole range of activities designed to increase their awareness of environmental and conservation issues.)

The key questions remain. What should the company be projecting/communicating to society, and to customers? How is the company perceived by outsiders and stakeholders? Is the management's self-perception in terms of the company's market position and so on realistic? All these have a significant bearing on corporate promotion (see Case 8.16). Management must realise the importance of fulfilling promises made in advertising, for example, and must understand how corporate endorsement can be used to strengthen a brand image. If an advertising promise is unfulfilled, a company can, in the extreme, actually become a hostage to its own advertising slogan.

CASE 8.17

In 1990, General Motors Corporation of the USA (GM) undertook a research survey into public perceptions of, and attitudes towards, its corporate identity in the UK. The aim of this research was to establish how far GM corporate identity was related to, and of benefit to, the market position and sales of the GM brands, and to assess the quality and standing of the GM corporate logo in relation to other major car manufacturers. The survey showed that while the corporate identity of GM was generally clearly recognised and esteemed, there was a very low comprehension of which were the major GM brands. (Vauxhall, for example, was still perceived by many UK respondents as just another British car!)

As a result of these survey findings, GM management sharpened up the GM corporate logo, but specifically highlighted the main GM brands such as Vauxhall and Opel as part of that logo with the caption, 'Backed by the worldwide resources of General Motors'. Subsequent surveys showed that, not only did public awareness of GM brands improve, but brand sales appreciably increased as a result over the following two-year period.

■ Corporate culture and corporate image

These are essential components of corporate promotion. Corporate culture has been defined in one analysis as:

the pattern of habits, goals, concepts, ideas and behaviour that are found within a company. It is strongly influenced by the formulas which management develops to the benefit of the company. In a successful enterprise, the culture reflects the market situation ... Thus, the corporate culture should harmonise with the commercial environment. When this changes, the culture has to change as well, if the company is to survive.

(Mattehart, 1989)

This analysis is significant in that it was done in the context of the airline business. The management of a leading European airline realised that, in order to meet demands in an increasingly competitive environment, the company needed to develop a new organisational culture in terms of attitudes and work practices, allowing for greater flexibility and responsibility for decision-making at lower levels of management, and involving more decisions by front-line personnel. Of course, this was not implemented without considerable investment in both internal and external communications (videotapes, brochures, symposia and so on), and it will take time to reach fulfilment. It is also significant that culture-changes of precisely this sort have now been tried in companies in other sectors, with (so far) beneficial effects on morale, planning and market operations. Furthermore, corporate promotion has a role to play in fostering this cultural change.

Image concerns the identity or corporate-personality and reputation of the company as it is perceived by customers and others, in terms of their expectations of the company. Corporate identity has been defined as:

more than an outward picture (or symbol); it must show inner values and convictions, because only then can it achieve its most important objective: to encourage people to direct positive attention towards the company and its products; only that creates a lasting image which in turn is a good basis for a favourable buying decision.

Image and culture, therefore, largely determine what sort of corporate identity is communicated to customers and to the community. Perceptions of this identity, combined with the record of service and quality typically delivered by the company, make up the reputation of the company in its major markets. Case Example 8.18 illustrates the importance of this image-building.

CASE 8.18

International Telephone and Telegraph Corporation (ITT), headquartered in New York, faced a serious image problem in the early 1970s. A majority of the public was unaware of the firm and its variety of business activities. Furthermore, many of those who were aware of ITT had a rather blurred image of the firm, primarily because of confusion between the ITT and AT&T (American Telephone and Telegraph) names.

In 1974 ITT began a multi-year, multi-million-dollar advertising campaign aimed at building a distinct and favourable image for itself in the eyes of the public. The campaign involved a series of television and print advertisements that employed very creative approaches to convey memorable messages and slogans, such as 'The best ideas are the ideas that help people'. ITT's campaign won praise from advertising critics and received numerous awards and honours over the years (including the CLIO and EFFIE awards). By 1982, ITT was spending over $10 million per year on its corporate image-building campaign.

To assess the potential impact of the advertising campaign on the public, ITT retained the services of Yankelovich, Skelly & White, Inc., a marketing research firm well known for its expertise in conducting public opinion polls. Yankelovich, Skelly and White conducted a benchmark survey in 1974 to assess the public's views just before the start of the advertising campaign. The survey involved telephone interviews of a national sample of 1500 respondents. Similar surveys, using fresh random samples of respondents, were conducted at least once a year thereafter in order to monitor changes, if any, in the public's perceptions about ITT. A summary of the findings from the surveys showed, for instance, that, while only 68 per cent of the respondents in the January 1974 survey felt that ITT was one of the largest companies, 85 per cent of the respondents in the November 1978 survey felt so; other responses also reflected a change to more positive attitudes towards ITT on the part of the public as a result of this campaign.

All these aspects require positive attitudes and planning on the part of management, and consistent investment in communication, particularly promotion, to convey clearly to the community the developing nature of the company's activities. And, indeed, the topicality of these aspects is borne out by the increasing attention to designing new, sharper corporate logos, and consistent graphic designs which they represent.

And much of this activity in corporate promotion is based on experiential and survey data. Many MNCs have shown that corporate image-building over many years has sustained their strong market positions and has aided sales.

■ Conclusions

The focus of this final chapter has been international product and market management, and the communications mix. The parameters used by companies in implementing portfolio analysis have been explained and illustrated in Case examples; essentially this approach is used by managers to assign resources to markets and industry sectors on the basis of perceived priorities in terms of industry attractiveness and competitive strengths. The pivotal role of the brand in the international marketing programme has been assessed, and its place within the overall mix. This scenario has led logically to a detailed analysis of the communications mix in the final section: the somewhat neglected role of international selling is given its due place, together with overseas representation, and the increasing importance of corporate promotion for international companies, particularly to the key constituencies described at the beginning of the section.

QUESTIONS

1. Explain how portfolio-analysis enables management to plan marketing operations with some degree of precision.
2. 'Market management is more important than product management'. Explain this assertion, and say whether or not you agree with it, and why, in international business.
3. What are the specific risks attaching to international product development and management, and how far can they be eliminated?
4. Explain the importance of the PLC in international marketing operations.
5. Corporate communications are complex: what priorities would you assign to communications with different stakeholders and why?
6. Explain how corporate promotion can materially support the international marketing programme.
7. How can the problems of originating and controlling an international advertising campaign best be tackled?

References

■ 1   International trade

European Bank for Reconstruction and Development (1995) *Economic Transition in Eastern and Central Europe*, London: EBRD.
Heckscher, E. (1935) *Mercantilism*, Allen & Unwin, London.
Helpman, E. and Krugman, P. R. (1989) *Trade Policy and Market Structure*, MIT Press.
Keesing, D. (1981) *Changing Composition of Developing Country Exports in World Order: Past and Prospects*, edited by Grossman, S. and Lundberg, E., London: Macmillan, pp. 82–116.
Ludlow, P. W. (1990) 'Global Challenges of the 1990s: Future of the International Trading System', *Economic Impact*, pp. 4–10.
Ohlin, B. (1933) *Interregional and International Trade*, Harvard, Cambridge, Mass.
Pass, G. L. and Sparks, J. R. (1977) *Trade and Growth*, Heinemann.
Porter, M. E. (1986) 'Changing Patterns of International Competition', *California Management Review*, Vol. XXVIII, No. 2.
Porter, M. E. (1990) *The Competitive Advantage of Nations*, Macmillan.
World Bank (1990) *World Development Report*, New York.

■ 2   International business: concepts and organisation

Czinkota, M. R. (1982) *Export Development Strategies*, Praeger.
Ellis, J. and Williams, D. (1995) *International Business Strategy*, Pitman.
Johanson, J. and Vahlne, J.-E. (1977) 'The Internationalisation Process of the Firm', *Journal of International Business Studies*, Vol. 8 (Spring/Summer).
Leontief, W. W. (1954) *Domestic Production and Foreign Trade: the American Capital Position Re-examined*, Economica Internationale, pp 3–32.
Macrae, H. (1993) 'European Industry – Performance and Prospects', *The Independent*, 16 November 1993.
Organisation for European Cooperation and Development (1992) *International Investment and Multinational Enterprises*, Statistical Report, Paris: OECD.
Porter, M. E. (1990) *The Competitive Advantage of Nations*, Macmillan.
Ricardo, D. (1813) *On the Principles of Political Economy and Taxation*, London.
Smith, Adam, *The Wealth of Nations*, Modern Library Edition, New York, 1990.
Tookey, D. (1985) *Export Marketing Decisions*, Penguin.
United Nations (1994) *World Investment Report 1993*, UN.

■ 3   The international business environment

Hanson, F. (1986) 'Psychological Theories of Consumer Choice', *Journal of Consumer Choice*, No. 3.

Jain, S. C. (1987) 'Environmental Scanning Systems in US Corporations', *Journal of Long Range Planning*, Vol. 17, No. 2.

Keegan, W. J. (1990) *Global Marketing Management*, 4th Edition, Prentice Hall. Reprinted by permission of Prentice Hall, Upper Saddle River, New Jersey.

Lee, J. E. (1976) 'Cultural Analysis in Overseas Operations', *Harvard Business Review* (March/April).

Moyer, R. (1968) 'International Market Analysis', *Journal of Marketing Research* (November).

Piercy, N. (1982) *Export Strategies: Markets and Competition*, Part 2, George Allen & Unwin.

Varadarajan, P. R., Clark, T. and Pride, U. M. (1992) 'Controlling the Uncontrollable: Managing Your Market Environment', *Sloan Management Review* (Winter).

Zeithaml, C. P. and Zeithaml, V. A. (1984) 'Environmental Management: Revising the Marketing Perspective', *AMA Journal of Marketing*, Vol. 48, No. 2.

■ 4 International business strategy

de Bono, E. (1978) *Opportunities: A Handbook of Business Opportunity Search*, London: Associated Business Programmes/European Services Ltd.

Bonsiepe, G. (1973) *Development through Design*, Vienna: United Nations Industrial Development Organisation (UNIDO).

Bruce, M. and Roy, R. (1991) 'Integrating Marketing and Design for Commercial Benefit', *Marketing Intelligence and Planning*, Vol. 9, No. 5.

Cunningham, M. T. (1985) 'An Interactive Approach to Competitive Strategy in European Markets', Proceedings of IMP Research Seminar, Uppsala University, September 1985.

Hamman, A. and Mittag, H. (1985) 'The Marketing of Industrial Technology through Licensing', Proceedings of the 2nd IMP Research Seminar on International Marketing, Uppsala University.

Kravis, I. and Lipsey, R. W. (1971) *Price Competitiveness in World Trade*, Columbia University Press.

Porter, M. E. (1985) *Competitive Advantage: Creating and Sustaining Superior Performance*, Macmillan.

Quinn, J. B. 'Managing Innovation: Controlled Chaos', *Harvard Business Review*, Vol. 63, No. 3 (May/June).

Rapp, W. V. (1973) 'Strategy Formulation and International Competition', *Columbia Journal of World Business* (Summer).

St John, C. H. and Hall, E. H. (1991) 'The Interdependency Between Marketing and Manufacturing', *Industrial Marketing Management*, Vol. 20.

Simmonds, K. (1986) 'The Accounting Assessment of Competitive Position', *European Journal of Marketing*, Vol. 20, No. 1.

Wheelwright, S. C. and Hayes, R. H. (1985) 'Competing through Manufacturing', *Harvard Business Review*, Vol. 63, No. 1 (January/February).

■ 5 Planning for international expansion

Boddewyn, J. J. (1983) 'Foreign and Domestic Divestment and Investment Decisions', *Journal of International Business Studies*, Vol. 14, No. 3 (Winter).

Casseres, B. G. (1993) 'Managing International Alliances, A Conceptual Framework', Harvard Business School.

Contractor, F. J. (1986) 'An Alternative View of International Business', *International Marketing Review* (Spring).

Contractor, F. J. (1987) 'Why should Firms Cooperate? – The Strategy and Economic Basis for Cooperative Ventures', in *Cooperative Strategies in International Business*, Lexington Books.

Harringan, K. P. (1984) 'Joint Ventures and Global Strategy', *Columbia Journal of World Business* (December).

Hopkins, D. S. (1981) 'The Marketing Plan', Conference Board.

Majaro, S. (1980) *Marketing in Perspective*, George Allen & Unwin.

UNCTAD (1993) *World Investment Report*, UN.

■ 6 Financial aspects

Berry, L. L. *A Model of Service Quality Gaps*, Texas: A&M University.

Buzzell, R. D. and Gale, B. (1987) *Profit and Performance Improvement*, Strategic Planning Institute, Harvard.

Cornell, B. and Shapiro, A. C. (1983) 'Managing Foreign Exchange Risks', *Midland Corporate Finance Journal* (Fall).

Cosse, T. J. and Swan, J. E. (1986) 'Strategic Marketing Planning by Product Managers – Room for Improvement', *Journal of Marketing* (Summer).

OECD (1992) Report, *Host Government and Cooperation in Investment Issues* (adapted), Paris.

Organisation for European Cooperation and Development (1992) *International Investment and Multinational Enterprises*, Statistical Report, Paris: OECD.

Parasuraman, A., Zeithame, V. A. and Berry, L. L. (1985) 'A Conceptual Model of Service Quality and its Implications for Future Research', *Journal of Marketing*, Vol. 49 (Fall).

Sevin, C. H. (1965) *Marketing Productivity Analysis*, McGraw-Hill.

Windle, A. and Sizer, J. (1985) *Exporting for Profit: A Guide to the Financial Evaluation of Export Opportunities*, National Economic Development Office (NEDO) UK.

■ 7 Managing international operations

Arterian, S. (1990) 'How Black and Decker Defines Exposure', *Business International Money Report* (December).

Bartlett, C. A. and Ghoshal, S. (1993). 'What is a Global Manager?' (September/October).

Corfield, Sir K. (1984) *World Communications – Tomorrow's Trade Routes*, Conference Proceedings of the British Computer Society and the Department of Trade and Industry, London.

Daniels, J. D. and Radebaugh, L. H. (1995) *International Business: Environments and Operations*, 7th Edition, Copyright, Addison-Wesley Publishing Company, Inc. Reprinted by permission of Addison-Wesley Publishing Company, Inc.

Department of Trade and Industry (1985) *Countertrading*, DTI Project and Export Policy Division, HMSO.

Ford, D. and Farmer, D. (1990) 'Make or Buy – A Key Strategic Issue', *Journal of Long Range Planning*, Vol. 19, No. 5, pp. 54–62.

Humes, S. (1992) *Managing the Multi-National – Confronting the Global – Local Ethical Dilemma*, Prentice Hall.

Meyers, G. C. and Holusha, J. (1986) *When it Hits the Fan: Managing the Nine Crises of Business*, Houghton Mifflin.

Root, F. R. (1982) *Foreign Market Entry Strategies*, AMACOM.

Root, F. R. (1987) *Entry Strategies for International Markets*, Lexington.

US Department of Commerce (1985) *US–Europe Countertrading*, Report of International Trade Commission.

Wiechmann, U. and Pringle, L. G. (1979) 'Problems that Plague the Multi-National Marketer', *Harvard Business Review* (July/August).

■ 8 Developing international marketing

Allio, R. J. and Pennington, M. W. (eds) (1979) *Corporate Planning Techniques and Applications*, AMACOM, American Management Associates.

Gur-Arie, O. and Taylor, J. R. (1982) *Portfolio Analysis of the Brand Level*, Proceedings of the 9th International Research Symposium European Society for Opinion and Market Research, Aix-en-Provence, France.

Hansen, N., Gronhaug, K. and Warneryd, K. E. (1990) 'Excellent Marketing: the Concept, its Measurement and Implications', *Marketing and Research Today* (June).

Harell, R. and Keifer, R. O. (1981) 'Market Portfolio Analysis', MSU *Business Topics*, pp. 5–15.

Henzler, H. and Rall, W. (1986) 'Facing Up to the Globalisation Challenge', *The McKinsey Quarterly* (Winter).

Martenson, R. (1986) 'Future Competition in a Cross Cultural Environment', *European Management Journal*, Vol. 4, No. 3.

Mattehart, A. (1989) *Multi-National Corporations and Corporate Cultures*, Horseshoe Press.

Mickwitz, G. (1959) *Marketing and Competition*, Cyckereit, Helsingfors, Finland.

Pitcher, A. E. 'The Role of Branding in International Advertising', *International Journal of Advertising*, No. 4.

de la Torre, J. (1975) 'Product Life Cycle as a Determinant of Global Marketing Strategies', *Atlanta Economic Review*, Vol. 25 (September/October).

Index